Human Levitation

A True History and How-To Manual

Preston Dennett

Artwork by Kesara

4880 Lower Valley Road, Atglen, PA 19310 USA

Other Schiffer Books by Preston Dennett
Supernatural California
UFOs Over California
California Ghosts

Ouija is a registered trademark of Parker Brother's Games.

Published by Schiffer Publishing Ltd.
4880 Lower Valley Road
Atglen, PA 19310
Phone: (610) 593-1777; Fax: (610) 593-2002
E-mail: Info@schifferbooks.com

For the largest selection of fine reference books on this and related subjects, please visit our web site at **www.schifferbooks.com**
We are always looking for people to write books on new and related subjects. If you have an idea for a book please contact us at the above address.

This book may be purchased from the publisher.
Include $3.95 for shipping.
Please try your bookstore first.
You may write for a free catalog.

In Europe, Schiffer books are distributed by
Bushwood Books
6 Marksbury Ave.
Kew Gardens
Surrey TW9 4JF England
Phone: 44 (0) 20 8392-8585; Fax: 44 (0) 20 8392-9876
E-mail: info@bushwoodbooks.co.uk
Website: www.bushwoodbooks.co.uk
Free postage in the U.K., Europe; air mail at cost.

Designed by Mark David Bowyer
Type set in Bernhard Mod BT / Souvenir Lt BT

ISBN: 0-7643-2547-7
Printed in China

14.95

Contents

Introduction

Do humans have the ability of physical levitation? Can people actually fly through the air without mechanical devices of any kind? While mainstream science has failed to provide proof, history says otherwise. *Hundreds* of credible firsthand accounts of levitation are now on record from many different cultures across the world, starting from ancient history and continuing to the present day.

Levitation, when seriously considered, is often thought to be the sole realm of saints, yogis, and mediums. However, today many modern accounts have surfaced involving housewives, businessmen, farmers, young children, and other seemingly normal people.

Levitation episodes have taken place consistently throughout recorded history across the entire world and have been treated differently by each culture. Some explained the accounts as a natural human talent. Other cultures concluded that levitation is caused by spirits. Some explained it as communion with God, others as possession by demons or the Devil.

Pantanjali. This Indian sage lived more than 5,000 years ago. He wrote the *Yoga Sutras*, the foundation of yogic practice. Two of the sutras include instructions on how to levitate. His is the first recorded historical reference to the phenomenon of levitation. (Self-Realization Fellowship)

The history of the phenomenon itself is also fascinating. Probably the earliest historical reference to levitation comes from Patanjali, an Indian sage and author of the *Yoga Sutras*, the foundation of Yogic practice. Patanjali lived about 2,500 years ago, and wrote at that time that levitation is one of the eight great psychic powers, or *siddhis*, which come naturally to the yogi on the pathway towards enlightenment.

Early records of levitations were also kept by the Catholic Church. Accounts of levitating saints reach as far back as the first century and stretch to the late 1900s. Also, throughout the Middle Ages, the Catholic Church kept records of levitations among people supposedly possessed by the Devil or involved in witchcraft. At that time hagiography, or religious biographies, was the dominant form of literature, thereby numerous accounts of levitations were recorded for posterity.

John van Bolland (1596-1665) was the founder and first editor of the massive *Acta Sanctorum,* an official and comprehensive hagiographic collection on the lives of the saints. After his death, the project was continued by a group of Jesuit scholars called the *Bollandists*. The first volume was published in 1643, and contained multiple accounts of levitating saints.

In 1746, Benedictine Abbot and religious scholar Augustin Calmet published a series of scientific works on various paranormal subjects including ghosts, life after death, premonitions, and more. One of his works, *The Phantom World*, contained a section about the levitation of saints, and is probably the earliest treatment of the subject.

In 1756-59, religious scholar Reverend Alban Butler, published his massive multi-volume study, *Lives of the Saints,* detailing the biographies of hundreds of saints, many of whom were reported levitators.

The first in-depth study and analysis of levitation was made in 1842 by J. J. von Goerres, an expert on Catholic mysticism. Goerres collected and published a list of seventy-two cases of levitating saints in his book, *Die Mystique, (The Mystical Life)*.

Within a few years of this, the phenomenon of Spiritualism spread across the world like wildfire, and prominent scientists, including Sir William Crookes and Charles Richet, began to methodically study accounts of levitations, even conducting controlled laboratory experiments. In January, 1875, Crookes compiled and published a list of forty levitating saints in the *Quarterly Journal of Science*.

Also in 1875, the term "levitation" first appeared in the Oxford dictionary, originating from the Latin word *levis,* meaning "light." Other terms used include *rapture, elevation, ascension, suspension, transvection,* and *ecstatic flight*.

In 1894, French author Dr. A. Imbert-Gourbeyre, listed several more accounts in his book, *La Stigimatisation,* which was probably the most complete study of levitating saints to date.

Then the prominent French psychical investigator, Lt. Col. Eugene de Rochas (1837-1914), published a series of articles, *Receuil de Documents Relatif a la Levitation due Corps Humaine,* [A Collection of Documents Relating to the Levitation of the Human Body]. In 1897, he organized the articles into, *La Levita-*

tion, which became the seminal book on levitation, including for the first time, accounts from a variety of cultures. Rochas was later forced to resign his position as Administrator of L'Ecole Polytechnique as a result of his interest in and research into the occult.

In 1919, English author F. Fielding-Ould, wrote a comparative analysis of several accounts of levitating saints in his volume titled, *The Wonders of the Saints.*

The first truly comprehensive treatment of levitation came in 1928 with Olivier Leroy's landmark book, *La Levitation*, which followed up Rochas' research, listing two hundred cases of levitating saints, and a few involving yogis and mediums. Leroy's book sold well and effectively popularized the subject, fixing it permanently into the public consciousness.

French researcher Colonel Eugene De Rochas researched and wrote the first book ever to focus solely on accounts of human levitation. (*Mysteres.*)

The next study of the subject came in 1947 when Eric J. Dingwall published his book, *Some Human Oddities,* which contained a few chapters on levitation with a strong focus on the flights of St. Joseph of Cupertino, a sixteenth century Italian friar.

Then in 1952, Father Herbert Thurston published *The Physical Phenomenon of Mysticism,* presenting twenty additional cases of levitating saints, following up a few articles that he had published more than thirty years previously.

In 1966, leading English paranormal researcher Nandor Fodor published an extensive study of the subject in his massive volume, *Encyclopaedia of Psychic Science.* By this time, other prominent researchers jumped on the bandwagon, including D. Scott Rogo, Colin Wilson, Lynn Picknett, and others, each of whom conducted significant investigations of levitation accounts.

In 1980, Steve Richards published his small book, *Levitation,* which is one of the first modern treatments of the subject. Richards' book presents several historical and a few current accounts, and puts into understandable form some of the Yogic methods to achieve levitation.

In 1990, authors Rodney Charles and Ann Jordan conducted an extensive survey of world literature and uncovered numerous mythical and historical levitation accounts from various cultures across the world, the results of which are told in their book, *Lighter Than Air.*

Finally, in 1998, an anonymous researcher published a short, yet informative book titled, *Invisibility and Levitation,* using the pseudonym Commander X.

My own introduction to the subject of levitation began in 1985, after reading a brief paragraph about Saint Teresa of Avila and Saint Joseph of Cupertino. Both were saints born in the 1500s. Both were reportedly seen by multiple witnesses on numerous occasions to levitate during religious trances.

At first I assumed these were isolated cases. Furthermore, they seemed unbelievable. If levitation were actually true, I thought, then there should be modern accounts. Obviously levitation wasn't possible, I reasoned, because science would have revealed this fact by now.

My interest in levitation took flight in 1990 when a good friend revealed that she had experienced a spontaneous levitation event as a child. *This is a new twist*, I thought. While I had never really taken levitation seriously, I thought that if by some small chance it were possible, then only a highly advanced spiritual being could attain such an incredible feat. But here was someone I had known for years telling me that she had actually levitated. I was certain she wasn't lying or misperceiving. The only other logical explanation was that she *wasn't* lying, that she had actually levitated. For the first time, I began to take these accounts seriously. Was levitation truly possible?

So I started doing research. To my surprise, I found there was little current information on the subject. The number of full-length works on the subject could be counted on one hand, and all proved very difficult to locate. More importantly, none were truly comprehensive. The last major study was conducted nearly eighty years ago!

I did find several original accounts scattered throughout books and magazine articles, but these precious, rare nuggets came few and far between. Firsthand accounts of levitation, I discovered, were exceedingly hard to find. This was especially true of modern-day accounts, which of course, carry the most evidential weight.

So I began to ask everyone I know, "What do you think of levitation? Have you ever flown?" Most people looked at me like I was crazy. I quickly realized that people are much more inclined to believe in UFOs, ghosts, ESP, or life-after-death than levitation.

But I kept searching, and persistence paid off. I was eventually able to locate several people who claimed to have experienced levitation episodes. These were neither Buddhist monks nor enlightened masters, but normal people who were themselves bewildered by their experiences.

It soon became obvious that levitation did not belong only to the realm of the spiritually enlightened. If so many different types of people experienced levitation, then it should be possible for *anyone* to do it.

After more than ten years of investigation and research, I had collected hundreds of accounts of levitation. Now I was faced with the opposite problem—too many accounts! While levitation accounts were rare, they weren't *that* rare. In fact, after reviewing all the available evidence on the subject, one soon realizes that there is an embarrassingly large amount of evidence supporting the validity of levitation. Embarrassing because levitation should have long ago been accepted by mainstream science. The evidence is, in the truest sense, overwhelming.

This book is an attempt to compile a comprehensive history and chronology of levitation events, to determine if levitation is real, what it is, to study the mechanics of how levitation takes place, who experiences it and why, and, finally, to present any possible methods to initiate levitation. I am confident that this is the largest collection of levitation reports ever assembled and the most complete analysis of the phenomenon.

More than 350 cases are presented. They are organized both chronologically and topically.

Is levitation real? As you will read, it certainly seems to be real. Definitely the levitators and witnesses to the levitations claim that it is.

At first I assumed there was little evidence other than anecdotal stories. I later learned that there are far many more witnesses than I first imagined. Furthermore, many of the witnesses are extremely credible. I learned that levitation events have been performed in front of eminent scientists (including Nobel prize winners) under controlled laboratory conditions. And finally, I was surprised to find cases of levitations that have been repeatedly photographed and even filmed. Obviously, *something* is happening here, but actual levitation?

The scientists and researchers who have taken the time to study the phenomenon have usually come away convinced. A surprisingly large number of researchers have gone on record in support of levitation.

Leading modern researcher Steve Richards writes, "Does man fly?...the evidence is that he probably does."[1]

Way back in the seventeenth century, Zacchias, the physician for Pope Innocent 10th, wrote, "It is possible to admit the suspension of the body in space, under the action of an invisible force, not being contrary to the laws of nature."[2]

Medieval religious scholar Augustin Calmet writes, "We have in history several instances of persons full of religion and piety, who, in the fervor of their orisons, have been taken up into the air, and remained there for some time....We cannot reasonably dispute the truth of these ecstatic trances and elevations of the body of some saints, to a certain distance from the ground, since these circumstances are supported by so many witnesses."[3]

Colonel Rochas writes, "The phenomenon of the rising of the human body, or levitation to use today's term, appears to be one of the most extraordinary psychic forces that our generation has tried to define. Meanwhile, the reality of it has been demonstrated by a number of impressive testimonies."[4]

Olivier Leroy writes, "Following a quasi-general tradition, ancient and uninterrupted, the human body has been capable, with certain individuals, at certain moments, of raising itself up into the air, and sometimes to travel there, without visible support, without controllable action from any physical force. Today, we call this phenomenon levitation."[5]

Pioneering levitation researcher Father Herbert Thurston writes, "I have taken note of the names of something over two hundred persons alleged to have been physically lifted free from the ground in ecstasy. In about one third of these cases there seems to be evidence which, if not conclusive, is to say the least respectable....If only the facts are attested by witnesses for whose good faith we can answer there seems no possible ground for resisting the conclusion that the most universal and familiar of all the physical laws which govern our material existence in this world has over and over again been suspended by some agency external to the person affected and wholly spiritual in its nature."[6]

Mircea Eliade, a leading authority of shamanism, reveals a cross-cultural belief in levitation. "Levitation characterizes Siberian shamanism [and] is found elsewhere [and] can be regarded as a typical feature of shamanic techniques in general....Shamans and medicine men, to say nothing of mystics, are able to fly like birds and perch on the branches of trees. Siberian, Eskimo and North American shamans fly....All over the world, indeed, shamans and sorcerers are credited with the power to fly, to cover immense distances in a twinkling, and to become invisible....In this connection, we may remember that the levitation of saints and magicians is also attested in both the Christian and Islamic traditions. Roman Catholic hagiography has gone so far as to record a large number of 'levitations' and even of 'flights'....Ascension and magical flight have a leading place among the popular beliefs and mystical techniques of India. Rising into the air, flying like a bird, traveling immense distances in a flash, disappearing – these are some of the magical powers that Buddhism and Hinduism attribute to arahats, kings and magicians. There are numerous legends of flying kings and magicians."[7]

Patricia Treece, an authority on modern mysticism, writes, "Can a human being anywhere actually defy gravity to rise, unsupported, from a few inches to much higher? Even at the outer limits of physiology, can this be considered within human potential? To answer that, let me say for starters there are a goodly number of nineteenth and twentieth century testimonies....A phenomenon that has been with us for centuries, entire groups, at times, have left depositions that someone levitated....Tibetans, Hindus, Moslems, Spiritualists, and Transcendental Meditators join Orthodox and Catholic Christians in claiming levitators. A universal myth? I prefer to take this universality as suggesting this mystical phenomenon is *not* a myth but exists at the outer limits of human psychophysical potential."[8]

Writes researcher Lynn Picknett, "Throughout recorded history, there have been incidents that prove levitation to be possible, rare perhaps, but nevertheless well-attested."[9]

Modern levitation researchers Charles and Jordan agree. "For countless people throughout history, flying was not merely a dream but an empirical reality, and many of their flights have been carefully documented."[10]

Researcher Brian Inglis states simply, "The historical evidence is extensive."[11]

An authority on witchcraft, Montague Summers writes, "It is significant that the belief in the nocturnal transport of sorcerers is practically universal and exists among savage races as strongly as amongst civilized people....In hagiography, this is a recognized and not unfrequent occurrence, and very many instances are noted by the Bollandistes in their immense work on the lives of the saints. It is not too much to say that some hundred such cases [of levitation] have been known."[12]

Controversial author and Tibetan mystic, T. Lobsang Rampa, writes, "Levitation is a very real thing indeed, it is not something out of science fantasy or science fiction or whatever you want to call it; it is not the pipe-dream of a person who has had too much alcohol!"[13]

Author Richard Hatcher Childress writes, "People have been personally defying gravity for thousands of years. Incidents of levitation have been recorded in many ancient Hindu, Babylonian, Chinese, and Egyptian texts....Other incidents of levitation, starting in the middle ages, are fairly numerous....Today, levitation still makes the news."[14]

Leading paranormal researcher, Nandor Fodor, writes, "The phenomenon was known from ancient days. Instances of levitation are recorded both in the Old and New Testaments, while in the walking of Jesus on the water, a feat duplicated by many of the saints, we find a plain illustration. The power is claimed today by wizards of many savage tribes, by mystics in the East, and it has been repeatedly demonstrated, in less sensational degrees, by many modern mediums. These furnished the first proof acceptable to science that the miracles of rising in the air, recorded in the life of saints, ecstatic, 'witches,' and victims of 'demoniac' possession rest on a solid basis of fact."[15]

The late well-known author and researcher, D. Scott Rogo, writes, "Stories about human levitation are not rare. It can purportedly be produced by the shamans of Asia, and also occurs during cases of 'demonic' possession. It is perhaps the most commonly mentioned miracle in yogic and Tibetan Buddhist literature and in the lore of the Roman Catholic saints."[16]

Michael Murphy writes in *The Future of the Body*: "Levitation of the human body has a long history in Christian lore and has been said to occur among adepts of other religions....belief in the phenomenon has persisted for at least two millennia in the shamanic and religious traditions....There exist, it seems to me, enough compelling anecdotes about the phenomenon to warrant our considering it as a human possibility."[17]

Paranormal investigators Bob Rickard and John Michell write, "There is no doubt in our minds that the phenomenon of human flight does, on occasion, take place....Clearly there is some natural force, unknown to our present science, by which people can achieve levitation....this force has been recognized, studied and made use of."[18]

Modern paranormal researcher Tim Beckley is also persuaded that levitation is a reality. "There are those, I'm convinced, who are not bound by earthly laws that most mortals have made for themselves. These adepts and avatars, if you want to call them that, have learned to do things which most of us can only dream of. They can make themselves invisible. They can leave the ground and travel in the air by levitating their physical form."

Anonymous researcher Commander X writes, "Stories about human levitation are not rare....Reported instances of levitation can be found in many ancient texts as well as modern literature on the paranormal. The power of levitation is not exclusive to Saints and other holy people. The power could be dormant in all of us, needing only the proper catalyst to set it in motion."[19]

World-famous psychic Sylvia Browne writes, "One of the most interesting facets of levitation is the diverse cross-section of belief systems in which the phenomenon has been recorded. Mediums, shamans, and mystics have reported levitations for thousands of years, but then so have Hindus, Buddhists, yogis, Brahmans, Japanese Ninjas, Indian fakirs, Catholic saints, Christians, and followers of Islam."[20]

Finally, author Cassandra Eason uncovered a few modern reports of levitating children. As she writes, "The trouble with children is often that they do not know their limitations….Many children have broken bones to show for their early attempts at flying before they learned the rules. But some can remember breaking those rules and getting away with it."[21]

What exactly is levitation? Simply defined, it is human flight without the aid of *any* physical device. Several inferior types of levitation include "finger levitations," the so-called "Indian Rope trick," and "stick levitation." Many credible UFO witnesses also report being levitated by a beam of light from a UFO. There are also many forms of stage or street levitations. These levitations are done using various optical tricks including mirrors, wires, or other devices. In 1974, Ed Balducci revealed a simple technique whereby anyone can appear to levitate a few inches off the ground. If performed correctly, it can be very convincing. I have personally fooled a number of people using the Balducci method.

True human levitation, however, is done with the body and mind alone, and that is what we are primarily concerned with here.

How does levitation work? A close analysis of the evidence reveals underlying patterns that are present in virtually every case. The accounts are remarkably consistent and the experience seems to be the result of a specific set of circumstances. In other words, levitation is no accident. While there are processes at work that have yet to be identified, there has been some progress made. By closely analyzing the recorded cases, I believe that some of the secrets behind the mechanics of levitation can be revealed.

Can levitation be initiated? The answer is a resounding, yes! In fact, different cultures each have their own unique approach to the attainment of levitation. As we shall see, there are many different methods you can use to initiate your own levitation experience.

After studying all the accounts, it becomes clear that levitation can be broken down into seven main categories:

ONE: Ecstatic Levitation

Most commonly experienced by Saints or the very religious, this type of levitation involves the witness experiencing a state of divine union with God. The episodes usually (but not always) occur after years of prayer and devotion and may be provoked by exposure to religious paraphernalia, nature, music, or during prayer, at which point the witness falls into an ecstatic trance. The body may become rigid as it is slowly lifted up into the air where it remains suspended for the duration of the trance, which can last from minutes to hours. In some cases, visible light is emitted from the body. These states are usually involuntary, unexpected, and uncontrollable. They are believed by the levitators to be caused by the grace of God.

TWO: Meditative Levitation

Most commonly experienced by yogis, ascetics, shamans, mystics, sorcers....This is differentiated from ecstatic levitation in that it is an apparently fostered talent, one that is *intentionally* cultivated, controlled, and developed through specific techniques involving breath-control, meditation, fasting, chastity, mantras, or other methods. It is presumably internally generated by the power of the human organism and is controllable. Otherwise, it seems closely related, or nearly identical, to ecstatic levitation.

THREE: Crisis Levitation

This type of levitation is reported by all kinds of people regardless of culture, age, race, sex, religion, or level of spiritual development. It occurs during a time of emergency or trauma, or in some cases illness, saving the witness from injury or death. The episodes are typically of brief duration and are not controlled. They are usually attributed by the witnesses to guardian spirits or angels.

FOUR: Mediumistic Levitation

This occurs to all people, but most often to so-called psychic mediums. The episodes are usually brief, lasting a few seconds to a few minutes. Like meditative levitation, mediumistic levitation is controllable, though this is not always the case. However, it is differentiated from meditative levitation in that it *appears* to be generated by an outside force, usually postulated as spirits or ghosts, or sometimes God or the Devil, as opposed to being internally generated. It also differs from meditative levitation in that it occurs with little or no spiritual training from the witness.

FIVE: Spontaneous Levitation

This category involves those levitations that seem to have no obvious trigger. Occurring most often to young children, it can happen at any time. It usually lasts only moments and there is little control over the events, but they may return briefly, on and off, for a period of months. They seem to occur more commonly to people who have strong spiritual inclinations.

SIX: Sleeping Levitation

This rare form of levitation occurs only when the percipient is asleep. It is reported by all kinds of people, and can last for seconds, minutes, or longer. The levitator remains in a horizontal floating position. Sometimes the levitator may awaken. In most cases the levitation is witnessed by others.

SEVEN: Traveling Levitation

Also called running levitation or supernatural agility, this form of levitation involves rising not so much upwards as *forwards*. It is reported in many different

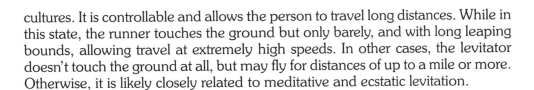

cultures. It is controllable and allows the person to travel long distances. While in this state, the runner touches the ground but only barely, and with long leaping bounds, allowing travel at extremely high speeds. In other cases, the levitator doesn't touch the ground at all, but may fly for distances of up to a mile or more. Otherwise, it is likely closely related to meditative and ecstatic levitation.

These seven types of levitation have occurred in virtually every culture in the world. Levitation is a mystery, but it is one that is worth exploring, don't you think? To be able to fly, wouldn't that be exciting? As we shall see, many people claim to have levitated. Many more claim to have witnessed it. Do you think you could do it? Are you willing to try?

1. The Emergence of a Phenomenon

Some of the earliest accounts of levitation are wrapped up in legend and myth, making it difficult to determine if the story is fiction, non-fiction, or a mixture of both.

For example, Jesus and Buddha. Most people agree that these two men actually lived and walked upon this earth. Both are also reported to have levitated and performed numerous other miracles that are still remembered today. The problem is, this occurred a very long time ago, and a great many legends have sprung up around them. One can't very well interview Jesus or Buddha. How much credit should we give to these accounts?

History is replete with such larger-than-life figures, especially when it comes to levitation. Many early accounts, however, are filled with symbolic imagery. Other tales seem to be metaphorical.

And still levitation was apparently such a spectacular display that, like other unusual events, it stood a good chance of being recorded for posterity. Even with the limited scientific understanding of these early cultures, they still recognized that levitation was a truly miraculous event—one which had the potential to reveal many secrets about what it means to be human.

For this section I have included only accounts that pre-date the thirteenth century and seem to rise above *pure* fantasy. In other words, each of these people actually lived and their accomplishments are recorded in written historical documents. And as time goes on it becomes increasingly apparent that the reports originate from genuine events.

The earliest recorded account comes from Kuang Che'eng Tzu, an early practitioner of Taoism in China around 179-157 B.C. As the story goes, the Emperor of China, Wen Ti, summoned Kuang Tzu by messenger with questions about Taoism. Tzu refused to answer the messenger, saying that the emperor should meet him in person. The emperor was reportedly insulted and traveled to confront Kuang, saying, "Even though you are a man of Tao, you are still my subject. If you are unable to bend low, how shall you be exalted? It is in my power to bestow poverty and abasement as well as riches and rank."

Kuang Che'eng Tzu replied by clapping his hands and rising into the air. He told the Emperor, "Poised thus between heaven and earth, having my abode in neither, nor belonging to the race of mortals, how can I be subject to your sovereignty, and how can your Majesty cause me to be rich or poor, of high or lowly station?" The Emperor was overcome with humility and bowed before Kuang Che'eng Tzu.[22]

Most of the early recorded levitations are particularly dramatic, which is perhaps why they are still remembered today. Such is the case of Brother Schnoudi, an Egyptian monk from the first century BC. A controversial figure in religious history, Schnoudie was best known for organizing raids against Pagan temples and destroying them. He was eventually arrested and brought before the north Egyptian court. It was there that the first recorded "court levitation" took place. According to his biographer, Visa, as Schnoudi began to plead his case he was "raised up in the air by the angels of the Lord up to a height where he could make himself heard."

Needless to say, Schnoudi's levitation had the desired effect, uniting the court in amazement, and winning him his freedom.[23]

Some early levitations accounts are surprisingly detailed when one considers how long ago they occurred. In the year 430, Saint Zosime was traveling through the desert in Egypt when he encountered the well-known hermit, Marie the Egyptian. As a young woman, Marie worked as a prostitute and lived a life filled with lustful pursuits. She was reportedly a prostitute not for the money, but because she enjoyed the sex. Then one day, she attempted to walk into a church and was thrown backwards by an invisible force. Repeated attempts to enter had the same effect. This experienced changed her life, turning her to religion and asceticism. She eventually became a hermit and lived alone in the desert, which is where Zosime found her.

After talking for a while, Zosime and Marie decided to pray together. Saint Zosime had finished his prayers, and looking up, was "seized by a great fear" to see that Marie the Egyptian was kneeling in prayer, "floating at one cubit [eighteen inches] from the ground."[24]

St. Aedh (d589) grew up as a swine herder. When his father died, his brothers forced him off the estate, which they kept for themselves. He took up a religious life, at which he prospered, eventually becoming Bishop. He set up monasteries and was widely influential, partly due to the many miracles ascribed to him. He was well known for his supernatural healing abilities, allegedly turned water into wine, and on several occasions, experienced "transportation through the air."[25]

St. Milburga (d700) was the founding Abbess of Wenlock in Shropshire. Her monastery flourished under her care, and Milburga became widely known for her humility and wonder-working. She was reportedly graced with the gift of healing, and is said to have cured a blind person, and resuscitated a young child. She had power over wild beasts, and birds often landed on her hands and shoulders. According to *Butler's Lives of the Saints*, she also experienced numerous levitations.

Shankara, a well-known Indian philosopher and mystic, lived from 788 to 820 A.D. According to one of his biographers, Madhava-Vidyaranya, Shankara had the ability to levitate. On one occasion, he desired to visit Mandana, another philosopher in a distant city. Shankara traveled to this location via levitation. First he clearly visualized his intended location and then lifted up into the air and, "traveling through the skies, reached the splendid city of Mahismati, which had gained great reputation as the residence of Mandana. Admiring the beauty and splendor of the numerous buildings of the city, he descended from the skies even like the sun at the close of the day, in a lovely wooded park of that place."

Then, locating Mandana's residence, Shankara flew through a high tower window. Mandana was astonished as the gates to his residence were locked and it should have been impossible for Shankara to gain access.[26]

A similar account comes from Padma Sambhava, a Buddhist missionary and ordained monk circa the 700s. Sambhava is credited with the establishment of Tantric Buddhism. He spent the first half of his life in study, and the second half in teaching. According to biographer Evans-Wentz, Sambhava used levitation as a way to interest people in his teachings.

On one occasion, he reportedly levitated before a group of nuns outside their monastery. The nuns were shocked to see "a smiling youth sitting on a rainbow…. he landed in the garden and all the nuns bowed before him." Not surprisingly, Sambhava was invited into the monastery to share his teachings.

Sambhava's reputation grew. During a conflict between a group of Buddhists and a non-Buddhist King and his hundreds of followers, the Buddhists prayed to Sambhava for help. Samhbava reportedly showed up, "coming down through the branches of the trees like a great bird."

Sambhava then engaged the non-Buddhists in a debate, and after giving a demonstration of his magical abilities, was invited by them to teach the Buddhist doctrines to adjacent Monarchs and their kingdoms.[27]

Tongjung Thuchen lived in the eighth century and is credited with the discovery of the *chod* practice to achieve enlightenment. Even today his teachings are followed by students of Tibetan Buddhism. By the time he was six years old, Thuchen had already achieved a complete understanding of the teachings. By age twelve, he was meeting with other enlightened masters in the dream state to receive their teachings. He soon became well-known for his high level of spiritual development and displayed several supernatural abilities, including levitation. Writes Tenzin Wangyal Rinpoche, "Many times when he walked, his feet did not touch the ground, and he could walk very, very fast, using the power of his prana."[28]

Andrew of Salus (880-946) was born a Scynthian slave. According to his biographer, Andrew was sometimes seen to levitate while in prayer. Salus's biographer interviewed the witness to the levitation, Epiphane, who later became a patriarch at Constantinople.[29]

Luke of Soterium or Saint Luc the Young (890-946) was a Greek monk who worked first as a shepherd. From an early age, he lived an "austere and contemplative" life. He often gave up his own meals to feed the hungry, and even stripped himself of his own clothes to give to the poor. When he worked to sow seeds, he took half the seeds and scattered them over the land of the poor. Following his father's death, he left home and was imprisoned as a runaway slave. Fortunately, he regained his freedom, and, at age eighteen, became a religious ascetic, isolating himself and living as a hermit. His mother objected at first. But as time passed, she became increasingly curious to see why her son insisted on always being alone. One day she followed him and observed him in contemplation, floating above the ground in prayer. Not believing her eyes, she returned the next day and observed another levitation. She finally acquiesced and allowed her son to follow the religious life. Later, there were so many witnesses to Luke's "miracles" that he was given the name, "Thaumaturgus" or *wonder-worker*.[30]

While many levitators led hermetic lifestyles, others were very influential in society. St. Dunstan (910-988) was a nobleman who became a Benedictine monk, advisor to King Edred and Archbishop of Canterbury, England. As a young student, he was accused of practicing "incantations." This led to his expulsion from school. His uncle persuaded him to embrace a religious life; however, Dunstan refused. Then he was stricken with what appeared to be leprosy. When he miraculously recovered, Dunstan followed his uncle's advice and became a monk, and later an abbot. A towering figure in religious history, Dunstan single-handedly revived and reformed English monasticism and changed the course of English history. He was also one of the first recorded saints who levitated. Writes Calmet, "A little time before his death, as he was going up stairs to his apartment, accompanied by several persons, he was observed to rise from the ground, and as all present were astonished at the circumstance, he took occasion to speak of his approaching death."

Three days later, on May 17, 988, Dunstan died as he had predicted.[31]

Other reasons there are early re-cords of levitations are not only because an event was so spectacular, but also because the witnesses to the events were of high social standing. This next case occurred in 1036 to St. Richard, the abbot of St. Vanne de Verdun, and was witnessed by a French Duke and several other influential citizens. As the story goes, St. Richard performed mass and became slowly elevated above the ground while in the presence of Duke Galizon, his sons, and "a great number of lords and soldiers."[32]

India, as we shall see, has a long tradition of levitation. Sometime in the tenth century, Appolonius of Tyana traveled through India. According to his diary, he and his disciple, Damis, viewed the Brahmans of India "levitat-ing themselves in the air, at the height of two cubits, not to astonish (as they defend themselves from this kind of allegation), but because, according to them, all this they do at some distance

St. Dunstan was a highly influential figure in early English history. He was seen to levitate three days before his death in 988. (Mary Evans Picture Library)

from the earth is in honor of the sun and more praiseworthy of God."[33]

Damis and Appolonius viewed another levitation involving a complex cer-emony with multiple levitating Brahmans. The ceremony began when several

Brahmans approached a river, removed their clothes and applied a peculiar perfume or lotion onto their bodies. This caused their bodies to warm up so that they were covered in perspiration and began to steam. At this point, they threw their bodies into the river, cleansed themselves, and advanced to a predetermined location. They formed a circle and began to beat on the ground with sticks as they chanted a song. After a few moments, the ground beneath the Brahmans appeared to tremble, and the Brahmans lifted up in the air "to the height of two cubits." The levitation lasted as long as the Brahmans were singing, after which point they descended to the ground.[34]

Another early account is that of Simon Magus, a self-proclaimed Sumerian Magician. He performed an incredible levitation display over a Roman amphitheater. According to the Acts of Peter, "Suddenly a dust was seen afar off in the sky, like a smoke, shining, with rays stretching from it. And when he drew near to the gate, suddenly he was not seen; and thereafter he appeared, standing in the midst of the people."

On another occasion, Simon Magus was seen to elevate himself before a crowd of people, including several nobles, until suddenly, he was dashed to the ground, reportedly breaking his leg. Magus allegedly lost his powers after a confrontation with St. Peter.[35]

An early, undated account comes from Sulpice Severe, who wrote in *The Constitutions Apostoliques,* "I have seen a possessed person elevated in the air in a way that the feet didn't touch the ground, the arms extended at the approach of the relics of Saint Martin."[36]

Yet another early account of uncertain date occurred during the initiation ceremony of Emperor Julian the Apostate. The initiator, a philosopher named Maxime, fell into a trance and tilting his head back, rose slowly into the air, where he remained suspended above the ground. Julian approached. Maxime grabbed him and both men were levitated into the air together.[37]

Levitation can sometimes be harmful to the percipient simply because it has a tendency to generate controversy. A typical case involves Al Hosayn-Ibn-Mansour (d993), who was actually brought to trial and executed. During his trial, a witness to the prosecution, Al-Hallaj, who was the servant of Al-Hosayn, testified to the vicar that he had, in fact, observed his master to levitate above the ground while in prayer.[38]

Most early accounts involve meditational or ecstatic levitation, though again, very few kept detailed written records. The earliest recorded first-person narrative involving levitation comes from Milarepa (1052-1135), a well-known Tibetan Buddhist. His firsthand biography is still in print today. Milarepa reached enlightenment after many years of study and meditation on Buddhist scriptures. Along with enlightenment came several miraculous powers, including the power of flight.

Writes Milarepa, "After further intensive practice and meditation there began to develop in me certain Powers, those of transforming myself into any shape I desired and of being able to fly through the air....At first these powers manifested themselves only in my dreams but as I went on, eventually I found I was actually able to fly in broad daylight and go where I would to meditate."

Like many early levitators, Milarepa sometimes displayed his talents to amazed onlookers. Says Milarepa, "I passed over a small village called Langda, where a man was plowing with his son who saw me and cried out, 'Father, look at that fantastic thing! A man flying through the air.'"

The father warned his son not to watch the so-called holy man as he was "cunning and obstinate."

The son replied, "If a man can fly, obstinate or not, there is no greater spectacle than that! So look, Father!"

Another translation: "One day I was flying thus and was passing over a village where lived a distant relative of mine....He and his son were out plowing the field as I floated over them....the son happened to look up and saw me and cried, 'Look, there's a man flying!'

"'What of it?' said the father angrily. 'Why are you standing there like one moonstruck? It's only that rogue Mila, a good-for nothing starveling, son of a wicked woman from near here. Out of the way and don't get under his shadow, and carry on with your job.' The father was dodging about at the time, too, trying to avoid being covered by my shadow. But his son answered him back, 'I don't mind whether a man is good for nothing or not, just so long as he can fly; that's a most wonderful thing for a man to be able to do.' And he went on gazing up at me!"

Shortly after learning to levitate, Milarepa went into hiding. As he writes, "[I]f I stayed where I was when it was known that I could fly, people would come flocking to me to see me work miracles and fame and prosperity would impede any further progress."[39]

Saint Bernard of Clairvaux (1091-1153), the son of a nobleman, was a physician, author, preacher, and Abbot. Although he was very strict and austere, his holiness attracted numerous disciples. His sermons converted so many people to religious order that parents tried to prevent their children from attending. His reputation as a spiritual advisor grew until he, like St. Dunstan, became one of the most powerful personalities in Europe, consulting with Kings, Popes, and other rulers. He was a major force in shaping the political and religious thought of Western

St. Bernard of Clairvaux was a leader in religious history and an advisor to Kings, Popes, and heads of State. He sometimes experienced levitations while preaching. (Mary Evans Picture Library)

Europe. He is reported to have experienced many supernatural events, including miraculous healings and control of wild beasts. Part of his popularity lay in the fact that he, according to Von Goerres, occasionally experienced levitations while preaching.[40]

In the 1100s, teacher, Sufi philosopher, and biographer, Ibn al-Arabi, wrote about the life of his companion Zainab al-Qal'lyyah, a well-known ascetic and holy person. According to al-Arabi, he often traveled with al-Qal'lyyah in Mecca and Jerusalem. He described her as exceedingly intelligent and devout. Most interesting here, however, is that while in a state of prayer, al-Arabi witnessed al-Qal'lyyah levitate. This occurred only during the Prayer of Invocation. Al-Qal'lyyah would rise several feet in the air in rapt prayer, then after she was finished, would float slowly down to the ground.[41]

Another account told by al-Arabi is that of Ibn al-Hakim, a preacher in Tunis during the 1100s. According to the story, Ibn al-Hakim's duty was to announce the hour of prayer each day with a small cough. However, one day, al-Hakim was late. Bashir, the water-carrier went to look for him and saw al-Hakim float down out of the sky. Ibn al-Hakim coughed gently to begin the hour of prayer and warned Bashir not to tell anybody about his levitations until after his death, a request repeated by many levitators.[42]

Christina the Astonishing (Admirable) (1150-1220) was a Flemish nun whose levitations were of such a dramatic and bizarre character, they are still remembered today. She and her two older sisters were orphaned at an early age. As a young girl, she worked to guard the flocks in the field. However, she soon became very religious, and in the fervor of her prayers, began to fall into trances during which she would barely move and her breathing was nearly imperceptible.

At age twenty-one, she suffered a particularly severe fit, and was thought to have actually died. She was put in a coffin and prepared for burial. While mass was being read for her in church, she suddenly arose from her open coffin and "soared to the roof of the church." The entire congregation understandably panicked and fled the church, until the priest finally ordered her to come down. After descending, Christina reported a lengthy near-death experience during which she visited the heavenly realms and was given the choice to stay in heaven or return to life and serve God and pray for the salvation of lost souls. Christina chose to return.

After the experience, she was often seen hovering near the rafters of the roof in order to avoid human contact, which she now abhorred. Writes Calmet, "From then she could not bear the effluvia of the human body, and rose up into trees and on the highest towers with incredible lightness, there to watch and pray."

Christina's levitations were so numerous that her parents weighted her body with heavy chains in an unsuccessful attempt to halt the flights. Many other attempts were made to confine her, but she always escaped. She fled into the fields, onto the tops of towers, church roofs, the tops of tall poles, and all the highest points in the area. Her ability to levitate was observed by all those who lived in the vicinity. Some thought her mad. She would crawl into tiny spaces, run screaming through the town, swim in the icy rivers, hold flames over her flesh without being burned, and perform other strange behaviors.

Christina also had the rare talent of running levitation. Writes Calmet, "She was so light in running, that she outran the swiftest dogs."

Her strange behavior lessened in her old age and she spent the last years of her life in the convent of St. Catherine at St. Tround, dying at age eighty-four. Her biography was written eight years after her death by Thomas de Cantimpre, who interviewed dozens of firsthand eyewitnesses to her incredible feats.[43]

As history progressed, the accounts of levitations became better recorded and less mythical. The vast majority of these accounts come from Catholic Saints.

The reports of levitating saints are particularly compelling for a number of reasons. First, they come from people with a high-level of credibility. Second, they were often written down in detailed historical records. Third, many of the saints levitated repeatedly. Fourth, their levitations were witnessed by large numbers of people. And finally, the accounts from independent sources match each other with highly specific details. All of this makes it difficult to explain these accounts as mere fantasy or exaggerations.

Whether or not one believes the accounts now, it is obvious that at the time, people did believe these events were taking place. These levitations, although certainly controversial, were taken very seriously by the people of that time.

The fact that so many saints are reported to have levitated may seem like an enigma. Why only saints?

One way to answer this question is to turn it on its end and look at it from another perspective. One of the qualifications to make sainthood was performing a miracle. In other words, the reason that so many saints are reported to have levitated could be because those who levitated were canonized as saints. Throughout Europe, the cultural interpretation of the phenomena was dominated by the Catholic Church.

Another reason could be that many other cultures were experiencing levitation, but it remained largely unrecorded. The Catholic Church seems to have been largely alone in keeping detailed written records of these rare events.

St. Dominic (1170-1221) was an Italian preacher and founder of the order of Preaching Brothers. He is credited with bringing religion to the newly forming urban centers of Europe. He was religious from an early age and spent much of his time in church, studying, praying and "weeping for the sins of others." After seven years of contemplative life, he became very active by forming his own religious order. He soon became known not only for his stirring sermons, but for his miracles. On Ash Wednesday, in 1218, he is credited with reviving a young man who had been killed from a horse accident.

Often, levitations are verified when the levitator fails to arrive for his/her prescribed duties. When St. Dominic once failed to show up for mealtime, the Prior ordered another monk to retrieve him. The monk returned saying that St. Dominique was levitated in prayer. Skeptical, the Prior followed the monk back to St. Dominic's cell and verified the levitation himself. On several other occasions, he was seen to levitate during Holy Communion. His biographer, Mother Francis Raphael, writes, "Often, in rapture, he was seen raised above the ground; his hands then moved to and fro as though receiving something from God, and he was heard exclaiming, 'Hear, O Lord, the voice of my prayer when I cry unto Thee, and when I hold out my hands to Thy holy temple.'"[44]

St. Edmund of Abingdon (1180-1240) was the archbishop of Canterbury and advisor to King Henry III. From an early age, he devoted himself to the study of God. He took a vow of chastity, and immersed himself in religious scholarship, at which he excelled quickly. According to Abingdon's chancellor, St. Richard de Chichester, he observed Abingdon in the chapel in a state of intense prayer, "raised high in the air with knees bent and arms stretched out." Of the truth of this case, Herbert Thurston wrote, "….there can be little doubt."[45]

Probably one of the most famous and popular saints of all times is St. Francis of Assisi (1181-1226). St. Francis was the son of a wealthy silk merchant. He gave up his title and dedicated his life to God and the love of all creation. He soon became an enormously popular preacher. His extraordinary charisma garnered him a massive following. He was the first recorded person to receive the wounds of Stigmata. He was also seen to levitate on numerous occasions.

One such flight was recorded in 1223 in Grecchio. Brother Leo was charged with providing Saint Francis with food and water. He testified that he saw St. Francis rise more than six feet above the surface of the ground. On several other occasions, he saw St. Francis hovering outside his cave. Often it appeared that his body was glowing with light.

At other times, Brother Leo reports that St. Francis would levitate among a nearby grove of Beech trees. As the saint rose slowly, Brother Leo confessed that he would sneak up to St. Francis, kiss his feet and pray for a blessing. According to Brother Leo, on at least one occasion, St. Francis levitated so high among the trees that he was no longer visible among the crowded branches.

On one reported occasion, St. Francis reportedly fell into an ecstatic trance, and grabbing Brother Masseo, pulled him into the air with him. Some authors, however, have disputed this episode.

St. Francis was also well known for his vow of poverty and charity. On yet another often-quoted occasion, he visited a wealthy and powerful landowner whom he apparently wished to convert. Apparently knowing that he would levitate, St. Francis began to pray before the man. As expected, St. Francis quickly rose into the air. And as St. Francis evidently hoped, the wealthy landowner was so impressed, he took a vow of poverty, gave away all his possessions, and became one of the many followers of St. Francis.[46]

St. Francis was so influential that two of his contemporaries also began to levitate. Phillipin the Blessed reportedly fell into ravishments during which his body would float up among the tallest oak trees, as affirmed by the brothers of his monastery.[47]

Pierre of Monticello (also contemporary to Saint Francis) was witnessed by Servadeo D'Urbin, the guardian father of the convent of Ancone, to levitate at six cubits above the stone tiles of the church while in contemplation before the crucifix.[48]

At the same time that St. Francis was experiencing his miracles and changing the lives of thousands, Saint Lutgard [Lutgardis] [Ludgard](1182-1246) lived a quiet life as Belgian nun. Her parents entered her into a convent at age twelve because they had no money for her to marry. At age twenty, she had a vision of Christ which caused her to renounce worldly life. She then experienced numerous ecstatic levitations that were witnessed by her fellow nuns. Writes Thurston, "Sometimes during her frequent ecstasies, she would be upraised from the ground, or a strange light would be seen above her head."

She was asked to become abbess, but declined, preferring to live a humble life. Today, however, she is considered by many religious scholars to be one of the leading mystics of the thirteenth century.[49]

As we have seen, many early levitators are powerful and influential members of society. Such is the case of Gilles the Blessed of Santarem (Giles) (1190-1267). The son of the governor of Portugal, Gilles first shunned religion in favor of science and medicine. He soon studied physics, alchemy, and then necromancy and other so-called "Black Arts." After having a horrific nightmare, Gilles changed his dark ways. He burned all his magical books and potions. He then joined the order of Saint Dominique and organized a monastery. Seven years of penitence followed, until Gilles began having divine visions, ecstasies, prophecies and levitations.

While staying at the home of Dame Pichena, he experienced a fit of ecstasy and was levitated. All the residents of the home were astonished, and fearing that Gilles might fall, they attempted to pull him down. To their surprise, they were only able to budge him slightly.

The scene caused a huge uproar, and hundreds of people converged to view the levitation. The residents of the house were unable to stop the stampede of spectators who even climbed onto the roof of the house and dangled over the edge to view Gilles through the windows.

When Gilles finally returned to his senses and learned what had happened, he left secretly in the middle of the night. Gilles, like many other levitators, preferred to keep his episodes a secret.[50]

It should be clear by now that levitation events occur in a wide variety of cultures. While Europe, and in particular Italy, accounts for most of the early cases, several came from eastern countries. An undated twelfth century account is attributed to Indian sheikh Djilani from Baghdad who reportedly held séance-like meetings during which he would be elevated above his seat.[51]

Another undated twelfth century account is that of the Iranian Saint, Qutb uddin Haydar. He was credited with numerous abilities, including incombustibility, the ability to withstand intense cold, and levitations. He was often seen meditating on inaccessible roofs and tree-tops.[52]

Levitation as a phenomenon emerged very early in history, starting in the second century BC, and continuing at a regularly increasing rate. The next centuries would bring more levitations and more controversy.

2. Levitations in Early History

As time marched on into the thirteenth and fourteenth centuries, levitation events became more numerous and better recorded. However, there was still no serious investigation into the phenomenon. As a consequence, levitation would remain largely unexplored and unexplained for centuries to come.

Jalalu d'Din Rumi (1207-1230) was a Persian saint, philosopher, poet, and founder of the Order of Mevlevi Dervishes, who are perhaps best known for their spinning technique of meditation. Rumi levitated first as a child. One day he and his friends climbed up to the rooftop as they had many times before. On this occasion, however, they began to discuss the possibility of flying when Rumi suddenly flew upwards, disappeared into the clouds, and reappeared moments later. Later, he was said to levitate whenever he became deeply absorbed in prayer or devotion, at which point he would rise from his chair and start whirling. Reportedly, the other devotees were only able to stop the levitations by playing music.[53]

St. Philip Benizi (1233-1285) was the only son of a noble Italian family. As a child, he studied medicine and philosophy. One day in church, he had a vision that inspired him to become a lay brother. Although he preferred to be alone and in contemplation, he climbed quickly up the church hierarchy, and several years later, he was appointed the head of the Servites in Pistoia, Italy. His sermons were very effective and caused many sinners to convert to religion. He became so popular that he was considered to become Pope. Upon hearing this "bad news," he fled the church and lived in a cave in the mountains for three months until the "danger" had passed. He was reportedly seen to levitate on several occasions.[54]

The thirteenth century produced several other levitators. Saint Douceline (1214-1274) experienced frequent ecstatic levitations which were witnessed by reputable observers including Jacques Vivaud, the Senior of the Castle of Cuges, and his son, who reported that she was so high up, they could kiss the bottoms of her feet—which they did with great devotion. Another witness, Raimon du Puy, observed her in levitation, and kneeling down, measured a distance of one palm (the width of one hand) between her and the floor.

Numerous other people witnessed her levitations. On the Feast of Assumption, she was seen to rise up from the ground and travel over the entire choir, as if following an imaginary procession. On many occasions, she was seen partially levitated, balanced on the tips of her toes, lifted in ecstatic rapture.[55]

Jutta of Prussia (1215-1264) was a well-known hermit and ascetic. After being widowed, she gave up her considerable wealth to the poor and lived in seclusion where she experienced numerous visions and levitations. Reportedly, her ecstasies occurred twice daily and were often accompanied by levitations which were witnessed by her neighbors.[56]

Very little is known about Humiliano of Florence (1219-1246), other than he lived very austerely, and reportedly experienced levitations.[57]

Ambrose Sausedonius (Ambroise Santedonis) (Sienne) (1220-1287) was an Italian Priest. Born paralyzed to two highly distinguished families in Siena, he experienced a miraculous healing at an early age. This developed in him a religious piety and a desire to help the sick and poor. At age seventeen, he joined the Dominicans. He excelled in his studies, and he soon became a popular teacher, preacher, and mediator. He was reported to have levitated on two separate occasions, both while preaching. His biographer admitted to the levitations, but theorized that perhaps the witnesses were the victims of a "divine hallucination."[58]

St. Bonaventura (1221-1274) was an Italian Cardinal and influential author. He devoted much of his life to formal prayer, which he considered of paramount importance to spiritual happiness. As he wrote, "A spiritual joy is the greatest sign of the divine grace dwelling in a soul." Bonaventura reportedly experienced at least one levitation, which was observed while he was researching the life of St. Francis. He was canonized in 1482.[59]

St. Thomas of Aquinas (1227-1274) was an Italian Friar and associate of St. Bonaventura. He became a powerful religious figure, often consulting with Louis IX on important state matters. He was also a prolific author, and his writings eventually became the official teachings of the Catholic Church. He was reportedly very humble and holy. At three hundred pounds, he was overweight and was called by some, "The Dumb Ox."

From age five to thirteen, Aquinas lived in a monastery. He then went to the University of Naples where he studied and taught art and science. After attending the university, he joined the Order of Preachers and spent much of his time in prayer. It was around age nineteen, when his fellow friars first noticed mysterious "rays of light" which appeared around his head while he was in prayer. Later in life, he experienced numerous ecstatic levitations accompanied by visions. The levitations are well-verified, with names of witnesses and firsthand testimonies. His biographer and friend, Guillaume de Thoca, reports that several times he saw Aquinas levitated from the ground in ecstasy. Other witnesses include Brother Jacques and Brother Dominique. In 1269 in Paris, he was levitated in prayer for so long that scores of people gathered to watch the spectacle. St. Aquinas was known mostly for his piety and humility. He often said that he learned more at the foot of the crucifix than from all the books he had ever read.[60]

Bentivoglio the Blessed (d1232) was born to wealthy parents, but joined the Franciscans and took a vow of poverty. His sermons were so effective, that numerous members of his own family turned to religious life. He was known for his religious fervor, his piety, and several miracles. The best attested of these was reported by Parson Masseo, who observed Bentivoglio levitating while in prayer deep in the forest where he had apparently hidden himself to avoid observers.

As in several other cases of levitation, the witness converted his religion and joined the Franciscans.[61]

While many levitators were deeply religious or spiritual, they didn't necessarily start that way. Peter [Pierre] Armengol the Blessed (1238-1304) came from a family of Spanish counts and ran away to join a group of bandits. One day, his group of bandits came upon and was about to rob Armengol's father. Realizing the error of his ways, Armengol was consumed with guilt, changed his life, and became a monk. He then devoted his life to prayer and asceticism. Any free time was spent ransoming captive prisoners. Witnesses reported that he often levitated during prayer.[62]

St. Albert of Trapani (1240-1306) was a Sicilian Priest who became famous for his fervent preaching, practice of austerities, and miraculous manifestations, among them, levitation. Writes Calmet, "During his prayers [he] rose three cubits from the ground."[63]

Gerardesca the Blessed (d1243) was seen elevated at fifteen feet in height. The witness was initially very frightened by the spectacle, but the "graceful singing" of the ecstatic quickly calmed her fears.[64]

Saint Marguerite of Cortone, Tuscany (Margaret of Cortona) (1247-1297), like many of the Saints, led a particularly colorful life. She was a Franciscan nun who worked as a nurse. As a child, she was abused by her stepmother and ran away from home. She was then seduced by a young Italian knight with whom she lived in sin as his mistress. After his tragic murder, she repented and became a nun, living very ascetically and often mortifying her flesh. She was later credited with numerous miraculous healings and was widely sought for counsel by people across Italy.

One day, she was seen weeping about her mistakes and praying for forgiveness. Her prayers reached such a fervor that she rose up three feet into the center of the room, while the household members looked on with awe. As in other similar cases, she was supernaturally informed of the exact time of her approaching death.[65]

St. Agnes of Montepulciano (1268-1317) was born in Tuscany, Italy. From as young as she could remember, she was attracted to religion, and at age nine, she convinced her parents to place her in a convent. She rose quickly up the ranks, and at the unheard of age of fifteen, she was appointed abbess. She was extremely devout, spending much time in prayer, eating only bread and water, and sleeping with a stone for a pillow. She later became prioress of her own convent, where she reportedly experienced "levitation and performed many miracles." The levitations were often witnessed by many of her fellow sisters, and usually took place in front of the crucifix.[66]

Blessed Gerard Cagnoli (1270-1345) was the only son of noble Italian parents. His parents died young, leaving him an orphaned but wealthy teen-ager. Relatives strongly persuaded him to marry, but instead, he slowly gave away his considerable wealth. By age forty, he was living the life of a pilgrim and hermit, spending most of his time in the wilderness. He subsisted solely on bread and water, slept on a wood plank, and scourged his flesh until it bled. Around this time, he became known for several miracles. On one occasion, he apparently manifested a feast of food. On another, he made a broken glass dish whole by holding it in his hands. He was also sought after to perform healings. On many occasions, he was seen in a state of ecstasy "surrounded with light and raised from the ground."[67]

Saint Robert of Solentum (Salente) (Palentin) (1273-1341) was an Italian Abbot. On one occasion, he was seen in levitation while in church. One of the monks uttered an exclamation of surprise, which startled Robert and ended the levitation. According to Calmet, "St. Robert de Palentin rose also from the ground, sometimes to the height of a foot and a half, to the great astonishment of his disciples and assistants."[68]

That levitation is within the grasp of any person is illustrated by the following colorful account. Franco Lippi of Grotti the Blessed (1211-1291) of Italy was reportedly a violent, insubordinate, and lazy child. He spent the first half of his life with a group of bandits, committing a series of violent crimes. Then, at age fifty, he lost his eyesight. This caused him to become deeply spiritual. His eyesight then miraculously returned. He continued to live an extremely ascetic and austere lifestyle, flagellating himself, and wearing only sackcloth. He was eventually admitted as a lay brother into the Carmelites, where he became famous for his asceticism, faith, visions, and miracles. He experienced a particularly dramatic levitation following a vision of the Virgin Mary in his room. He fell into ecstasy and began to levitate and emit so bright a light that his fellow monks came running, thinking there was a fire. On another occasion, he was seen reciting the Psalms with such devotion, that he was lifted three feet from the ground. These incidents, and others, made him famous across the city of Siena.[69]

Bartholus of Vado (Bartholomew Buonpedoni of San Gimignano)(d1300) decided to become a priest after having a vision of the Lord. In 1280, he contracted malignant leprosy. He was forced to leave his order, and retired to the leper-house of Celloli where he served as chaplain. He was often seen levitated there during contemplation.[70]

Ibn Battuta, a fourteenth century Arabian geographer, historian, theologian, botanist, and author, left a particularly detailed account of a Far East levitation demonstration. During his travels, Battuta visited Delhi, India, where he was the guest of the Sultan, Abul Mujahid Muhammad Shah. The Sultan had invited several honored guests, including Battuta, to view the feats of the Sultan's yogis. What happened next was vividly engraved in Battuta's memory. He later wrote a vivid description of the event: "The sultan ordered me to sit. I sat down. He then said to the yogis, 'Verily this illustrious man has come from a distant country; show him what he has not seen.' They said, 'Yes.' One of them squatted and lifted himself high up in the air in such a way that he remained over us in a squatting posture. I was astonished at this and became frightened and fell on the ground. The sultan ordered that I should be administered a medicine which he had with him. Thus I recovered and sat up, but the yogi was still in the same squatting position."[71]

Blessed Peter of Treia (d1304) was born of poor parents and joined the order of Franciscans at an early age. He was a popular and effective preacher, reportedly converting many sinners and attracting large crowds to hear his speeches, during which he sometimes foretold future events. Once, while praying fervently at the convent of Ancona, his superiors observed him "rapt in ecstasy and lifted from the ground."[72]

Marguerite of Castello the Blessed (d1320) was born blind and hunchbacked, and spent the first fourteen years of her life held captive by her parents in a walled-in room. At age fourteen, she was abandoned by her abusive parents, and was taken in by nuns at the convent of Citta del Castello. Her extreme austerity, however, caused her to be expelled. She later joined the Dominicans where she founded a children's school. She was credited with numerous miracles of healing and levitation. Her fellow sisters reported that she was often levitated while in prayer more than a foot from the ground, where she would remain for long durations.[73]

Not much is known about the life a young woman named St. Flora (d1347) of Beaulieu, France. She resisted her parents' attempts to have her married, and instead, devoted herself to God. She was later torn between religious and secular life and became very depressed. The nuns in her priory ridiculed her mercilessly. However, her religious fervor grew and she began to receive "divine favours." On one occasion, she fell into a three-week-long ecstasy, during which she needed no food or water. Sacred objects were once teleported to her presence. And once while meditating on the Holy Ghost, Flora was "raised four feet from the ground" and "hung suspended in the air for some time while all were looking on."[74]

St. Catherine of Sienna (Sienne) (1347-1380) was an extremely influential spiritual leader, who gave counsel to Popes, princes, priests, soldiers, and the common man. She is credited with helping to heal the "Great Schism" which had divided the western Church for forty years. When the Black Death swept across Europe, she cared for the sick and dying. She often treated those who nobody else would help, including victims of leprosy.

Catherine, the twenty-third child in her family, devoted her life to spirituality from age six, when she had a vision of the Lord. By age twelve, she had built a hermitage in her backyard. Around that time, she fell into her first ecstatic trance and felt herself levitated until her head hit the ceiling. Her parents tried everything they could to dissuade her from her religious obsession, but to no avail. They finally gave up and gave Catherine her own small room, in which she spent most of her time praying intensely. She also fasted and slept on hard wooden boards.

As an adult, she continued to have regular mystical experiences, usually following communion or her practice of depriving herself of food, sleep, and comfort. Her numerous levitations were often witnessed by her fellow nuns, who verified the miracles by placing their hands between the floor and the floating Catherine.

Her biographer, Joergensen, gives a vivid description of one of her levitations: "Beginning to pray, she found herself in a new and strange state where everything disappeared around her and she had the feeling of hovering in a world of bright light. She had the impression of being lifted up, little by little, from the ground, higher and higher. Finally her head hit on the ceiling which woke her."

On August 18, 1370, following communion, she remained levitated above her bed, which was witnessed by three people. Caffarini, one of the witnesses to her feats, reports that her levitations sometimes exceeded several meters.

Leroy considered her case to be particularly reputable. Herbert Thurston wrote, "The evidence for St. Catherine of Siena's levitations seems quite overwhelming."

During her ecstasies, Catherine occasionally gave long spiritual discourses, much in the manner of today's trance channelers. Some of these discourses were later published as the *"Dialogues of Saint Catherine"* and are today considered spiritual classics. Interesting here are the comments Catherine made regarding levitation.

Like many channelers, Catherine spoke as if she were channeling God. "The perfect soul lives in constant union with God....Many times the body is raised from the ground because of this perfect union that the soul has made with Me, as if the body had lost its weight in order to become light. Actually, it lost none of its weight, but as the union of the soul with Me is more perfect than the union between the body and the soul, the force of the spirit fixed in Me raises the weight of the body from the ground." Catherine of Sienna died at age thirty-three. She was canonized in 1461.[75]

As can be seen, extreme religious devotion can lead to levitation. Certainly, most of the early levitation cases seem to indicate this. A typical example is St. Vincent Ferrer (1359-1419), a Spanish Missionary. Ferrer was highly educated and wrote several well-received treatises. When the city of Barcelona suffered from a famine, Ferrer predicted that ships would bring food in two days. Although his prior censured him for making predictions, he was right, and Ferrer's reputation as a holy man was assured. His sermons were so powerful, listeners often wept uncontrollably or fainted with emotion. Ferrer was seen on at least one occasion to levitate during prayer, his body encased in a cloud of light.[76]

St. Coleta of Ghent (1381-1447) was a Flemish Abbess who founded more than nineteen convents and was well known for her holiness and spiritual wisdom. She had numerous instances of precognition, supernatural luminosity, healing, taming of wild beasts, predicted her own death, and also experienced many ecstatic levitations. Many monks testified in the Acta Sanctorum that she was seen to hover in the air, sometimes attaining such a height that she disappeared from view. She was canonized in 1807.[77]

Pierre-Jeremie of Panormo (Palerme) (1381-1452) was a Sicilian friar. Following his death, his companions wrote his biography, reporting that he often levitated during prayer. At times his body also became luminous. On one occasion he levitated in his room, at which time his body became so bright, that his superior believed (as in several other cases) that there was a fire, and getting no response, broke down the door to get in.[78]

Catherine Columbina (d1387) was a Spanish Abbess. Her case is particular interesting because her levitations were used by St. John Columbino, teacher of the Jesuits, to inspire other nuns to join the Jesuits. According to Calmet, "It is related of her, that sometimes she remained in a trance, and raised up two yards from the ground, motionless, speechless and insensible."

According to her biography, on Christmas Eve she experienced a two-hour-long levitation during which her body emitted a soft white light.[79]

St. Antonine Pierozzi (1389-1459) was the Archbishop of Florence, Italy, and had no qualms about exerting his power and influence. He created many reforms, abolished gambling, fought usury, established aid for the poor, and helped victims of natural disasters. He was considered a very holy man and was known to have produced several miracles, among them levitation. His levitations usually occurred during contemplations, at which time his body also became luminous. His trial for canonization contains the testimonies of several firsthand eyewitnesses.[80]

Saint Pierre of Regalati (d1456) joined the Franciscans at age thirteen, against his mother's wishes. His fellow friars soon singled him out as being particularly fervent. Pierre then undertook severe austerities, which served to increase his piety. He soon began to have frequent ecstasies in which he was "often raised from the ground." During some of these occasions, his body would emit an intense light. Regalati's levitations reportedly lasted for several hours.[81]

Nicolas of Ravenne (d1398) was a Dominican monk who experienced levitations while saying mass or preaching, reaching an elevation of about one foot.[82]

Another brief case comes from Guilemette de la Rochelle, (fourteenth century), a well-known spiritual leader who, while in meditative contemplation, was seen to be "lifted into the air more than two feet."[83]

Saint Francois de Paule (Francis of Paola) (1416-1507) became a friar at age thirteen. Two years later, he moved into a remote cave and lived as a solitary hermit. His reputation for holiness and miracles grew quickly, and he soon became a well-known thaumaturge who was often consulted for spiritual advice by many royal figures. He was credited with numerous miraculous talents, including the gift of prophecy, immunity to fire, the ability to read people's minds, and levitation, which usually occurred during prayer. Several prominent witnesses attest to his levitations. King Ferdinand the First of Naples observed him suspended in the center of his room, his body emitting beams of light. Ann de Beaujeu, the daughter of Louis XI, also testified to having seen Saint Francois de Paul in levitation.[84]

Blessed Giles of Lorenzana (1443-1518) of Naples, Italy, was born to working class parents, and turned to religious life while still a child. He spent most of his time in silent prayer, during which time wild beasts would often approach him. He then began to experience prophecies and perform miraculous cures, which attracted a steady stream of visitors. Among the most famous of his miracles is levitation. He was reportedly often seen "raised from the ground" while in prayer.[85]

Osanna Andreasi of Mantus (1450-1505) was an Italian nun who experienced her first miracle—a vision of Paradise—at age five. From this early age, she devoted her life to God and spent most of her time in private prayer and penance. When she began having ecstasies, her concerned parents thought she had epilepsy. Later, as a young woman, she resisted her family's wish for marriage and instead became a Dominican nun. She experienced many visions of Jesus Christ, during which she was seen to levitate while in prayer. Her fellow preachers sometimes saw her walk a few inches above the ground as she went to church.[86]

Jean-Ange Porro the Blessed (1450-1506) spent his entire life as a hermit in Milan, Italy. He was reportedly seen by his servant to be raised up to the height of a man.[87]

J. Savaranola (Savonrole) (1452-1498) was a Dominican monk who reportedly had levitations while in prison. According to his biographer, the jailer found Savaranola in ecstasy, freed from his chains, surrounded with light. The scene so impressed the jailer that he converted to Christianity.[88]

Saint Diego (d1463) was born from poverty, and lived an austere life as an Observant Friar. He worked in the Canary Islands as a teacher and missionary. He also worked as a caretaker, and was credited with the miraculous healing of many sick friars. He reportedly had a levitation upon seeing the painting, "The Miracle of San Diego," which is currently found in the Louvre Museum in France. The levitation was observed by three witnesses, and as in several other cases, his body was bathed in light.[89]

Columba of Rieti (1468-1501) was an Italian nun whose unusual reputation began early in life, when a dove alighted on her head during her Baptism. Her parents set her up to get married, but she cut off all her hair and refused. She had secretly vowed herself to God at age ten. She later became a Dominican nun and practiced austerities, reportedly living on only a few berries each day. She founded a monastery, and became famous for mediating local conflicts, prophecies, her ability to cure the sick, as well as her ecstatic visions, during which she would sometimes levitate. Her confessor, Sebastien de Perousse, reported that he personally witnessed her levitations, saying that on these occasions her body was "carried sweetly towards God." She died at the young age of thirty-four.[90]

Christine Ciccarelli of Aquila (1480-1543) of Abruzzi, Italy, took a vow of chastity and joined a convent while still a child. An Augustine nun, she was known for her humility, virtue, charity, and holiness. She spent many hours in prayer, and often displayed knowledge of future events. She had at least two recorded levitations, one during which she was raised five feet above the ground while in prayer, and another during which she fell into a levitating ecstasy for twenty-four hours, one of the longest-recorded levitations. Her popularity was such that upon her death, a huge crowd of people attended her funeral.[91]

Blessed James of Illyria (d1485) was reported to have levitated on several occasions. As in other cases, this usually occurred during prayer.[92]

Brother Antoine de Saint-Reine (fifteenth century) worked as a gardener at a Franciscan convent. He was seen on several occasions, praying in the garden where he would rise to the tops of the tallest trees. On another occasion, he was seen levitating on the road before a tree, staring at a crucifix nailed onto the trunk.[93]

So closes the early accounts of levitation. The sheer number and consistency of the reports suggests that most of the events happened as described. The first recorded accounts come almost exclusively from Europe and Asia, with the majority coming from Italy. The official explanation adopted by most of Europe was that God was responsible for the manifestations. Those who levitated were often canonized as saints. In Asia and the Far East, however, levitation was generally considered a human talent, although one that lies deeply latent, activated only by arduous spiritual devotion and strict asceticism.

The reaction to the levitations was generally positive. There are almost no accounts of levitators being vilified. On the contrary, the levitators were considered to be extremely wise and holy, and levitation displays were used to convert people towards spirituality.

The next few hundred years, however, brought more accounts. Not only did the number of accounts increase, so did their credibility and number of witnesses. And as different cultures were faced with the enigma of levitation, they began to react in different ways. While many levitators were still considered to be saints or spiritually advanced, others, it was believed, were unfortunate victims of diabolical or demonic possession. Also the tradition of covering up levitation events became widely practiced.

3. The Levitating Royal Family of Hungary

While acts of levitation have been recorded numerous times throughout history, it was still a rare and spectacular event that occurred sporadically to people who seemed to have no relation to each other. However, for every rule there are exceptions. In this case, the exception is the Royal Family of Hungary. For some unknown reason, numerous members of the Hungarian Royal Family have apparently inherited the ability to levitate. While there are some cases of levitators who have known each other, there are only a few other cases (which we shall explore later) in which levitation runs in families.

The first known levitator of the royal family was Saint Stephen I, (978-1038) King of Hungary. Stephen I was an enormously influential leader. Shortly after taking the throne, he restricted the power of the nobles, expanded the church, outlawed adultery and blasphemy, abolished pagan customs, considerably reduced crime, and ordered all couples outside of religious order to marry. Despite his strictness, he was also known for his extreme generosity, and reportedly walked the streets in disguise, distributing alms to the poor. He never started a war, but successfully repelled every attempted invasion. He was very religious and spent much of his time in prayer and meditation. Stephen was only one of several members of this royal family who reportedly had the ability to levitate. In 1030, on the night before a big battle, the King was seen praying in his tent, raised high above the ground. On other occasions, he would pray in his tent, which would itself be elevated along with him.[94]

Ladislas I, (1041-1096) King of Hungary, was the next levitator from the royal family of Hungary. Also a very successful leader, he expanded the borders of Hungary, and repelled numerous attempts at invasion. His piety, strength, and courage made him a national hero. His ability to levitate was first discovered by a servant who was waiting for Ladislas to finish praying in a chapel. When Ladislas failed to exit the chapel, the servant entered and found his master in prayer, levitated above the ground. From the moment of his death, he was honored as a saint.[95]

More than one hundred years later, the Royal family produced yet another levitator. St. Elizabeth, Princess of Hungary (1207-1231), had her marriage arranged at age four. Although she married and later had children, she led a very religious and ascetic life. She was widely known for her acts of charity. In fact, she gave so much of her massive wealth away to the poor that she was accused of mismanaging her estate and was forced to leave. She then joined the Franciscans, and took a lifetime vow of poverty. Her levitations reportedly occurred on several occasions upon encountering an image of the Virgin Mary. She died at age twenty-four.[96]

Many of the early levitation cases involved powerful and respected people in society. St. Hedwig (1174-1243) was the daughter of Count Berthold of Bavaria, and through her sister, was Aunt to St. Elizabeth of Hungary. At age twelve, she married the Duke of Pologne. She founded numerous hospitals and monasteries, including the first woman's monastery in Silesia. She was also an influential peacemaker and mediator. Following the death of her husband, she joined a monastery, and lived very ascetically, wearing only a light tunic and going barefoot even in snow. She soon began to exhibit miracles including healings, predicting her own death, and levitation. According to her biographer, she was seen one day raised above the earth, surrounded in light.[97]

Agnes of Bohemia (1205-1281) was the Princess of Bohemia. Her mother was sister to King Andreas II of the Royal Family of Hungary, making St. Elizabeth of Hungary her first cousin. Agnes dedicated her life to helping the poor. She refused to marry Emperor Fredric II, and instead, became a nun. She worked tirelessly building hospitals, convents, and attending to the poor. According to her biographer, she was sometimes lifted off the ground during contemplation. On one occasion, Sister Benigne and Sister Prisque saw Agnes levitate in the convent garden. She rose up quickly and out of view. When she reappeared an hour later, she refused to reveal where she had been.[98]

Princess Margaret of Hungary (1242-1270) gave up her comfortable royal life to become a nun. She volunteered for the most menial jobs, and spent much of her time caring for the sick and praying. She lived very austerely, depriving herself of food, sleep, and even sanitation. Her levitations occurred almost exclusively on holy days.[99]

Finally, Princess Margaret's sister, Blessed Helena (1235-1298), also reportedly levitated, making her at least the seventh member of the Royal family to do so. As of yet, no other members of the Royal Family of Hungary have admitted to levitation events.

St. Elizabeth, Princess of Hungary, noted for her charity and holiness, is only one of several members of the Royal Family of Hungary who have experienced levitations. (Mary Evans Picture Library)

4. The
Saints Come Marching In

As humanity entered medieval times, the majority of *recorded* levitation accounts still originated from Catholic saints. However, increasingly, detailed records were kept and more levitators began to write their own autobiographical accounts. No longer is there any doubt that the accounts are non-fiction. The levitators are clearly describing what happened to them in their own words. As one reads their obviously sincere testimonies, it becomes increasingly difficult to deny that levitation occurs. Over and over again, men and woman describe the same experience. And again, many of the levitators were extremely influential people in society.

In this chapter, we shall focus only on cases of medieval levitating saints.

St. Angela Merici (1470-1540) of Italy is credited with founding the first teaching order of women to be established in the church. Both her parents died at age ten, leaving her to be raised by her uncle. Three years later, her older sister died. Then when she was twenty-two, her uncle died. After a vision, she devoted herself completely to God and joined a Franciscan tertiary, where she practiced extreme austerities. One day she became appalled by the ignorance of local children, and decided to start a small school. Her efforts prospered, and before long, she founded other schools. She also exhibited a number of supernatural gifts, including at least one levitation event. Writes Thurston, "As she was assisting at Mass, shortly afterwards she fell into a prolonged ecstasy and was seen by a great number of persons to be upraised from the ground." She was canonized in 1807 and is known today as the Foundress of the Company of Saint Ursula.[100]

St. Cajetun (1480-1547) of Vicenza, Italy first worked as a senator, but at age thirty-three, joined the priesthood. He eventually became very influential, and is today best known for his sweeping reforms of the Catholic Church, as well as his tireless aid to the poverty-stricken. He was reported to have experienced many supernatural graces, and was sometimes seen levitated while deep in prayer.[101]

St. Ignatius Loyola (1491-1556), born of noble heritage, was a Spanish Soldier who turned to religion through remarkable coincidence. At age thirty, his leg was shattered by a cannonball, forcing him to take several months to recuperate. Normally anti-religious, he was so bored that he picked up a book about the saints. The book totally changed his life, inspiring in him a desire to be like them. He gave away all his belongings and took a vow of poverty. He stopped washing, became a vegetarian, deprived himself of sleep, food and comfort, and spent long hours in prayer and contemplation. Thus began his steady rise to spiritual giant. He later founded the Jesuits and devoted his time to teaching spiritual conversion through meditation. His order was enormously successful, expanding as far as China, Japan, India, and North and South America. As McBride writes, "Ignatius founded the most successful educational order in modern history."

He later wrote extensively on spirituality, including his best-known and most influential work, *Spiritual Exercises,* and had many visions and levitations. John Pascal testified during the process of Canonization that he observed Loyola deep in prayer, raised more than one foot above the ground. The nuns at the Saint Jerome convent in Barcelona reported that Ignatius would spend long hours in contemplation before the altar, and would sometimes levitate there.

Calmet wrote that Loyola often "remained entranced by God, and raised up from the ground to the height of two feet, while his body shone like light. He has been seen to remain in a trance insensible, and almost without respiration, for eight days together."[102]

St. Ignatius Loyola was a highly influential figure in religious history. Numerous witnesses have seen him in a levitating state. (Mary Evans Picture Library)

St. Peter [Pierre] Garavita of Alcantara (1499-1562) of Spain became a Franciscan friar at age sixteen. He practiced many austerities, sleeping without a mattress, sometimes in a sitting position. He put so much vinegar and salt in his food that he eventually lost all sense of taste. He ate no meat, drank no wine. He wore only one tunic, and when it was being cleaned, he remained naked. He was finally forced to limit his austerities when his health began to suffer.

Like many levitators, his episodes occurred spontaneously during religious services. Peter's episodes, however, were particularly memorable as they were of long duration, often lasting up to three hours.

Most of his levitations took place took place in front of the church altar or in the convent garden. During some of his levitations, his body appeared to glow brightly.

On one occasion, he was seen by several shepherds and peasants levitating before a roadside cross. On another, he and a fellow brother reportedly walked across the Guadiana river, which was flooded and impassible by normal means. During yet another memorable levitation, St. Alcantara was lifted far above the level of the trees with his arms crossed against his chest. As he hovered overhead, hundreds of small birds were seen to flock around him, chirping loudly.[103]

St. Francis Xavier (1506-1552) was the youngest member of a large wealthy family in Pamplona, Spain. He attended the University of Paris, and later met St. Ignatius of Loyola. As an apparent result, he himself, turned to religious life and became a missionary. St. Xavier eventually traveled across the world, and became one of the most influential missionaries in history. He was enormously popular, not only for his missionary work, but for his

St. Peter of Alcantara, Spanish mystic and Franciscan friar, levitating to a crucifix, circa 1560. (Mary Evans Picture Library)

charity and care for the sick. He was also reported to have experienced several episodes of precognition and was seen to levitate on several occasions. He was canonized in 1622, at the same time as St. Philip Neri, St. Ignatius Loyola, and St. Teresa of Avila, all levitators.[104]

Saint Catherine de Ricci (1522-1589) suffered from a variety of painful diseases as a child, which she overcame by intense prayer. At age twenty-five she became prioress of a Dominican monastery near Florence, Italy. Although she was uneducated, she soon earned a reputation for holiness and spiritual wisdom, and was widely sought for advice by high-ranking religious officials, including three cardinals each of whom later became Pope. She experienced regular ecstasies during which she would act out various religious scenes while in a trance. Most famous for her wounds of the stigmata, she also experienced levitations that were reportedly viewed by numerous witnesses. She was a friend of Saint Philip Neri, himself a levitator. She was canonized in 1747 by Benoit XIV, who also published her biography.[105]

Throughout the Middle Ages, levitation accounts remained dominated by religious mystics. St. Luis Bertrand (1526-1581) was a Spanish Missionary who became a well-known preacher. He aided victims of the Black Death, and according to his biographer, Batholome Avignoni, had the gift of prophecy, speaking in tongues and levitation.

During one instance, Bertrand was traveling with his servant when he asked the servant to wait at the edge of a field of corn while he prayed. Bertrand then went into the field out of view. At that point, a local resident came along the road and saw the servant waiting patiently. He questioned the servant who replied that Bertrand was praying in the field. Intrigued, the resident climbed onto a nearby hill to search for the preacher. He found him in the center of the field, floating just above the tops of the corn stalks, ravished in ecstatic levitation. Like other levitators, St. Bertrand had attempted unsuccessfully to cover-up his levitation events.[106]

St. Bernardino Realino (1530-1616) was an influential Italian lawyer. At age thirty-four, he joined the Jesuits and later became rector at Lecce College. In his later years, he gained a reputation for extreme holiness and at least one particularly well-recorded levitation. Like many levitators, he attempted to keep the experience a secret. However, by pure coincidence, there was an outside witness to the event, Tobias Da Ponte, a minor noble who gave away his secret. Da Ponte's obviously sincere testimony presents a very compelling case for the reality of levitation.

Da Ponte was a prominent citizen of a nearby town who, in 1608, had gone to visit Realino for spiritual guidance. While waiting in the lobby, Da Ponte saw a strange illumination coming from the door of Realino's chambers. He opened the door and peered inside. To his amazement, he saw Father Realino hovering two or three feet above the floor in a kneeling position, his body glowing with light. He was whispering a prayer with his face turned upward.

Da Ponte felt that he was intruding on a very private moment. He quietly closed the door and waited outside the room.

Later, Da Ponte was called before a church inquiry regarding the canonization of Father Realino, during which he was forced to reveal what he had seen. The court repeatedly asked Da Ponte if he was sure that he wasn't hallucinating or misperceiving—had he actually seen Realino levitate? Under oath, he testified, "The thing was so clear, unmistakable and real, that not only do I seem to see it still, but I am certain of it as I am speaking now or see those around me."

Da Ponte elaborated. "I noticed the light that filtered through the ajar door not one time, but two, three and four times, before this theory came to me. Then I wondered how there could be a fire in this room because the rays of light that escaped could only come from a great fire, like when the blacksmiths hammer red-hot iron on the anvil. I stood up on purpose and pushing open the door I saw with my own eyes Father Bernardino raised from the ground as unmistakably as I now see your illustrious Lordships."

The witness was asked a final time if he had exaggerated, misperceived or lied out of pure devotion. Da Ponte replied, "This that I have said is the entire truth, pure and simple, with neither exaggeration nor fiction."[107]

Saint Pascal Baylon (1540-1592) grew up as a shepherd but joined the Franciscans at age twenty. He was immediately recognized for his purity and goodness. He later wrote a popular book of prayers, and became wildly popular for bestowing many miraculous healings on the sick and diseased. Baylon also reportedly fell into ecstatic fits during which he was seen to levitate. Brother

Andreas Rodriguez claimed to have witnessed one such levitation inside the church.[108]

St. John a Cruce [of the Cross] (1542-1591) was a Spanish Priest. The son of a silk-weaver, he later joined the Carmelites. He had a long, controversial career and was eventually sent to prison where he wrote many works that are today considered to be great spiritual classics. His only known levitation occurred with St. Teresa of Avila.[109] (see below).

St. Philip Neri (1515-1595), like other saints, often levitated during acts of devotion to God. Specifically because his displays of levitation invariably caused a spectacle, Neri limited his public devotions. He would pray only briefly in public before being overwhelmed by ecstasy. Because of this, however, his levitations were often viewed by large numbers of witnesses, making his episodes among the best verified in medieval history.

Neri, despite his extreme popularity as a spiritual leader, was exceedingly humble. He would regularly go out in public wearing his clothes inside out, barefoot, or with only half his beard shaved, in order to dispel any thoughts of pride or vanity.

Neri also lived very austerely, and this apparently awakened within him numerous psychic gifts. Writes Alban Butler, "Many sick persons were restored by him to health, and on several occasions he prophesied future events—all of which came to pass. He lived in such constant touch with the supernatural that sometimes it was with the greatest difficulty that he could pursue his worldly avocations. He would fall into an ecstasy when saying his office, when offering Mass, or even while he was dressing."

During one service, Neri was saying Mass and floated a foot off the ground. The crowd allegedly gasped and one child cried out, "I think that father must be possessed; see how he stays in the air!"

The child's mother told her child to be quiet, and said, "It is a saint in ecstasy."

After the service, St. Neri was approached by a witness who asked him how the levitations were possible, and wondered if he was actually possessed as the child had said. Neri reportedly laughed and replied, "True, true, I am possessed."

On one occasion, while praying for the healing of a child, a crowd of people saw Neri's body become luminous and float up to the ceiling of the room.

One of the most credible witnesses to Neri's levitations is Cardinal Paul Sfondrate, who reported to Pope Paul V that he saw Neri in prayer, levitated to the height of the ceiling. Another witness, Gregoire Ozes, saw him levitating in a cloud of light before the tombs of the Apostles at the Vatican.

One day, Neri was asked by Father Antoine Galloni, one of his disciples and biographer, what it felt like to be levitated. Neri replied that it felt as if he was taken hold by somebody and "wonderfully lifted." On occasion, Neri's ecstasies lasted so long that acolytes would leave for an hour's break and return to find him still in trance.

Calmet writes that Neri was levitated "sometimes to the height of several yards, and almost to the ceiling of his room, and this quite involuntarily. He tried in vain to hide it from the knowledge of those present, for fear of attracting their admiration, and feeling in it some vain complacency."

When Neri fell sick, he was seen by his attendants to rise "about a palm" above his sickbed.[110]

St. Camille de Lellis (1550-1614) of Italy was born when his mother was nearly sixty years old. He grew up to be a large man, six feet and six inches tall, but a disease in his leg left him with a permanent limp. He fought in the Turkish war and then became addicted to gambling. This vice took over his life so that, by age twenty-four, he was completely destitute, even losing the shirt off his back in a gamble. This caused him to re-think his life, and one year later he decided to join the Capuchins. He was denied because of his diseased leg, so instead, he worked caring for the sick and infirm. Despite being denied a religious life, he became widely known for his piety and holiness. When famine and plague struck Rome, De Lellis became famous for his care for the afflicted. He reportedly experienced ecstatic levitations while in prayer. He was canonized in 1746 by Benoit XIV.[111]

St. Joseph of Leonissa (Leonessa) (1556-1612) became a missionary and preacher at age eighteen. He lived very austerely, eating only bread and water for three days each week. He was known for preaching to and caring for Christian galley-slaves. He was arrested numerous times for preaching Christianity to Muhammedans and Moslems, and as a result, was tortured and banished. He retired in Leonissa, Italy, where he was sometimes seen by his fellow priests in contemplation before the altar, his body hovering above the floor and glowing with light. He died at age fifty-eight of cancer. He was canonized in 1745.[112]

St. Mary Magdalen Dei Pazzi (1566-1607) joined the Carmelites at age fifteen. At age sixteen she became seriously ill. Afterwards, she became subject to ecstasies. According to Delaney, "She had the gift of prophecy and the ability to read people's minds and to perform miracles of healing. Her utterances while in ecstasy and descriptions of her revelations were copied down by some of the sisters in the convent and later published."

She also experienced occasional levitations, some quite dramatic. Her biographer and confessor, Father Cepari, wrote that on May 3, 1592, she ran into the choir and suddenly leapt up into the air, rising up to a height of no less than thirty feet. She landed on a cornice, reached up and removed a crucifix that had been placed up there, hugged it to her chest, and floated slowly back down. Father Cepari wrote that this sort of event happened repeatedly.

He also wrote that the nun often seemed to defy the laws of gravity while walking through her convent, and would move "with incredible swiftness from one place to another, mounting and descending the stairs with such agility that she seemed rather to fly than to touch the earth with her feet."

Once during a levitation, a bystander questioned her. Dei Pazzi shouted out the answer, then said apparently to herself, "They can't hear me down there; it is too far off."

St. Dei Pazzi was canonized in 1669. Her body still lies in an uncorrupted state in a shrine at her convent in Florence, Italy.[113]

St. Giacinta Mariscotti (Hyacintha) (1585-1640) was born into a wealthy Italian family. Although she was schooled at a convent, she showed no interest in religion. And when a marriage was arranged between her younger sister and the Marquis Cassizuchi, Mariscotti became furious. When she continued her tirades, her family forced her into a convent. While Mariscotti wore a habit, she refused to live like a nun or give up her lavish lifestyle. She equipped her cell at the convent with all the comforts money could buy and lived with total disregard for the rules of the convent. She lived this lifestyle for ten years, until one day, going to confession, she became filled with remorse and the desire to change. She gave away everything and underwent a complete conversion.

Before long, however, she began to slip back into her indulgent ways. At this point, she became terribly ill, which she interpreted as a sign. She again repented and this time the conversion was permanent. She lived the rest of her life with cruel disciplines, constant fasting, sleep deprivation, and long hours of prayers. This did little to help her health, and her sisters marveled at her continuing survival.

S. GIACINTA MARISCOTTI V.

Nobile Romana del Terz Ordine di S. Chiara Nata nel 1585. morta nel 1640. Canonizzata nel 1807. Il di cui Corpo si venera in S. Bernardino della Città di Viterbo.

Roma, presso G. Antonelli Via del Corso N.º 228 229.

FIG. 17.

Italian nun, St. Giacinta Mariscotti is seen by onlookers to levitate before a crucifix. (Mary Evans Picture Library)

She persevered, and became the mistress of novices, a powerful fundraiser and philanthropist, and helped establish hospitals for the aged, diseased, and poverty-stricken. She was seen by her sisters to levitate on numerous occasions.

Saint Michael of the Saints (1589-1625) of Catalonia announced when he was six years old that he was going to be a monk. His mother had just told him the story of St. Francis. His parents thought it was a passing fancy, but St. Michael had made his decision. After his parents died, he lived with his uncle and worked as a merchant. However, his attraction to religion was so strong, that in 1607, he joined the Trinitarian Friars in Barcelona. His devotion was so impressive that he soon became superior of his convent where he experienced numerous ecstatic levitations that were easily provoked by the mere mention of God. He died at age thirty-six.[114]

Saint Pierre Clavet (Claver) (1589-1654) is best known as the Apostle of the Negroes, though he called himself the Slave of the Negroes. He was a missionary in Cartegena, Spain, which at the time, was dominated by the brutal and inhumane slave trade. Clavet worked tirelessly to ease the suffering of the captive slaves, to move their status up from being treated like animals to human beings. Each time a slave-ship entered the ports, Clavet was there with his band of volunteers, distributing food, water and medical care to the enslaved men, women, and children.

Throughout his life, he was credited with supernatural gifts including prophecy, the ability to read minds, and levitation. He reportedly experienced numerous luminous levitations. He was seen to pass one entire evening floating in the air in a position of prayer, clutching a crucifix. Once, while very ill, he experienced a levitation from his bed.[115]

While most levitators were looked upon as being divinely inspired, this wasn't always the case. The following case is a good example of how levitation can be interpreted in different ways. Saint Marie Madeline of Cordoue (sixteenth century) was a Franciscan Abbess, a contemporary of Saint Teresa and an advisor to the wife of Charles the Fifth. She was canonized forty years after her death.

Often during religious ceremonies, she was seen to levitate "more than three cubits above the ground." According to Leroy, however, "she was bound since childhood by a diabolical pact from where came all her prestige...among them was levitation."[116]

Whatever the explanation may be for the levitating saints, it is difficult to deny that the phenomenon exists. Several of these cases, in particular, St. Neri and St. Realino provide considerable circumstantial evidence, including sworn affidavits from multiple witnesses and firsthand testimonies. While the skeptic may choose to view these cases as the naïve superstitions of a medieval culture, this theory becomes increasingly untenable as we advance through the centuries.

5. The Devil Made Me Do It

While many people were eventually canonized as Saints, partly as a result of their levitations, others were not so lucky. Writes Fodor, "In ancient rituals, levitation is mentioned as a sign of possession. Charges of witchcraft or bewitchment usually followed the manifestation."

While it may seem understandable that a deeply spiritual person might levitate, when seemingly normal (or non-religious) people began to levitate, other explanations were raised, including spirits, demons, and the Devil. Society's struggle to deal with these bizarre events sometimes led to unfortunate consequences.

In most cases, a levitation event occurs to a single person. However, in a few rare cases, entire groups of people have experienced levitation episodes. Society found these types events particularly difficult to ignore. One such incident occurred in 1491, when an entire convent of nuns in Cambrai, France became apparent victims of demonic attack.

For a period of four years, the nuns would spontaneously fall into fits during which they would run uncontrollably through the countryside. They were observed by the residents of the area to "shoot up into the air" where they would perch on roofs and onto the tops of trees "like cats." Many would also announce future events that soon came to pass.

While it is certainly unusual for an entire convent of nuns to begin levitating, the Cambrai incident is not unique.[117]

In the mid-1500s, following Lent, a number of nuns at a convent in Uvertat-Hoorn, France began falling into convulsive fits, during which they were unable to maintain their balance, and crawled around uncontrollably on the ground. Many reported being pulled out of their beds by an unseen force. These effects escalated until some of the nuns were lifted up into the air for brief moments and then dashed brutally to the ground. Others were thrown up into the treetops and when descending, would levitate upside-down to the ground. Many of them reported an unusual itching or burning sensation in the souls of their feet.

The entire ordeal is highly reminiscent of the earlier Cambrai incident. In both cases, the phenomena were explained as attack by demonic forces. In both cases, the activity ceased after a few months.[118]

While the two above cases are virtually unknown, the drama would repeat itself 150 years later. In 1635, Thomas Killegrew, an English playwright, visited a convent in Loudun, France, where another group of nuns were suffering from "demonic possession." Killegrew observed several of the nuns during their demoniacal episodes, and also stood in on several exorcisms. He was most impressed by the way the nuns' bodies contorted, and on at least one occasion, appeared to defy gravity. He writes, "...as she [a possessed nun] lay on her back, she bent her waist like a tumbler and went so, shoving herself on her heels after the friar; and many other strange unnatural postures, beyond any that ever I saw or could believe possible for any man or woman to do. Nor was this a sudden motion, and away, but a continual thing which she did for above an hour altogether; and yet not out of breath, nor hot with all the motions she used."

While this wasn't a full levitation, Abbot Leriche reports that he observed two of the possessed nuns truly levitate during two separate exorcism ceremonies.

Because the series of events at Loudun were so dramatic, they attracted a great deal of attention and controversy. Abbot Bremond visited the convent and observed no levitations. However, Dr. Francois Pidoux of Poitiers, France attended several exorcisms and reports that he saw several of the sisters throw themselves down upon the ground and levitate together.[119]

While it was sometimes acceptable to levitate spontaneously, those who sought to learn how to do it were on much shakier ground. Witches belonged to one group of people who earned the reputation for having the ability to fly. The stories of flying witches may have basis in historical fact. In a few rare cases, the use of strange ointments appear to be integral to the levitation of witches. Some researchers believe that these "flying ointments" were actually hallucinogenic drugs, which caused the user to hallucinate that they were flying, or even having an out-of-body type experience, and in fact, the evidence for this is fairly conclusive. The ingredients for some of these ointments have been discovered to actually contain hallucinogenic herbs. However, as we shall see, a few cases involving ointments point more towards the levitations being objective physical events. One of the earliest references comes from the folk-tale of the Kashmir, whose fables involve yogis that could fly through the use of "sacred ointments." Most other cases, however, involve witchcraft.

An early case occurred in 1526, when a young lady in Rome was accused of witchcraft and sorcery. In his treatise, *On Witchcraft,* Paul Grilland, who was a witness to the trial, asserted that the accused flew in the air after anointing her limbs with a "certain magic liniment."[120]

Nearly one hundred years later, in 1617, Collette Dumont was accused of witchcraft after confessing her ability to levitate. She claimed that the Devil had given her an ointment which, when rubbed on her body, gave her the ability of flight. After applying it, she said she would go outside and be instantly carried into the air to her appointed destination. Although her assertions were unproven, Dumont was found guilty and executed.[121]

Probably the most dramatic case involving "flying ointments" occurred sometime in the late 1600s. Several men and women were brought to trial, accused of sorcery in the town of Navere, France. One of the Council, in order to prove the veracity of the accusations, promised to pardon any defendant who agreed to perform magic in his presence. A young woman agreed on the condition that she was given back her bottles of ointments that had been taken from her.

This was agreed upon, and the young lady climbed up a tower with the commissioner. Once she reached the upper window, she applied the lotion at various points on her body. She called out to the sky, "Are you there?"

All those present were shocked to hear a loud disembodied male voice reply, "Yes, I am here."

The young lady began to make curious motions with her hands and arms, and then running down the staircase on all fours like an animal, "...she took flight, and the assistants followed her with their eyes until she faded from sight off into the horizon."

The scene caused an uproar, and the commissioner immediately announced that whoever captured the young sorceress would be given a "considerable sum of money."

This began a massive search. Two days later, several shepherds found the accused woman in a field a few miles away. She was returned to the court. The commissioner asked her why, with her ability to fly, she didn't go further. The lady replied that her flights were not controlled by her, but by her master.[122]

A brief case of a flying witch occurred in 1692, when a young woman from Salem, Massachusetts was executed for witchcraft, after she confessed to having falling off her broomstick while in flight."[123]

Cases of flying ointments are particularly rare. Much more common are mediumistic levitations, which in medieval times, usually meant you were possessed by the Devil. And in fact, these types of levitation events are often provoked by exorcism rituals. In 1591, a young French girl named Francoise Fontaine experienced a dramatic levitation incident that was recorded in the *Bibliotheque Nationale de Paris*. The incident was particularly memorable because it took place in a courtroom (as have several levitations) and was witnessed by numerous officials. According to one of the witnesses, "....Francois walked but six paces into the court, and we together with our clerk entered the office where the judge's chair is and the sitting is held, and, as our clerk was beginning to write the present report that we were dictating to him, he cried out and showed us Francois, who was near the door of the court, whom we all saw raised about two feet off the floor, upright, and at once she fell down on the ground, flat on the back, with her arms spread out crosswise, and afterwards she was dragged, with her head foremost, still on her back, along the court, without anybody touching her or standing near her, as witnessed La Prime, the jailer, Nicolas Pellet, servant of the jailer, his wife and several prisoners who came into the court, a thing which amazed us much."

The Provost quickly began to read the Gospel of St. John to exorcise what he believed were demons possessing the girl. Fontaine's body lay prone on the floor. Suddenly, her body arched, began crawling around and then, "...all at once the body of Francois was raised off the floor, three or four feet high, and borne horizontally, face upwards along the court, without anything to support her. When we saw the body make straight for us, thus suspended in mid-air, it threw us into such a fright that we withdrew into the office of the court, locking the door behind us and reading the Gospel of St. John down to the end."

To the shock of the witnesses, the levitation continued. "The body kept following us through the air up to the office, against the door which it struck with the soles of its feet, and then was carried back through the air, with the face upwards and head foremost, out of the court. This gave such a fright to the jailer, the servants, our archers and many prisoners…that they fled, some into the prison, some into the street, after shutting the doors behind them; and the body of Francois was carried out of the court and remained in the passage of the prison, between the door of it and the street door which the fugitives had shut in their flight. We considered this with great astonishment, till one guard and other prisoners opened the door of the prison and said they would help us, which enabled us to get out of the office and court, having thus found Francois lying on the ground close to the prison door."

Following this incident, further exorcisms were immediately attempted. Each resulted in a levitation. On the first attempt, Fontaine was given the Holy Sacrament. "Francoise, kneeling down, had been most alarmingly carried away, without being able to take the Sacrament, opening her mouth, rolling her eyes in her head in such a horrible way that it had been necessary, with the help up five or six persons, to pull her down by her dress as she was raised into the air, and they had thrown her down onto the floor."

A second attempt provoked the same results. "…she was again snatched off the floor, higher than the altar, as if she had been taken by the hair, in such a strange way that the bystanders were much amazed, and would never have thought of witnessing so frightful a thing, and they all knelt and began saying prayers."

A third and final attempt also failed. "…for the third time [she was] carried over a large bench that was before the altar where Mass was said, and lifted up into the air towards where a glass had been broken, with her head downwards and her feet upwards, without her clothes being upset, through which, before and behind, was belching forth much water and stinking smoke [steam]…and for some time thus carried through the air, till at last seven or eight men had taken hold of her and brought her to the ground."[124]

Exorcism levitations can be particularly dramatic. In 1612, at Beauvais, France, an exorcism took place to cure a young lady of what appeared to be demonic possession. The exorcist was Father Pot, of the Jacobin religion, who later wrote that during the procedure, "…she was levitated into the air, her feet off the ground, and was bellowing horribly." The attendees rushed to her aid and attempted unsuccessfully to pull her down.[125]

Another case is that of Elisabeth de Ranfaing, born in 1592. When she became widowed as a young woman, she devoted her life to caring for the sick, in particular prostitutes who were victims of venereal diseases. Through her efforts, the Maison de Refuge was founded, which is today a powerful institution of research and healing into dermatology, cancer, and other diseases.

While she was a powerful force of goodness, Ranfaing also suffered from demonic or diabolical possession and would fall into fits during which she would be struck or even levitated. In September, 1619, she fell into a fit and was levitated in front of numerous people of high social standing, causing a huge spectacle.

As time went on, levitation accounts involving normal people began to appear in greater numbers. In 1657, Mr. Jones, a twelve-year-old resident of Shepton-Mal-

In September, 1619, widow, nurse, and victim of possession, Elisabeth De Ranfaing, was seen to levitate before numerous witnesses. (Mary Evans Picture Library)

let village in England, fell into "fits" during which he would levitate. As the report reads, "He would be carried by invisible means from one room to another, and sometimes wholly lifted up, so that his body hung in the air, with only the flat of his hands placed against the ceiling. One afternoon, being at the house of one Richard Isles, he went out into the garden, and there in the sight of Isles' wife, was raised up into the air, and transported over the garden wall for about thirty yards, falling at length as one dead at the door of a neighboring house."

Jones' episodes lasted for about one year and then ceased. Residents in the village believed that the boy had been possessed by the spirit of a dead woman. Fortunately, he fully recovered.[126]

Twelve-year-old Mr. Jones was lucky. Around this time, numerous levitators were treated not as saints or even victims, but as criminals. In 1661, four years after Mr. Jones' levitations, Mary London, a young servant girl became subject to hysterical fits. She was put on trial in Cork for witchcraft after observers saw that she was "removed strangely, in the twinkling of an eye, out of her bed, sometimes into the bottom of a chest with linen, under all the linen, and the linen not at all disordered." On other occasions, she was transported onto the roof of the house, where she was forced to wait until somebody located a ladder.[127]

During a Salem, Massachusetts witch trial the same year, Margaret Rule was accused of witchcraft after several Salem residents had observed her levitating. On one occasion, her body was lifted out of bed "wholly by an invisible force, a great way towards the top of the room where she lay."

On at least two occasions, observers tried unsuccessfully to stop her levitations. As one witness said, "...not only a strong person hath thrown his whole weight across her to pull her down, but several other persons have endeavored with all their might to hinder her from being so raised up."

On the second occasion, an invisible force "pulled her up to the ceiling of the chamber, and held her there before a numerous company of spectators who found it as much as they could do to pull her down again."[128]

Another witchy case occurred in 1663, when Julian Cox was put on trial for witchcraft after a witness testified that she had seen her fly into her room through the window.[129]

Thankfully, most levitators escaped this kind of treatment. In any case, spectators usually had the same reaction, which was to attempt to end the levitation. One account of a mediumistic levitation from 1665 occurred to an anonymous young man in Ireland. As the report reads, "Glanvil tells a strange story of a gentleman's butler in Ireland, who was thought to be haunted by spirits, that threatened to carry him away, and who was actually one day raised from the ground in the presence of several persons, including Mr. Valentine Greatrakes. Mr. Greatrakes and another lusty man clapped their arms over his shoulders, one before, and the other behind, and weighed him down with all their strength; but he was forcibly taken up from them, and they were too weak to keep their hold, and for a considerable time he was carried to and fro over their heads, several of the company still running under him, to prevent his receiving hurt if he should fall. At length, he fell, and was caught before he came to the ground, and had by that means no hurt."[130]

Another well-recorded case of mediumistic levitation occurred in 1682 to Francis Fey, a young man from Spraiton, Devon County, England. Employed as a servant in the home of Mr. Phillip Furze, Fey had no problems until a female ghost appeared in the Furze household. Poltergeist-type manifestations soon followed and seemed to center around Fey. On several occasions, Fey was thrown from his horse by the ghost, which would also rip his clothes or remove his hat.

Then came the levitations. As recorded by Fey's neighbor, "When the young man was returning from his labour, he was taken up by the skirt of his doublet by this female daemon, and carried a height into the air. He was soon missed by his Master and some other servants that had been at labour with him, and after diligent enquiry no news could be heard of him, until at length (near half an hour after) he was heard singing and whistling in a bog or quagmire, where they found him in a kind of trance or extatick [sic] fit, to which he hath sometimes been accustomed (but whether before the affliction he met with from this spirit I am not certain.) He was affected much after such sort, as at the time of those fits, so that the people did not give that attention and regard to what he said as at other times; but when he returned again to himself (which was about an hour after) he solemnly protested to them that the daemon had carried him so high that his master's house seemed to him to be but as a hay-cock, and that during all that time he was in perfect sense, and prayed to Almighty God not to suffer the Devil to destroy him; and that he was suddenly set down in that quagmire. The workman found one shoe on one side of the master's house, and the other on the other side, and in the morning espied his [hat] hanging on the top of a tree; by which it appears he had been carried a considerable height, and that what he told them was not a fiction."[131]

A case of apparent mediumistic levitation occurred in 1720 to Patrick Sandilands, the young son of Lord Torphichen, in Calder, Scotland. Without any warning, he suddenly began to suffer from spells where he would become "bewitched" and levitated. As the reports says, "...what chiefly drew attention was his tendency to rise entranced into the air, which was so great that his sisters had to watch him, and sometimes could only keep him down by hanging to his skirts. In time the 'disease'—for so it appeared to be—passed away, and the young man going to sea rose to the command of an East Indiaman."[132]

The case of Nancy Wesly in 1716 in Epworth, England began as a typical poltergeist haunting. What made this particular account remarkable, however, was that the victim of the haunting was the daughter of the Victor of Epworth Vicarage. Because of his high social standing, the paranormal events became well known, especially when the Vicar's daughter, Nancy, began to levitate. Although most of the paranormal activity centered around the Vicar's other daughter, Hetty, it was Nancy who was often seen "elevated" in the presence of her family members.[133]

In 1738, Monsieur Delacour, a respected French missionary, traveled to Indochine. While there, he performed a number of exorcisms on locals who were suffering from what he diagnosed as demonic possession. During one of these exorcisms on a young child, Delacour provoked a remarkable feat of levitation. As in other cases of possession, Delacour found that he could command the possessed person to perform certain feats, which would be completed with alacrity. As he later wrote to his superiors of the incident, "While engaged in my exorcism, I suddenly had the idea to ask the Devil in Latin to move the possessed to the ceiling of the church. Specifically, this was to be done with feet upwards and head pointing down. Immediately, the body became rigid, and the possessed was unable to use his limbs. He was propelled to a pillar in the middle of the church, and with his feet close together, pushed with his back towards the pillar. All this occurred while his hands remained out of use. He was transported to the ceiling in the wink of an eye, much like a weight that is forcibly pulled upward. Throughout all this, the man remained seemingly passive. He hung from the ceiling, his feet flat up against it, his head downwards....I kept him in this manner, up in the air for more than a half hour, but I did not have the steadiness to leave him there any longer. I was, in any event, very frightened by what I had observed. I ordered the Devil to put the possessed back on his feet without any damage whatsoever. He immediately tossed him down at me on the ground, like a package of dirty laundry, completely unharmed."[134]

In 1761, the Richard Giles family of Bristol, England experienced a poltergeist attack centered around their two young children. As in many such severe cases, levitation was also involved. "They were struck, dragged, pelted, bitten, throttled, stuck with pins, and slobbered over. On occasions, several men could not hold them down as they rose into the air."[135]

A more modern and unsettling case comes from French occultist, Eugene Vintras (1807-1875), founder of the infamous Church of Carmel. Vintras was first employed as the foreman of a cardboard factory. However, following a series of visions of St. Michael and other religious figures, he quit his job and began a cult, attracting many followers. Vintras claimed to be the reincarnation of Elijah, and he prophesized that in the future there would be a great explosion which would signal the beginning of Hell on Earth. His followers revered him as a saint, and he was seen by numerous witnesses in a state of levitation. Today, however, his name is more commonly associated with Satanism. He was accused of performing sacrilegious masses during which he and other members were nude and engaged in sex acts.

While in some cases, levitation appears to be the result of intense prayer or meditation, the above much rarer cases show that this is not always the case. Clearly there is some outside force that is initiating the suspensions in these cases. While most of the early cases of levitation involve ecstatic or meditational levitation, later on we shall find that medi-

Controversial French occultist, Eugene Vintras levitates before his own specialized altar. (Mary Evans Picture Library)

umistic ability (communicating with spirits) plays an increasingly powerful role in the manifestation of levitation.

6. Saint Teresa of Avila

Of the more than 332 known levitators, one person who rises above the rest is a Carmelite nun named Saint Teresa of Avila (1515-1582). Although she lived nearly five hundred years ago, her feats are still remembered today, undoubtedly due to the fact that she was a prolific author and an incredible mystic. Her works today are considered classics of mystical literature and are still in print.

Although St. Teresa tried to hide her strange abilities, large numbers of people witnessed her levitations, several of who left recorded statements. These accounts, and Teresa's own extensive autobiographical descriptions of her levitations, make her case among the best documented in all of history.

St. Teresa became a nun at an early age. However, it wasn't until she turned forty, after viewing a shallow complacency among her fellow sisters, that she became seriously dedicated to spirituality. Despite suffering from ill health, she left her convent and traveled across Spain founding the "Reformed Communities of Carmelites" a strict and devout institution.

St. Teresa of Avila, probably the most famous "flying nun" in history. (Self-Realization Fellowship)

St. Teresa spent much of her time in daily mental prayer. It was during these long prayer sessions that she first experienced levitations. She didn't like them, as they were frightening, awkward and distracting, and she prayed that her "episodes" would stop. As she later wrote, "Do you think it is a small disturbance for a person to be very much in his senses and see his soul carried off...and even the body...without knowing where that soul is going, what or who does this or how?"

To her annoyance, these episodes continued. On several occasions, St. Teresa called out to her fellow Sisters to assist her. They would obligingly hold her down so that services could continue. On other occasions, she ordered everyone out of her convent when she felt an approaching episode.

St. Teresa received Holy Communion thousands of times. On rare occasions, she would sometimes rise into the air and hover. Bishop Yepes revealed one incident which occurred when she was about to receive the Host from Don Alvaro of

Mendoza, the Bishop of Avila. Just as the wafer was to be placed on her tongue, Teresa's body began to quickly rise. She reached out and grasped the grille, and the Bishop quickly administered the sacrament. Several witnesses watched the levitation. Teresa quickly realized her predicament and threw herself to the ground.

Teresa's levitations were recorded by other witnesses. Under oath, during a church inquiry into Teresa's life, Sister Anne testified, "On another occasion, between one and two o'clock in the daytime, I was in the choir waiting for the bell to ring, when our Holy Mother entered and knelt down for perhaps the half of a quarter of an hour. As I was looking on, she was raised about half a yard from the ground, without her feet touching it. At this I was terrified, and she, for her part, was trembling all over. So I moved to where she was and I put my hands under her feet, where I remained weeping for something like half an hour while the ecstasy lasted. Then suddenly she sank down and rested on her feet, and turning to me, she asked who I was and if I was there for a long time. I responded, yes. She ordered me under obedience to say nothing of what I had seen, and I have, in fact, said nothing until the present moment."

At least nine other firsthand witnesses also testified to Teresa's levitations, some saying that Teresa's body was luminous. These episodes were common enough that St. Teresa was sometimes seen clutching the ground in a vain attempt to keep from levitating. One priest reported that she observed Teresa levitate while standing in a choir with the other nuns. As he watched, she grabbed at the floor mats to hold herself down, but still rose into the air still holding the mats.

During another occasion, St. Teresa was listening to St. John of the Cross (1542-1591) speak of the Trinity. Suddenly, he levitated, and St. Teresa, caught up in the rapture, floated up in a kneeling position to meet him. At that moment, Sister Beatrice walked in and saw them both hovering in an ecstatic trance. The incredible event was later memorialized in a painting hung in the church.

What does it feel like to levitate? Few people have left as complete and vivid a description as St. Teresa of Avila. As she writes in her 1565 autobiography, which her superior ordered her to write, "When I tried to resist these raptures, it seemed that I was being lifted up by a force beneath my feet so powerful that I know nothing to which I can compare it, for it came with a much greater vehemence than any other spiritual experience and I felt as if I were being ground to powder. It is a terrible struggle, and to continue it against the Lord's will avails very little, for no power can do anything against his....If we resist it out of humility, the same effects follow as if we had given it our entire consent.

"These effects are very striking. One of them is the manifestation of the Lord's mighty power; as we are unable to resist His Majesty's will, either in soul or in body, and are not our own masters, we realize that, however irksome this truth may be, there is One stronger than ourselves, and that these favours are bestowed by Him, and that we ourselves, can do absolutely nothing. This imprints in us great humility. Indeed, I confess that in me it produced great fear—at first a terrible fear. One sees one's body being lifted up from the ground; and although the spirit draws it after itself, and if no resistance is offered does so very gently [with great sweetness] one does not lose consciousness—[the senses are not lost]—at least, I myself have had sufficient to enable me to realize I was being lifted up. The majesty of Him who can do this is manifested in such a way that the hair stands on end."

Again, Teresa tried to resist the levitations, but found it impossible to do so. As she writes, "No means of resistance is possible....with rapture, as a rule, there is no such possibility: often it comes like a strong, swift impulse, before your thought can forewarn you of it or you can do anything to help yourself; you see and feel this cloud, or this powerful eagle, rising and bearing you up with it on its wings. You realize, I repeat, indeed see, that you are being carried away, you know not whither. For, though rapture brings us delight, the weakness of our nature makes us afraid of it, and we need to be resolute and courageous in soul, much more so than for what has been described. For, happen what may, we must risk everything, and resign ourselves into the hands of God and go willingly wherever we are carried away, whether we like it or not. In such straights do I find myself at such a time that very often I should be glad to resist, and I exert all my strength to do so, in particular at times when it happens in public.... Occasionally I have been able to make some resistance, but at the cost of great exhaustion, for I would feel as weary afterwards as though I had been fighting with a powerful giant. At other times, resistance has been impossible: my soul has been borne away, and indeed as a rule my head also, without my being able to prevent it; sometimes my whole body has been affected, to the point of being raised up from the ground.

"This has happened only rarely; but once, when we were together in choir, and I was on my knees and about to communicate, it caused me the greatest distress. It seemed to me a most extraordinary thing and I thought there would be a great deal of talk about it; so I ordered the nuns (for it happened after I was appointed Prioress) not to speak of it. On other occasions, when I have felt the Lord was going to enrapture me (once it happened during a sermon, on our patronal festival, when some great ladies were present) I have lain on the ground and the sisters have come and held me down, but nonetheless the rapture has been observed. I besought the Lord earnestly not to grant me anymore favours which had visible and exterior signs; for I was exhausted by having to endure such worries and after all (I said) his Majesty could grant me that favour without its becoming known....for it is entirely supernatural and comes from His hand, and, as I have said, is in no way acquired by me."

Teresa also wrote about the peculiar mental and physiological effects of her levitation episodes. "Let us now return to raptures, and to their most usual characteristics. I can testify that after a rapture my body often seemed as light [buoyant] as if all weight had left it; sometimes this was so noticeable that I could hardly tell when my feet were touching the ground. For, while the rapture lasts, the body often remains as if dead and unable of itself to do anything: it continues all the time as it was when the rapture came upon it – in a sitting position, for example, with the hands open or shut. The subject rarely loses consciousness: I have sometimes lost it altogether, but only seldom and for a short time. As a rule the consciousness is undisturbed; and though incapable of action with respect to outward things, the subject can still hear and understand, but only dimly, as though from a long way off."

St. Teresa's levitations may have occurred a long time ago, but as can be seen, they are very well documented. Leroy, who declared his skepticism of the majority of cases wrote, "We can leave our prejudice aside and clearly admit this case." Herbert Thurston was also skeptical of many hagiographical accounts, but said of St. Teresa, "To my thinking, the most satisfactory example of this phenomenon is to be found in the case of St. Teresa....The importance of her case lies in the fact that not only was she seen by others raised in the air, but that she herself bore witness to the reality of these levitations. At the same time no one who has studied her life and writings will be disposed to question either her good faith or common sense."[136]

7. Medieval Flying Nuns and Monks

During the Middle Ages, levitation was still treated, at least in Europe, as an event to be regarded with awe or fear. There were still no studies of the subject and very little understanding of the causes. The church explained it simply as either a Divine favor or a demonic torment. It was only because of the popularity of hagiography that many of the accounts came to be recorded at all.

However, levitation is, of course, in no way limited to the saints. Many undecorated monks, friars, priests, nuns…etc., experienced levitations and never received saintly status. Still, most of the cases do originate from deeply spiritual nuns and monks and other religious persons. In this chapter, we shall examine thirty-three medieval cases of this kind.

Ladislaw of Gielniow the Blessed (Stanislaw) (1440-1505) was an influential preacher and missionary, famous throughout his native Poland. In 1498, an army of 70,000 Turks and Tartars threatened to take over the country. Ladislaw preached to the population to trust God and pray. When the army of 70,000 was suddenly decimated by floods and blizzards, Ladislaw was given credit. There are several reports of Ladislaw levitating while in prayer. But his most dramatic levitation occurred on April 4, 1505, as he preached the Passion. In the middle of the sermon, he became insensible and fell into an ecstatic trance. The congregation watched in amazement as his body rose above his chair and remained suspended in the air, hanging with his arms outstretched as if crucified. After a few moments, he sunk back into the chair and awoke, totally exhausted. He died exactly one month later. His is only one of many cases involving pre-death levitations.[137]

Eustochium of Padua (1443-1469) was born into scandal: her mother was a nun who had been seduced and impregnated in sin. As a young woman, she joined the convent where she was born. She was deeply religious, but throughout her life, experienced violent poltergeist-like manifestations which caused her to be treated with fear and contempt. On one occasion, she terrified her sisters when she was transported through the air up onto a beam high on the ceiling, where a fall would have caused grievous injury. On other occasions, she was "lifted into the air and then let fall like a stone." She died at age 29, at which time a "celestial fragrance" was emitted from her body. She was re-interred three years later, still in an incorrupt state.[138]

Archangela Girlani (1460-1494) showed herself to be religious from an extremely early age. At that time she vowed to remain a virgin and devote her life to God. By the time she was a teenager, she was already prioress of her convent. She later founded a convent in Mantua, Italy, where she spent the rest of her life. She was profoundly fervent in her prayer, and on a great many occasions, she was observed in her cell "rapt in ecstasy and raised several yards from the ground."[139]

Blessed Antonia of Florence, Italy (d1472) married at an early age, but was soon widowed. Her family urged her to remarry, but instead she joined a convent. She excelled quickly and within one year, was put in charge of the convent of St. Anne. Despite her strictness, she attracted more than a hundred nuns to her convent and was deeply loved by her community. Writes Alban Butler, "Antonia at times was seen to be in ecstasy and upraised from the ground, and once a fiery globe appeared to rest upon her head and to light up the place in which she prayed."[140]

Blessed Louisa Albertoni (1473-1533) was born of Italian nobility. She married a nobleman and bore three daughters. Upon her husband's death in 1506, she became a nun and spent her entire days weeping in prayer. She gave away all her wealth, and would often hide gold coins in bread loaves which she distributed to the needy. In the last three years of her life, she fell into a daily series of ecstasies, during which (according to her biographers), she was often "raised physically from the ground."[141]

Bernard Scammacca (d1486) was born into a noble family in Catania, Sicily. As a young man he led a wild and sinful life. After seriously breaking his leg in a fight, he underwent a complete conversion, turned to God and joined the Dominican order. Here he spent all his time in intense, fervent prayer, and was a model of obedience, humility and penitence. Later, he became famous for various miracles. Birds would reportedly perch on his arms. He regularly foretold future events that came to pass. He was also seen on several occasions to be "raised from the ground in prayer."[142]

Thomas of Villanova (1488-1555), Archbishop of Valencia, Spain, grew up to become a professor of philosophy. At age twenty-eight, he joined the Augustinian friars where he taught courses in divinity. He lived austerely and spent much of his time in prayer and contemplation. He experienced frequent raptures, which he tried unsuccessfully to hide. He is also credited with one of the longest observed levitations. While holding the missal, a book of Roman Catholic prayers, he floated into the air for an alleged duration of twelve hours. During this time, the levitation was confirmed by the archbishop, the clergy, and a great number of citizens of the village of Valence. When he finally sank down, he apologized to the onlookers saying that he had simply lost his place. He was apparently unaware that twelve hours had passed.[143]

Bartholomew of Anghiers (d1510) was an Italian friar who habitually hid himself in forested areas to avoid detection of his ecstatic levitations. Apparently, he was unsuccessful as his levitations are still remembered today.[144]

Salvator de Horta (1520-1567) was a Spanish friar. Orphaned at a young age, he became a shoemaker, and at age twenty, joined the Observant Franciscans, where he served as cook. Here he grew spiritually with leaps and bounds. He soon became well known for his miracles of healing and levitation, which were so numerous, that he was eventually persecuted for thaumaturgy. Still thousands trekked to him to be healed.

His best-recorded levitation took place at the home of Antoine Vughet, who had invited Salvator for a meal. When Salvator broke open a pomegranate and saw the perfect arrangement of the purple seeds, he saw the beauty of God's divine plan in them and immediately fell into an ecstasy. Within seconds, he was insensible and levitated above his seat. Vughet jumped up and gathered his neighbors to view the amazing spectacle.[145]

Nicholas Factor the Blessed (1520-1583) was the son of a Sicilian tailor. His father wanted him to go into business, but Factor chose instead to join the Friars Minor in his home town, and later moved to Spain. According to his biographers, Factor practiced such extreme austerities, he was investigated by the Inquisition. According to Alban Butler, "His raptures, miracles and visions were so frequent that St. Louis Bertrand said he lived more in Heaven than on earth." He was widely known across Spain and was regularly consulted by King Phillip II. According to his biographers, Factor's raptures were sometimes accompanied by aerial ascensions.[146]

Conradin de Brecia the Blessed (d1529) was the superior of the convent of Brescia. During a revolt, when the town was held in prohibition, Conradin went against the rules and as a consequence was thrown in prison. It was while in his cell, during prayer, that he was seen to levitate.[147]

Caspar de Bono (1530-1604) was born into poverty. He failed as a silk merchant and became a soldier. The many hardships he suffered during battle caused him to become increasingly religious, and he began to spend more and more time in prayer and meditation. One day he was so badly wounded, he felt he was about to die. He vowed that if he lived, he would join the Minims, an austere and humble religious order. After his recovery in 1560, he joined the group. His superiors were deeply impressed by his devotions and virtues, and he was ordained within a year. He lived his life with prudence, charity, and humility. According to his biographer, P. A. Miloni, de Bono also experienced ecstatic raptures during which his body would be physically levitated into the air.[148]

John de Ribera the Blessed (1532-1611) was the son of the viceroy of Naples. He was educated at Salamanca University where he taught theology. At age twenty-five, he was ordained a priest. A few years later, he became bishop, and then archbishop, and finally viceroy. He is most famous for the Edict of 1609, which enforced the deportation of the wealthy Moriscos from Valencia. According to his biographer, Castillo, he experienced ecstatic levitations that only became publicly known following his death and process for beatification.[149]

Alphonsus Rodriguez (1533-1617) spent his youth studying with the Jesuits, but the death of his father forced him into the family's wool business. Then, in a space of two years, his mother, wife, and child died. Overcome with grief, Rodriguez took his only surviving son and went to live with his very religious sisters. Here he underwent a religious conversion and began to pray and practice austerities daily. He later became a lay-brother and excelled in his virtues of prayer and obedience. Before long, he was widely known for his piety and holiness. Among his students was Peter Clavet, who would later experience levitations himself. In his later years, Rodriguez experienced regular raptures during which his body would be levitated above the ground.[150]

Marguerite Agullona (1536-1600) was a well known ecstatic and stigmatic who experienced at least one particularly memorable episode of levitation. One day during services, she glimpsed a painting of a crown of thorns. She fell into a trance and rose up in the air before the painting. The other sisters looked on in amazement as her body swayed slightly with the breeze. Numerous residents entered into the church for the specific purpose of viewing her levitation, which lasted several minutes.[151]

Ursule Benincasa the Blessed (1547-1618) became, according to Imbert-Gourbeyre, an "ecstatic" at the young age of ten years. She fell into hysterical fits, during which onlookers believed she was demonically possessed. She underwent a ritual of exorcism, during which she was levitated and cured of her condition.[152]

A very well recorded early levitation occurred to Francis Suarez (1548-1617), a Spanish Priest and professor of divinity at the University of Salamanca. Suarez was observed by a fellow priest, Jerome De Silva, to levitate.

Again, like most early levitators, Suarez experienced ecstatic levitations during prayer, and attempted to keep them secret. This case is particularly interesting because it contains a detailed testimony by a highly credible witness. It all began when De Silva was sent by his superiors to fetch Francis Suarez for an important matter.

De Silva approached Suarez's room. Says De Silva, "Across the door of his room I found the stick which the Father usually placed there when he did not wish to be interrupted. Owing, however, to the order I had received I removed the stick and entered. The outer room was in darkness. I called the Father but he made no answer. As the curtain that shut off his working room was drawn, I saw through the space left between the curtain and the jambs of the door a very great brightness. I pushed aside the curtain and entered from the inner apartment. Then I noticed that a blinding light was coming from the crucifix, so intense that it was like the reflection of the sun from glass windows, and I felt I could not have remained looking at it without being completely dazzled. This light streamed from the crucifix upon the face and breast of Father Suarez and in this brightness I saw him in a kneeling position in front of the crucifix, his head uncovered, his hands joined, and his body in the air five palms above the floor on a level with the table on which the crucifix stood. On seeing this I withdrew, but before quitting the room I stopped bewildered, and as it were beside myself, leaning against the door-post for a few moments. Then I went out, my hair standing on end like the bristles of a brush, and I waited, totally beside myself."

A few moments later, Suarez exited. He was not happy to see De Silva. Says De Silva, "When the Father heard that I had entered the inner room, he seized me by the arm, then, clasping his hands and with eyes full of tears, he implored me to say nothing of what I had seen, at any rate, as long as he lived. I asked permission to tell my confessor. He consented easily to this as my confessor was his. My confessor advised me to write this account in the form that I have said, and I sign my name to it because all that it contains is true."

Later, there was a church inquiry on the canonization of Father Suarez, and De Silva was ordered to reveal what he had seen. De Silva testified and signed an affidavit swearing to the event.

Herbert Thurston regarded this case as particularly credible, writing, "No one, I think, will be disposed to regard this piece of evidence as contemptible."[153]

Other cases are much less detailed, but still worth mention, such as that of Marie Raggi (1552-1600), a Dominican nun who experienced ecstatic fits, stigmata, and luminous levitations.[154]

Francois Dorothee of Villa (1558-1623) was Prioress of a Spanish Dominican monastery. She apparently levitated on numerous occasions which were not witnessed by outside observers. However, it was only a matter of time before her secret was revealed. One day, one of the residents of the monastery saw her in levitation. As the witness later testified, "The mother Dorothea stayed at the choir after morning. I wanted to stay also in order to keep her company. She made me swear to leave. About one hour after midnight, I saw Mother Dorothea raised in the air to the height of one and a half cubits, her face glowing and her body surrounded with a resplendent light. This ravishment lasted two hours. When it ceased, our mother knocked on the pew to call me. Believing that she was ignorant of my presence, I said nothing, but she called me by my name. I approached and I kneeled before her feet. Then she put her hand on my head and said, 'Pay good attention that I command you on God's behalf not to tell anybody, during my life, of this that you have seen. Our Lord would not be happy. I give you this warning because I know you want to speak, but since God has confided in you his secrets, it is necessary that you know to guard them with fidelity.'"[155]

St. Laurence [Lorenzo] of Brindisi (1559-1619) was born in Naples. He was put into a religious college where he made rapid progress. He learned more than seven different languages and memorized most of the Bible. He founded numerous missions, cared for victims of the plague, was chaplain general of a large army, and an influential peace-maker. He was also incredibly devoted and when saying mass, often fell into ecstatic raptures during which he would sometimes be seen to levitate.[156]

Dominique Ruzzola de Jesus-Marie (1559-1630) joined the barefoot Carmelites at a very young age, rose quickly up the ranks and eventually became the leader. He was reportedly gifted with prophecy and levitation. In 1593, he began to experience ecstatic levitations which lifted him so high, that the other monks were just able to reach the bottoms of his feet.

He could apparently feel the onset of his levitations and would often throw himself to the ground in order to stop them from occurring.

During one such occasion, one of the witnesses to his levitations grabbed him out of concern, and was lifted momentarily up with him, but fell to the ground. While visiting the court of Philip II, he experienced an ecstatic levitation. The king approached and was able to lift his body as if it were a feather.[157]

Jacquette de Bachelier (1559-1635) joined the Franciscans at age twenty-five. One morning, the other monks came running into the church to find her raised up in the air, glowing with a light that lit up the entire interior of the church.[158]

The Blessed Marie Acarie of the Incarnation (1566-1618) was attracted to religion from an early age, but instead became married to a French aristocrat and raised six children. She was an active philanthropist and, following the death of her husband, joined the Carmelites. She was intensely charitable, extremely spiritual, and at age twenty-eight, announced that she had achieved a complete spiritual union with God. She experienced occasional visions and ecstasies, one of which was so powerful it resulted in a three-hour-long levitation. Afterwards Marie was left very weak. Her biography was written by her son. She was beatified in 1980.[159]

For whatever reason, this particular period in history provided a flood of levitators. Damien de Vicari (1569-1613) was a Franciscan monk who was seen one night in levitation, his body glowing near the ceiling of the church.[160]

Leonard da Lettra (1569-1621) was a Dominican priest who reportedly experienced a levitation while praying before a crucifix.[161]

St. Martin de Porres (1579-1639) followed many occupations including barber, surgeon, wardrobe-keeper, nurse, and more. He founded an orphanage and a hospital, and spent much of his time attending to the poor. He soon became well known for supernatural gifts including multiplying food, bilocation, and several instances of "aerial flights."[162]

Blessed Humilus of Bisignano (1582-1637) grew up as a farm laborer. At age eighteen, he decided to become a priest. It took nine years for him to be accepted as a lay brother by the Observant Friars. Before long, Humilus began to display paranormal talents. Writes Alban Butler, "He in fact became so celebrated for miracles and the prudence of his opinions that not only did learned men come to consult him, but he was sent for to Rome by Pope Gregory XV." When Pope Gregory XV died, his successor Pope Urban VIII retained the services of the humble lay brother. After an illness, however, Humilus returned to his home in

Calabria, where he remained the rest of his life. On numerous occasions, he was seen to fall into ecstasies and levitate.

The power of levitation to affect people who touch the levitator is illustrated by the following account. Jeanne Rodriguez of Jesus-Marie (1584-1650) became a nun at age sixty. She soon fell into ecstatic trances during which she would act out complete religious scenes and reportedly levitate. On one occasion, she was so weak with illness that she needed two assistants to help her walk. Suddenly, she experienced a levitation and all three people were carried in levitation "ten stone's throw."[163]

Doubtless, the number of levitations is much greater than most people realize because of one simple reason: many (most?) levitations are covered-up. A few accounts leak out by sheer luck, as in the following well-known case. A Dominican nun by the name of Maria Villanie (1584-

Humilio Bisignano was consulted by two Popes and was credited with numerous miracles. In this sketch from 1630, he has a vision of the Virgin and child, and is levitated. (Mary Evans Picture Library)

1670) fell into ecstatic trances and began to levitate. She also left a detailed written record of her levitations in a personal letter to a priest dated 1618. "On one occasion when I was in my cell I was conscious of a new experience. I felt myself seized and ravished out of my senses and that so powerfully that I found myself lifted up completely by the very soles of my feet, just as the magnet draws up a fragment of iron, but with a gentleness that was marvelous and most delightful. At first I felt much fear, but afterwards I remained in the greatest possible contentment and joy of spirit. Though I was quite beside myself, still, in spite of that, I knew that I was raised some distance above the earth, my whole body being suspended for a considerable space of time. Down to last Christmas Eve (1618) this happened to me on five different occasions."

Villanie wrote that she believed these episodes were "favors from heaven" and that she had told nobody up until that point.[164]

Jean Massias the Blessed (John Macias) (1585-1645) was a Spanish shepherd. As a result of a vision, he moved to Peru where he worked on a cattle-ranch. He then joined the Dominicans as a lay brother and porter. He soon became famous for his austerity, the gift of healing, and levitation. He reportedly experienced levitations while praying at night in the church. On one occasion, a novice entered the lay brother's darkened chamber and received a terrifying shock when he walked directly into Massias' legs and feet as he hung suspended in the air.

He was revered by all who knew him and upon his death at age sixty, the whole city of Lima, Peru mourned.[165]

Again, many of these early accounts are very brief as in the following three cases. J. S. Piscator (d1586) was a Roman Professor and orator, who reportedly experienced ecstatic levitations.[166]

Luc de Medina del Campo (sixteenth century) was a Spanish Franciscan who, according to his biographer, Arturus, fell into ecstatic trances during which his body would levitate and become luminous.[167]

Alphonse Rubius (d1601) was a Franciscan monk whose levitations reached such a height that the other monks were able to pass to and fro beneath his feet.[168]

The case of Maria Coronel de Agreda (1602-1665), however, is much more detailed. Agreda is probably most famous for her abilities of bilocation. She was often seen aiding and preaching to the North American Natives while still remaining in her cell in Spain.

Agreda was also seen to fall into trance and levitate. During her levitating trances, her fellow nuns discovered that if they blew in her direction her body swayed with their breath. Her levitations typically occurred following spiritual lectures, when hearing spiritual music, or during communion.

Agreda tried so hard to resist her "trance levitations" that she vomited blood. Typically, she would levitate about a foot off the ground for several hours' duration. The levitations were so long that De Agreda's fellow nuns regularly showed her off to visitors.

Her friend, Bishop Ximenes Samaniego, describes in detail his experiences with Agreda: "The raptures of the servant of God were of this nature. The body was entirely bereft of the use of the senses, as if it were dead, and it was without feeling if violence was done to it; it was raised a little above the ground and as light as if it had no weight of its own, so much that like a feather it could be moved by a puff of breath even from a distance. The face was more beautiful than it normally appeared; a certain pallor replaced the naturally swarthy hue. The whole attitude was so modest and so devout that she seemed a Seraph in human form. She frequently remained in this state for two or even for three hours." Leroy counts Agreda's case as among the most credible.[169]

And a final medieval case: Andrew Hibernon the Blessed (d1602) was of noble Spanish heritage, but his parents were so poor that they had to hire him out to support the family. After several years of hard work, he saved enough money to provide a large dowry for his sister. However, while taking the money home, he was robbed of every cent. This theft caused him to realize the worthlessness of material things, and he converted to religion and joined the Franciscans as a lay brother. He spent the rest of his life largely hidden in prayer and penitence. He later became a powerful preacher, converting many to religion. He was also widely known for his prophecies and correctly predicted the date of his own death. During his process for beatification, several witnesses testified that he experienced levitating raptures and would often be seen fully raised from the ground in prayer.[170]

8. The Flying Friar of Europe

The most famous levitating saint of all times, perhaps rivaling even St. Teresa of Avila, is undoubtedly St. Joseph Desa of Cupertino (Giussepe Desa of Copertino, Italy) (1603-1663). At first, Desa seemed an unlikely candidate for sainthood. He was born into poverty. His father, a carpenter, sold their home to pay for debts and died soon after Joseph's birth. Joseph was reportedly withdrawn, excitable, dim-witted, and deformed in his feet. As a child, his nickname was "the Gaper" because of his vacant, slack-jawed expression. However, even from an early age, Desa showed a strong interest in religion, and reportedly experienced his first "ecstatic trance" at age eight.

At age seventeen, he was apprenticed to a shoemaker, but was fired for incompetence. He was rejected twice by the Franciscans because he was unable to perform simple menial tasks. He

S.Joseph a Cupertino Ord.Min.S.Francisci Convent. in Missæ celebratione sæpissime in aerem elevatur.
Michaelang.Ricciolini del. Nic.Guttierez sculp.

St. Joseph of Cupertino, the "flying Friar" of Europe. More than seventy levitations were recorded in his life. (Mary Evans Picture Library)

kept dropping dishes, letting the fire go out, and falling into ecstatic fits during which he was unable to work.

His transformation occurred after finally being hired as a stable-boy by the Franciscan Friars at Cupertino. He became devoutly religious and spent much of his time in prayer. He lived very ascetically, wearing a hair-shirt, often eating only twice a week, and flagellating himself so that his body was covered with wounds. At age twenty-two he was admitted, by a stroke of luck, to the novitiate. It was then that his levitations began.

Desa's levitations were so numerous and witnessed by so many people of high credibility that they are very difficult to dismiss as anything but true. Desa would sometimes levitate when he was exposed to anything of a religious nature. The mere sight of a statue or painting could send him aloft, as could the sound of prayer or religious music. On each occasion, he would let out a characteristic shriek and then float quickly upwards.

During several of his levitations, he was so overcome with ecstasy that he would embrace heavy stone statues and lift them up into the air with him. He would mistake a fellow monk for famous religious personages, grab the monk and carry him into the air.

His first recorded levitation occurred while saying Mass at a monastery in Naples. Mass had just begun when he fell into a trance and levitated from a corner of the church and flew across the room to the altar. The event was observed by several stunned witnesses.

After that, the levitations came fast and furious. While visiting Assisi, he entered a monastery to pray when he sighted a painting of the Virgin Mary. He instantly rose into the air and floated fifteen feet over a group of more than a dozen witnesses.

He was also observed levitating in the open air. On one reported occasion, while walking outside, he observed a baby lamb, which sent him into ecstasy. A fellow brother, seeing Joseph's reaction, handed him the lamb. Joseph grabbed the lamb, placed it on his shoulder, and ran into the garden. The other priests followed, eager to see if the ecstasy would result in a levitation. As they predicted, Joseph rose into the air with the lamb and hovered in a kneeling position among the trees for a duration of two hours.

Joseph's levitations were easily provoked. On one occasion, a priest, Antonio Chiarello, uttered, "Oh, how beautiful God has made heaven." Desa promptly rose up and perched on the thin top branches of an olive tree where he remained for two hours. Chiarello finally had to fetch a ladder to get Desa down.

One Christmas Eve, shepherds in the church played religious music on their pipes, launching Desa an estimated forty feet across the church to the high altar. As one witness, a shepherd, testified, "We then saw brother Joseph, he was so joyous, starting to dance to the sound of the music. But all of a sudden he gasped and uttered a loud cry. At the same time, he rose up in space in the middle of the church, flying like a bird to the main altar...a good twenty-five meters. But the most amazing part of the affair was that the altar was covered with lit candles. Brother Joseph flew, set himself among the candles, and disturbed neither candle nor candlestick. He stayed thus so, kneeling above the altar, hugging the altar in his arms for about fifteen minutes. Then he descended from the altar disturbing nothing. He went away from us, his eyes pouring tears. All of us were saying, 'My brothers, that was enough to be blessed by the love of God.' We were all afraid and astonished from this devotion. I said to myself, 'It certainly is a miracle.'"

Several nuns also observed this occasion, and began screaming, "he will catch on fire." They were assured by Brother Lodovico, who had observed Joseph's flights on prior occasions, that he would not be burned.

On one famous occasion, Joseph flew among the burning candles along the altar and yet remained unharmed. (Catholic Forum)

On the Feast of Saint Francis, Desa was seen levitating while holding a lit candle, passing fourteen paces through the air in front of several startled monks. Once, upon seeing the cross, he flew fifteen feet up into the air and remained suspended on the edge of the pulpit, hugging the cross.

Desa was able to exert some control over his flight path. On one occasion, he flew around several lamps and ornaments that obstructed his way to the altar. Upon seeing the levitation in progress, Desa's superior ordered him back, and Desa promptly reversed his path and landed back in the place he had just vacated.

When he was in one of his episodes, his brothers would sometimes try to rouse him by pricking him with needles or burning his flesh. Desa took no notice, and afterwards would laughingly apologize for his state.

On July 15, 1657, he experienced a recorded levitation upon seeing the cupola of the Notre-Dame de Loretta. He cried out, raised six feet up from the ground, and flew nearly one hundred feet into an almond tree.

The sight of an altar often sent him into a levitating trance. This occurred on at least fifteen known occasions. Another altar-induced levitation was particularly memorable because at the time, he had not levitated for two years. His ecstasies and levitations had ceased after a hostile superior repeatedly humiliated and persecuted him. However, during a visit to Assisi, the sight of the image of the Virgin Mary on the altar sent him sailing fifteen yards to embrace her.

On still another occasion, officials guarding the holy relics of Saint Francis saw Joseph approach. As soon as he saw the relics, he uttered a cry and flew up backwards over their heads, landing behind them on the stone tiles.

Often, Desa appeared to be unaware of his surroundings during his trances. On one occasion, a priest observed Desa levitating, and a slipper fell off his foot. Desa took no notice.

Joseph levitated whenever exposed to religious items. On one occasion, he spied several men trying to lift a heavy wooden cross. He instantly flew several yards and raised the cross with ease. (Mary Evans Picture Library)

Another instance of levitation was particularly memorable. A thirty-six foot cross had been constructed, but due to its immense size and weight, ten men were unable to lift it and put it in the stand that had been built along the roadside outside of Cupertino. Desa, however, observed the cross from the doorway of the church. As soon as he saw it, he "rose like a bird into the air," flew seventy yards, and lifted it up "as if it were a straw" and put it in its place.

On another occasion, his gaze fell upon a statue of Jesus. He let out a yell, fell into an ecstatic trance, floated eight feet off the floor, and grasped the heavy stone statue, which he lifted up. Still holding the statue, Desa floated down the hallway to his room.

Desa would sometimes grab other people and carry them into the air. On one such occasion, he heard religious music, provoking an attack. Desa rushed up to the confessor, and grabbing his hands, they both flew up to the center of the room.

Once he saw a wax statue of the infant, Jesus, above the altar. He cried out, flew up to the statue, and, clutching it to his chest, floated about the room for several minutes in numerous different postures.

Another similar event occurred in the Church of Santa Chiara in Cupertino. Several novitiates were being honored with a festival. Desa then heard the Latin words, "Veni Sponsa Cristi" (Come Bride of Christ), when he felt a levitation coming on. "Giving his accustomed cry, he ran towards the convent's father confessor, Raffaelle Palma, who was attending the service, and, seizing him, grasped him by the hand and....finally both rose into the air in an ecstasy, the one borne aloft by Joseph, the other by God Himself...one being beside himself with fear but the other with sanctity." Reportedly, this sort of event happened on several occasions.

On another occasion, Desa reportedly cured Balthazar Rossi, a local madman. Formerly a prominent citizen, the man had gone insane and had to be physically bound to prevent him from hurting himself and others. Joseph untied the man and told him to have no fear. He then grabbed him and levitated with him for a period of fifteen minutes, after which, the man was cured of his insanity.

Joseph's reputation grew and he was often called to pray for the sick. On one occasion, while praying for a patient, he rose up into the air and came back down on a table crowded with dishes. In May of 1649, while attending a patient's deathbed, Joseph was seen to levitate while in prayer.

While praying in the church of Saint Gregoire in Naples, he uttered a loud cry, startling all those present, and flew up to the altar. He was seen to levitate before images of the Virgin on several occasions—one of these levitations reaching a height of thirty feet.

Father Juniper reported that he saw Joseph levitate while listening to the boys' choir. As they sang, Joseph approached and floated a few inches above the ground. The boys stopped singing and surrounded Joseph to pass their hands beneath his feet.

Often when he said Mass, Joseph was seen to balance on the tips of his toes in ecstasy.

Joseph Desa's levitations became wildly famous all across Europe and enormous crowds gathered to witness the miracle of the flying friar. His fame caused many people of high social standing to come and view the events. His levitations were viewed by numerous officials, including several cardinals, the duke of Medina de Rio-Seco and the daughter of Charles Emmanuel I the Great, duke of Savoy, Catherine of Austria, and others. Probably the most significant witness was none other than Pope Urban VIII. During this visit, while kissing the pontiff's feat, Desa rose into a levitating trance. Pope Urban VIII was so impressed that he declared that he had witnessed a true miracle.

Johann Friedrich, the Lutheran Duke of Brunswick, traveled to Assisi for the expressed purpose of viewing Desa's levitations. Friedrich, not being Catholic, had to be sneaked into the church. As he watched, Desa gave out his customary cry, floated slowly into the air, moved backwards and then towards the altar

St. Joseph levitated in front of Pope Urban, causing the Pope to exclaim that he witnessed a "true miracle."

where he returned to the ground. Friedrich was overcome with emotion and began to cry. He returned the next day and observed Desa levitate again for a period of fifteen minutes. Friedrich was so impressed by what he had witnessed that he converted to Catholicism.

Another memorable levitation occurred in 1645. The Spanish Ambassador to the Papal Court had heard about the levitating saint and called for a meeting.

According to Ghezzi, "In 1645, the Spanish ambassador to the papal court, the high admiral of Castile, passed through Assisi to see Joseph. After speaking with the saint in his cell, he returned to the church and told his wife, 'I have spoken with another Saint Francis.'

"Upon hearing this, his wife also wanted to meet Joseph, and at her request, his superior commanded him to go up to the church and speak with her. 'I will obey,' said Joseph, 'but I don't know whether I'll be able to speak,' and he hastened to comply.

"Scarcely had he entered the church when, looking up to a statue of Mary Immaculate on the altar, he flew about twelve paces over the heads of those present to the foot of the statue. After remaining there sometime in prayer, he flew back with his customary cry and returned to his cell. The occurrence amazed the admiral and his wife, and their retinue."

According to some accounts, the admiral's wife actually fainted and needed strong smelling salts to recover.

Another early description of Desa's levitations is the following, "Several religious, whom he helped fold a habit worn by St. Francis, saw him hover in the air above their heads. Others saw him suspended on a cornice in the chapel of St. Francis, about eight feet from the floor. One day, while a priest was preaching in the chapel of St. Ursula, Joseph flew from a balcony that jutted out in front of the altar. He remained suspended in a kneeling position before the tabernacle until at his superior's command he flew back to the balcony."

Many other witnesses are listed by name, including the Bishop Martelli of Spoleto, Bernardino Benaducci, and Archange Rosimi, each of who testified under oath to having seen Joseph in flight. The Bishop of Spoleto wrote, "The ecstasies of which he was favored are known by all the world. I have seen him, and several people of my house have seen him as have I, raised up four fingers from the ground."

When the Spanish Ambassador and his entourage came to visit, Joseph levitated over their heads, causing the Ambassador's wife to faint. (Mary Evans Picture Library)

Desa's antics had become so famous that they created considerable controversy. He was known across Europe as the "flying friar." Church superiors feared that he was becoming a cult figure. Growing crowds of people continued to flood into the area and follow him everywhere. So many people came that temporary housing had to be erected to contain the increasing throngs of spectators.

Around this time, Desa was accused by his superiors of seeking publicity and trying to create false miracles. He was investigated by the Inquisition, and the decision was made to put Desa in isolation. For more than thirty-five years, he was forbidden to say mass, take part in processions, choir practice, or anything that might cause one of his episodes. He was shielded from religious icons of any kind, and was moved from one friary to another to avoid spectators. He was eventually returned to his original friary where he remained in virtual seclusion.

Even these precautions weren't enough to stop the levitations or the crowds of followers, who somehow managed to locate him. St. Joseph Desa of Cupertino's levitations are among the most numerous of all levitators, with more than seventy recorded episodes. They are difficult to account for, unless they are true.

Although he left no written record of his impressions, he often referred to his episodes as "my giddiness." He believed that his levitations were a kind of illness, and once apologized to an awestruck witness by saying, "my body is out of order."

More than a hundred years following Desa's death, Pope Benedict XIV examined the eyewitness accounts of the levitations. The report on Desa in the "Acta Sanctorum" was in excess of 1,000 pages in length and listed seventy separate flights. Although normally skeptical of so-called "miraculous" events, the Pope wrote, "Eyewitnesses of unchallengeable integrity gave evidence of the famous uplifting and prolonged flights of [Saint Joseph] when rapt in ecstasy."

Prosper Lambertini was one of the investigators at Joseph's trial for canonization. He also came away convinced. "At the time when I exercised the functions of the Promoter of the Faith in the Sacred Congregation of the Rites, they examined the cause of the venerable servant of God and examined his virtues there. Following that, I resigned from the functions of the Promoter, the question resolved in a favorable manner. In this cause, the eyewitnesses—whose integrity is above suspicion—deposed on the subject of the very famous elevations from the ground, the grand aerial flights of the ecstatic servant of God."

Joseph Desa's levitations continued until his death at age sixty. Desa's doctor, Francesco Pierpauli (Pierpaoli), testified to church officials that he witnessed several levitations. During one examination with two other doctors, Desa spontaneously entered into ecstasy and rose three feet above the chair. Pierpauli attempted to pull Desa down but was unable to do so. Pierpauli told church officials that this event happened three times, and that each time, Desa was "rapt out of his senses." As Pierpauli testified before Church officials, "I noticed that he was raised about a palm over the said chair, in the same position as before the rapture. I tried to lower his leg down, but I could not; it remained stretched out....To better observe Father Joseph, I knelt down on my knees. The nurse observed with me. The both of us recognized that Father Joseph was very obviously ravished out of his senses and that from the start he was truly and actually suspended in the air as I have said. He had been a quarter of an hour in this situation when Father Silvestro Evangelista of the monastery of Osimo came up. He observed the phenomenon for some time, and commanded Joseph to come to himself, and called him by name. Joseph then smiled and recovered his senses."

The doctor also testified that Desa was floating a few inches above his bed when he died.

Desa's case is among the strongest on record. Leroy writes, "If there is a cluster of cases on levitation which appear from the outset compact and varied enough in order to resist the testing of the proposed rules, it is manifestly that which we find in the life of Joseph of Copertino....the existence of Joseph of Copertino appears to have been organized in order to prove the existence of levitation, because of the number and the variety of the phenomena, and the diversity of the places where they were produced, joined with an intellectual quality, social and moral, of the witnesses who verified them....In order to reject these witnesses, it is necessary to admit to an organized hoax or a collective hallucination of unbelievable power."

Alban Butler writes, "St. Joseph's life was one long succession of ecstasies, miracles of healing and supernatural happenings on a scale not paralleled in the reasonably authenticated lives of any other saint...St. Joseph of Cupertino, in both the extant and number of these experiences, provides the classical examples of levitation, for, if many of the earlier incidents are doubtful some of those recorded in his later years are very well attested."

Herbert Thurston writes, "It is very difficult to believe that they [the witnesses to Cupertino's levitations] could have been deceived as to the broad fact that the Saint did float in the air, as they were convinced they had seen him do, under every possible variety of conditions and in many different surroundings."

Most researchers who have examined Desa's case reach similar conclusions. Religious writer Norman Douglas writes, "The witnesses were not ignorant, being upstanding men whose testimony should not be treated lightly."

Patricia Treece calls Cupertino's case "absolutely authenticated" and "as well attested as accounts can get."

Joseph Desa was canonized in 1767, and is now the patron saint of air travelers, pilots, and students. At least four biographies have been published on his life.[171]

9. Seventeenth Century Levitating Saints

As humanity climbed out of the Dark Ages and into the Age of Reason and Enlightenment, levitation was still recorded mainly only among the very religious. And, although there was a definite growth of scientific knowledge and discovery, no scientists were quite ready to examine the phenomenon. However, ignoring the cases didn't make them go away. What follows are twenty-three cases of seventeenth century levitating saints.

Thomas of Cori (1603-1709) was born in the Italian countryside to poor parents. He worked first as a shepherd, but joined the Observant Franciscans at age twenty-one after his parents died. He occupied a remote friary in the mountains near Subiaco for the rest of his long life. Here he spent many hours praying, in penance and preaching to the locals. He also began experiencing ecstasies and became "gifted with levitation." On one well-remembered occasion, he levitated while giving communion. According to the spectators, he rose up without warning, and so quickly, that they feared he would strike his head on the rafters. He floated for a few moments and then floated gently downwards and continued distributing communion.

He was also seen to experience a luminous levitation on his deathbed.[172]

Jeanne-Marie of the Cross (1603-1673) became an ecstatic at age thirteen. She often experienced ecstatic fits following communion. On occasion, these were accompanied by levitations in full view of stunned witnesses. [173]

Saint Bernard Latini of Corleone (1605-1667) was first a shoemaker, but then became one of the best swordsmen in Sicily. In 1632, after wounding a police officer and about to be imprisoned, he took sanctuary in a church, and there experienced a spiritual catharsis. He was later admitted as a Capuchin lay brother. To purge himself of guilt and sin, he practiced extremely severe austerity and penances. This activated within him numerous supernatural gifts including prophecy, healing powers (mostly of animals) and levitation. One day he was praying with the other brothers when he suddenly flew up to the main altar in full view of everyone present. A huge crowd

B. Thomas a Cori O. M. O. mire elevatus dum Eucharistiam ministrab.
Parisotti a Pasquino N.º 9.

Saint Thomas of Cori levitates while administering the Eucharist. (Mary Evans Picture Library)

gathered to watch the marvelous spectacle, several of the witnesses coming up to touch his clothes, as if to verify with their fingers what their eyes couldn't believe.[174]

Saint Francois de Saint-Nicholas (1608-1678) experienced occasional ecstasies while saying mass. On one occasion, this was accompanied by a levitation. On another, he was seen to float up to the ceiling.[175]

Passitea Crogi (d1615) was a Siennese nun whose ecstasies began when she was a very young child. Before long, she began to levitate. When asked how these levitations occurred, Passitea replied that angels appeared to her and spoke with her, sometimes supporting her in the air. Her levitations were remarkable in that she was occasionally observed to travel considerable distances without her feet moving to make steps; instead she appeared to glide from place to place. One particularly memorable incident was observed by Sister Diodata who went hiking with Crogi on a rainy day. After they returned, Sister Diodata's feet were covered with mud while Crogi's feet didn't have even a "speck" of mud on them, although they had both traveled the same path.

Several people went on record as witnesses to her levitations, including her fellow nuns, Sister Felipe and Sister Maria Francesca, who said she was usually raised up between nine and twelve feet above the ground. One of her levitations lasted for three hours and was accompanied by luminosity.

Probably her most remarkable levitation occurred while staying at the home of Duchess Sforza. Passitea Crogi experienced a sudden rapture that lifted her to the height of six feet. Duchess Sforza was so impressed that she had everyone present sign an affidavit attesting to the truth of the event.[176]

Saint Marianne of Jesus of Paredes (1618-1645) was orphaned at an early age and turned to religion. She lived ascetically, eating a minimal amount and sleeping only three hours a night. As we have seen, asceticism can activate certain psychic powers. Paredes found that she had the gift of prophecy and to display "miracles." This sometimes took the form of luminous ecstatic levitations. She died at age twenty-seven, and was canonized more than three hundred years later, in 1950.[177]

Marguerite Parigot of the Saint-Sacrament (1618-1648) experienced occasional levitations during which her body appeared to become luminous. She was also gifted with supernatural agility. On one occasion, she was seen to literally fly up to the ceiling of her room. Numerous residents of her convent witnessed the levitations, which occurred during prayer. During one incident, a sister crept forward and, to assure herself of the reality of the levitation, passed her hands underneath the kneeling form of Marguerite. On another occasion, Father Amelote reported that Sister Marguerite was raised from her bed and "suspended in the air between the mattress and the ceiling, without being able to protect herself from this invisible force."

Marguerite was apparently able to levitate at will as she was once seen by her fellow sisters levitating to reach some grapes that were beyond her reach. One year before her death, Marguerite experienced an hour-long levitation before the crucifix, in full view of her fellow sisters.[178]

Sister Beatrice Mary of Jesus (1632-1712) was a Spanish nun who was often seen to levitate while kneeling in prayer before the altar. Other nuns who witnessed the levitations also noticed that Sister Beatrice would sway back and forth with the currents of air in the chapel.[179]

Marie Paret (1636-1674) was a Dominican nun who experienced luminous ecstasies that were sometimes accompanied by levitations. She was also seen to descend staircases without touching the steps.[180]

Francois de Posadas the Blessed (1644-1714) was forbidden by his father from becoming a friar and was instead forced to work in the family's grocery business. When his father died, he entreated his step-father to let him join the order. His step-father refused and sent him to learn a trade. When Francois was nineteen, his step-father died and Francois finally became a Spanish Dominican. Although he was a prolific author, he was best known for his preaching, which sometimes reached such a fervor, that his body would reportedly glow and float off the ground. These luminous levitations also occurred during mass. He revealed some of his impressions to his confessor saying, "I don't know if I've left the ground; I don't know what's happening to me."[181]

St. Joseph Oriol (1650-1702) of Barcelona, Spain was religious from an early age. He excelled scholastically, and after receiving his doctorate in theology, he lived a life of extreme asceticism, subsisting only on bread and water for twenty-six years. He had no possessions in his cell, not even a bed, sleeping on the floor only three hours each night. He gave much money to the poor. He was widely sought after for spiritual advice and healings. His fame and reputation as a healer spread so widely that his confessor forbade him to perform them in church because of the disturbances they caused.

He also experienced numerous visions and prophecies, as well as regular levitations during prayer. In 1698, he stunned a group of sailors with his spontaneous levitation. The priest was sailing home from Marseille, France when he suddenly fell into an ecstatic trance and floated above the decks of the ship. The sailors attempted to pull him back to the deck by climbing up the shrouds. The owner of the boat, Raphael de Baladas de Blanes, wept at the sight—and also whenever he recounted the story. Oriol was canonized in 1909.[182]

One brief case: Onofrio de Fiamenga (d1639) was a Franciscan lay brother who reportedly experienced luminous levitations.[183]

The power of fervent prayer is exemplified in the following dramatic case. Bonaventure of Potenza (1651-1711) was an Italian Friar who experienced levitations during his life and stigmata upon his death. Abbot Daras was a firsthand witness to Potenza's levitations and left a vividly written record. "When he said his first mass, he started to cry and his body lifted up from the ground as though to approach God. When he spoke of the sufferings of our Lord, of His love for mankind, his eyes appeared to shoot flames, his feet not touching the ground. The chair itself on which he sat left the ground and raised up with him."

Abbot Daras reported that, in 1711, after being given an apple, Potenza sniffed the apple, fell into a trance and rose into the air. On another occasion, he levitated following contemplation. Writes Daras, "His eyes became enflamed, perspiration poured from his entire body and he elevated himself from the ground and stayed suspended for twenty minutes above the steps of the altar."[184]

Saint Pacifico Divini of San Severino, Italy (1653-1721) was orphaned at age five and left to be raised by a strict and abusive uncle, who treated him more like a servant than a nephew. At age seventeen, he joined the Observant Friars. He became very popular for his simple, direct sermons and for being able to read the minds of his penitents. At age thirty-five, illness left him crippled and nearly blind and deaf. He retired to the friary at San Severino, devoting the remainder of his life to prayer, fasting, and self-mortification.

He then began to experience ecstasies, prophecies, and levitations. He was seen on several occasions to levitate while praying before the altar. Father Felix Pascal reported that in December, 1714, he was attending mass with Pacifico when his body began to glow and then levitated one foot above the floor for a period of five hours. The levitation ended only after the superior of the convent commanded the ecstatic to return to the ground.[185]

Saint John Joseph Calosirto of the Cross (1654-1734) of Naples joined the Franciscans at age sixteen. As a child, he often retired to the attic of the family home where he fasted and prayed. After joining the religious order, he excelled quickly, impressing his superiors with his fervency of prayer, obedience, and humility. By age twenty-three, he became a well-known confessor, and was later instrumental in settling numerous high-level disputes. After he had a vision of a departed lay brother, he became endowed with supernatural gifts, including healing, prophecy, telepathy, and multiplication of food. He was also said to have the "supernatural gift of levitation."

In his advanced age, he needed a walking stick to get around. On one occasion, he was jostled in a crowd of people and lost his walking stick. At this point, he prayed and was levitated in front of the crowd to beneath the pulpit and then to the door of the cathedral. His walking stick was then seen to float back into his hand, much to the amazement of the crowd.

His levitations were sometimes particularly elevated, almost always exceeding the height of six feet. Like St. Joseph of Cupertino, he would let out a loud shriek before he rose into the air. In 1728, as he followed a procession in Naples, he was seen to rise upwards and walk in empty space. As Herbert Thurston writes, "One would be inclined to dismiss such a tale as pure fable from beginning to end, if it were not that there seems to be good evidence that St. John Joseph was himself on very many occasions seen raised in the air, sometimes a few inches, sometimes five or six feet, and once to the roof of the church, while in 1728, he took part in a procession, making believe to walk, but in fact, we are assured, carried through the air in ecstasy a distance of two miles half a foot or more above the ground."

St. John Joseph was so popular that he was constantly followed by large crowds of people, each seeking his advice or blessing. Followers constantly attempted to cut or even bite pieces of his religious habit. He correctly predicted his death at two o'clock a.m., on March 1, 1734.[186]

Ange d'Acri the Blessed (1669-1739) was drawn to religion early in life, but was unable to endure the ascetic lifestyle. However, his spiritual ardor grew, and he became a Capucin missionary, well known for his fervent prayer. He experienced at least four known levitations. In 1722, while preaching, he became ravished in ecstasy and floated above the platform where he remained suspended for several minutes. This same incident happened on two other occasions. One episode occurred when he saw the altar, fell into ecstasy, and reportedly flew ten feet up to the cross. He also reportedly had the abilities of prophecy, reading men's minds, bilocation, and supernatural agility.[187]

Saint Veronica [Ursule] Giuliani (1676-1727) of Italy was a Capucin nun who worked teaching novitiates. Even from an early age, she was very religious. By age six, she regularly donated her own food and clothes to the needy. Her father tried hard to get her to marry, but at age seventeen, she was allowed to join the convent. She became increasingly fervent in her prayers, when at the age of twenty-one, she received the wounds of the stigmata. She was put into a hospital for treatment, but the wounds failed to heal. When her situation began to cause attention, she was investigated by the Bishop of Citto de Castello, who declared her wounds authentic. She experienced regular levitations in the convent garden as well as numerous other mystical events. Her episodes caused such an uproar that she was examined on several other occasions by various ecclesiastic authorities. Researcher Herbert Thurston wrote that her case was among the best-verified cases of physical mysticism in all of Catholic hagiography. Giuliani left a written account of her life by order of her confessor, and her influence as a mystic was felt throughout the eighteenth century. She was canonized in 1839.[188]

Marcelline Pauper (1668-1708) became a nun at age twenty-two and experienced so many mystical events that her superior commanded her to write the details of her life. While she refused to discuss her levitations, believing them to be the effect of a nervous condition, others, including sister Juliette Bernardino, reported seeing her elevated above the ground during prayer.[189]

Therese of the Cross (d1673) experienced numerous levitations which were easily provoked by exposure to anything religious. Her levitations were typically several hours long. Because of this, she was forced to change convents several times, then was accused of sorcery, and lived much of her life in total isolation. She was finally taken back by a monastery in Liege, where she lived the remainder of her life in peace.[190]

Sometimes levitations are accompanied by peculiar physiological effects. Blaise de Caltanisetta (d1684) was a Franciscan monk who experienced particularly dramatic levitations during which his chest would expand, his body would shake from head to foot, and he would cry out loudly as he was lifted upwards. Spectators report hearing loud noises "like two stones striking together" coming from his body.[191]

Saint Paul Francois Danei of the Cross (1694-1775) was best known as an outstanding preacher, and was also admired for his holiness and self-debasement. He was regarded by many as a living saint because of his supernatural gifts of prophecy, healing, bilocation, and reading men's minds. He was unbelievably popular, and was followed by huge crowds who fought to touch him or even get a piece of his clothes as a relic.

Danei also experienced numerous highly dramatic levitations. Most of these occurred while praying before the altar, during which his body would become weightless, rise to the ceiling, and emit light.

According to his own account, once, while traveling through the winter wilderness, he was overcome by weariness. He lied down to pray, and found himself elevated and transported to his destination.

One of his most remarkable levitations occurred while giving a sermon. He was seen to step off the raised platform and to walk in empty space above the stunned audience.

On another occasion, concerned on-lookers tried to halt a levitation. While having a conversation about God with his fellow priests, Paul-Francois began to tremble, become insensible, and exhibit all symptoms of an upcoming ecstasy. One of the priests recognized this, jumped up and tried unsuccessfully to hold Paul-Francois down in his chair. As one of the priests who was there later wrote, "Despite his efforts he began to levitate with the chair whose feet reached the top of my head, which made me believe that he must have been raised up about six feet. He stayed a rather long time in ecstasy. When he recovered, I noticed a little trembling in the upper part of his body, then he came back down little by little with the chair on which he sat."

St. Danei himself wrote advice on how to achieve a spiritual state conducive to ecstasy. "If you cannot spend much time at prayer, no matter: to act well is always to pray well. Be attentive to your duties, and at the same time be attentive to God by frequently purifying your heart in the immense ocean of divine love."[192]

A late 1600s account comes from Father Dominic De Jesus-Marie [Carme Dechaux], who was observed on one occasion to be raised up to the ceiling of his cell for the duration of one day and night. At one point during the levitation, De Jesus-Marie was accosted by a skeptic who, thinking it was a trick, reached up and seized the father by the feet. To the shock of the unnamed skeptic and the amusement of the onlookers, he was borne aloft with De Jesus-Marie, and then becoming afraid, released his grip and fell down, injuring himself.

One particularly compelling and memorable levitation of Dominic reportedly occurred in the presence of the King Phillip II of Spain, the Queen, and the entire royal court, members of whom stepped forward and blew their breath upon the father's body, making it sway back and forth "like a soap-bubble."[193]

By this time, the evidence in support of levitation, although still anecdotal, is very persuasive. In particular, the cases of Passitea Crogi, Bonaventure of Potenza, and others offer impressive testimonials from highly credible witnesses. Clearly, the events which occurred to these people were so unusual that their legacy remains today.

10. The Miracle of Saint Liguori

Saint Alphonse-Marie de Liguori (Aldophis) (1696-1787), although not well known among the levitating saints, remains one of the strongest cases on record for the veracity of the phenomenon. He experienced numerous levitations, two of which were witnessed by extremely large numbers of people, several of whom left convincing written testimonials.

Liguori grew up with little interest in religion. Instead, he was a precocious student of the law. By age sixteen, he was already a successful lawyer. Eight years later, he had a perfect record, winning every case he represented. Then, in 1720, he lost an important case because of a simple, stupid mistake. This mistake made him think deeply about what he wanted to do with his life. As a result, he left his practice (against his father's wishes) and became deeply religious. He was ordained as a priest at age thirty. He soon became a very popular confessor and preacher, and founded numerous missions throughout Naples.

Today he is credited with many miracles, including visions and prophecies which were later verified as accurate. And, of course, levitations.

His most famous levitation is undoubtedly the one that took place in December, 1745. While preaching before more than two thousand people, Liguori fell into ecstasy and rose several feet above the platform. The crowd fell into stone silence, then began to cry out, "Miracle! Miracle!" During Liguori's trial for beautification, multiple witnesses testified to this event including Father Garzilli and brother Dominique Corsano.

In 1756, again while preaching before a crowd of more than a thousand people, he experienced another levitation. Again, the crowd became very emotional. One witness, Father Casanova wrote, "We saw his body glow, his eyes fixed, ravished in ecstasy, to rise two palms above the chair, appearing as though an angel was flying him to heaven. This ravishment lasted for more than five minutes, during which erupted an indescribable emotion, the sobbing of the audience mingling with cries from all sides of, 'miracle!'"

Father Criscuoli says, "I am knowledgeable enough to know this happened. I particularly remember the complete transformation of two quarters of the town." Criscuoli elaborated, reporting that many prostitutes and drunkards changed their ways and improved their moral standing as a direct result of the "miracle."

Another witness, Francois de Stefano says, "All the people saw him, as I myself saw him, that he experienced a state of ecstasy. His eyes were turned to the sky, and his body raised up more than two palms."

The quality and number of testimonies avowing to Liguori's levitation leaves little doubt of their veracity. Wrote brother Verdesca, "At the beginning of 1762, I went one morning to order to recite, as is the custom, the office with him. Upon entering his room, I saw him elevated two or three palms above his chair, half-kneeling, half-sitting. He had his arms extended, his eyes open and raised towards the sky, his face glowing brightly as though transfigured. I entered quietly into the room and kneeled between the armchair and the bed in a way which allowed me, in turning my head, to watch his figure. The ravishment lasted about a quarter of an hour, but for me this seemed only an instant. All the while, my eyes streamed tears. I considered this spectacle very heavenly, he expressing a profound gasp and crying out, 'My God! My God!' He recovered at this moment and found himself on his chair in his normal state. I burst out sobbing, at which he noticed my presence and became confused. Turning towards me, he said with a gentle but reproachful tone, 'Unfortunate you were there! Above all, tell no one what you have seen.'" De Stefano reports that Liguori seemed disoriented as a result of the levitation.

Another witness, Father Majella, apparently prevented a levitation. As he reports, "In March, 1770, I attended his mass. That morning I saw him more excited than usual and as though in kind of fear. He recited the prayers of the Holy Mass up to the canon with an ineffable devotion. I knelt to celebrate the Holy Sacrifice, and I stopped a moment to observe. As soon as I saw that the consecration didn't happen, I raised my eyes and I saw him leaning his elbows on the altar, holding the host in his hand, without saying the words of the sacrament. In raising my head a little, I was able to see his face. The eyes were opened hugely and fixed on the cross, all of this revealing an animation which made me shudder. Then I discovered that he was touching the ground only by his toes, as if he was going to take flight. Completely beside myself and not knowing what to do, I went to call brother Romito or the servant Alex, and not finding them, returned to the altar. The servant of God was still in the same position. I then took him, as I had under similar circumstances, and shook him strongly, pulling him by his cassock. This movement made him recover. In leaving his ecstasy, he heaved a great gasp of love and pronounced the consecration. He finished the mass with the fervor of an angel."

Father Volpicellim reported that he once accidentally provoked Liguori into levitation by speaking to him of the love of God.

In October, 1784, Father Tannoja observed Liguori—now severely ill with rheumatism—levitating and left this detailed account: "...Alfonse was before the altar of the Very Holy Sacrament. I heard him move his feet as if he slid across the pavement; this sound began again a few moments later, and suspecting that something supernatural was happening to him, I glanced to the side and I saw him elevated in the air above his chair....I noticed the same levitations several times. In order to assure myself of this in a more thorough manner, I placed myself in the same location for several days, after careful consideration, and I saw the same transports in the air which recurred with the speed and the ease of a light feather."

Shortly before he died, Liguori had a levitation on his deathbed. This occurred after he was told that the chapels were so crowded with visitors, the drivers deserved to be called the real saints.

Only one year after his death, a trial was held to consider Liguori's canonization. A total of ninety-two witnesses testified to having seen Liguori in levitation. He was canonized in 1839.[194]

11. Levitations
In the East

While the levitations of Catholic Saints comprise the majority of early accounts, levitation is present in virtually all cultures. Second to Europe are the countries from the east and Far East. The eastern levitations display a marked difference from the European levitations. While the saints usually levitated only during ecstatic trances, eastern levitators often levitated at will, and also showed a higher degree of control over their flights. Most cases appeared to be meditational levitation, involving levitators who had learned to control the ability.

Rabbi Hayyim Vital (1542-1620) of Safed, Palestine was a disciple of the Kabbala and an influential author. He wrote mostly of the Kabbala, but also wrote some autobiographical material which was later reproduced in *Jewish Mystical Testimonies*. In his work, Vital wrote of an Arab who was the custodian of a mosque and a well-known anti-Semite. One morning, this Arab approached Vital, fell to his knees and begged for a blessing.

Vital was amazed and reminded the Arab that he, Vital, was a Jew. According to Vital, the Arab replied, "I now know that you are a godly and holy man. For I am custodian of a mosque. Last night at midnight I went out of the door of the mosque to relieve myself. The moon was shining so brightly at the time that it was as clear as noon. I raised my eyes and saw you flying through the air, floating for an hour above the mosque—you yourself, without any doubt."[195]

Levitators who openly displayed their abilities were understandably becoming increasingly rare. Lha-Tsu Ch'em-Bo (1595-1661) was born in Kongbu in southeastern Tibet. From an early age, he lived a monastic life. He founded a monastery near Nepal and authored several Buddhist texts.

He was reportedly seen levitating by his many servants as he traveled through the mountains of Sikkim, founding temples, monasteries and shrines. In 1641, Ch'em-Bo became a Lama. In 1648, he had an audience with the first Dalai Lama to whom he demonstrated his ability to levitate. By this time, his reputation as a levitator was so well-known that he was nicknamed "lha-tuns num kha Jig-may," or "the reverend god who fears not the sky."[196]

An interesting account from the 1700s is that of Shaikh Muhammad Quaili, a holy man from Sudan. According to Musa Was Rayya, Quaili led them each morning in prayer. One morning he was late and when he finally showed up, he was levitating, as Rayya says, "between heaven and Earth."

Rayya watched with astonishment as Quaili floated up over the doorway, hopped up and down on the ground a few times and entered the hut. Said Rayya, "The Shaikh came out of the [hermitage] in a distressed state, and counseled me to keep my mouth shut about what I'd seen."[197]

India has produced a number of well-verified levitation accounts. One is the case of Lahiri Mahasaya (1828-1895), known as the "incarnation of Yoga."

Author Paramahansa Yogananda was able to obtain a firsthand interview with Srimati Kashi Moni, the widow of Mahasaya. Says Moni, "It was years before I came to realize the divine stature of my husband. One night in this very room I had a vivid dream. Glorious angels floated in unimaginable grace above me. So realistic was the sight that I awoke at once; strangely, the room was enveloped in dazzling light. My husband, in a lotus posture, was levitated in the center of the room, surrounded by angels....Astonished beyond measure, I was convinced I was still dreaming. 'Woman,' Lahiri Mahasaya said, 'you are not dreaming...' As he slowly descended to the floor, I prostrated myself at his feet."[198]

Ramakrishna (1836-1886) was a well-known "great Master" who lived near Calcutta, India. He espoused teachings of God-realization. Ramakrishna claimed that people with a firsthand knowledge of God could attain "wonderful powers," among them levitation.

According to Ramakrishna's biographer, his nephew, Hriday was one of the few witnesses to the levitations. One evening, Hriday decided to follow his uncle to a site near the eastern bank of the Ganges that was used for religious practices. As he followed, Hriday was stunned to notice that Ramakrishna's body grew suddenly luminous and then lifted up into the air. Hriday rubbed his eyes in amazement, but his uncle remained in the air. According to the report, "His shining figure was moving through the air, his feet not touching the ground."[199]

A similar impressive account was supplied by Joshi Ootamram Doolabrahm, who traveled to India in 1856, to research Hindu theories of chemistry. He was eventually guided to the residence of a Hindu ascetic by the name of Narayenanand.

After much persistence, Doolabrahm convinced Narayenanand that he was genuinely interested in Yoga and not just idly curious. Narayenanand agreed to instruct him, at which point there followed no less than two years of discourse. Doolabrahm reports that during this two-year period, he observed Narayenanand levitating on more than one occasion. Writes Doolabrahm, "[He] was an ascetic who practiced Yoga and ecstatic trances, and I became one of his disciples...Here was a man about thirty-five years old, medium height, of very handsome appearance, with an intelligent expression and particularly rosy cheeks that I never saw such a human face until then. His head was shaven and he wore a saffron-colored robe of the ascetics."

Doolabrahm reports that he learned "many of the secrets of nature, and I was able to convince myself, by numerous proofs, of the abilities of man to dominate the forces, as my teacher practiced, among other things, pranayama, or the suspension of the breath."

While practicing this, Doolabrahm observed Narayenanand levitating. "His body would rise from the ground to the height of four fingers, and remain suspended in the air for four and five minutes at a time, while I was allowed to pass my hand beneath him three or four times, to satisfy myself beyond a doubt that the levitation was a positive fact."[200]

Sometime in the 1860s, Bubu Khrisna, then a ten-year-old child from Benares, India, witnessed several levitations involving one of his relatives. Writes Khrisna,

"One of my relatives, Amarchand Maitreyer, was known in the village for the practice of Yoga Dharma or the Law of Union with God. This venerable old man was able to elevate his body into the air a foot and a half above the ground, and stay suspended thus so more than a quarter of an hour. His two small sons and me...we asked him, with a child's curiosity, the secret of this phenomenon. And I remember well what he told us, that by Khumba Yoga, the human body becomes lighter than the air which surrounds it, and can then float above the ground. This explanation was sufficient for us."[201]

In 1866, the Chief Justice of Chandernagore, France, Louis Jacolliot, became interested in the accounts of Indian Fakirs and their alleged ability to levitate. He traveled across India to view these so-called "miraculous displays" in a scientific, objective manner. He was determined to discover if the stories of levitation were true or fanciful, and insisted that he was just "a simple recorder of facts."

Jacolliot eventually located a holy man in Benares, India by the name of Co-vindasamy. The Indian holy man proceeded to astound Jacolliot with a number of unexplained feats, including apparent telepathy and telekinesis of small objects. Jacolliot made further visits to determine if Covindasamy was hoaxing or not.

On one occasion, as Jacolliot was leaving, he saw Covindasamy levitate. His report, when published, caused a sensation, and is now considered a classic case of levitation. "The fakir stopped in the doorway...and folding his arms, he was lifted—or so it seemed to me—gradually, without visible support, about one foot above the ground. I could determine the exact height, thanks to a reference mark upon which I had fixed my eyes during the short time the phenomenon lasted. Behind the fakir hung a silk curtain...and I noticed that the fakir's feet were as high as the sixth stripe. When I saw the rising begin, I took my watch out. From the time the magician began to be lifted until he came down to earth again, about ten minutes elapsed. He remained about five minutes suspended without motion...Now that I have reflected on this strange scene, it is impossible for me to explain it otherwise; my sense of reason refused to accept it."

On another occasion, Covindasamy performed "stick levitation" for Jacolliot. "Leaning upon the cane with one hand, the Fakir rose gradually about two feet from the ground. His legs were crossed beneath him, and he made no change in his position, which was very like that of those bronze Statues of Buddha that all tourists bring from the Far East....For more than twenty minutes I tried to see how Covindasamy could thus fly in the face and eyes of all the known laws of gravity; it was entirely beyond my comprehension; the stick gave him no visible support, and there was no apparent contact between that and his body except through his right hand."

Before departing, Jacolliot asked Covindasamy if he was able to levitate at will. Covindasamy replied, "The Fakir can lift himself up as high as the clouds."

"How can he obtain this ability?" Jacolliot asked.

Covindasamy replied, "It is necessary that he stays in constant communication, through contemplative prayer, and a higher spirit descends from the sky."[202]

A somewhat amusing account of an involuntary levitation was reported in 1885 by Bavadjee D. Natts, who had traveled to India to study Indian mysticism.

Natts located an ascetic, and together, they planned to travel to an ashram in south India. They hiked to the location.

Just before reaching the ashram, the ascetic received a psychic warning to leave the area immediately. The ascetic refused and insisted on continuing towards the ashram. A few minutes later, he learned to regret his decision. Writes Natts, "He felt a powerful hand which took hold of him; and in a half-minute he was carried out of the forest, to the other side of the river and tossed unconscious on the ground."

Natts had to hike for an hour to locate his companion and guide, whom he found lying on the ground, weak and shaken. The ascetic then tried again to penetrate into the area near the ashram. Again he was lifted up and transported a long distance from Natts, who again had to hike to find him.

But that was not Natts's only experience with levitation. A few months later, he and another companion went searching for another yogi. They located a yogi named Ramagiri Swami who agreed to teach them yoga. They studied under him for a few months.

As the weeks passed, both Natts and his companion became curious about one unusual fact: every morning at three a.m. yogi Ramagiri Swami left his house and hiked secretly towards the nearby river. Natts and his friend decided one day to follow the yogi to see what he was doing by the river. They should have known better than to try and outwit a yogi.

Writes Natts, "That evening, when we went to his house, the yogi smiled and said to us, 'You want to know what I do by the river; very well! You don't have to resort to espionage; I will go to look for you tomorrow and we will go together.'"

The next morning, all three went to the river. Natts and his companion watched the yogi remove his robe and bathe in the river. He instructed them to do the same, which they did. Then, looking around them, they both simultaneously realized that Ramagiri Swami was missing.

Writes Natts, "We looked for the yogi, but it was impossible to find him.... We called likewise in vain. We believed then that he had entered into the river and that he was drowned, when we saw appear, on the surface of the water, the shadow [reflection] of the beautiful form of the mystic draped in his yellow clothes. We raised our eyes and glimpsed him, laying totally stretched out as if he was laying on a layer of air about thirty feet over our heads. At that moment, we saw him slowly descend until he sunk gently on the water; he then washed himself and returned to the house with us....Since this day, we have seen the yogi raised up and floating on the water for about two and a half hours each morning. This experience continued for a month."[203]

A particularly credible account of a late 1800s levitation comes from Seenath Chatterjee, who was entertaining a Tibetan Lama in his home in India. Chatterjee met the Lama when he came begging for food at his door. Chatterjee gave the Lama some food, and, on a whim, asked if the Lama possessed any psychic powers.

The Lama asked what exactly Chatterjee would like to witness. Chatterjee asked if he was able to levitate. It was then that Chatterjee saw something he would not soon forget.

He took the Lama into the back room. They shut the door and closed all the curtains. The lama then stripped down to his underclothes and sat in the full lotus posture. Says Chatterjee, "…he brought the thumb of each hand into contact with the ring-finger and, his hands against the abdomen, sat erect, turned his eyes upward, and remained for awhile motionless. His next action was to work his body with a wriggling motion, at the same time drawing several very deep breaths. After the third or fourth inhalation he seemed to retain the breath in his lungs, and for a half-hour was motionless as a statue of bronze. Then a succession of nervous shiverings ran through his body lasting perhaps three minutes, after which he resumed his state of immobility for another half-hour. Suddenly he, still retaining his sitting posture, rose perpendicularly into the air to the height of, I should say, two cubits—one yard, and then floated, without a tremour or motion of a single muscle, like a cork in still water. His expression was placid in the extreme, that of a rapt devotee, as described by eye-witnesses in the biographical memoirs of saints."

Chatterjee watched in amazement for several more minutes, until he suddenly felt guilty for asking for such a display. At that exact moment, the Lama descended, took in four deep breaths and stood up, laughing at Chatterjee's obvious puzzlement. The Lama then replied that levitation was actually a "commonplace siddhi" and that many of his amateur students were able to perform the same feat.[204]

Dr. John L. Nevius was a missionary in China. While there, he studied cases of possession among the primitive peoples. He wrote that "Chinese wizards are carried by invisible power from place to place. They ascend to a height of twenty or fifty feet, and are carried to a distance of four or five li."

A "li" corresponds to a one-third of mile. If true, accounts like this give films like *Crouching Tiger, Hidden Dragon* a strong historical basis.[205]

One of the highest altitude levitations was published by psychical researcher, Perovsky-Petrovo Solovovo, who reported that an Indian fakir was levitated to the height of a hundred feet, while in the presence of a crowd of witnesses.[206]

By far, most of the eastern levitations have taken place in India. And as time marched on, further Indian levitation cases would grab the attention of the modern world, bringing more adventurers to the country to observe and study the phenomenon.

12. Sorcerers and Shamans

One of the most obvious patterns concerning the phenomenon of levitation is the fact that it is present in virtually all cultures across the world. While accounts involving European saints and eastern yogis reach back thousands of years, most primitive cultures left little or no written records. The majority of cases from these cultures were actually recorded by European explorers, usually missionaries and anthropologists. Despite the lack of early written records, a surprisingly large number of cases have been collected. By far, the majority of these come from the dark continent of Africa.

An early example is that of Dengbagine, an Azande medicine man from Africa. He served in the court of King Mabenge of Sudan in the early 1800s. Dengbagine was known for his incredible supernatural powers. As the story goes, Dengbagine grew so powerful that King Mabenge and his followers feared him and finally decided to execute him.

Dengbagine allowed himself to be seized, bound with stones, and thrown into the river. What happened next was evidently remembered for years. Dengbagine rose to the surface, freed himself of the stones, and walked on the surface of the water. He performed a mystical dance and then rose into the air before the astonished onlookers. He rose higher and higher until he was a speck in the sky and disappeared, never to be seen in the kingdom again.[207]

In the late 1800s, English magician and skeptic, Harry Kellar, toured the world, exposing fakery in several mediums. Then in 1870, Kellar traveled to Africa to visit a Zulu witch doctor who allegedly had supernormal powers. Kellar asked to see a levitation.

The witch doctor sat down on the floor of his hut, closed his eyes and went into a trance. Says Kellar, "...to my amazement, the recumbent body slowly arose from the ground and floated upward in the air to about three feet, where for a while it floated, up and down."

Afterwards, the witch doctor floated back down and stood up. Kellar had to admit that he could not explain the levitation and found no evidence of trickery.[208]

While levitation appears in a wide variety of cultures, their approaches to the phenomenon can be very different, often involving unique, complex rituals. A typical example occurred in central Africa in January, 1893. Anthropologist Richard Hodgson traveled to Africa where he had the opportunity to observe a bizarre ritual that culminated in a levitation.

The ceremony commenced with two Zulu men, one a sorcerer and the other a young apprentice, each standing several feet distant from the other. Each then took a rope with a stick tied to the end. They then began to spin the devices over their heads. Hodgson could hardly believe what happened next. "When their two flailings began to knock against each other, a flash of light was produced, or rather a small flame which appeared to pass from one stick to the other. At the third spark, there was an explosion, then the stick of the young Zulu fell to pieces, he himself falling lifeless to the ground."

The sorcerer grabbed a handful of weeds and waved them around the head of the unconscious man. Hodgson watched as the weeds suddenly burst into flames. The sorcerer passed the burning herbs around the man's head. Writes Hodgson, "To my great amazement, I saw this body detach slowly from the ground and float in the air at an average of three feet in height. It rose and fell according to the slow or rapid passes made with the burning herbs, and when the herbs were consumed by fire and fell to the ground in ashes, the body of the Zulu fell in turn. Some magnetic passes practiced by the sorcerer on the young man sufficed to wake him up; he stood up with the appearance of having suffered from the experience and became subdued."[209]

As we have seen, the majority of primitive culture accounts come from religious missionaries. Another such account comes from Father Trilles, who traveled through Africa to convert primitive tribes to Christianity. While in Congo, he stayed with the Bouiti tribe, whose initiates claimed to have the ability to stay suspended one meter above the ground for a period of up to ten minutes. Although he didn't view these feats, he did see members of the Ngil tribe raise themselves up to the top of tall poles—a tradition reminiscent of some of the "pole saints"—and a feat that he felt must involve a "kind of levitation."[210]

Yet another missionary, Father Picarda, traveled to Zanzibar where he investigated the case of a young sorcerer who claimed to have been levitated involuntarily to the top of one of the tallest baobab trees, where he was found bound tightly with cord.[211]

Ngudeng was a famous African sorcerer who died in 1906. He reportedly had the ability to levitate which he acquired through long fasts and solitary meditation. He was called a *gwan kwoth*, or "possessor of the spirit." To explain his levitations, he claimed that an air spirit would take possession of his body. On these occasions, Ngudeng was observed to "climb into the air without support."[212]

Many other levitation accounts come from the continent of Africa. In 1907, Claire-Germaine Cele, a young Bantu native girl from Natal, Africa, orphaned and raised by missionary nuns, began to levitate shortly following her first communion. She displayed the ability to understand foreign languages, read minds, and would also fall into trances during which she would curse and mock the nuns and priests. The attacks eventually became so severe that an exorcism was ordered. Around this time, the levitations began.

During the reading of the exorcism rituals, the priests observed Cele to rise six feet above her bed. According to a report on the case written by the exorcists: "Germana floated often three, four, and up to five feet high in the air, sometimes vertically, with her feet downward, and at other times horizontally, with her whole body floating above her head. She was in a rigid position. Even her clothing did not fall downward, as would have been normal; instead, her dresses remained tightly attached to her body and legs. If she was sprinkled with holy water, she moved down immediately, and her clothing fell loosely onto her bed. This type of phenomenon took place in the presence of different witnesses, including outsiders. Even in church, where she could be seen by everyone, she floated above her seat. Some people tried to pull her down forcibly, holding on to her feet, but it proved to be impossible."

The exorcists were also stunned to see Cele's body actually change shape, sometimes elongating like a snake. An exorcism ritual headed by Father Erasmus cured Cele of her condition. According to Erasmus, the demon signaled its departure with another act of levitation which was observed by no less than 170 witnesses in the mission chapel.[213]

In 1975, explorer and author Douchan Gersi traveled across the world, visiting primitive cultures and studying their beliefs and supernatural practices. On one occasion, he visited a sorcerer in a small village in Zaire, Africa where he witnessed what appeared, at first, to be a typical nighttime fire-walking ceremony. Instead, it turned out to be much more complex. Writes Gersi, "Overcome by collective frenzy, the worshipers began jumping over a large campfire, and then walking on its coals without being burned. When it came his turn to do the same, the village sorcerer dove into the fire, in the same way a diver plunges into the water, but instead of falling into it, he remained three feet over the fire, parallel to it, long enough for me to ask myself what was happening. Then, as if in slow motion, his body moved until he was standing erect again, his feet touching the live coals, and he walked away."

Gersi noticed that the sorcerer seemed physically exhausted. The next morning, Gersi asked him how the levitation occurred. The man said calmly, "That happens sometimes, when spirits are there," but he refused to elaborate.[214]

Levitation seems to be particularly prominent in many primitive African cultures. Another well-verified modern case occurred in 1984. At that time, a German film crew traveled to Toga, Africa to film Nana Owaka, a local sorcerer who claimed the ability to levitate. Owaka promised to give a demonstration for the film the crew was shooting, *Journey into the Beyond*.

Owaka first meditated all day. He then placed a circle of leaves and twigs in a clearing next to the beach and sat in the center of the circle.

As one of the witnesses says, "Just as the sun was setting, Owaka started to stir. A villager lit the circle of twigs and flames shot up. Drums began beating wildly. Then we were hardly able to believe our eyes as Owaka stood and rose straight upward! It was as if he were being lifted up on a pillow of air. He simply hung there as if suspended, with nothing above or below him."

Owaka's body then sank back down in the center of the circle, and the demonstration was over. The crew filmed the event from two different angles. After reviewing the film, no evidence of trickery was found. According to Father Andreas Resch, a Catholic Priest and director of the Institute of Frontiers of Science in Insbruck, Austria, "I have invited different teachers of physics to look at the film and not one has been able to detect anything artificial which would have made this sorcerer levitate. I think the best proof for levitation to date is this film."[215]

As part of the research for this book, I conducted a long search for the film. After weeks of searching, I finally located a copy. To my delight, it was a well-put-together documentary, focusing on a wide variety of occult subjects, including mediumship, astral projection, telekinesis, psychic surgery, possession, hypnosis, and—one of the last segments—levitation. The producers had obviously saved the best for last.

Unlike many stage levitators, Nana Owaka was obviously the "real deal." He appeared to be a middle-aged man of African ancestry, with short hair, beard, and mustache. He wore a colorful red and orange robe and a tight knitted cap, no shoes. He, at first, refused to do any levitation demonstrations. Only after being repeatedly asked did he finally relent, and only upon the condition that the location of his little fishing village remain undisclosed. Once that was agreed upon, he left the area to meditate all day and ask the "Water Gods" for permission to do the religious ritual.

Meanwhile, for the half-dressed inhabitants of the rural village, the excitement was not about the upcoming levitation, but the visit by the German film crew, who were eyed with curiosity by everyone.

Once darkness had fallen, the ceremony began. The six-foot wide circle of twigs was lit on fire, while Owaka stood in the center. The natives began drumming and chanting around the circle with increasing intensity. Owaka stood with his arms in a *T*, and a tense expression on his face. He craned his neck upwards, grimaced, and began to breathe heavily and sweat. Suddenly and slowly, he rose up into the air. He ascended about two feet, hovered for twenty seconds, drifted back and forth slightly, and then returned back down. Five seconds later, he rose into the air again and floated for about thirty seconds. At this point, a second cameraman approached and filmed Owaka close-up from the side. Owaka then returned to the ground. This process was repeated one more time. Owaka floated about twenty-five seconds, then fell to the ground, exhausted.

The segment is approximately five minutes in length, with the levitation part lasting about one minute. The film is truly astounding. Unfortunately, because of its age, the quality of the film is not the best. Also, because the incident took place at night, it is difficult to see anything other than Owaka himself being raised from the ground. Overall, the film evidence combined with the testimony of the film crew makes the case very impressive. Says the film crew, "There seems to be absolutely no question of any possible deception or illusion. We cannot find any device by which Owaka could be lifted from above or supported from below during this amazing feat."[216]

While Africa dominates the accounts from primitive cultures, other cases come from America, Australia, Asia, and some of the island countries. Again, if not for various missionaries, many cases would never have been recorded at all. One such case comes from Father Papetard, a French missionary in Oregon, during the mid-1800s. For the first time, cases of Native American levitations were being observed by the outside world. According to Papetard, he personally witnessed Native American sorcerers rise three feet into the air and walk on the tops of the pampas grass plants.[217]

An interesting early 1900 account comes from Adolphus P. Elkin, an anthropologist and author who specialized in Australian Aboriginal shamanism. In his book, *Aboriginal Men of High Degree,* he revealed that Australian medicine men were able to levitate by sending an invisible magical cord into the sky which pulled them upwards. Elkin was able to locate a specific case: "A Wongaibon clever man, lying on his back at the foot of a tree, sent his cord directly up, and 'climbed' up with his head well back, body outstretched, legs apart, and arms to his sides. Arriving at the top, forty feet up, he waved his arms to those below, and then came down in the same manner, and while still on his back the cord re-entered his body."[218]

Another Australian account was first revealed by field anthropologist Mr. A. W. Howitt, who studied the cultures of various Australian tribes. He found a strong belief in levitation among all of them. He eventually earned the trust of a magician named Mundauin, from the Kunai tribe, who provided a firsthand account. Mundauin told Howitt that spirits would levitate him and reveal information on the movements of neighboring tribes. Mundauin also produced eyewitnesses who supported his account.

Howitt learned of other alleged levitations from neighboring tribes. Members of the Bwiti tribe were supposedly able to rise to a height of several feet for a duration of fifteen minutes during certain wizard ceremonies. Again Howitt obtained a few firsthand accounts. He was told the case of one sorcerer who was found in the top of an inaccessible tree following a séance. He also located a sorceress of the Wotjobaluk tribe who claimed the ability to speak with the dead and to levitate. Witnesses reported that she would be supported by invisible spirits with whom she conversed.[219]

In the early 1900s, Russian author, Sergei Shirokogoroff studied Tungus, Siberian shamanism. According to him, levitation episodes happen frequently in ceremonies. "The shaman becomes 'light' and can spring into the air with a costume that may weigh as much as sixty-five pounds, yet the patient scarcely feels the shaman tread on his body. This is explained by the magical power of levitation."[220]

In the early 1900s, Max Freedom Long, author and expert on the Hawaiian Kahuna culture, spent eighteen years in Hawaii studying the magic rituals of various Kahunas. During his research, he uncovered at least one firsthand case of levitation. According to Long, the best Kahunas had a deep understanding of the workings of the astral world and were able to manipulate astral energies with incredible ease. Concerning one case, he writes, "A Kahuna of an unidentified class made quite a name for himself in outlying districts of Oahu by putting a girl into a trance in which she was levitated about the room."[221]

The country of Haiti has long been a stronghold for the practice of the Voodoo religion. It should come as no surprise that this culture has produced some astounding accounts of levitation. One outstanding example comes from explorer and author Douchan Gersi, who has made it his life's work to study mysticism in primitive cultures. In the mid-1970s, Gersi and his wife attended a Haitian Voodoo ceremony involving a *houngan,* or witch-doctor. Gersi and his wife sat on a bench watching the ceremony. They could scarcely believe what happened next. Writes Gersi, "I had hardly finished talking when the woman sitting just behind me jumped over my head and, her body shaking like a puppet, floated in the air just in front of us, five feet off the ground, for a long time—much longer than the laws of gravity would allow....The woman was sitting on a bench set against the wall. She suddenly jumped in the air, and passing over my head, floated from behind me to about twelve feet in front of me, where she stayed suspended in the air for at least ten seconds, about five feet from the floor. From there, she moved to my left and finally hit the ground about twenty feet away....And then instead of falling down vertically, she was thrown to the other side of the sanctuary....During the whole time that she was 'floating' (she moved about thirty-four feet from her seat to her landing, in an L-shaped pattern), she never touched the ground....It was, literally, as if the woman had been grabbed by an invisible force that shook her body before throwing her to one side. My wife and I pinched each other to be sure we were not dreaming."[222]

While Gersi had traveled across the world and seen many paranormal events, this act of levitation left him astounded, and he vowed to do further research. He was incredibly successful and was able to witness and photograph numerous Voodoo ceremonies during which levitation occurred. These meetings were normally closed to the public, but Gersi was able to convince the houngans of his sincerity and was allowed to attend.

A few years after the above incident, he witnessed an even more dramatic levitation episode. Again, he was attending a nighttime Haitian Voodoo ceremony involving chanting and rhythmic dancing. Writes Gersi, "All the worshipers were dancing in a frenzy, jumping and violently shaking their bodies. Suddenly the body of one of the dancers stopped wriggling and began moving as if in slow motion. Then the man, his body completely vertical, slowly started to rise in the air as if he were weightless breaking away from the rest of the people, who were still dancing frantically. Once he was above the crowd, still in a vertical position and dancing in slow motion, he slowly began to turn upside down. Once he was upside down—with his head about six feet off the ground—he suddenly traveled through the air with amazing speed, hurtling toward the tree on one side of the plaza and landing, still upside down, on the tree trunk, halfway between the ground and the tree's lowest branches. And in this upside down position he began climbing the tree until he reached the first branches, where he set himself upright again. To the cheers of the worshipers, he got down from the tree as if nothing had happened."

Gersi actually filmed the incident, though his camera mysteriously malfunctioned during the levitation part of the episode, a phenomenon that has occurred repeatedly whenever he attempted to photograph a ceremony. Still, he insists that there was no possibility of trickery. He approached to within six feet of the levitating man, looking for ropes or sticks or anything that could explain the levitation. He also noticed that the man's shirt didn't hang downwards and appeared to be levitating with the man.

Gersi later saw many other Voodoo ceremonies during which levitation occurred. Writes Gersi, "In later years as I traveled extensively throughout Haiti, I saw men and women levitate numerous times. And I now believe in the reality of what I saw, although I have no explanation for how it happens. And I know that it is not just a freak phenomenon but a reflection of the powers of the human mind over matter....Moreover, since I saw this phenomenon on many occasions, I had the opportunity to study it very carefully. After sufficient incidents, I went beyond the state of awe and surprise that might have clouded my first impressions, and was able to observe the situations with calm rationalism, to search carefully for possible fraud, and even to approach the subjects close enough to see the reality of what was going on."[223]

Gersi later learned about the existence of a secret sect of people on Haiti called *the Flying Men*. The members of this group reportedly have the ability to dematerialize and teleport great distances. Gersi was able to contact a member of the sect and was actually taken to one of their gatherings. While there, he claims to have witnessed several people literally appearing and disappearing—and walking through walls—in front of his eyes. While this is more properly termed teleportation, it could also be categorized as an advanced form of levitation.[224]

As can be seen, each culture approaches the phenomenon within the confines of their own worldview. And despite vast cultural differences, the phenomenon itself remains remarkably consistent.

13. More Levitating Saints, Nuns, and Monks

By the time the 1700s and 1800s came along, humanity had overcome the Dark Ages and embraced the Age of Enlightenment. As reason began to blossom in the public consciousness, accounts of levitation were not only widely recorded across the world, but the first glimmerings of scientific analysis began to illuminate the cases. Religious scholars like Augustin Calmet began to collect the accounts of levitating saints and provide comparative analyses.

Even more significant was the continuing rise of the mediumistic accounts. While the saints still dominated the records, their numbers were slowly giving way to the mediumistic accounts. Whether this is a matter of cultural interpretation, it is difficult to say.

While the age of reason brought scientific analysis, it also marked the beginning of the decline of the influence of the Catholic Church. And, as organized religion lost its sway over the populace, the number of levitating saints correspondingly diminished. At the same time, it remained dangerous to be associated with levitation, which was sometimes still believed to be the work of the Devil.

This chapter presents thirty cases of ecstatic levitations from the 1700s and 1800s. While the huge number of similar levitation accounts is somewhat repetitive, these new cases bring greater detail and impressive firsthand testimonials. Furthermore, each case has unique elements and adds one more piece of evidence to both establish the validity and solve the mystery of levitation.

Jean-Baptiste de Mastena (d1713) was a Franciscan monk. He was seen to levitate while sweeping, while praying before the altar, and while in his room in contemplation.[225]

Saint Marie-Francoise des Cinq Plaies (1715-1791) was a Franciscan nun who became very religious at the age of four years, during which she started praying late into the night and falling into ecstasies. As a child, she experienced numerous ecstatic levitations. On another occasion, when she was very ill, she took a short walk. An ecstasy seized her and she was seen to run with an "abnormal" speed and agility through the countryside.[226]

Father Anthony Margil (d1726) spent his life as a missionary in Mexico and Guatemala. His biographer, Giuseppe Gusman, wrote of him, "A soul which was so inflamed with the love of God could not fail to be constantly absorbed by celestial delights and ravished out of itself in the ecstasies which are the ordinary privilege of Christ's holy servants. Of these happy transports he had familiar experience, and very often it happened that his soul in the vehemence of its flight towards God carried with it heavenwards the dead weight of the body, so that he was actually raised from the ground."

Gusman presents the testimonies of several witnesses. Maria Treio saw him in prayer, raised six inches above the ground. John de Armiso saw him raised one foot in the air while saying mass. During the confession of a sick nun, he spoke to his patient with such vehemence as to be lifted into the air. Rose de Rivera reported that Margil was meditating on the beauty of her garden when he cried out, "Wonderful! Wonderful!" and was lifted into the air in ecstasy. Brother Jerome Garzia reported that he observed the father in front of the church altar, raised in the air with arms extended like a cross, whirling around at high velocity. John of Jesus Surraine Birriesa went to look for him in church and found him suspended so high in the air that the bottom of Margil's robe brushed his head. On another occasion, John of Jesus saw Margil lifted a foot and a half above the ground.

While some of these accounts are second-hand and Thurston considered them unreliable, he does admit that Birriesa was interviewed firsthand, and, therefore, the case has been included.[227]

Didacus the Blessed (Diego) (1743-1801) was a Capuchin Preacher in Spain. He grew up with religious leanings that became cemented upon reading about the lives of the saints. His powerful sermons drew huge crowds of people from all walks of life. He spent most of his free time devoted to the sick, the poor, and the imprisoned. He was reported by many to have "the gift of levitation." While he was preaching about the love of God, he would suddenly be "raised supernaturally into the air," at which time he would request assistance to be pulled down. Whenever he finished his sermons, the crowd would converge in an attempt to touch the holy man or obtain a piece of his clothing. He was declared by many to be a living saint, but was beatified in 1894, ninety-three years after his death.[228]

One of the most astounding levitators to float above this earth was St. Gerard of Majella (1726-1755), a well-known spiritual advisor from Caposele, Naples, Italy. Researcher Alban Butler called him, "the most famous wonder-worker of the eighteenth century." Certainly he is one of today's most popular saints. As a child, Majella spent most of his time praying in his bedroom. He lived a lifestyle of extreme asceticism, wearing heavy chains, putting bitter herbs in his food, eating while kneeling on sharp stones, limiting his intake of food and other mortifications, including flagellation. He spent most of his life in charity and spiritual counseling. Although he never enjoyed good health, dying at age twenty-nine, Gerard is credited with a huge number of miracles, including heal-ings, prophecy, telepathy, control over nature, multiplication of food, invisibility, bilocation, and levitations—the last of which were typically caused by religious ecstasies. While this list of abilities is long, there is an even longer list of firsthand witnesses to Gerard's incredible talents, all of which made him hugely famous and highly sought after.

One levitation occurred on the eve of the feast of the Most Blessed Trinity. Gerard became entranced as the choir started chanting. He shouted out to the nuns, "Oh Sisters, let us love God!" At that point, he looked upwards and rose several feet into the air.

One day, during his travels, he visited the home of Anna Scoppi in Melfi, where he saw a picture of the Virgin Mary high on the wall. He shouted out, "Oh,

Donna Anna, what a beautiful virgin you have!" He then rose off the ground to the level of the picture, which he kissed lovingly. Anna Scoppi promptly fainted.

Later on another occasion, he visited the picture gallery of the Canon Capucci. When he saw a particular painting of the Virgin Mary, he was instantly elevated to the height of the painting, which he embraced, saying, "How beautiful she is! See how beautiful she is!" All those present were moved to tears.

On April 20, 1753, he glimpsed an image of Christ on the cross and levitated in front of several stunned witnesses. On yet another occasion, he requested a beggar to play a particular song on his flute. The beggar obliged and the song sent Gerard leaping and dancing and finally into a levitating trance.

Sometimes the oddest events would send Gerard into ecstasy. On one occasion, he was harshly insulted by Camillus Bozzio, a Canon of Conza. Instead of being dismayed, Gerard returned to his chamber and prayed with such humility that he was raised into the air, an event witnessed and attested to by Bozzio himself.

Probably his most famous levitation was witnessed by archpriest Don Salvador at Oliveto, at whose home Gerard was visiting. One evening, Salvador entered Gerard's room to announce dinner and saw Gerard floating three feet in the air, deep in prayer. Salvador quietly left and returned later to find Gerard still floating. The whole family began to weep with amazement as they waited for the humble lay brother.

Later, Gerard exited his room, apologized for his lateness to dinner, and asked them not to wait. Don Salvador marked the height of the levitation on the wall to memorialize the event.

Gerard's levitations sometimes involved considerable distances. Two workers told all who would listen that they saw Gerard rise up from the ground and fly to a church three-quarters of a mile distant. Another witness to a long-distance levitation was Rosaria Bertucci. One day, she walked with Gerard to confession. According to Bertucci, she observed Gerard enter a roadside chapel. Moments later he walked out and floated up into the air, then flew more than three-fourths of a mile to the convent, one of the longest recorded flights.

Gerard Majella was enormously popular in his time and still is today. He was canonized in 1904. Several books have been written about his life.[229]

Saint Benedict Joseph Labre (1748-1783) of France was attracted to religion from an early age. His parents urged him to study Latin and Science, but Labre became enamored by the Holy Scriptures and the lives of the saints. With his parents' reluctant consent, he left home at age eighteen to locate and join an austere religious order. To his disappointment, he was rejected by several religious orders. He finally decided, instead, to travel to Europe's major holy places. He took a vow of poverty and homelessness, and soon became well known for his holiness and devotion. His fame grew and though he visited Germany, Switzerland, France, Spain, and numerous other shrines throughout Europe, he was known widely as the "Beggar of Rome." He was observed to levitate on several occasions. On one instance, he was visiting a chapel to pray and was seen to rise a few inches above the floor. Several onlookers remarked about Labre's "strange behavior" to the sacristan, who casually replied, "The saint is in ecstasy," and returned to his sweeping duties.

Often, Labre was seen in ecstasy, not levitating, but balanced in physically impossible positions.[230]

A very well verified case of levitation is that of the French Saint, Andrew Fournet (1752-1843). Told in Fournet's biography, his levitations were recorded by several witnesses. Leroy, after studying the accounts of levitating saints and rejecting the vast majority of them, wrote, "The levitations of the blessed Hubert Fournet appear to me to merit a serious examination."

Fournet grew up as a mischievous child who resisted becoming a priest or a monk. He joined the army, but was bought out by his parents and then hired as a clerk. Fired from this last position, he relented and began to study theology and later became a priest. Fournet then gave away his possessions and spent his time sermonizing. As he grew older, he began to exhibit a wide variety of supernatural phenomenon, including multiplication of food and levitation.

He first began levitating at age sixty-eight during religious services. Sister Marie-Alexandrine testified during his trial for beatification that she saw Fournet levitate during each mass for eight consecutive days.

Lafleur-Peignon of Paizay reported that during mass, Fournet, "appeared like a bird which took flight and his feet didn't touch the ground."

An anonymous nun testified that Fournet was "more than once raised above the ground."

One well-known episode occurred when Fournet was conducting stations of the cross in the church of La Puye. Sister Ludvine was in attendance and witnessed the amazing event. As she testified, "I was following him with a candle with another Sister appointed to that office. At the tenth station, as the Father began to preach, I saw him raised above the floor. As I was close to him, I could see easily the light streaming between his feet and the pavement of the church. He was not lifted a foot, but more than half a foot, above the floor. I was quite bewildered, and I could not help saying with emotion to the Sisters near me, 'Oh! Oh! Look at the Father in the air!' The Sisters beckoned me to keep silent and not disturb the ceremony....I could observe the prodigy quite at my ease, for it lasted all the time the Father preached at the tenth station."

On another occasion, Fournet was preaching to a procession of children and parishioners along the roadside. Fournet spoke of the "Bliss of Paradise" when he suddenly was lifted up into the air. The audience was overcome with emotion and wept at the sight. Several nuns were called to testify to this event.

One reported, "All of a sudden, the children cried out and told sister Saint Vincent de Paul, 'My sister, look now at the Father, he is in the air.' She ordered their silence, saying, 'I see him well, but don't say anything.' And she came very gently to warn me, because I held my eyes lowered, hearing the father who spoke with extreme animation and devotion. I then saw him elevated at a foot and a half above the ground, and he lowered little by little. That evening, several sisters who knew of it spoke in the community."

Still another nun reported, "Father Andre spoke of the goodness of heaven; we heard him very distinctly…while he spoke, I heard a lady next to me exclaim that the good Father had climbed into the sky; she appeared very moved and started crying. Her exclamation made me very attentive to what was happening. Then I very distinctly saw the Father above the people who were before me.…It was impossible for me to see him thus so unless he had been elevated above the ground.…For several days we spoke of this feat which I have come to tell, but the sisters told us to speak no more because the good Father, they said, wasn't happy to learn that we had spoke of it. Later sister Saint Vincent de Paul told us about it very often as a thing that she had clearly seen and of which she was perfectly aware. She spoke of it as a thing very assured."

Sister Saint Vincent de Paul reported her impressions of the event: "I listened to the sermon of the servant of God without looking at him when one of the children of the first communion who was next to me cried out, "My sister, the Father is raised up above the ground!' I looked, then I saw, in fact, the servant of God, who wasn't touching the ground, and who held himself raised up about a foot above the small stone on which he stood. I saw and very clearly observed the servant of God in this position. I was four or five paces from the good Father, and nobody was sitting between him and me to obstruct me from observing him at my leisure. I went to warn a sister who was a few paces from there and I told her, 'Look now, the Father is raised up in the air.' This nun was sister Saint Martin who then started to watch him with me. But at this moment, the servant of God already began to be a little less elevated and approached the ground. From the moment when, warned by the child, I saw the servant of God above the ground, until the moment when I saw him again returning his feet to the ground, ten to twelve minutes passed, during which I carefully observed this levitation above the ground."[231]

Mary Magdalen Postel (1756-1846) was a French saint and founder of the Sisters of the Christian Schools of Mercy. She devoted her life to education and also sheltered numerous fugitive priests in her home. She was reportedly seen by several nuns to levitate. Postel was ordered by her Superior to explain one of her levitations in which she was allegedly transported several miles over the bay between the two small French villages of Gateville and Barfleur.

Under oath, Postel testified that she heard a voice say, "Do not fear." At that instant, she was lifted up into the air and transported. As she reported, "There was neither man, nor boat, nor horse. When God wills a thing, it is done. After hearing the voice, I was carried away in no time."

Postel's niece, Adelaide Lamare confirms her levitations. One day, pushed by curiosity, she spied through the window and the keyhole and saw Postel in levitation. As she says, "Indeed, my aunt is a saint; that night she was again lifted up from the floor and suspended with bent knees in the air, her eyes lifted to heaven and her face quite transfigured."

Other witnesses include sisters Xavier and Aimable, both who were waiting for Postel, and peeking through the keyhole, saw her in levitation.

Postel was canonized in 1925. Her biographer, M. A. M. Legoux, based her biography on the various trials leading up to her canonization.[232]

Abbe Claude Dhiere (1757-1820) was the Director of the Grande Seminaire of Grenoble, France. According to his biographer, Mademoiselle De Franclieu, Dhiere experienced ecstatic levitation trances while performing mass. He was often levitated in full view of his astonished students. Writes Franclieu, "...it was usually at the Memento of the living and the dead that, when enraptured, his feet did not touch the floor."[233]

Seraphim of Serov (1759-1833) was a great Russian saint, healer, and prophet. He was sought by many for spiritual counsel and healings. At age twenty-five he became a hermit. He took a vow of silence and didn't speak for the next eighteen years. Then, in 1825, a vision of the Virgin Mary healed him and instructed him to offer himself as a spiritual counselor and healer.

A famous incident occurred in 1831 when a young boy, Nicholas Motovilov, was brought alone to his cell for a healing. Suffering from chronic rheumatism, the boy was almost completely paralyzed. St. Seraphim instructed him to pray and not turn around while he himself also prayed. Not surprisingly, Nicholas sneaked a glance and to his shock, saw the holy man floating in the air. He let out a gasp, capturing the Saint's attention. Seraphim finished the prayer, sank to the floor and instructed Motovilov not to tell anybody what he had witnessed. Motovilov kept his word, and didn't tell anyone until after Seraphim's death.

Like many levitators, Seraphim tried unsuccessfully to keep his levitations a secret. On another occasion, he was preaching to a small group of nuns when he evidently felt one of his episodes coming on. As one of the nuns later wrote, "One day we were crossing a field and the grass was very high; Father Seraphim was walking ahead of us and enlarging on his subject....He suddenly stood still and told us to go on ahead. We did what we were told, but, inquisitive as we were, we turned around to look at him. We were dumbfounded; the Staretz was walking about two feet above the grass....We threw ourselves at his feet while he himself was urging us, 'O my joys, don't tell anyone about this as long as I am still alive!'"[234]

As history progressed, accounts of levitations became more numerous and detailed. One case that was thoroughly examined by church officials comes from Anne Catherine Emmerich (1774-1824). She was a nun in a strict Augustinian convent in Germany. Emmerich often fell into religious ecstasies that caused her to levitate.

She was reportedly so devoted, that she even levitated while she was performing cleaning duties. As she says, "In my duties as sacristan, I was often lifted up suddenly, and stood on the highest points of the church, on the windows, the carving, and the cornices, cleaning and dusting where humanly speaking no one could go. I was not frightened when I felt myself thus raised and held up in the air, for I had always been accustomed to my angel's assistance."

There are different translations of Emmerich's brief autobiographical levitation testimony. In another translation, Emmerich reportedly wrote, "When I was doing my work as a vestry nun, I was often lifted up suddenly into the air, and I climbed up and stood on the higher parts of the church, such as windows, sculptured ornaments, jutting stones. I would clean and arrange everything in places where it was humanly impossible. I felt myself lifted up and supported in the air, and I was not afraid in the least, for I had been accustomed from a child to being assisted by my guardian angel."

Like other levitators, Emmerich was not happy about these levitations. She actually witnessed a levitation by one of her fellow sisters, Magdalen Dei Pazzi, in the same convent. She was so struck by the "perilous" nature of the flight that she decided to take "every precaution not to yield to these states."

Although Emmerich was able to use her levitations in a practical way, on other occasions, she would lose control of her body. She would faint to the ground or become totally rigid. Whenever she levitated, she felt profoundly dissociated. As she said, "I know not that I have a body. I am often quite joyous." While there has been some controversy that Emmerich's levitations were exaggerated by her secretary, her case matches those of other ecstatics.[235]

St. Maddalena di Canossa (1774-1835) of Verona, Italy, was born into nobility. As a child, she was stubborn and hot-tempered. As a young woman, she tried to become a nun, but was forced to return home. Once home, however, she took a vow of poverty and for the rest of her life worked tirelessly to help the poor, sick and abandoned. She later became subject to fits of ecstasy, and on at least one occasion, was seen to levitate before a crucifix.[236]

Marie Crucified of Jesus (1782-1826) of Naples was a stigmatic and according to Imbert-Gourbeyre, "was seen suspended in the air several palms above the ground."[237]

Joachima de Mas Y de Vedruna (1783-1854) of Spain was born into a noble family. She was a busy and energetic child, and at age twelve, she presented herself at the front door of the local Carmelite convent and demanded to be admitted. She was refused. Instead, at age sixteen, she married, and by age thirty-two, had produced eight children. One year later, she had a vision that her husband would die within the year, which he did. She then devoted her time to praying, charity, and caring for the sick. Instead of joining an existing convent, she founded her own order, called the Carmelites of Charity.

During her trial for canonization, it was revealed for the first time that she had experienced several luminous levitations. According to the sisters of her chapel, she was often seen "lifted from the floor in ecstasy, her head ringed with light." These levitations were also witnessed by her children and several of her fellow nuns. As one second-hand witness reported, "One time Sister Apollonia Camps, now dead, with whom I lived, told me that she saw the Servant of God who was reciting some prayers in the Holy Trinity in ecstasy, all resplendent [with light] and at the same time raised from the earth. Also, in another instance, Sister Teresa Casany, now dead, with whom I lived, told me that one night, she observed a great splendor in the cell of the Servant of God. Recalling that the Sisters' rule called for little light to be used in the cells, she raised the curtain of Mother Joquina's cell and, with wonder, observed the servant of God luminous and raised in the air higher than the bed on which she slept."[238]

St. Gaspar del Bufalo (Caspar) (1786-1837) of Rome, Italy was an ascetic from early childhood. He became a very influential preacher, even converting bandits who had been sent to assassinate him. Del Bufalo was often seen in ecstasy, and sometimes in levitation. In 1824, priest Domenico Silvestri, then an altar boy reported, "My aunt assured me that she had seen Father Gaspar risen above the altar steps about four or five inches (half a hand's span) after the consecration."

In 1827, Silvestri witnessed a levitation firsthand. "Praying before the tabernacle, he was suddenly observed to start as if an electric shock had transfixed his body. Immediately he rose almost a hand's span above the ground. Neither knees, hands, nor any other part of his body was in contact with any surface."

Del Bufalo was seen to levitate on at least one other occasion. Several miraculous cures are also attributed to him. He was canonized in 1954.[239]

Many levitators are profoundly influential people. St. Joseph Benoit Cottolengo of Italy (1786-1842) started a small hospital to care for the poor, old, deaf, blind, mentally ill, chronically diseased, and crippled. Over the years, his little hospital expanded until it became a large and powerful medical institution.

Cottolengo experienced several witnessed levitations. Once after being assaulted, he returned to his room. Another nun testified during Cottolengo's trial for beatification that not hearing any noise from his room, and not receiving any response after knocking, she entered and found the priest in ecstasy, elevated above the ground. Following this, the nun testified that she saw Cottolengo in levitation on several other occasions, usually on Holy days or after Cottolengo had mortified himself in prayer. Leroy singled this case out among hundreds as being worthy of attention. Cottolengo was canonized in 1934.[240]

Saint Jean-Marie Baptiste Vianney (1786-1859) of Dardilly, France began his career as a shepherd, then a soldier, and finally a priest. He soon became a very influential spiritual director. He was very strict in his austerities and discouraged worldly activities of any kind, even including dancing. He reportedly had the ability of prophecy and reading men's minds and experienced numerous other paranormal events, including multiplication of food and poltergeist attacks. More than three hundred people visited him daily for advice, with a waiting list sometimes eight days long. The city of Lyons had to maintain a ticket office just for those who wanted to travel by train to meet him. Because of his extreme popularity, Vianney often spent up to sixteen hours a day in the confessional. Many specific examples are given of his supernatural knowledge concerning the lives of his confessors.

Vianney also experienced several levitation episodes. He woke one evening and, as he reported, "I left my bed bit by bit."

Once, while preaching, his body suddenly became luminous and he rose up into the air. The curator of the church who witnessed the marvel kept silent until he left the church, after which he told all who would listen. This incident was testified to under oath by Father Gardette, a chaplain. "About the middle of the exercise, when M. Vianney was saying the Act of Charity, my brother saw him rise into the air, little by little, until his feet were above the ledge of the pulpit. His countenance was transfigured and encircled by an aureole."[241]

Another solid case of levitation is that of Marie de Jesus (the Mother of Bourg) (1787-1862) which offers, according to Leroy, "impressive guarantees of truth." Her nephew, Mr. D'Hulst, reported that his aunt was seen "elevated over the ground on several occasions and in front of the eyes of all the sisters of her community, notably when they spoke before her of the 'love of God.'"

Marie tried to resist the raptures, but—like other levitators—soon discovered that it was impossible, and she gave in to her ecstasies. These trances sometimes ended in a levitation during which time her body became rigid and she retained the same position in which she had started. Once after levitating, she returned to her senses and realizing that she had created a spectacle, said humbly to herself, "Oh, wretched and miserable creature, look what you have done."

Several members of her family saw her in levitation and early levitation researcher, Dr. Imbert-Gourbeyre, also made her personal acquaintance.

On one occasion, she was seen to levitate with her stool, until reaching a certain height, the stool fell and broke into several pieces which were saved as evidence. D'Hulst separately interviewed the nuns who witnessed this last levitation, and was assured by each of its veracity. The stool itself was saved and is today held and memorialized at the Chappelle du Maison Mere du Congregation at La Souterraine, in France.[242]

Michael Garicoits the Blessed (1797-1863) of Bayonne, France, was born to peasants and worked as a shepherd. His desire to become a priest was thwarted by the extreme poverty of his family. His grandmother, however, recognized something in Michael and was eventually able to arrange his acceptance. In 1823, he joined the priesthood and became a professor of philosophy. He experienced numerous half-levitations, where he would balance on his toes in ecstasy, and several full-blown levitations which were widely witnessed by church members and local residents. He was canonized in 1947.[243]

Several early undated levitation accounts that probably date around the 1700s were recorded by Augustin Calmet. Writes Calmet, "We have known a good monk, who rises sometimes from the ground, and remains suspended above it, without seeking to do so, especially on seeing some devotional image, or on hearing some devout prayer, such as 'Gloria in excelsis Deo.' I know a nun to whom it has often happened in spite of herself, to see herself thus raised up in the air to a certain distance from the earth; it was neither from choice, nor from any wish to distinguish herself, since she was truly confused at it….We see similar trances and elevations in the Life of St. Bernard Ptolomei, teacher of the congregation of Notre Dame of Mount Olivet; M. Nicole, in his letters, speaks of a nun named Seraphina, who, in her ecstasies, rose from the ground with so much impetuosity, that five or six of the sisters could hardly hold her down."[244]

Levitations in the 1700s cannot be discussed without mention of Cornelius Otto Jansen (1585-1638), a Dutch Roman Catholic theologian whose writings on the teachings of St. Augustine took Europe by storm. The writings were enormously popular, and not only changed the way people practiced religion, they started a popular cult of religious hysterics known as "Jansenists" or "Jansenist Convulsionaries."

Jansenists were known for their trances and bizarre behavior, including self-flagellation. Often entire groups of Jansenists would fall into trance-states, at which point, their bodies would convulse and thrash about in inhuman positions. The cult became so influential and widespread, and its activities so bizarre, that Pope Innocent the X condemned the movement, and labeled Jansen a heretic.

By this time, however, the damage was done. Throughout the early 1700s, thousands of Jansenists roamed the streets of Paris. At one point, it took more than 3,000 volunteers to control the group's movements. The Jansenists themselves exhibited numerous, apparently superhuman, abilities. They were able to withstand heavy blows from stones, hammers, chains, metal rods, or other objects. Some were reportedly unable to be cut by knives. Others became clairvoyant. Miraculous healings of all kinds were reported. And then, of course, there were the levitations. Writes researcher, Michael Talbot, "One of the levitators…was so forcibly lifted into the air during his convulsions that even when witnesses tried to hold him down they could not succeed in keeping him rising up and off the ground."[245]

Another firsthand account comes from Mademoiselle Thevenet, a well-known Jansenist. As described by Dom La Taste, "She would levitate herself from time to time, seven or eight feet high up to the ceiling, and in levitating herself, she carried two persons three feet above the ground, pulling her down with all their strength. An event most marvelous, yet in one sense, a horrible event! While Mademoiselle levitated her head high up, her skirt and shirt twisted around, as she had herself. Her normal character never brought about such effects, or is she able to bring them about?"

Mademoiselle Thevenet also experienced the rarest form of levitation—sleeping levitation. Writes La Taste, "From time to time, when she was sleeping, her head and her feet would raise up together several feet in height."[246]

Saint Paulin, in *The Life of Saint Felix de Nole,* reports that he observed a possessed person to walk upside down against the archway of a church, levitating in such a manner that even his clothes stayed stuck to his body.[247]

In his book, *Levitation,* Rochas relates a case involving an anonymous missionary, who says, "I saw an Indian whom I had to baptize, transported, all at once, to the road that led to another church."

Another interesting case comes from Flechier of Aurillac, France and involves a house-servant who accused his master (who was up for an important election) of having practiced magic. In particular, the servant reported that his master would sometimes "elevate himself from the ground." This usually happened when he went to church and on a few occasions, happened in full view of all present.[248]

And so closes the accounts levitations from the 1700s. While skepticism is a necessary condition for scientific progress, cases like Fournet are impossible to ignore.

Again, although these incidents occurred a long time ago, the tantalizing records remain. Clearly something important was going on here.

Levitation cases were now being reported by a wider variety of people, including young children. As history progressed, the accounts dramatically increase in number and credibility. Before the 1800s, levitation accounts were usually given only brief mention, and there had been no serious comprehensive studies of the phenomenon. The nineteenth century, however, was the age of science and discovery. And as the levitation accounts continued to mount, people were forced to take them more seriously. For the first time, scientists began to look into the phenomenon, objectively documenting and researching the accounts. As a direct result of this, accounts of levitation dramatically increased in number and credibility, giving further weight to the idea that these are actual experiences being described, and not fantasy.

The 1800s also brought a dramatic drop in the number of levitating saints, which seemed to give way to mediumistic accounts. Fodor writes, "The levitation of mediums represents a simple continuity of age old experience."[249]

The 1800s produced at least six more impressive cases of levitating nuns and monks. Marie de Morel (1812-1863) was a well-known stigmatic who was sometimes seen to skim along the floor on the tips of her toes instead of walking. This was witnessed by Mr. E. Demoy, a law professor at the faculty of Munich, who wrote, "Her hands joined, her head and eyes raised towards the sky, her knees and body bent forward, she appeared to be carried by angels who supported her invisibly because the inclination of her body trespassing against the laws of balance, and she made nearly no impression on the rug."[250]

St. John Bosco (1815-1888) was an Italian priest, teacher, and preacher. He made it his life's work to care for neglected boys. He founded dozens of schools and churches across the world. He became well known for a wide variety of supernatural manifestations, including prophecy, visions, and healing. Several firsthand eyewitness accounts are on record describing episodes during which his body would become luminous. He reportedly had supernatural strength and could hammer nails into wood with his bare fist. He lived very ascetically, eating very little and never sleeping more than five hours per night.

Bosco devoted his life to helping the poor, sick, and uneducated. His entire life was spent in service to others.

In December, 1878, altar boy, Evasio Garrone, observed Bosco praying before the altar. Suddenly, he watched Bosco rise slowly above the floor until he could barely reach him. Garrone ran and summoned another priest. They both arrived in time to watch Bosco descend slowly to the floor. Garrone was so impressed that he decided to enter the priesthood.

Bosco's sermons were so effective that at least two of his pupils also began to levitate. On one occasion, Bosco and another priest entered the church to find one of these students levitating before the altar. At their approach, the student came out of his trance and came down gently to the floor. Bosco turned to the priest and replied, "These things seem to be of the Middle Ages, and yet they happen even now."

Even into old age, Bosco had the ability of running levitation. He regularly covered miles on foot, and remained very athletic. Although he was in his seventies, he was still able to run faster than anybody else around. Pope Pius said of him, "In his life the supernatural almost became the natural, and the extraordinary, ordinary." Upon his death, more than 40,000 people attended his funeral. Numerous volumes have since been written about his life.[251]

The 1800s also brought some of the first accounts of levitations in the New World. Father Francis Xavier Seelos's (1819-1867) of Maryland, United States, main claim to fame is that he often appeared to glow while preaching. There are numerous firsthand witnesses claiming that Seelos actually emitted light from his body. And of course, there are the levitations. Following Seelos's death, Andreas Franz revealed that he had seen him in levitation. "On one occasion, I went into the chapel at Cumberland, and there I saw the Servant of God on his knees with his arms extended, and, as it seemed to me, elevated from the ground about a foot."[252]

Francis Luycks (1824-1896) was a Flemish Benedictine, better known as Abbot Paul. Early in his career, he gained a reputation for his extreme holiness and love of God. Like many people who levitate, Luycks exhibited a wide variety of other paranormal abilities including healings, telepathy, precognition, odor of sanctity and luminosity. As a testimony to his healing powers, Luycks kept a room full of various crutches, canes and braces that were discarded by healed patients.

Luycks' levitations were an equally spectacular display, impossible to miss. One witness to his levitations later testified to an event: "I raised my eyes and to my great astonishment, I saw Father Paul standing before me in ecstasy, raised a considerable distance above the ground, and holding the sacred host. I cannot tell how long he continued in this attitude, but I think it was at least five minutes."

Luycks experienced rapturous levitations on a regular basis. He apparently could feel the episodes coming on as he would distract witnesses by telling them to "look at those beautiful pigeons,"—at which point, he would fall into ecstasy and levitate to a height of a few feet for a period of about ten minutes.

In 1889, another witness reported the following levitation. "In the course of the conversation he suddenly stopped and exclaimed, 'For the love of Jesus!' and as if rapt in ecstasy he was raised about three feet above his chair and remained thus eight or ten minutes; then he slowly descended upon his chair and resumed the conversation."

Luycks also experienced occasional episodes of traveling levitation. A community of nuns at Bruges reported that "they noticed that the Reverend Father while passing from one room to another, hardly moved his feet but seemed to glide over the floor rather than step upon it."[253]

Brother Andre Bessette (1845-1937) of Montreal, Canada was a well-known healer. A man by the name of Moise Poirier often visited Brother Andre and spent the night with him. In 1945, on his death-bed, Poirier revealed that he had seen Bessette levitating above his bed on at least two occasions.[254]

Mary of Jesus Crucified (1846-1878) was observed on numerous occasions to levitate. Although she was somewhat overweight, the nun was seen to rise up to the tops of the lime trees in the convent garden, perching on a small branch at the top in rapt meditation. Several witnesses say that her levitations began with incredible swiftness.

As one nun testified, "Sister E. told me one day that she was in the garden with the servant of God who said, 'Turn around!' She barely turned her head and, looking back, she saw her already sitting on the top of the lime tree, on a small branch, balancing herself like a bird and singing of divine love."

Another witness to her peculiar levitations testified, "I saw her one time in ecstasy at the top of a lime tree, stopping at the tip of the highest branch which normally would not be able to support her. Her body shined brightly! I saw her come back down the tree like a bird, from branch to branch, with lightness and modesty. I noticed that the branches of the lime tree were very small and should have broken under the weight of the servant of God who was rather heavy."

Other witnesses also testified to watching the nun flit from branch to branch like a bird. On one occasion, her ecstasy ended while she was still in the tree and she needed a ladder to get down. During another occasion, her superior called her out of ecstasy, and the nun was only able to descend from the tree with great difficulty. On some occasions, she came down so quickly, she left her sandals up in the high branches.[255]

As can be seen, there is no shortage of levitating nuns, monks, priests and other flying religious persons. And while this may appear to be a phenomenon confined to a bygone era, we will later explore several modern cases that are currently taking place.

14. The Man Who Could Fly

Arguably, the best-recorded case of levitation in all of human history comes from a remarkable man, Daniel Dunglas Home (1833-1886). As a child, Home had many psychic experiences which culminated in his becoming the single most influential spiritual medium of his time. Home's fame rose from the simple fact that he was able to produce a wide variety of inexplicable paranormal events virtually on demand. By his early twenties, he was already a highly celebrated figure and traveled across the world, keeping audience with numerous heads of state, kings, queens, leaders in art, literature, religion, science, and politics. He met with Elizabeth Barrett Browning, Mark Twain, and even the Pope. Tolstoy witnessed a levitation, writing in a letter to his wife, "Home was levitated in his chair. I held his feet while he floated over our heads."

Not once was Home ever caught in any trickery.

While many people during Home's era were able to produce physical spiritualistic phenomena such as table-lifting, table-rapping and even apparitions, none were able to equal Home's abilities. He not only produced all of the above phenomena, but much more, including miraculous healings, glowing lights coming from his body, superhuman strength, incombustibility, elongation (a feat duplicated by a few saints) and most importantly here, levitation.

Daniel Dunglas Home was an enormously influential medium, holding audience with leaders in politics, religion, science, royalty, literature... His claim to fame rested on his ability to regularly produce a huge variety of spiritualistic phenomenon, including more than 100 instances of levitation. (Mary Evans Picture Library)

Home was a normal child, though of delicate health. His career as a spiritual medium was assured when as a young child, he experienced considerable poltergeist-like activity in his Connecticut home. By the time he was a teen-ager, Home was already holding séances and giving readings in the local neighborhood. During the sittings, virtually the entire range of spiritualistic phenomena were produced. His popularity grew so quickly, that it was clear to him that this would be his life's work.

Home himself was surprised when he first began levitating at age nineteen. It occurred in 1852 during a séance at the home of Mr. Cheney in South Manchester, Connecticut. As expected, many manifestations were produced. Then, as one of the sitters said, "Suddenly, and without any expectations on the part of the company, Mr. Home, was taken up in the air! I had a hold of his hand at the time, and I and others felt his feet—they were lifted a foot from the floor! He palpitated from head to foot apparently with the contended emotions of joy and fear which choked his utterance. Again and again he was taken from the floor, and the third time he was carried to the lofty ceiling of the apartment, with which his hand and head came into gentle contact....I omitted to state that these latter demonstrations were made in response to a request of mine that the spirits give us something that would satisfy everyone in the room of their presence. The medium was much astonished and more alarmed than the rest..."[256]

Home had never levitated prior to this incident and had no reason to expect a repeat performance. However, it did happen, again and again, and in full view of countless credible witnesses, placing Home among the most celebrated levitators of all times.

In 1857, Home visited Count and Countess De B. in Biarritz, France. During a séance there, he again levitated. Writes Home in his 1864 autobiography, *Incidents in My Life,* "The lady of the house turned to me and said abruptly, 'Why are you sitting in the air?' and on looking we found that the chair remained in its place, but that I was elevated two or three inches above it, and my feet were not touching the floor. This may show how utterly unconscious I am at times to the sensation of levitation. As is usual when I have not got above the level of the heads of those about me, and when they change their position much, as they frequently do in looking wistfully at such a phenomenon, I came down again, but not till I had remained so raised about a half-minute from the time of its being first seen. I was now impressed to leave the table and was soon carried to the lofty ceiling. The Count De B. left his place at the table, and coming under where I was, said, 'Now, young Home, come and let me touch your feet.' I told him I had no volition over the matter, but perhaps the spirits would kindly allow me to come down to him. They did so, by floating me down to him, and my feet were soon in his outstretched hands. He seized my boots, and now I was again elevated, he holding tightly, and pulling at my feet till the boots I wore, which had elastic sides, came off and remained in his hands....Since I wrote the narrative of this, I have applied to the Count for his verification of it, and I have his letter stating its correctness."[257]

In 1859, Home visited Bayswater, England where he conducted a séance. One of those present was J. G. Crawford, then a very vocal skeptic. After the session, however, Crawford changed his tune. As he later wrote, "...a very curious affair took place, an explanation of which I cannot hazard a conjecture. Mr. Home remarked, 'I feel as if I'm going to rise.' The room was quite dark. He said, 'I am getting up,' and as I was only a few feet from him, I put out my hand to him; I indubitably felt the soles of both his boots some three feet above the level of the floor. On doing so, he said, 'Don't touch me, or I shall come down.' Of course, I instantly desisted, but down he came. In less than five minutes after this, he remarked, 'I am again ascending,' and from the sound of his voice, we could but not infer that he was actually rising towards the ceiling of the anteroom. He then appeared to float under the archway, then to rise to the cornice of the room we were sitting in, and we heard him quite distinctly make three marks on the ceiling....Then he came softly down, and lay stretched out with his back upon the table, in which position we found him when the gas was lighted, and when we distinctly saw the marks on the ceiling which we had heard him make."[258]

In 1860, during a session in London, Home again gave a remarkable demonstration of his levitation abilities. Said one witness, "After a pause, Mr. Home said he felt as he were about to be lifted up; he moved from the table and shortly said, 'I am rising'—but we could not see him—'they have put me on my back.' I asked, will you kindly bring him, as much as possible, towards the window, so that we may see him; and at once he was floated with his feet horizontally into the light of the window, so that we all saw his feet and a part of his legs resting or floating on the air like a feather, about six feet from the ground, and three feet above the height of the table. He was then floated into the dark; and he exclaimed, 'They have turned me around, and I am coming towards you.' I saw his head and face, the same height as before, and as if floating on water instead of air. He then floated back, and came down."

Moments later, Home levitated again. "I went, and sat beside him; he took my hand; and in about a minute, and without any muscular action, he gently floated away from me, and was lost in the darkness. He kept talking to us to let us know where he was. We heard his voice in various parts of the room, as if near the ceiling....I next saw a shadow of his body on the mirror as he floated along near the ceiling. He said, 'I wish I had a pencil to make a mark on the ceiling. I have made a cross with my nail.' He came down near the door, and after a pause, he was again taken up, but I did not see him, but heard his voice as if near the ceiling. Again he came down, and shortly returned to the table we were at."[259]

While Home often performed his levitations in darkened rooms, this was not always the case. In many cases, the light was more than sufficient for the sitters to see Home's figure rise upwards.

In July, 1860, Home held a séance at the home of a prominent Englishman in London, England. One of the attendees was James Wason of Wason Buildings, in Liverpool, England. Writes Wason, "...Mr. Home stated he was being lifted up in the air and he crossed the table over the heads of the parties sitting around it. I asked him to make a mark with his pencil on the ceiling. He said he had no pencil. I rose up and said I would lend him mine, and by standing and stretching upwards I was enabled to reach his hand, about seven feet distant from the floor, and I placed therein a pencil, and laying hold and keeping hold of his hand, I moved along with him five or six paces as he floated above me in the air, and I only let go of his hand when I stumbled against a stool. Mr. Home, as he floated along, kept ringing the small hand-bell to indicate his locality in the room, which was probably forty by thirty feet, and I saw his body eclipse two lines of light issuing from between the top of the door and its architrave.... Mr. Home was replaced, as he stated, with the greatest care and gentleness in the chair from which he rose, but this I could not see."[260]

Also in 1860, an anonymous gentleman wrote to *Cornwall Magazine* describing his observations of Home's levitating abilities. "Mr. Home was seated next to the window. Through the semi-darkness his head was dimly visible against the curtains, and his hands might be seen in a faint white heap before him. Presently, he said in quiet voice, 'My chair is moving—I am off the ground—don't notice me—talk of something else,' or words to that effect. It was very difficult to restrain the curiosity, not unmixed with a more serious feeling, which these few words awakened; but we talked, incoherently enough, upon some indifferent topic. I was sitting nearly opposite of Mr. Home, and I saw his hands disappear from the table, and his head vanish into the deep shadow beyond. In a moment or two he spoke again. This time his voice was in the air above our heads. He had risen from his chair to a height of four or five feet from the ground. As he ascended higher, he described his position, as first perpendicular, and afterwards horizontal. He said he felt as if he had been turned in the gentlest manner, as a child is turned in the arms of a nurse. In a moment or two more, he told us that he was going to pass across the window, against the gray, silvery light of which he would be visible. We watched in profound stillness, and saw his figure pass from one side of the window to the other, feet foremost, lying horizontally in the air. He spoke to us as he passed, and told us that he would turn the reverse way, and recross the window; which he did. His own tranquil confidence in the safety of what seemed from below a situation of the most novel peril, gave confidence to everybody else; but, with the strongest nerves, it was impossible not to be conscious of a certain sensation of fear or awe. He hovered round the circle for several minutes, and passed, this time perpendicularly, over our heads. I heard his voice behind me in the air, and felt something lightly brush my chair. It was his foot, which he gave to me to touch....He now passed over the farthest extremity of the room, and we could judge by his voice of the altitude and distance he had attained. He had reached the ceiling, upon which he made a slight mark, and soon afterwards descended and resumed his place at the table."[261]

J. M. Gully, another witness to the same incident, writes, "I can state with the greatest postiveness that the record made in the article is in every particular correct; that the phenomena therein related actually took place in the evening meeting; and, moreover, that no trick, machinery, sleight-of-hand, or other artistic contrivance produced what we heard and beheld. I am quite as convinced of this last as I am of the facts themselves. Only consider that here is a man, between ten and eleven stone in weight, floating about the room for many minutes—in the tomb-like silence which prevailed, broken only by his voice coming from different quarters of the room, according to his then position—is it probable, is it possible, that any machinery could be devised—not to speak of its being set up and previously made ready in a room, which was fixed upon as the place of meeting only five minutes before we entered it—capable of carrying such a weight about with the slightest sound of any description?...even when the room was comparatively darkened, light streamed through the window from a distant gas-lamp outside, between which gas-lamp and our eyes Mr. Home's form passed, so that we distinctly perceived its trunk and limbs; and most assuredly there was no balloon near him, nor any machinery attached to him. His foot once touched my head when he was floating above."[262]

In 1861, Home again visited London, England. As usual, his schedule was full of appointments for séances. During one séance involving seven sitters, Home was again levitated. Says one witness, John Jones, "Two of the three gas-lights were now put out—and the fire burning brightly, gave a subdued light in the room. Mr. Home then became cataleptic in his hands and arms: he was raised from his seat till he stood upright, and then he rose vertically till he was a foot above the floor—his head level with the chandelier—this was repeated twice, but he did not rise higher."[263]

Yet another witness to yet another levitation writes, "...he [Home] exclaimed, 'They are raising me; do not look at me till I am above the level of the table, as it might have the effect of bringing me down.' Almost at the same moment, Mr. Home was raised up and floated in the air at the height of about five feet, touching one gentleman on the head slightly as he passed, but on approaching the window he came again gently to the ground. He remarked, 'Their strength is hardly great enough yet, but I feel that it will be soon.'...His arms were raised above his head, he was again lifted about two feet off the ground and carried towards the window, and when there, he was raised to within about eighteen inches of the ceiling. After remaining floating for about two minutes, he descended, but on coming near his chair, he was again elevated, and placed in a standing position in the center of the table....in about a minute both Mr. Home and the small table were elevated a fourth time in the air, about a foot off the surface of the large table, and, after remaining in that position for about a minute, he descended and resumed his seat."[264]

W. M. Wilkinson attended several meetings with Home and witnessed levitations on more than one occasion. He writes, 'I was well convinced also of the alleged power of mediums to float in the air, by having had one come down on my chest, as well as having on other occasions had hold of his hand, whilst he was floating about in the room."[265]

William Howitt was a spiritual investigator and also attended several of Home's levitations. Says Howitt, "Mr. Home was lifted about a foot from the ground, but did not float, as he frequently does, in the strongest light."[266]

During his stay in England, Home made his residence with Mrs. P., who witnessed no less than five separate levitations. As she later wrote in her diary, "Mr. Home's arms were raised, and he walked to the end of the room, where he was lifted off the ground, and raised until his feet were on a level with the top of the chiffonier, between four and five feet off the ground. I distinctly saw his body carried along erect in the air, it then returned to its former place, where it remained some time—at length it floated forwards in the air, passed behind the gas chandelier which was suspended in the center of the apartment, and he descended gently upon the floor, close to the chair in which a lady was sitting. She said that when she saw him, he was about four feet from the ground. When he descended his arms were paralyzed, but in a short time they returned to their natural state."[267]

Mrs. P. also witnessed a rare luminous levitation. As she wrote, "Mr. Home was now led to the end of the room, which was very dark; he was raised from the ground, a beautiful star was visible, and also one like a small comet. He said a star was on his forehead, and one on each hand; we saw the three very bright, and many others glancing about. He was fixed against the wall. The luminous appearance was so distinct as to render the papering on the wall perfectly distinct; and then he floated along the room and was placed on his knees on the sofa; again he was carried up....[and] floated along the room."[268]

And a third occasion, "Mr. Home was raised from his chair erect into the air, and descended on a foot-stool. Then he was drawn to the other end of the room, and raised in the air until his hand was on the top of the door, thence he floated horizontally forward, and descended."[269]

A fourth occasion, "Mr. Home was raised from his chair, and carried up a little in an erect posture, and then put down again."

And a fifth occasion, "Mr. Home was lifted up a little in his chair, and went into the trance. His arms were then raised, and he ascended about a foot from the ground, descended, and rose again a couple of feet. He leaned over until he touched Mrs. Home, and then he was carried up, his body being bent forward in a circular form, until his head was above the center pane in the large window; he ascended some feet and came down again. It was quite light in the window, and we were close to it."[270]

From 1867 to 1869, Lord Adare, a young British nobleman accompanied Home on his adventures and observed several outstanding levitations. He later wrote a privately published book on his experiences with Home, which was soon withdrawn from publication due to the intense controversy it generated.

On December 13, 1868, the most controversial and famous of Home's levitations took place in which he was levitated out the window of a five-story building in London and back in through another window. The event was witnessed by Lord Adare, Lord Lindsay, and Charles Wynn. The levitation was so spectacular that it was widely criticized as being impossible, yet all three witnesses insist it actually took place.

On December 20, 1868, Adare reports that he and several other witnesses saw Home rise out of his seat and float to the ceiling in full view.

On still another occasion, Adare witnessed a very rare outside levitation. As he writes, "Presently we all saw him approaching and eventually raise off the ground....He floated by in front of us, at a height which carried him over the broken wall, which was about two feet high. There could not be a better test of being off the ground, for as he crossed the wall, his form was not in the least raised, but the movement was quite horizontal and uniform. The distance that we saw him thus carried must have been at least ten or twelve yards."[271]

Several influential scientists studied Home's abilities and came away convinced. One of these was Russian scientist, Alexander von Boutlerow. Using a weighing device, von Boutlerow discovered that Home could change the weight of a one-hundred pound table to fluctuate from seventy pounds to one-hundred-fifty pounds. Home achieved this remarkable feat by resting his fingers lightly on the tabletop.[272]

Another scientist who came away convinced was Professor Robert Hare of the University of Pennsylvania, perhaps best-known for his invention of the blow-torch.[273]

Still another prominent supporter of Home was Alfred Russel Wallace, who,

Daniel Dunglas Home's ability to levitate was demonstrated on hundreds of occasions across the world. Not once was he ever discovered performing trickery. He is also credited with other miracles including healings, elongation, incombustibility, and superhuman strength. (Mary Evans Picture Library)

independently of Charles Darwin, developed the theory of evolution.[274]

Home's supporters continued to grow. Lord Lindsay testified, "I once saw Home in full light standing in the air seventeen inches from the ground."[275]

In 1871, Sir William Crookes, a leading British scientist, decided to expose the fakery of spiritualistic phenomenon. He studied Home's abilities and observed firsthand levitations under controlled laboratory conditions. He was soon to become Home's biggest supporter. Writes Crookes, "There are at least a hundred recorded instances of Mr. Home rising from the ground in the presence of as many separate persons...This has occurred in my presence on four occasions in darkness; but I will mention only those occasions when the deductions of reason were confirmed by the sense of sight. On three separate occasions have I seen him raised completely from the floor of the room. On each occasion I had the full opportunity of watching the occurrence as it was taking place.

"On one occasion, he went to a clear part of the room, and after standing quietly for a minute, told us he was rising. I saw him slowly rise up with a continuous gliding movement and remain about six inches off the ground for several seconds, when he slowly descended. On another occasion I was invited to come to him, when he rose eighteen inches off the ground, and I passed my hands under his feet, round him, and over his head when he was in the air.

"On several occasions, Home and the chair on which he was sitting at the table rose off the ground. This was generally done very deliberately, and Home sometimes tucked up his feet on the seat of the chair and held up his hands in full view of all of us. On such occasions I have gone down and seen and felt all four legs were off the ground at the same time, Home's feet being on the chair. Less frequently, the levitating power extended to those sitting around him. Once my wife was thus raised off the ground in her chair."

Crookes became totally convinced of Home's abilities, although the idea was abhorrent to his scientific mind. As he wrote, "The phenomenon I am prepared to attest are so extraordinary and [so] directly oppose the most firmly-rooted articles of scientific belief—amongst others—the ubiquity and invariable action of the force of gravitation—that, even now, on recalling the details of what I witnessed, there is an antagonism in my mind between reason, which pronounces it to be scientifically impossible, and the consciousness that my senses, both of touch and sight, are not lying witnesses."

Crookes is emphatic, however, that Home did, in fact, levitate. "To reject the recorded evidence on this subject is to reject all human testimony whatever; for no fact in sacred or profane history is supported by a stronger array of proofs."[276]

Still another prominent scientist who studied Home was Dr. Hawksley, a well-known English physician. When Home came to visit the Hawksley's home, Hawksley witnessed him to levitate on a table "at least eight inches high." Hawksley was able to verify the levitation by passing his hands underneath the table legs. Writes Hawksley, "That which I have known of his [Home's] life and his abilities leaves me absolutely convinced of his veracity, his honesty, his good vigilance, and of the noblesse of his character."

As can be seen, there is no shortage of witnesses to Home's amazing feats of levitations.

Home has also experienced crisis levitations. One occurred as he was standing under a tree when "suddenly I was seized by the collar of my coat and vest, and lifted off the ground." Home was deposited a few feet to the side, at which moment, a large branch fell from the tree and landed where he had been moments earlier.[277]

On a few other occasions, he experienced partial levitations while

Despite intense ridicule, Nobel Prize winning scientist, Sir William Crookes conducted an in-depth investigation into Home's ability to levitate. He soon became Home's leading proponent, and also observed numerous levitation events firsthand. (Mary Evans Picture Library)

bedridden with severe respiratory illness. Says Home, "...many times when it would have been impossible to have moved me in bed, for fear of increased hemorrhage from the lungs, my head has been slowly lifted, and my pillow has been turned by unseen hands. This has been repeatedly witnessed by many persons."

Home himself is at a loss to explain the levitations, only that they are done by his spirit friends. Says Home, "For myself, I have no apology to offer for the occurrence of these unwonted manifestations in my own case. As will have been seen, they came to me quite unsought....I have not, and never had the slightest power over them, either to bring them on, or to send them away, or to increase, or to lessen them. What may be the peculiar laws under which they have become developed in my person, I know no more than others. Whilst they occur I am not conscious of the mode by which they are produced, nor of the sort of manifestation that is about to occur....beyond being of a highly nervous organization, there is nothing peculiar about me that I am aware of. I continue to have delicate health.....Especially I would say, that I do not on this account or on any other, consider myself morally superior to others, nor should any one believe that these phenomena come to me, or to others, on account of moral or immoral qualities."[278]

Home also notes the peculiar effect that human touch or light has on his levitations, which worked ideally during low light levels. Says Home, "Mr. Crawford mentions the circumstance of my immediately coming to the ground again on touching his feet. I have observed that this is invariably the case when I am touched, or even anxiously gazed at, until I have risen above the heads of those who are in the room, but after I have attained that height, their looking at me, or touching me, has no effect upon me. What the cause may be I cannot explain, but it may perhaps be some break in the magnetism which is caused in the former case, and which does not occur in the latter....I have been lifted in the light of day upon only one occasion, and that was in America. I have been lifted in a room in Sloane Street, London, with four gas-lights brightly burning, with five gentleman present, who are willing to testify to what they saw, if need be..."[279]

What exactly does it feel like to levitate? Home's description is one of the most detailed ever recorded. Says Home, "During these elevations or levitations, I usually experience in my body no particular sensations other than what I can only describe as an electrical fullness about the feet. I feel no hands supporting me, and since the first time, above described, I have never felt fear, though should I have fallen from the ceiling of some rooms in which I have been raised, I could not have escaped serious injury. I am generally lifted up perpendicularly; my arms frequently become rigid and drawn above my head, as if I were grasping the unseen power which slowly raises me from the floor. At times when I reach the ceiling, my feet are brought on a level with my face, and I am as it were in a reclining position. I have been frequently so suspended four or five minutes....on some occasions, the rigidity of my arms relaxes, and I have with a pencil made letters and signs on the ceiling, some of which now exist in London."[280]

As can be seen, Home's levitations were so numerous, so well documented, so widely observed by multiple independent highly reputable witnesses—it is very difficult to account for them unless they are true. As Olivier Leroy wrote, "With Daniel Home, it is particularly difficult to dismiss in doubt the totality of the testimonies which establish the reality of this phenomenon."[281]

While Home's reputation was occasionally attacked by skeptics, none was ever able to prove a hoax, nor provide even the slightest evidence of a hoax. One of the worst criticisms came from Count Spada, who, after witnessing Home levitate, wrote, "We think that Home exercises on the people present an entrancing fascination which makes them see something that isn't there."[282]

While Home's achievements remain unparalleled, except for perhaps by some of the saints, as we have seen, they are far from unique. In fact, around this time, the number of levitations dramatically increased, and were being reported across a much wider area.

15. The French Magnetizers

While levitation has occurred regularly for more than 2,000 years of history, for most of that time few people were willing to explore the subject. However, the scientific climate in mid-nineteenth century France was beginning to change. As numerous scientific fields blossomed and many amazing discoveries were made, the door opened for research into more esoteric topics. One particular phenomenon that gripped Europe was known as "magnetism." Made famous by German physician, Franz Anton Mesmer (1734-1815), magnetism involved a "curing" process during which the physician would control the flow of "animal magnetism" using a process of hypnosis and Reiki-like movements of the arms and hands.

In 1840, French doctor, Mr. Bourguignon, discovered by accident that when one of his patients entered into a hypnotic trance, and was "magnetized" using wide sweeping movements of his hands over her body, her movements began to mimic his own. This led shortly to a startling levitation episode. Writes Bourguignon, "I placed my hand two or three feet above the epigastria [of the patient] and the entire body left the ground and stayed suspended."

Bourguignon claims that he was also able to levitate his patient in a standing position. "I put my hand above her head and made her rise from the ground this way, and was able to pass my hand and a cane several times under her feet."

Bourguignon reports that he tried the experiment ten times and was successful on eight of them. However, he was unable to reproduce the effects with anybody else accept the one patient, who was, incidentally, severely ill with a respiratory infection. His colleague, Mr. Theron, attempted the experiment with his own patients and "was able to obtain the same results with a somnambulist, though not with any apparent consistency."[283]

In 1840, Mademoiselle Pourrat of Kiev suffered from fainting spells, which had left her bedridden. Her father, a physician, had read that magnetizing a patient could have beneficial effects. He proceeded to perform the required motions, and to the astonishment of all those present, the young lady was levitated two feet above her bed.[284]

In 1858, the influential French physician, Dr. Lafontaine, traveled across Europe investigating victims of convulsive fits, with the hopes of curing them through a process of magnetization.

One of his first cases involved a young girl from a large family in England. The girl in question exhibited many of the signs of hysteria, including, he was told, "extraordinary agility."

When Lafontaine arrived at her home, he found the patient lying in bed. She showed no movement and seemed to be barely breathing. As Lafontaine examined her, she suddenly sprang to life. Writes Lafontaine, "In one leap the young girl was in the middle of the room, her eyes wide open and fixed, gesticulating with her arms, raising herself on the tips of her toes and running across the room, then throwing herself on the ground, rolling in frightful convulsions, striking herself all over her body."

This type of behavior continued for several minutes, until she fell exhausted into the center of the room. Then suddenly, to everyone's amazement, "She leaped anew and ran like this through the room, perching her bare feet on the furniture, on the glasses, the cups, the globe of the pendulum, on all the fragile things that furnished the shelves, and all without breaking or disturbing anything…an instant after the convulsions exhibited themselves, her eyes expressed an unspeakable ravishment. She fell to her knees, her lips murmuring sweet words like a prayer. She was in ecstasy. The inspiration took possession of her; she recited verses, she composed others; she foretold facts and events that were going to happen; she levitated herself into the air and took flight; then finally, she fell again, sinking down, inert, without movement, without respiration. The fit was over; she had endured it for two hours."

Lafontaine stayed with the family for three months, during which he magnetized her using his hands and making passes over her body. After three months of treatment, her convulsions lessened and stopped completely. She had suffered from them for four years prior to Lafontaine's intervention.[285]

Lafontaine's research continued. In March 1858, he visited the small village of Morzine, near Chablais, France, where, a year earlier, an epidemic of convulsionaries had broken out among many of the women aged eleven to twenty. When Lafontaine arrived, he found twenty-six young girls (and one boy) falling into fits, during which they would run into the fields and "climb the trees with an extraordinary agility and balance themselves on the very tops of the highest spruce trees."

Lafontaine's attention was drawn to one girl in particular, Victoire Vullet, age seventeen. He observed her to remain in an ecstatic fit for several hours of the day, running back and forth with no fatigue. According to Lafontaine, she "leaped from one pine tree to another as would a squirrel or monkey."

As her case appeared to be the most extreme of the group, Lafontaine was appealed upon for help. He came to her home during one of her fits and observed her during her convulsions. He watched as she jumped on the tops of furniture in humanly impossible positions with an agility that seemed to necessitate levitation. He was finally able to approach the girl and placing his hand on her head, caused the convulsions to immediately dwindle. After thirty minutes of magnetizing her with wide passes, Victoire's fit stopped completely. Fifteen days of this kind of treatment stopped her convulsions permanently.

While Victoire was cured, the other victims continued to suffer. By 1860, the outbreak of demonic possession at Morzine had so overwhelmed the community that the Minister of Interior ordered an investigation, and demanded the inspector general control the situation.

One visitor who left a written record of the events was Hippolyte Blance. "Several of these children did things which appeared evidently against the laws of nature, for example, climbing with an unprecedented ease and speed up to the extreme tips of the tree branches, forty or fifty meters up, performing somersaults, leaping from one tree to another tree several meters distant, then descending head first, or holding themselves up with one foot on the extreme tip of one tree and another on another tree."

Blanc personally observed one young boy, Joseph, who began having fits immediately following the funeral of his father. "He climbed up an enormous spruce tree," wrote Blanc, "from which he dangled. Arriving at the top, he broke off the tip and did a headstand on the top, singing and gesticulating. His brother ordered him to keep quiet, and telling him that this was not the time to amuse himself when returning from his father's funeral. At this injunction, the child appeared to wake up, and seeing where he was, he became very afraid and lost, calling for help. The brother then changed his mind and cried out, 'Devil, put this child back right now so that he can come down!' The fit began again and soon the child ceased to cry and be afraid, and descended head first with the rapidity of a squirrel."

According to Leroy, sixteen of the patients were eventually cured through traditional exorcisms.[286]

In 1859, Lafontaine reported another case involving a young lady, Mademoiselle A., who would fall into somnambulistic trances. When Lafontaine arrived, he hypnotized the young woman and began magnetizing her. Meanwhile, the patient's mother started to play the piano. Interestingly, the piano music caused the patient to suddenly start shaking and then, as Lafontaine writes, "she leaped right up in bed, her eyes wide open and fixed. Then her feet glided along the edge of the bed without there being any movement of muscles. She moved softly beyond the bed and descended slowly, both feet at the same time and without any point of support until reaching the carpet, like she had been positioned on one of the those stage props used in the operas in order to bring down the angels from the middle of the clouds. Her entire body appeared to be supported by an invisible wire, with all her limbs rigid.

"I watched in the most profound amazement without understanding anything; but my eyes were wide open; my intelligence and reason vigilant and at their post. It wasn't possible for me to be in error. Her feet and legs were naked…Meanwhile, descending on the carpet, her feet continued to glide together, without the least movement or muscular contraction. She resembled a statue placed on the floor that one pulled by oneself, and which glided, without any shaking, like she had been set on a railway."

Lafontaine followed her, prepared to catch her if she fell. Her mother, suddenly seeing what was taking place, stopped playing the piano. Immediately, the patient fell to the ground senseless. Only by playing the piano were they able to provoke a response.

Lafontaine began performing his magnetizing procedures. After a half-hour, the fit was over. Three weeks of treatment appeared to leave the young girl completely healed.[287]

An undated account from the mid-1800s comes from Monsieur de Mirville of France who attended a magnetic exhibition during which he saw "sleepwalkers to fly up to the chandeliers."[288]

In his book, *Seer of Prevost,* Dr. Kerner reported that he was able to levitate Mademoiselle Hauffe by placing his hands above her and raising them upwards, somehow causing Hauffe's body to rise. Dr. Kerner asked his wife to try, and she obtained the same results. They then filled a bath with water and lay Hauffe down. They attempted to submerge her body with the help of the nurses, but were unable to do so.[289]

The French magnetizing era may have contributed to the inspiration of Colonel Eugene de Rochas who wrote his series of articles—and the first book ever on the subject of levitation. Olivier Leroy's landmark 1928 study was itself inspired by Rochas' research. In any case, as can be seen, French researchers such as Bourguignon, Imbert-Gourbeyre, Lafontaine, Rochas, and Leroy pioneered the study of levitation, and laid the foundation for modern levitation research.

Today, magnetizing patients using wide sweeping motions of the hands over the patient's body has faded away, at least in relation to levitation. However, the practice of Reiki and other forms of psychic healing are still popular, and may utilize the same or a similar force. This seems even more likely when one considers the fact that many levitators also display the ability to perform hands-on healings.

16. The Rise
of the Mediums

Spiritualism, or the belief and practice that people can communicate with the dead, has a long, colorful history. However, it wasn't until the 1850s when Spiritualism enjoyed a sudden and profound surge in popularity. For the first time, millions of people became exposed to a wide variety of mediumistic phenomena. Levitation being among the most dramatic, it attracted the attention of numerous scientists. Now that Daniel Home had popularized the phenomenon, more and more people were revealing their own ability to levitate. Levitation was now a phenomenon that was impossible to ignore. In fact, by the 1850s, the floodgates had opened and levitation accounts appeared in unprecedented numbers. Practically overnight, mediumistic accounts of levitation overtook all other forms of the phenomenon combined. In this chapter, we shall examine two dozen mediumistic accounts from 1850 to 1900.

In March 1850, the Phelps family of Stratford, Connecticut experienced a poltergeist attack centered around their twelve-year-old son, Harry. Objects constantly moved in his presence. Stones were thrown at the boy; his clothes were torn. According to the report on the case, "At times he was violently caught up from the ground until his head nearly struck the ceiling." On one occasion, he was thrown into the water cistern, and on another, was also levitated up into a tree.[290]

On March 25, 1850, the life of Helene-Josephine Poirier of Loire, France changed forever. She was an apprentice dressmaker, still in her teen-age years, and very religious. That evening, Poirier was woken by loud knocking noises in her bedroom. She ran and told her parents. Although they also heard the knocks, no cause could be found.

Over the next few months, the haunting activity increased until Poirier began to fall into trances during which her body would become rigid and be thrown to the ground by a strong force. Local doctors examined her and ruled out epilepsy, but were unable to diagnose the trance states. The activity continued on and off for no less than *eighteen* years, until 1868, when Poirier finally concluded that she was suffering from demonic possession. This conclusion was the result of a particularly violent series of incidents, including a levitation. On August 28, 1867, "reliable witnesses saw her levitated from the ground on two distinct occasions."

She underwent an exorcism ritual and one year later, in 1869, after nineteen years of suffering, was cured of her strange condition.[291]

Also in 1851, the Attwood family of Troy, New York began to hear knocking noises in their home that seemed to happen only in the presence of their five-year-old daughter. They soon discovered she was a medium and began conducting séances during which spirits would rap out intelligible messages. On one occasion, the child was seen to levitate. "Seated on a high chair, with her tiny feet resting on a footboard, the medium all-unconsciously munched away at her sweetmeats whilst the spirits lifted her about and moved her from place to place with the ease of a feather blown by the winds."[292]

In 1851, the Davenport brothers, Ira (thirteen) and William (eleven), of Buffalo, New York created a local sensation when dramatic poltergeist phenomena occurred wherever they went. "At times the children would be lifted up several feet in the air and kept suspended there for one or two minutes. The manifestations accompanied them everywhere; in the streets or stores; at their play or in bed, and were always of the wildest and most preternatural character."

On one occasion, Ira Davenport was seen by his family to levitate out of the back room of the house onto the street, for a distance of seventy feet. On another occasion, while delivering papers, Ira reported that he felt "queer." Seconds later, he fell into a trance and was floated for a distance of one and a half miles across the bank of the Niagara River, where he regained consciousness.

The Davenport brothers knew a good thing when they saw it, and decided to take financial advantage of their situation. They eventually became internationally celebrated mediums, touring the country and the world, displaying an incredibly wide variety of mediumistic talents. They were accused of fraud, though this was never conclusively proved. Houdini was their arch-skeptic, but admitted that he was never able to reproduce or explain their feats.

The very popular Reverend J. B. Ferguson attended many séances held by the Davenport brothers, and he staked his sterling reputation in support of the case. Writes Ferguson, "From as good testimony as I have of any fact that I can accept without personal knowledge, I believe that these young men have been raised into the air to the ceilings of rooms and have been transported a distance of miles by the same force and intelligence, or intelligent force, that has for eleven years worked in their presence so many marvels."[293]

The Davenport Brothers (Ira: far left; William: far right) were among the most celebrated physical mediums of their day. They discovered their mediumistic abilities as young children when they both began to spontaneously levitate. Here they pose before one of their cabinet demonstrations, circa 1864. (Mary Evans Picture Library)

By this time, the phenomenon of spiritualism had the attention of the entire world. Accounts of levitation were now newsworthy items. In 1853, the *New York Courier* printed an editorial recounting a levitation event. As the editorial reads: "We have the word of a gentleman of acknowledged high social and professional position, one whose bare word on any other subject we would receive without question, that he saw a man carried through the air for seventy feet at the height of three yards, although no one touched him or brought any mechanical power to bear on him."[294]

Also in 1853, the *New York Dispatch* printed the following account of a levitation: "Mr. Henry Gordon, a well-known physical medium for spiritual manifestations, being at a circle in this city one evening last week, was repeatedly raised from his seat and carried through the room, without any visible power touching him. The room was partially darkened, and the members of the circle could distinctly see him floating, with his lower extremities some two or three feet from the floor and some fifteen or twenty feet from the nearest person to him."

On another occasion, Gordon was seen by witnesses to be levitated for a distance of sixty feet.[295]

In 1864, in Philadelphia, Pennsylvania, yet another remarkable feat of levitation was performed by Henry Gordon in front of a crowd of people. It occurred during a church sermon, and Gordon was seated in the audience. Said one witness, "Mr. Henry Gordon...in the perfectly well-lighted room, rose in the air without any human aid, till the speaker beheld him floating so high that his feet just grazed the top of the seat, above which he hung in the air, where he swayed from side to side and turned gently around. By this time, the attention of the entire congregation was riveted on him, when he sank to the ground. The manifestation was imperfect on the part of the power that lifted him up, because it was afterwards declared by the spirits that they intended to have carried him over the heads of the entire congregation, and landed him in the rostrum, had the conditions permitted, but it seemed that the intense astonishment and agitation of the audience had broken the conditions of passivity necessary for the fulfillment of their design, and so he sank suddenly to the ground. Still there remained the phenomenon of his having been lifted up and suspended in the air without mortal aid, in a manner which no mortal could have achieved."[296]

A similar public levitation took place in 1853, and was reported by Dr. Cyriax from Berlin, Germany. At that time, he was visiting Baltimore, Maryland to attend a lecture by Mademoiselle French on the subject of spiritualism and trance-states. During the lecture, Dr. Cyriax and a hundred other witnesses watched French suddenly rise into the air. Dr. Cyriax leaves a particularly emotional and believable account of a mediumistic levitation. "...she was all of a sudden lifted up from the platform on which she had been standing, and carried towards the back of the room, all the while hovering at a height of about two feet over the floor. This spectacle of this phenomenon confirmed by my eyes, as it was the same moment by a hundred women and men, thrilled me. I saw before me, with full awareness, a person who, without moving a limb, the arms crossed and the eyes closed, hovering over the floor and was transported between two rows of seats, each one containing fifty people, then returning in the same way from the back of the room, up to the platform, and to continue her lecture as if nothing extraordinary had happened to her. I saw all the other people verify this phenomenon and everybody was as dumbfounded as was I. My senses were not deceived. This that I saw truly happened!…This phenomenon had such an impression on me that I didn't sleep the entire night. I found myself constantly faced with what I had seen and I searched vainly to explain it by the known natural laws." Later, Mrs. French would experience an astonishing episode of traveling levitation[297]

On December 7, 1855, ten people attended a séance in Boston, Massachusetts headed by medium Roland Squire. As reported by one of the witnesses, "The medium was lifted bodily from the floor at various distances, whilst we held him by either hand. He was lifted from the floor and placed, standing, on the center of the table, and again stretched upon his back thereon. Being seated in his chair, himself, chair and all, was elevated several inches, and hopped about the room like a frog. Suddenly it was lifted, medium and all, on to the center of the table. Again it was drawn up so high that the medium's head knocked against the ceiling; and finally the medium was thrown out of it upon the bed...."[298]

In October, 1856, several people held a séance at a private home in San Francisco, California. During the séance one of the members levitated. As one witness later wrote, "He was seized by the coat, and hurled forwards several yards in the room. He distinctly felt himself lifted by hands. He was thrown with a velocity that would have killed him had he not been lifted; but though thrown so far and the thing being done so quickly, it was evident he was carried, not thrown, and dropped so lightly that he did not sustain any other inconvenience than that of breaking upon our astonished eyes in a most undignified heap, in a remote corner of the room."[299]

In 1859, former Congressman Charles Cathcart of Indiana attended a séance and was quickly convinced of the validity of spiritualism and the physical phenomena it produced. He became even more convinced when his youngest son, Henry Cathcart, began to display mediumistic powers. These soon escalated into full-blown levitations during which the seven-year-old boy would be "tossed about the room like a feather. Lifted in the arms of the spirits, he would be carried to the ceiling, cornices, windows, perched up on the highest nooks in the rooms, or carried anywhere and everywhere beyond the reach of human arms to place him."

The other Cathcart children were greatly amused by the displays, and gleefully ordered the spirits to carry Henry to various places about the room. Henry himself enjoyed the experience, saying, "I'm not a bit afraid; take me again; take me again!"

Events took a bizarre turn, however, when the child began to fall into trances and "speak words of wonderful wisdom and beauty" that were well beyond his years. The mother became understandably concerned and put a quick stop to the sessions.[300]

On December 31, 1863, medium Charles Reed of Buffalo, New York impressed a group of eleven sitters when "...the medium was taken up bodily, and whilst the hands of both his neighbors still held on to him, he was lifted up as high as their extended arms—when dragged up from their seats, and standing—could reach. He was then suddenly dropped down, yet as if lifted rather than dropped, for his fall produced neither harm nor concussion, though a fall from such a height must have broken his bones. Again he was taken up several times, audibly striking his head against the ceiling, causing him to exclaim in some fear of being hurt, 'Oh, don't!' On one occasion, he was held against the ceiling for nearly a minute and a half, and then, as if to show the nature and care of the power that handled him, he was laid lengthwise on the top of the piano, whilst the music rack was still standing up, wholly undisturbed."[301]

An excellent mediumistic 1870 account comes from William Stainton Moses, professor at Cambridge University, author, religious scholar, and a founding member of the British Society of Psychical Research. His sterling reputation for honesty and integrity was vouched for by many prominent citizens.

William Stainton Moses was also a medium. He started out very skeptical, but after attending a few séances, he became convinced. He then began to exhibit his own mediumistic talent. He later levitated on numerous occasions in front of many influential citizens. Well-known pioneering paranormal investigator, Andrew Lang, investigated his case and concluded that Moses' levitations were a "miracle."

The levitations occurred exclusively during darkened séances. Writes Moses, "One day, June 30, 1870, I felt my chair moved away from the table and turned towards the corner where I had been seated, so that I turned my back towards the circle and faced at an angle towards the wall. Immediately the chair was elevated from the ground to a height—which after I was able to judge—came to be thirty to forty centimeters….The chair stayed suspended for some instants and then I felt myself leave it and climb still higher, then higher, in a movement very gentle and slow. I never had any apprehension and I never felt uneasy. I was perfectly conscious of what was happening and described the progress of the phenomenon to those around the table. The movement was very regular and it seemed to us a rather long time to complete."

Moses was able to take a pencil and make several marks high up on the wall, near the ceiling, verifying that he had actually levitated.

Moses himself left a vivid account of what it feels like to levitate. "My sensation was that of being lighter than the air. No pressure on any part of the body, no unconsciousness or entrancement. From the position of the mark on the wall, it is clear that my head must have been close to the ceiling. The ascent, of which I was perfectly conscious, was very gradual and steady, not unlike that of being in an elevator, but without any perceptible sensation of motion other than that of feeling lighter than the atmosphere, of being completely free." He also reported a slight difficulty in breathing and a tightness in his chest.

As in the cases of several Saints, Moses was seen on occasion to emit light from his body. Flowery perfume and other unusual odors were also emitted from his body, echoing the Saints and their "odour of sanctity."

Stainton Moses successfully levitated on nine separate occasions in front of multiple witnesses, under carefully monitored conditions, making his levitations among the best verified in history.[302]

In 1870, fifteen-year-old Florence Cook of London, England and her friends decided to conduct an impromptu table-tipping session, just for fun. To their shock, the table lifted easily into the air. A few minutes later, Cook herself was levitated in front of her young friends and tossed about the room before being set down. The incident propelled her into fame, and she soon became a well-known medium—a career that she held for many years. While she was able to produce other phenomena, she was never able to reproduce any feats of levitation. Her case eventually fell into disrepute after allegations of trickery.[303]

One of the most remarkable levitators of the late 1800s was Carmine (Carlo) Mirabelli, (1889-1951), the undisputed leader of Brazil's spiritualism movement. Mirabelli

Reverend Stainton Moses. He was able to levitate on more than ten occasions, each under strict conditions, making his case one of the best-verified in history. (Mary Evans Picture Library)

displayed countless psychic abilities from a young age, and had numerous credible witnesses vouching for his reputation, including his entire extended family and friends. Before long, he had conducted thousands of séances, producing virtually the entire range of mediumistic phenomena. Under trance, he was able to speak in no less than *twenty-eight* languages (three of which were dead languages) including seven dialects. Important here, however, is physical levitation, which he performed on several occasions.

During one séance, he was handcuffed to prevent trickery. He rose up in full view of several witnesses, and then disappeared, the handcuffs falling to the floor. Moments later, he appeared in another room in the same home. Two doors had to be unlocked to retrieve him.

At Sao Vicente, Mirabelli was tied to a chair by several scientists from the Academy Cesare Lombroso. After he had been securely fastened, Mirabelli and his chair rose from the ground and remained suspended in the air for two minutes at a height of more than six feet, during which time the witnesses were allowed to pass to and fro underneath.

Mirabelli's feats continued. According to Mr. Boqueroa, while driving through Santos, Brazil, he observed Mirabelli to levitate six feet above his automobile for a period of three minutes.

On one occasion, a levitation was photographed. The photograph shows Mirabelli hovering about three feet off the ground in a standing position. His face is turned upwards with an expression of awe and peace, as if he is beholding something of intense beauty. His arms are outspread in front of him in a posture reminiscent of the levitating saints. Some have claimed that the photograph is a fake, and that Mirabelli is standing on a ladder that has been airbrushed out of the photo. Either way, it is the first known photo of a levitation. Furthermore, there is more evidence pointing towards the validity of Mirabelli's case.

English researcher Guy Lyon Playfair performed extensive follow-up research on Mirabelli and (apart from the photo) came away convinced of the genuineness of the case. He writes, "One eminent Sao Paolo surgeon assured me that his father had seen Mirabelli leave the floor while sitting in a chair."

Playfair interviewed Mirabelli's son, Regene Mirabelli, who was a firsthand witness to a levitation event. One day, Regene peeked into his father's room and observed him sitting on the bed in a position of meditation. Says Regene, "As I watched him, his body

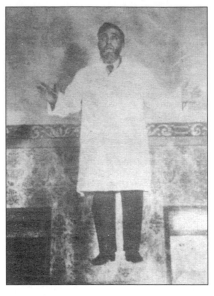

Carmine Mirabelli was Brazil's most popular medium and spearheaded the country's spiritualism movement. He levitated on numerous occasions. This controversial image is the first known photograph to show a person in a levitating state. (Playfair Archives)

began to rise up in the air, without changing position. Then he just stayed there, in mid-air, about a meter off the bed, his arms and legs still crossed....That was enough for me, and I ran off to tell mother as fast as I could."[304]

In the 1880s, English medium William Eglinton, born in 1857, exploded onto the spiritualism scene with his ability to produce "slate writings" of messages from the deceased. While this was his claim to fame, on several occasions he was also seen to levitate.

Eglinton started out very skeptical of mediums and ghosts. When his father started holding séances, Eglinton verbally attacked him, and called him a lunatic. His father told him to either leave the house during séances or join the investigation. Eglinton reluctantly joined, but only with the idea that he would stop the foolish and unreal activity from continuing. Instead, the table began dancing by itself, and Eglinton fell into a trance. To his utter shock, Eglinton found himself to be a powerful medium. In a space of a few months, Eglinton was producing a wide range of spiritualistic phenomena including materializations and levitations. He was besieged with so many requests for séances that he quit his printing job and became a fulltime medium.

His first levitation occurred during a séance in 1876. As described by Archdeacon Colley in the June 2, 1876 edition of *The Spiritualist,* "The medium was next entranced and carried by invisible power over the table several times, the heels of his boots being made to touch the head of our medical friend, Dr. Malcolm. Then he was taken to the further end of the dining room, and finally, after being tilted about as a thing of no weight whatever, was deposited quietly in his chair."

On March 16, 1878, Eglinton held a séance at the home of Mrs. Macdougall Gregory. During the session, Eglinton was not only levitated up to the ceiling, but was transported *through* the ceiling and into the room above, a rare though not unique event in the annals of levitation.

Another event was witnessed by magician Harry Kellar, who was perhaps best known for exposing the tricks of various fraudulent mediums. Kellar challenged Eglinton to perform a trick that "no conjurer could repeat." Eglinton agreed and a séance was conducted. At some point, during the session, Eglinton began to levitate. He reached out and grabbed Kellar, allegedly lifting him up into the air with him. Kellar was forced to admit that he was unable to account for the levitation. Said Kellar, "I went as a skeptic, but I must own that I came away utterly unable to explain, by any natural means, the phenomena that I witnessed on Tuesday evening."[305]

In 1884, Amy Fisher visited Eglinton and received messages from her deceased brother. Also during the séance, said Fisher, Eglinton levitated. As the report says, "She [Fisher] also had the bonus in the shape of spirit forms and a levitation—the medium rose so high that she had difficulty retaining her grip on his hand (and the odds are that she did not retain it, but did not like to say so). As the medium descended, she saw him lying in the air in a horizontal position."[306]

On yet another occasion, Eglinton levitated in the presence of the Emperor and Empress of Russia, the Grand Duke of Oldenburg, and the Grand Duke Vladimir. Writes Eglinton, "My neighbors had to stand on their chairs to follow me. I continued to rise until my feet touched two shoulders on which I leaned." Although not as famous as Home, Eglinton was clearly endowed with similar abilities.[307]

The unprecedented large number of levitation accounts began to attract the attention of more and more scientists. In 1887, Mr. B., a scientist and former student of L'Ecole Polytechnique, in France, discovered that a member of his family possessed mediumistic abilities. He took it upon himself to investigate his relative's abilities, which included the supernatural lifting of heavy tables four or five feet off the ground.

William Eglinton was a powerful physical medium, probably most popular for his ability to produce spiritual slate writings. He also sometimes spontaneously levitated during séances. (Mary Evans Picture Library)

On one occasion, during a séance, two guns next to the séance table were lifted by paranormal means, followed shortly by the medium. Writes Mr. B., "An instant later, we heard the medium cry out, 'I feel myself rising up.' Standing up from my chair, I saw his ascension right up to the ceiling, the length of which he did laying down, and my hand could travel under his body in its entire length, from the head to the feet. He came down slowly, and resuming a vertical position, he landed next to the table where we had found him after turning up the light on the gas lamp—his two feet positioned exactly in the narrow space which separated the two howitzers."

The medium was able to successfully levitate on two other occasions, during which he was actually pressed up against the ceiling of the room. He reported no sensation of being held and was at a loss to explain it.[308]

In 1888, English engineer Donald McNab observed and studied the repeated levitations of his two friends, Mr. F., a music composer; and Mr. C., a sculptor. Like many mediumistic levitators, the mediums were unable to levitate in bright light.

Writes McNab, "The medium, Mr. F. is frequently lifted into the air during his séances, but this happens most often to one of my friends, Mr. C., a sculptor who is also a medium. One time, he told us that he was lifted up in his chair. We heard the sound of his voice changing locations. We noted that he had heavy boots and that we didn't hear the least noise. Finally having turned on the lights, he found himself sitting on his chair, and then on the bed. Another time, having lighted up [turned on the lights] while he was levitated on the music stool, he fell heavily from a height of fifty to sixty centimeters, so heavily that the foot of the stool was broken."

To verify the levitation and ascertain their exact height while in complete darkness, McNab used an ingenious method. He placed a sheet of thin cloth material beneath Mr. C. When the levitation occurred, the witnesses lifted the sheet and made their measurements and observations. Writes McNab, "I can't believe that one can then raise any objection to this experience of the levitation of the medium, verified by the cloth held under the chair."

Numerous scientists witnessed these levitations, including Colonel de Rochas. Writes McNab, "In a séance, Mr. Montorgueil and in another Mr. De Rochas, passed their hands under the feet of the medium during his ascension, and were able to assure themselves that he had used no ordinary gymnastic moves."

Wrote another witness, Mr. Gaboreau, "Mr. McNab turned on the lights quickly, and as always, I saw the medium very breathless and sweaty, like he had come from carrying a burden…He had to pass over the table in order to come down next to me on my chair. I remember perfectly the fear of Mr. C., and I was convinced that he had passed over the table with his chair because the room where we were was very small, we filled it nearly completely with the table and chairs set all around. It couldn't have happened behind us without brushing against us, especially in the darkness.[309]

An undated 1800s account comes from Mrs. Volckman of England, who was levitated involuntarily during a séance with the American medium, Mary

Hardy, in the presence of Baroness Adelma Vay, Prince Albert of Solme, and several other witnesses.

Reports one of the witnesses, "Mrs. Volkman did not wish to take part in the experiments, so she retired to the back drawing room with the Baronness Adelma Vay and other visitors and left Mrs. Hardy with the rest of the guests in the front drawing room. Suddenly, however, Mrs. Volckman-Guppy was levitated and carried in sight of us all in the middle of the ring. As she felt herself rising the air she called out, 'Don't let go hands, for Heaven's sake.' We were just standing in a ring, and I had hold of the hand of Prince Albert of Solme. As Mrs. Volckman came sailing over our heads, her feet caught his neck and mine, and in our anxiety to do as she told us we gripped tight hold of each other and were thrown forward on our knees by the force with which she was carried past us into the center of the ring. The influence that levitated her, moreover, placed her on a chair with such a bump that it broke the two front legs off."

On another occasion, Mrs. Volckman-Guppy was levitated with medium Frank Herne. Writes witness Catherine Berry, "Mr. Hearn was floating in the air, his voice being heard near the ceiling, while his feet where held by several persons in the room, Mrs. Guppy who sat next to him being struck on the head by his boots as he sank into the chair. In a few minutes he recommenced ascending, and as Mrs. Guppy on this occasion determined if possible, to prevent it, she held his arm, but the only result was that she ascended with him, and both floated together with the chairs on which they sat. Rather unfortunately, at this moment the door was unexpectedly opened, and Mr. Herne fell to the ground, injuring his shoulder, Mrs. Guppy alighting with considerable noise on the table where, on the production of light, she was found comfortably seated though considerably alarmed."[310]

A remarkable late 1800s case of levitation occurred to an anonymous gentleman during a séance with English medium, Cecil I lusk. Writes one of the sitters, Gambier Bolton, "One of the observers (a man weighing quite twelve stones) was suddenly raised from the floor, with the chair in which he was sitting; and releasing the hands of those who were holding his hands, he was levitated in his chair, greatly to his surprise, until his feet where just above the heads of the other experimenters present. He remained stationary in the air for a few seconds and then slowly descended to the floor again. Fourteen observers were present."[311]

Another late 1880s account involves the somewhat violent mediumistic levitation of two sitters at a séance. As reported by one witness, Sergeant Cox, "Mr. Williams, although held firmly by myself on one side and a [man] on the other, was instantaneously lifted from his chair and placed in a sitting posture on the table. Mr. Herne was in like manner thrown flat upon his back upon the table, while his hands were held by two others of the party. While thus lying he was suddenly raised from the table, as if he had been flung by a giant, and thrown over the heads of the sitters to the corner of the room. The height to which he was actually thrown may be judged by this, that he knocked down a picture that was hung upon the wall, at a height of eight feet."[312]

A mediumistic account dated 1893, involves two Italian mediums, Alberto Fontana and Arturo Ruggiero, who levitated two of the sitters simultaneously—one of several cases on record in which three people have been levitated at one time.

The first séance took place in darkness and contained fourteen sitters, including several scientists. Writes one of the participants, Mr. Palazzi, "…all of a sudden and without any warning, the three people were lifted at the same time and carried onto the table, Mr. Fontana and Ruggiero standing up, Santangelo on his knees."

Writes Dr. Nicholas Santangelo, "When the medium Ruggieri commenced to rise I held him firmly by the hand, but seeing myself drawn with such force as almost to lose my footing I held on to his arms, and thus I was raised in the air with my companion, who was on the other side of the medium. We were all three raised in the air to a height of at least three yards above the floor, since I distinctly touched with my feet the hanging lamp which was suspended from the center of the ceiling....Yes, at Rome, me, myself, and without wings—I flew in the air, and this I then attest to in the face of God and all men."

Later on in the evening, further levitations of the mediums were obtained. Writes Palazzi, "During this time the medium was lifted above the table, the phenomenon established and verified by the majority of the assistants…we passed our hands several times under the feet of the medium, between his feet and the table. He was lifted about ten centimeters."

This feat was repeated a third time, and all participants again passed their hands under the medium, verifying the levitation.

At the end of the evening, the medium also exhibited the opposite of levitation, or increased weight. The combined strength of several men was insufficient to lift the medium from the floor.[313]

In the late 1800s, English medium Foster experienced several spontaneous levitations. According to one witness, Dr. Ashburner, "He grabbed my right hand and beseeched me not to quit my hold of him; for he said there was no way knowing where the spirits might convey him. I held his hand, and he was floated in the air towards the ceiling."[314]

And so closes the levitations from the 1800s. As can be seen, the accounts of levitation are no longer purely anecdotal. The feats of people like Mirabelli, Eglinton, Moses, and other mediums have been observed under controlled laboratory conditions. The validity of levitation is no longer the question. The real question is how does levitation occur and can it be duplicated?

As history progressed into the twentieth century, the number of levitation accounts increased in number and credibility, providing more answers to the secrets behind the phenomenon.

17. Eusapia Palladino and the Scientists

While the levitations of religious ecstatics are difficult to study—as they occur spontaneously—the levitation of mediums can be provoked and observed under controlled conditions. One medium who became world famous for her levitations was Eusapia Palladino (1854-1918), a poor woman from Naples, Italy. Palladino's levitations are among the best verified and most studied in history. She traveled across Europe for more than a decade, visiting (and convincing) one scientist after another, displaying her incredible mediumistic abilities under strict laboratory settings. Finally, after centuries of levitation displays, the phenomenon was getting the serious attention it deserved.

Palladino rose from obscurity to become one of the most famous spiritual mediums in history.

FIG. 40. EUSAPIA AFTER THE SÉANCE.

Eusapia Palladino is Europe's most studied medium of the nineteenth century. She was able to produce an incredibly wide variety of mediumistic phenomena. Her ability to levitate was verified by many leading scientists. (Mary Evans Picture Library)

She held local séances for years when her astounding abilities finally began to attract widespread attention. In 1889, Italian scientists, Lechavalier Chiaia and Mr. Tassil, and Spanish professor, Don Manuel Otero Acevedo, conducted a séance with Palladino in total darkness. Writes Chiaia, "Mr. Otero and Mr. Tassil, the closest to the medium, perceived the first unexpected ascension; because they felt her arms to rise very gently; and not wanting to let go of the hands of the medium, they held on to her during her ascension. This splendid case of levitation was even more so deserving of attention as it took place under the most rigorous surveillance and with the lightness of a feather."

Palladino then perched lightly on the table, in a trance state. The scientists were amazed at what was happening, and asked out loud if it was possible for Palladino to levitate again. Writes Chiaia, "Immediately, Eusapia was lifted ten to fifteen centimeters over the table, each of us were able to pass our hands under the feet of the magician suspended in the air."

The next event also astonished the scientists. Palladino's head rested on the edge of the table while the rest of her body extended horizontally in the air, without visible support. Writes Chiaia, "Although this was produced in darkness, this important feat

Charles Richet. A prominent scientist and Nobel Prize winner, Richet studied Palladino's case in-depth, and like most scientists who looked into her case, he came away totally convinced. (Mary Evans Picture Library)

was observed scrupulously, with the greatest care by all, and in a manner that rendered it most evident as if it had taken place in broad daylight."

Later Chiaia observed the same type of levitation under full light. As he writes, "Over and above this, I had the occasion to be a witness to a thing even more extraordinary. One evening, I saw the medium, extended in the state of the most complete catalepsy, holding herself in a horizontal position with only the head supported by the edge of the table for five minutes, under the light of gas lamps, in the presence of professor DeCintiis, the well-known writer, Dr. Capuano, Mr. Frederic Verdinois, and others." Palladino's fame was thus assured.

Three years later, in 1892, a half dozen eminent European scientists studied Palladino's abilities, including Giovanni Schiaparelli, the director of the Astronomical Observatory of Milan; Carl DuPrel, Doctor of Philosophy of Munich; Angelo

Brofferio, professor of Philosophy; Giuseppe Gerosa, professor of physics and two other particularly prominent scientists. Cesare Lombroso was an influential psychologist at the University of Turin and the founder of modern criminology. Charles Richet was a physiologist at the Faculte du Medicin in Paris and a soon-to-be Nobel Prize winner. All the above scientists observed Palladino under controlled conditions to levitate into the air with her chair, after which she was set gently down on the table. Writes Lombroso, "…the chair, with Eusapia in it, was not violently dashed, but lifted without hitting anything, on the top of the table and Mr. Richet and I are sure that we did not even assist the levitation by our force."

Using a scale, they were able to repeatedly record a reduction in Eusapia's weight under fully controlled conditions. On two occasions, while Richet and Lombroso held both her hands, Palladino levitated completely off the ground and was set on the table.

Palladino allowed her abilities to be studied by many other scientists of various disciplines including Matazewski, Ochorowitz, Colonel Rochas, Porro, Morselli, de Albertis, the well-known writer Dr. Capuano, Professor de Conties, Verdinois, the well-known researcher Hereward Carrington, Feilding, Baggaly, and many others, all of whom observed her to levitate fully or partially, or produce a wide variety of mediumistic phenomena. All came away convinced, making her one of the most studied and best authenticated levitators in history.

Writes Matazewski, "I became a witness to the levitation of the medium into the air in the middle of the room, without any support. She was then in a trance state, and was lifted up gradually, slowly and lightly into the air (all the while staying erect) and came back down just as slowly and lightly onto the floor.…Eusapia stayed a rather long time suspended in the air, for we were able to freely pass our hands under her feet in order to verify that she absolutely wasn't touching the floor. The height of the levitation was a few feet. The feat was repeated four times."

Mr. Ochorowiez witnessed a similar levitation. "Another feat more surprising and more rare was the complete levitation of the medium's person, held at all times by the hands and feet, levitated from the ground and carried with her, in a state of catalepsy, onto the table. In passing my hands under her ankle-boots, I was able to establish that between her and the table, there was a distance of four to five feet."

In 1895, Palladino allowed herself to be studied again by yet another spe-cially-selected commission of European scientists, including Mr. Sabatier, Dean of the Faculty of Sciences at Montpelier; Colonel de Rochas, administrator of L'Ecole de Polytechnique (also the future author of the first book-length study of levitation); Baron de Watteville, master of Physical Sciences and the law; Mr. Maxwell, proxy for General Limoges, and several others. Their experiments were successful, though Palladino was only able to levitate in darkness.

Writes Dr. Ercole Chiaia, "This woman rises in the air, no matter what bands tie her down. She seems to lie upon empty air, as on a couch, contrary to all the laws of gravity."

Like a few saints and Daniel Home, Palladino was also able to change her height, a phenomenon known as "elongation." Like other mediums, she was able to speak in different languages, and also would occasionally emit light or perfume from her body.

Scales were set up to measure Palladino's weight during a séance, which showed that she actually lost weight during and afterwards. On a few occasions, in her later years, she was sometimes caught using trickery. Nevertheless scientists were unable to account for most of the phenomena she produced. Writes Fodor, "The levitations of Eusapia Palladino are among the best observed cases."[315]

18. Iceland's
Greatest Levitator

In 1905, twelve-year-old Indridi Indridason (1883-1912) of Iceland created a furor in his home when a poltergeist repeatedly pulled him out of his bed and threw objects around in his presence. The activity began as the result of the boy attending a séance, during which he displayed unusually strong physical mediumistic abilities. Soon, the haunting escalated to the point when Indridason himself began to levitate.

One memorable incident occurred as Indridason was dressing himself in his bedroom. Finding himself flying uncontrollably through the air, he screamed for help. His guardian, Mr. Thorlaksson, came running and saw Indridason in full levitation. "Indridi is lying in the air in a horizontal position, at about the height of my chest, and swaying there to and fro, with his feet pointing towards the window, and it seems to me that the invisible power that is holding him in the air is trying to swing him out the window. I don't hesitate a moment, but grab the medium, and push him down onto the bed and hold him there. But then I notice that both of us are being lifted up. I scream to Thordur Oddgeirsson and ask him to come and help."

Together, the two men were just barely able to pull Indridason back onto the bed.

Realizing that something strange was happening to him, Indridason agreed to sit at further séances. His abilities grew in strength, and he soon became Iceland's single most influential medium, producing virtually the entire range of physical mediumship phenomena, including powerful levitations. In fact, during his early levitations he rose so quickly that his head often struck the ceiling.

Thorlaksson reported several other levitations during which Indridason remained seated on a couch or chair. During one séance, he and others observed the couch with Indridason on it levitate to the "height of a person's chest" where it remained for long enough to convince everyone present that no trickery was involved.

Indridason was usually able to initiate a levitation only in darkness, so scientists used elaborate and clever controls to verify his levitations. Writes Neilsson, a prominent preacher, "In order to substantiate these phenomena, we placed him in a basket chair, which creaked conveniently upon the least movement. We placed this at one end of the room and tight rows of chairs all across the room, so that any passage between the chairs was impossible. Then the sitters—and it must be remembered that we were sometimes more than 50 or more in number—sat down on all the chairs—the light being put out. Very soon the medium was levitated in the basket chair at a great distance from the floor—creaking in the chair being heard while it glided above our heads and was rather noisily deposited on the floor behind the chairs. Then the light was immediately lit and there sat the medium unconscious (in a deep trance) in the chair."

Indridason also displayed supernatural agility, performing complex gymnastic feats while in a trance state. Olafur Rosinkrans, a professional gymnastic instructor verified the feats and reported that they were well beyond his own considerable abilities. Indridason was able to perform these feats in bright light.

Numerous scientists and high officials examined Indridason, including a future Supreme Court judge, and Hallgrimur Sveinsson, the Bishop of Iceland. One prominent scientist was Dr. Gudmundur Hannesson, physician, founder of the Icelandic Scientific Society, and President of the University of Iceland. Hannesson was present during several of Indridason's levitations during which the medium was "drawn up into the air with his feet turned towards the ceiling and his head downwards."

At the time, the medium's hands were held by another man who reported that the medium was levitated with such force that he was barely able to hold on to his hands. This happened on several occasions. As the anonymous gentleman reported, "I myself while continuing to hold the medium was thrown with him into the air so that we crashed to the floor violently."

In his notes on the various séances, Hannesson remarked upon several other levitations of the medium. Of one occasion he wrote, "The medium's chair levitated a few times, but not with so much force that it could not be held down with one hand…damage or a scratch from the medium's chair in the corner indicates that the chair has levitated at least 35 centimeters."

On January 18, 1909, Neilsson was present when Indridason experienced a levitation during a séance in a darkened room. Writes Neilsson, "This time I and two others remained alone by the medium…in a kind of semi-trance, he said, 'Where are you taking me?' A little later we three heard his voice coming from close to the ceiling….Next all three of us clearly heard the medium being drawn along the ceiling of the room and made to knock his fingers on it. After a while, he was taken down and we were asked for light. He was lying prostate on the table, still being in trance."

During another séance, Thorlaksson asked if the spirits were able to levitate him personally. Writes Thorlaksson, "Immediately—just as I finished the last word—I felt as if something covered me completely but did not grasp me in any particular part of my body. At the same moment I crashed down on the floor on my hands and feet. This happened at such lightning in speed that I had no time to realize the route. I had no awareness until I fell down on the floor."

Dr. Loftur Gissurarson and Dr. Erlendur Harldsson of Reykjavik later studied Indridason's case in minute detail. Concerning his levitations, they write, "Levitation of a human body has sometimes been observed at séances of various celebrated mediums, but such reports have often been hotly debated. The levitations of Eusapia Palladino are among the best-observed cases, and the historic levitations of D. D. Home have been frequently quoted and referred to in the literature of psychical research. Some of the most astounding cases of levitation of which there are any records, however, are probably those of St. Joseph of Copertino…Indridason's levitations must be considered an important addition to these reports."[316]

19. The Levitation
Experiments of Baron Schrenk-Notzing

Baron Schrenk-Notzing. A German nobleman and a leading paranormal researcher, he conducted a highly influential series of strictly controlled levitation experiments with the young mediums Willy and Rudy Scheider. (*Mysteres*)

A sensational 1920s case comes from psychical researcher Baron Albert von Schrenck-Notzing (1862-1929). Schrenk-Notzing was a German aristocrat and prominent physician. He used his considerable wealth to undertake a series of well-controlled scientific experiments with the leading physical mediums of his day, including Eusapia Palladino, Eva C., and two young Austrian brothers, Willy and Rudy Schneider.

Schrenk-Notzing's rigidly controlled experiments with Willy Schneider, in particular, created a shockwave among local scientists. Prominent among these were Professor Holub, Professor Berse, Dr. Geley, and the well-known writer, Hans Muller, all of who conceded that Schrenk-Notzing's experiments with Schneider had proven that levitation is a fact.

Schrenk-Notzing's scientific approach to the subject was only part of what made his experiments so popular. The other reason was because his experiments actually worked! Time after time, under carefully controlled laboratory conditions, Schrenk-Notzing and his associates were able to provoke levitations in the teen-age medium.

Sudre, who spoke with one of the witnesses to the experiments, writes, "[Schneider] rose horizontally and seemed to rest on an invisible cloud. He ascended to the ceiling and remained five minutes suspended there, moving his legs about rhythmically. The descent was as sudden as the uplifting. The supervision had been perfect. Geley in his last journey to Vienna also witnessed a levitation of Willy at Dr. Holub's and he told me he felt absolutely sure of the genuineness of the phenomenon."

Because the levitations only took place in red light or near-total darkness, Schrenk-Notzing ingeniously stitched Schneider's clothes with phosphorescent pins, thereby allowing the witnesses to carefully observe Schneider's movements.

By 1927, Baron Schrenck-Notzing recorded no less than twenty-seven separate levitations of Willy Schneider in front of numerous reputable witnesses.

Writes Fodor, "The conditions of these experiments were very strict and the records unimpeachable. An electrical system of control made the phenomenon fraud-proof. The best evidence of this is the statements of a hundred profoundly skeptical, often hostile scientists who witnessed the phenomenon in 1922 and declared themselves completely convinced."

Here Schrenck-Notzing describes the processes involved in the levitations. "Willy gradually entered into an auto-hypnosis, accompanied by a very rapid contraction of the body, as if the subject was suddenly frightened. Often the passage to this state of somnambulism was so rapid that Willy didn't have time to finish the sentence he began. Sometimes when the medium wakes up, he continues the sentence and the conversation he began when he was awake. One has the impression that a strange and irresistible force takes control of the young man. The bodily state changes all of a sudden. The muscles which before were in a state of normal tension become hypertonic and rigid, producing clonic jerks in the arms, [and] the spasms' amplitude increases regularly before the appearance of the phenomenon....His body was entirely agitated, run through with cramps. Often the medium jumped from his chair and groaned like a man who wanted to lift a heavy weight."

Schneider's levitations began vertical. Once a height of about five feet was reached, Schneider's body would suddenly swing to a horizontal position and move back and forth about ten feet. The duration of the levitations was about thirty seconds.

One detail also noted was that during the levitations, Schneider maintained a penile erection. Interestingly, he lost his ability to levitate after going through puberty. His younger brother, Rudy, also showed similar abilities, though in a less spectacular fashion. Another curious detail was that the levitations were most successful when the group of sitters numbered about ten people and was evenly divided between men and women.

Baron Schrenk-Notzing continued to conduct his influential experiments until his death at age sixty-seven.[317]

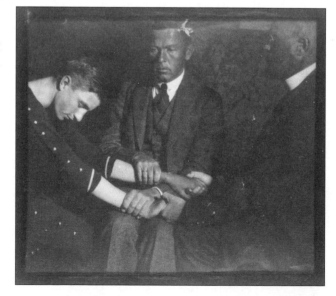

Willy Schneider (at left). When hypnotized into a trance state, Schneider was able to levitate on numerous occasions. (Mary Evans Picture Library)

20. Traveling Levitation

Writes medieval religious scholar, Augustin Calmet, "...Certain persons have what they call 'the garter', and by that means are able to perform with extraordinary quickness in a very few hours, what would naturally take them several days journeying. Almost incredible things are related on that subject, but the details are so circumstantial, that it is hardly possible there should not be some foundation for them."[318]

Writes Rampa, "Certain lamas, before the Communist invasion of Tibet, were able to cover long distances at fantastic speed. This is because they were able to do a minor form of levitation so that, their weight becoming appreciably less, they could leap perhaps fifty feet at one go. Thus, they progressed in fifty or a hundred-foot strides."[319]

Michael Harner, professor of Anthropology, expert on shamanism, and himself a practicing shaman, writes that Australian Aborigines and Tibetan Lamas both know the art of "fast traveling," which is achieved in a certain state of consciousness and is used for covering long distances in a very short period of time.[320]

Michael Murphy writes of Native American cases, "Ceremonial runs among the Papago and Pima on the Gulf of California have sometimes lasted for eight hours....These forty-mile runs of the Pima, however, are exceeded by the Tarahumara Indians of Mexico." The Tarahumaras were able to run non-stop for a period exceeding two days and two nights. Photographer Karl Kernberger observed the runs and said, "They didn't seem to be pushing themselves or crossing any pain threshold."[321]

Many firsthand cases have been recorded involving this unique type of levitation. An interesting mid-1800s account comes from anthropologist Thomas Buckley. Several early American explorers reported that Native American scouts were able to travel incredibly long distances through a method that came to be known as "Indian Running." This was a special technique that allowed the users to cover extremely long distances in short periods of times without becoming tired.

According to Buckley, he discovered that the Yurok Indians of northern California were practicing this form of levitation to traverse over the Siskiyou Mountains. Buckley observed them perform a kind of "effortless gliding" over the tops of Manzanita bushes. Their secret, they said, was to contact "unseen forces." They would then talk and sing to the trail, making it their ally, imagining the earth pushing against their feet helping them along. Using special breathing techniques and body motions, the runners were able to propel themselves along an invisible energetic rope.[322]

As can be seen, levitation appears in many countries and takes many forms. Traveling or running levitation has been reported in all kinds of cultures, starting from early history and continuing to the present day.

One of the earliest cases occurred in 1519. The famous scientist, Dr. Torrabla claimed that he traveled from Rome to Spain through the atmosphere "as fast as a horse beaten with a stick." Six years later, in 1525, he made a similar claim, telling the residents of Vallodolid, in the heart of Rome, that he had traveled through the air in order to render them assistance.[323]

In 1592, a Dominican Nun from Italy, St Mary Magdalen Dei Pazzi (d1607), a Carmelite Nun, was often seen using her gift of traveling levitation to navigate her way up and down the stairs of her convent.

Siennese nun Passitea Crogi (d1615) was often seen by her fellow nuns to "glide" from place to place without moving her legs. On occasion, these "flights" involved long distances. She also experienced ecstatic and luminous levitations.

Dominican nun Marie Paret (1636-1674) was often seen by her sisters to float down the staircase of her convent.

St. Bosco (1815-1888) was reported to levitate on several occasions. He also apparently had the ability of running levitation, as even into his old age, he was able to run faster than anybody else around.

Jean Edouard Lamy (1853-1931) was a French parish priest who experienced a wide variety of paranormal phenomenon. He often fell into raptures during which his body would sometimes become luminous. He also experienced traveling levitations, of which he left a rare firsthand description. "I have been...brought from one place to another without knowing anything about it. I used to say 'My God, how tired I am.' I was in my parish far away, often at night, and I found myself carried to the Place St. Lucian all at once....How it happened I don't know."

Witnesses also observed Father Lamy exhibit supernatural agility. At age seventy, he was seen to race briskly up to the top of a steep muddy hill to pray, and then speed back down. Reportedly the hill was too steep and slippery for the others to climb.[324]

Eric Dingwall was a leading paranormal researcher in the mid-1800s. He writes of the remarkable physical medium, Mrs. French, whose "controlling spirit" was allegedly none other than Benjamin Franklin. Mrs. French was well known for producing a wide variety of physical phenomena, including table lifting, spirit knockings, spirit paintings, and more. According to Dingwall, "On one occasion, it was said that she was transported, gliding just above the ground, from Brooklyn to New York."[325]

Another interesting Native American account was uncovered by anthropologist, Ruth Landes, who specialized in studies of the Ojibwa, an Alongonquin tribe in Western Ontario. She learned of an unusual woman in the tribe named Part-Sky-Woman who lived in the second half of the 1800s.

According to the tribe, Part-Sky-Woman won first place for nine straight years in the summer holiday games at Fort Frances, Ontario. When asked what her secret was, Part-Sky-Woman replied that after meditating on the death of her father, she was visited by a "cloud" spirit which gave her the ability of levitation. Whenever she wanted to run fast, all she had to do was call out to her guardian cloud spirit and "she felt her body light as a feather....as if she were running on air."[326]

David du Plesses (1905-1987) was a South African minister whom *Time* magazine called "one of the most prominent Christian leaders in the world." One day Du Plessis was conducting a counseling session when he heard a voice, the Lord, speak to him in his mind, telling him that he was needed immediately at a certain residence. He announced to all those present that he was needed elsewhere. He immediately left the location and started the mile-long walk to the house. Then something amazing happened. Writes Du Plessis in his auto-biography: "I went through the gate, and heard it click behind me. I turned left, the level way. And that's all I can remember. When I lifted my foot to run, I put it down and ended up at the man's house."

Du Plessis reports that he experienced a moment of disorientation and had a minor difficulty recalling where he had just come from. Recovering his bearings, he entered the house in time to resolve a pressing problem.

Unknown to du Plessis, however, his friends had tried to follow him. They heard the gate click and ran out after him, surprised to find him gone. Shouting his name and getting no response, they went directly to the location where they found du Plessis, who had already been there for twenty minutes! His friends expressed their astonishment, saying, "Impossible!"

Writes Du Plessis, "It was then that I realized I must have been transported by the Holy Spirit."[327]

Sister Mary of the Passion (Maria del Passione) was an Italian nun who died in 1912. In her life, she experienced stigmata wounds and other supernatural events. According to one of the nuns in Passion's order, "I was still a novice and on those last occasions when Suor Maria della Passione was able to come down to the choir to receive Holy Communion, the Reverend Mother Superior bade me take her back to her cell, because, as she was so ill, she had to return to bed almost immediately after Communion was given. Well, no sooner had we left the choir than I noticed that the servant of God, though she was in a most suffering state, mounted the stairs in an instant, as if she flew on wings, while I, who was in perfect health, could not keep pace with her, so much so that it seemed to me that she never touched the ground but that she really flew up the flight of stairs which led to her cell."[328]

An intriguing case of running levitation comes from anthropologist Carobeth Laird and is dated in the 1920s. In her studies of the Chemehuevis, a Paiute tribe in the Southern California desert, she learned that they had a select group of men labeled "swift runners." They were used as messengers because they were able to utilize supernatural means to cover long distances. Laird learned of a firsthand account concerning a man by the name of Kaawia, who still traveled "the old way."

According to Laird, several people who were friends of Kaawia were with him at Cottonwood Island in Nevada. Kaawia announced that he was going to a settlement at the entrance to the Gila River in southern Arizona. They said their good-byes and Kaawia ran off into the distance.

Knowing of Kaawia's ability of supernatural running, his friends decided to follow his trail. As the trail went over a dune, the tracks became less distinct. They then became increasingly further apart and shallower until fading out completely. When the witnesses finally reached the settlement many hours later, they asked about Kaawia. They learned that he had arrived only moments after leaving their group in Cottonwood Island, Nevada.[329]

In the early 1930s, Madame Alexandra David-Neel, a practicing Buddhist and explorer/author from France, spent twelve years traveling through Tibet in search of adventure. Her book, *Magic and Mystery in Tibet*, originally appearing in French, took the world by storm when she revealed that she was a firsthand witness to several astonishing paranormal events, including a dramatic display of running levitation. This case is probably the single most famous example of running levitation.

One day, as David-Neel traveled across a wide Tibetan desert area with her guide and servants, she observed a small black spot moving in the distance. She raised her binoculars and saw that it was a man moving towards them with "an unusual gait [and] extraordinary swiftness."

David-Neel paid careful attention to what happened next. As she later wrote, "...he had nearly reached us, I could clearly see his perfectly calm, impassive face and wide-open eyes with their gaze fixed on some invisible far-distant object situated somewhere high in space. The man did not run. He seemed to lift himself from the ground, proceeding by leaps. It looked as if he had been endowed with the elasticity of a ball and rebounded each time his feet touched the ground. His steps had the regularity of a pendulum."

The man ran on by, seemingly oblivious of their presence. David-Neel's guide explained to her that the man possessed the siddhe of *lung-gom* or "fleetness of foot" and told her that such people, after years of meditation, are able to "sit upon an ear of barley without bending its stalk or to stand on top of a heap of grain without displacing any of it. In fact the aim is levitation."

Later, on the same trip, David-Neel and her group came upon another man, totally nude, sitting alone in the forest wearing a heavy iron chain. As soon as the man saw their group, he quickly ran away. David-Neel's guide explained that the man also possessed the siddhe of *lung-gom*. He told her, "...as a result of long years of practice, after he has traveled over a certain distance, the feet of the lung-gom-pa no longer touch the ground and that he glides on the air with extremely celerity....They wear these chains to make themselves heavy, for through the practice of lung-gom, their bodies have become so light that they are always in danger of floating in the air."

Her guide further explained that to achieve the running levitation, the *long-gom-pa* had to maintain a deep trance while breathing rhythmically in cadence to a mental recitation of a mystic chant. No distractions were permitted. The levitator can neither speak nor look to either side, but must keep his gaze fixed on a single distant point.[330]

Even today, native cultures continue to practice this ancient mystical art. From 1970 to 1973, Dr. David Reed Barker, an anthropologist formerly at the

University of Virginia, lived in Nepal to study the Tibetan culture. While there, he observed lamas well-advanced in age climbing extremely steep slopes with incredible ease and swiftness that it appeared to be "paranormal" or "a form of levitation."[331]

As can be seen, traveling levitation is a worldwide phenomenon, appearing in a variety of cultures, starting in early history and continuing to the present day. It seems to be particularly prevalent among indigenous and so-called primitive cultures. In most cases, these cultures have developed similar procedural methods for achieving this state of consciousness.

21. Crisis Levitations

As we have seen, levitation is not an accidental event. A specific set of circumstances are almost always present. For example, in the majority of cases a trance state seems to be a prerequisite condition to achieve levitation. Again, however, for every rule there are exceptions. In this case, the exceptions are crisis levitations. Under this category, no trance-state is necessary and an accident is what provokes the event. Another major difference is that, normally, levitation serves no benefit to the levitator other than to move him from place to place, or to amaze anybody who may be lucky enough to witness the event. With crisis levitations, however, the event often serves to rescue the levitator from serious injury, or in some cases, actually save the levitator's life!

A crisis levitation is defined as a levitation event which occurs during a crisis (usually falls or illness), thereby rescuing the levitator. Like all categories of levitation, these cases stretch back centuries and continue to the present day.

One of the earliest known cases occurred in 1620. Author Moller wrote that two protestant ministers were attending to a young woman who lay ill in bed when she suddenly turned and leapt up from her bed, remained suspended in the air for a short time, and slowly floated back down.[332]

Crisis levitations are particularly interesting because of their intrinsic dramatic nature. Levitation is dramatic enough, but when you combine it with a crisis, the experience is not soon forgotten. In the following case, a woman became lost, but was rescued in a very unusual way. Margaret Hallahan (1802-1868) of London, England was orphaned at age ten and spent the next twenty-seven years working as a maid. At age forty, following a series of health problems, she recovered and devoted her life to helping the poor. She eventually founded numerous schools, orphanages, and a hospital. One snowy evening in 1843, Hallahan was returning home along a path. In the darkness, she accidentally lost her way and ended up in pond of mud and ice. She was unable to free herself and prayed for help. Suddenly, and in an instant, she found herself back on the path. Hallahan was convinced that she had been "supernaturally carried."[333]

It is not unusual for survivors of disasters to credit their survival to Divine Intervention. While some cases may be pure luck, others seem to involve a genuine "miraculous" event. Saint Anthony Claret (1807-1870) from Spain was a successful businessman who gave up his career to become a priest. Later he became a well-known spiritual leader, archbishop of Santiago de Cuba, Spain and confessor to Queen Isabella II. He reportedly exhibited the ability of healing and prophecy. Claret reports that his decision to join the priesthood was inspired by an incident of what appears to be a crisis levitation. Claret writes that after working hard for several months, his health was suffering. So he went to the ocean and walked along the coast to relax. Suddenly, a huge wave knocked him off his feet, and swept him out to sea. Writes Claret, "I saw in moment that I was far from shore, and I was amazed to see that I was floating on the surface, although I didn't know how to swim. I called out to the Blessed Virgin and found myself on shore without having swallowed even a drop of water. While I was in the water, I had felt exceedingly calm, but afterwards, on shore, I was horrified at the thought of the danger I had escaped through the help of the Blessed Virgin." Claret was canonized in 1950.[334]

We have already examined the case of Daniel Home, who himself experienced a crisis levitation that whisked him out of the way of a falling tree branch.

Madame Helene Petrova Blavatsky (1831-1891) achieved worldwide fame as a medium, psychic, mystic, and

Madame Helena Blavatsky. Probably most famous for founding *Theosophy;* as a teen-ager, Blavatsky experienced a crisis levitation which saved her life. (Mary Evans Picture Library)

the founder of Theosophy. Throughout her controversial career she experienced numerous paranormal events, including one possible crisis levitation, which she believed saved her life. Sometime in the mid-1840s, Blavatsky went horseback riding near her home in Russia. The horse suddenly jolted, causing Blavatsky to lose her balance. She fell from the saddle and her foot became caught in the stirrup. According to Blavatsky, her horse was traveling so quickly that she should have been killed instantly. Instead, something incredible happened. She distinctly felt a "strange sustaining power" which miraculously held her up "in defiance of gravitation," thereby saving her life. She later wrote extensively about the mechanics of the phenomenon of levitation.[335]

Saint Frances Cabrini of Italy (1850-1917) was born into poverty, and devoted her life to the service of humanity. She traveled the world founding schools, hospitals, and orphanages. She is credited with numerous miracles, including putting out a fire at an orphanage by making the sign of the cross with her hand. As a child, Cabrini was playing by the banks of the Venera River when she accidentally fell into the swift-moving current. Unable to swim, Cabrini was sure she was about to drown. Instead, she felt invisible arms grasp her firmly out of the water and deposit her gently several feet from the side of the river. Cabrini believed she was levitated through "supernatural" means.[336]

In 1898, the ship "Bourgogne" sank in the Atlantic, taking with it many lives. One of the survivors was an anonymous nun who, when asked about the last moments of passenger Joseph Baumann, reported that she saw him praying with two other Dominicans, his body glowing and elevated above the decks. Unfortunately, Baumann was never seen again.[337]

One of the earliest 1900 crisis levitation accounts comes from an anonymous woman who was interviewed by Hugo Muensteberg for his book, *Psychotherapy*. The event occurred following a visit from a faith healer to cure an illness (not described). After the healer departed, the patient lay in bed when she was suddenly overcome by a strange feeling. As the woman reported, "I suddenly had a sensation of being lifted up or rising slowly and becoming lighter in body. A rush of power that I have no way of describing to you filled me. I seemed to be a tremendous dynamo in the air several inches above the ground and still ascending, when I noticed everything around me becoming prismatic and more or less translucent. I could have walked on water without sinking. Matter seemed to be disintegrating and dissolving around me. I remained in this state for about three hours, my consciousness seeming to have reached almost cosmic greatness.... At the end of the day, towards twilight, the condition left me, and like the sudden dropping of a weight, I struck the ground, the same dull, ordinary person of ordinary experience."

The only other change noted by the lady was that her illness had completely disappeared.[338]

In 1937, housewife Blanche F. Swisher of Iowa City, Iowa decided to go comfort her sick friend and neighbor, Dolly. She grabbed her coat and made the short trip to her friend's home. As she was walking to the doorway, Swisher had an experience she'd never forget. Little did she know, she was about to experience a crisis levitation that would save her from serious injury. As she wrote in a letter to *Fate* magazine, "...I hurried up the cement steps. Suddenly I stumbled and started to fall—right on my face and glasses. In mid-air, however, I was stopped. It seemed incredible as I was stopped with my body in a slanting position, much as the motion of a horse in a race is stopped in the movies. I was lowered gently until my hands touched the cement step. Extremely puzzled, I stood up, continued up the steps and burst in on Dolly."

Both were amazed by the occurrence. Swisher speculated that maybe she had just been saved from a terrible fall by her guardian angel. Both she and Dolly were amazed again when Swisher revealed why she had actually come over to Dolly's house. She had wanted to read to Dolly the 91st Psalm, which says: "He shall give his angels charge over thee, to keep thee in all thy ways; they shall bear thee up in their hands, lest thou dash thy foot against a stone."

An amazing coincidence, thought Swisher. But the experience was so unusual that she began to doubt herself. As she says, "I pondered over the incident for days, until I'd just about talked myself out of believing what had happened."

As if in response to her doubts, a few days later, Swisher had a repeat performance. As she says, "...I was hurrying down a flight of stairs that had just been waxed. My heel slipped and I fell backward, expecting, in a flash of fear, to hit the back of my neck or head in a terrific blow. Instead I was lifted as if on wings, turned and gently eased down, landing on my knees. I stood up, feeling ashamed of my doubts, saying, 'Thank you, I shall never doubt again!'"

Not surprisingly, Swisher reports that the 91st Psalm is now her favorite. She has had no other levitation episodes before or since.[339]

A poignant case of crisis levitation took place during World War II in a German concentration camp to a man by the name of Israel Spira, a Hasidic Rabbi. During the holocaust, Rabbi Spira along with millions of other people, was captured by the Nazis and put into a concentration camp. Spira survived forced labor, malnutrition, "selections," disease, and other cruel tortures. On one occasion, Rabbi Spira and other prisoners were woken up in the middle of the night, put into a long single file line, and ordered to jump across a large pit. Those who failed to cross the distance to the other side fell into the pit and were executed by machine-gun. While the very strong and young were able to cross the distance, many were not. As Spira approached, his friend next to him in line said, "Spira, all of our efforts to jump over the pits are in vain. We only entertain the Germans...Let's sit down in the pits and wait for the bullets to end our miserable existence."

Rabbi Spira turned to his friend and told him that they must obey the will of God, and pointed out that the worst that could happen was they would enter the "world of truth."

According to the account, as told in *Hasidic Tales of the Holocaust,* "The rabbi and his friend were nearing the edge of the pits...filling up with bodies. The rabbi glanced down at his feet, the swollen feet of a fifty-three year old Jew ridden with starvation and disease. He looked at his friend, a skeleton with burning eyes.

"As they reached the pit, the rabbi closed his eyes and commanded in a powerful whisper, 'We are jumping!' When they opened their eyes, they found themselves standing on the other side of the pit."

Spira's friend expressed his surprise and asked him how he was able to cross the distance. Spira replied, "I was holding onto my ancestral merit. I was holding onto the coattails of my father, and my grandfather, and my great-father of blessed memory...tell me my friend, how did you reach the other side of the pit?"

His friend replied, "I was holding on to you."

Rabbi Israel Spira survived the Nazi concentration camps and moved to Brooklyn, New York where he lived into his late nineties.[340]

In the 1950s, housewife Martha Sherman was hiking near her rural Arkansas home on a trail that bordered a thirty-five foot cliff. Suddenly she slipped and her body hurtled over the edge of the cliff. Expecting to be killed, she was shocked instead to find herself suddenly floating. It is a perfect example of a crisis levitation. As she wrote in a letter to *Fate* magazine, "In one terrifying moment, I visualized myself lying badly injured at the bottom of those precipitous falls, helpless, until some hours later when I might be missed and discovered. But miraculously, this did not happen. Instead, I felt myself caught in mid-air, spun gently around and deposited as lightly as a feather on the very same rock from which I had just started."

Sherman was stunned and it took her a few moments to understand what had happened to her. She had been somehow levitated and it had saved her life. The realization that she had levitated instantly sparked the memory of an event that had occurred years earlier in her childhood.

When she was a little girl, Sherman remembers actually flying. As she says, "Memories came flooding back to me of long ago when, as a schoolgirl on my way back to class, I had felt myself lifted softly into the air (in much the same way) and set down gently some twenty feet farther on the sidewalk for no apparent reason. I briefly thought that perhaps it had been to show me that such things were possible, but I decided that it had been a figment of my imagination and said nothing about it."[341]

Levitation can come in many forms. A unique case of a crisis levitation comes from none other than Long John Nebel, the famous radio personality. Throughout the 1960s, his hugely popular late night radio program was a magnet for the weird and unusual. One evening, he received a call from a gentleman who had a very strange story to tell.

The gentleman explained that he had been in an auto accident three years earlier, and his right leg was amputated above the knee. Shortly after the accident, however, he discovered that not only could he still feel his "phantom limb," he could *use* it. He told Nebel, "I can now materialize a psychic right leg and walk without the aid of my crutches!"

Nebel was incredulous, but having heard many unbelievable but true accounts, he asked the man to visit his New Jersey station and prove it. This usually weeded out the hoaxers, so Nebel was surprised when the man showed up the next night. Writes Nebel, "He was a well-dressed man in his mid-forties. The bottom half of his right trouser leg was neatly folded back and pinned. There was nothing below his knee….As soon as we hit the air I asked him to repeat his story of the previous night. The story hadn't changed. He insisted there were times when, by summoning his psychic powers, he could produce a leg and actually walk with this invisible limb."

Nebel had a few more questions and asked for a demonstration. Then came the caveat. Nebel was not surprised when the gentleman said that he had little control over the force, and didn't know when it would happen. Disappointed and suspecting a hoax, Nebel turned to his microphone and continued the show with other topics. Meanwhile, the gentleman remained in the studio, attempting to materialize his "psychic leg."

Writes Nebel, "About fifteen minutes later my engineer, who sat facing me behind the window in his control booth, began waving his arm furiously. I didn't know what in the world he was doing as he continued gesticulating frantically, a look of stunned amazement across his face….Then I saw. First, out of the corner of my eye, then right in front of me. This man, the man whose right leg had been removed years ago, was walking toward the door. He was not using crutches. His trouser leg was still pinned up. He walked as if he had two legs but there was only one. He didn't falter as he headed toward the door. He maintained a strong, purposeful stride. I kept on talking into the microphone. I had to. All I remember seeing is the one-legged man reach the door, open it, wave good-bye to me and disappear into the night.…It takes a lot to jar me, but what I saw literally sent a shock wave running through every inch of my body."

Nebel looked down in amazement at the man's crutches lying on the floor. He motioned his engineer to follow the man outside to see what had happened. The engineer ran outside and watched as the man walked to his car, got in, and started blowing the horn. The engineer approached. The man apologized and asked for his crutches, saying that his psychic leg had dematerialized. The engineer retrieved the crutches and the unidentified man drove away.

Nebel was left stunned. "We had both seen it. We compared notes. All we could do was shake our heads in amazement. I had no explanation then. I haven't any now. If it was some sort of put-on, it was the best I've ever come across. As far as I'm concerned, I did see a one-legged man walk across that studio floor without any visible means of support. If there is any 'normal,' logical or scientific explanation for what transpired that night, I'd like to know it."[342]

An astonishing 1970s case of crisis levitation comes from businessman Robert Monroe of Virginia. Monroe is best known for his research and books about out-of-body experiences. Like many advanced astral-travelers, Monroe has also experienced levitation. As he writes, "In our house at Whistlefield Farm, there was a screened in porch off the living room. To get to the porch, one had to go through two double doors and down a series of flagstone steps that led to the porch at a lower level. These steps were quite steep, the difference in floor height being approximately four feet.…One morning, with my arms full of books and papers, I walked out the entrance to the porch and stumbled. My left foot crossed over in front of my right, and I dove headlong in the direction of the flagstone floor of the porch. As I fell I was unable to get my arms out in front of me. I remember thinking, 'Well, this will certainly end up with a fractured skull or a broken neck.'

"About six inches from the floor, my fall was suddenly arrested and I landed on my head and shoulders very lightly on the flagstone floor, no heavier than if I had simply put my head down very carefully. The rest of my body then draped down afterward, drifting as gently as a feather. I lay there for a moment wondering what had happened. I felt my head and my shoulders and there was no pain, no mark, no bruise, nothing. I stood up, picked up my books and papers, looked at the place from where I had fallen, and tried to figure some answer. Something had cushioned my fall, but I certainly was not consciously aware of what it was."

Monroe was unable to account for the levitation, but he was absolutely convinced it was unusual. His feelings were confirmed when it happened again. Says Monroe, "Some months later in the middle of winter, a similar event took place. I was walking down the front steps, which had been reportedly cleaned after a snow, slipped and started to fall. This time I was not quite so surprised when I again landed very lightly."

Monroe then knew that he hadn't imagined the levitation. Whatever the cause of the experience, he knew it was real. And yet, he was reluctant to experiment. As he says, "There have been only two such events, and I don't think I will deliberately try to fall experimentally. Just another one of those 'as yet' unexplained moments."[343]

An equally amazing case of a crisis levitation was presented in the television program, *Miracles and Mysteries*. Sometime in the 1970s, a young couple went hiking along the coastal cliffs in northern California. It was late afternoon when they finally scaled to the top of a loose sandstone and shale cliff. They then started climbing down. But because of the darkness, they took the wrong route and ended up stuck on the cliff-face, which was rapidly crumbling beneath them. Suddenly, the man slipped and fell nearly one hundred feet to his death. The woman

Robert Monroe was a businessman and electronics engineer who wrote three books about his out-of-body experiences. On two occasions, Monroe experienced dramatic levitations. (The Monroe Institute)

began to scream in terror as she felt herself slipping and falling. Then suddenly, she felt a strong force press her up against the cliff face and slowly lower her down. She is absolutely adamant that somebody invisible carried her down the cliff. Once she reached the base of her cliff, she saw an amazing sight. The lifeless body of her boyfriend lay on the ground surrounded by several glowing figures. The girlfriend saw that one of the figures was the spirit of her boyfriend. The others appeared to be angels. They gave her a long loving look. Her boyfriend waved goodbye and they all disappeared.[344]

In 1975, Sister Dolores Cazares of southern California was vacationing in France when she experienced a crisis levitation that saved her life. She was crossing the street when a motorcycle appeared and was about to run her over. Cazares insists that she was about to be crushed when suddenly, in mid-stride, she found herself on the opposite side of the street. The motorcyclist sped away. Cazares was convinced that the Lord had lifted her out of the path of the oncoming vehicle. She received further validation of her supernatural rescue immediately after the event. According to Cazares, two men standing nearby had seen the whole incident. Afterwards, they followed her and continued to stare intently at her for the next several blocks, obviously amazed by what they had observed.[345]

In 1984, author and mental health advocate Chris Costner Sizemore had a remarkable experience with a crisis levitation. As she writes in her autobiography, "Nothing seemed to herald that the day would be anything other than ordinary. I had been alone at our Herndon home and had worked vigorously, cleaning the house. By late afternoon, I decided to take a shower before Dan got home from work. So I went to the upstairs bath, undressed, and adjusted the faucet controls to produce a steady hot flow of water. But as I stepped into the shower stall, my foot rested on some soap residue and I slipped. I could feel my feet sliding out from under me. Fearing the fall, I panicked. Just as suddenly, however, I was startled when I felt my body being jerked back into a standing position by what seemed to be a pair of strong hands that lifted me along both sides of my rib cage. Despite an immediate sense of relief as having been spared of possible injury, I was terrified. Who had done this? None of my family was home and the house was locked tight. Had some stranger entered the bathroom? I slowly turned to see. But no one was there."

The next morning, Sizemore found physical evidence of the event. As she says, "I discovered blue bruises, like handprints, on both sides of my ribcage. Again I was frightened, and at first, I was determined to tell no one."

Sizemore, however, couldn't get the incident out of her mind and finally decided to write to well-known parapsychologist, Stanley Krippner, Ph..D., to whom she related her experience. Krippner wrote back, "Of course I found your experience in the shower interesting [though it] is not all that unusual....I feel that some people reach such a high degree of personal and transpersonal [development] that they are able to pull upon inner/outer resources in times of great emergency. Whether these resources are 'spirits' or elements of our own subconscious is debatable."

It should be noted that Sizemore has experienced a number of paranormal incidents and for many years suffered from Multiple Personality Disorder (now called Dissociative Identity Disorder) due to severe trauma in her childhood. At the time of her incident, she was already cured.[346]

An incredibly similar modern case (exact date not given) occurred to an anonymous woman from the United States. In a letter to researchers Bill and Judy Guggenheim, she related that one day she was out walking when she tripped. She knew that she was about to fall and hurt herself when she felt a strong pair of hands grab her from behind and lift her back up. She believed it was the spirit of her husband who saved her from a terrible fall. The next day, she discovered dark bruises on her arms, exactly where she had felt herself grabbed and pulled to safety.[347]

A typical case of a crisis levitation occurred in July, 1986, to sixteen-year-old Heather Bonser of Laurel, Montana. The incident occurred while she was vacationing in Holland. She was hiking with a large group along a narrow mountain trail when she started to lag behind. She realized she was alone. Then it started raining. Says Bonser, "Footing was slippery and it was slow going. I finally reached the goat trail on top. I was tired and breathing heavily. I could barely see through my rain-spattered, befogged glasses. I stepped forward and paused. Something was wrong. My right foot was in mid-air when it should have been on the ground. I took off my glasses to see more clearly and looked down the side of the mountain into a pile of black rock far, far below. I felt my body stiffen with fear and a scream began to form in the back of my throat. I was half-over the cliff, balancing in the air. In that moment I knew I was going to fall. A strange unearthly feeling came over me and I instinctively closed my eyes. The next thing I remember was someone shaking me. I opened my eyes—it was the 'caboose' guide asking me why I was screaming. I looked around and realized I was standing in the middle of the goat trail, several feet from the edge where I had been perched only moments before. I couldn't believe it! I began to cry as a flurry of emotions came over me."

Bonser is totally convinced that something saved her life. "Although I cannot explain it logically, something moved me those few feet away from certain death."[348]

Crisis levitations are among the most dramatic of all levitations. Why some people experience them and others do not remains a mystery. Nor is it clear if the levitations are generated by an internal mechanism of the human body or by external forces. In any case, crisis levitations are the most helpful of all forms of the phenomenon, showing again that the human organism has access to incredible powers that we have only begun to explore.

22. Sleeping Levitations

Many people talk in their sleep. A lesser number of people are sleep-walkers, with some of these people performing a wide variety of activities. However, only a few extremely rare cases exist of people who are "sleep-levitators." And yet, it has happened often enough to earn its own category.

One early case occurred in the mid-1800s to Jansenist, Mademoiselle Thevenet of France. She had already experienced several levitations; however, on some occasions, she would levitate in her sleep. Writes La Taste, "From time to time, when she was sleeping, her head and her feet would raise up together several feet in height."[349]

A rare account of sleeping levitation occurred in 1909 to a Mr. Slade. According to Slade's roommate, Dr. Kettredge, he personally witnessed Slade levitate from one bed to another while sound asleep. Incidentally, Slade was able to affect the direction of a compass needle by passing his hand over it.[350]

A modern account of sleeping levitation occurred in the mid 1980s in Alvarado, Texas. A group of young ladies were attending a class in self-awareness. One evening, one of the students, Dana X., spontaneously levitated while in her sleep. A witness to the event approached the teacher of the center, Helen Hadsell, who had, by coincidence, experienced levitation firsthand. The student asked Hadsell, "Do you know what I saw—or thought I saw—last night? Dana was floating in mid-air about a foot above her cot. My cot is beside hers. I got so scared I couldn't move. I didn't know what to do. I was afraid she might fall and hurt herself. Everyone else was asleep, so I just sat on my cot and watched. In about half an hour, she floated back down to her cot and turned over. She never did wake up."

As the student confessed to the teacher, Dana and another student walked in and the other student told Dana that she had become frightened when she, too, saw Dana floating in her sleep; and wasn't she scared of falling?

Dana blushed and revealed with embarrassment that both she and her mother had a problem with levitating in their sleep. On several occasions, Dana had seen her mother levitating. Sometimes while she was napping on the couch, she explained, her mother's body would rise several inches in the air.

Shortly following the birth of a child, Dana's mother experienced another dramatic levitation. Dana observed her mother floating along the ceiling. She ran to her father in terror. The entire family ran into the room and the father reached up and pulled Dana's mother down to the bed. The father calmed the children down and asked them to pray for their mother so that "the Devil cannot take her away."

Says Dana, "Grandmother was already on her knees, kissing the rosary she always carried in her pocket....Grandmother and Dad told us never to tell anyone. 'People just won't understand,' they insisted. We never did and I have never told this to anyone before now."

Dana clearly remembers the first time she levitated—in this case a crisis levitation. She was eight years old and had the chicken pox. She was running a fever and wasn't aware of what was happening. However, as she says, "Several days later my mother told me that I floated like she did, but not to worry. The angels would take care of me because I was a good girl and the Devil could not get me. She assured me that I was the only one of her children that the Devil was trying to get because I was so much like her."

The teacher told Dana that, in her opinion, the ability to levitate was "a gift of the spirit" and that "I am absolutely sure of one thing: the Devil is not out to get you if you have this gift."

Following the experience at the center, Dana reports that to her knowledge she has experienced no other episodes for several years.[351]

In 1992, Doretta Johnson of Indiana experienced a dramatic levitation. At the time, she and her family were in the midst of a severe poltergeist haunting in their home. However, one evening, she woke up from a deep sleep to find herself levitating.

"About one o'clock, I was awakened from a deep, heavy sleep. My entire body was tingling in a pleasant sort of way. Then I realized I was almost paralyzed. I couldn't move my hands or legs, not even my lips. I tried to say 'Ron' but couldn't form the word with my mouth. The next thing I was aware of was more frightening. I was not touching the mattress, but hovering above it, floating slowly away from it. In panic, I closed my eyes and tried to will my lips to speak. At last, the word 'Ron' came out and I fell back onto the mattress as though I had been dropped. 'It's just your powers,' my husband said. 'You were levitating.'"

Throughout her life, Johnson has exhibited numerous other psychic abilities, including precognition, and, as reported with some Saints and mediums, on one occasion, she emitted light from her body, a phenomenon observed by numerous witnesses. Her case was studied by a wide variety of investigators including demonologists, ghost-hunters, psychics, and scientists. One parapsychologist, William Roll decided to test Johnson's GSR (Galvanic Skin Response.) A normal person has a GSR of forty. While in meditation, Johnson's GSR measured an unbelievable zero. Roll remarked that this meant that there was no electromagnetic resistance. Could it be that Johnson's ability to levitate is because she is a good conductor of whatever energy causes the phenomenon?[352]

A 1996 account comes from an anonymous teenage boy from Los Angeles, southern California, who revealed that he had woken up on at least three occasions to find himself hovering about two or three feet above his bed. Each time, as soon as he woke up and realized he was levitating, he fell quickly back into bed. He declined to be formally interviewed and prefers not to think about his experiences.[353]

Sleeping levitation, although rare, may provide an important clue to the mechanisms behind the phenomenon. These cases confirm again that levitation is somehow connected to the trance state—as sleep itself is the ultimate trance state.

23. Walking on Water

While walking on water is not levitating in the air, it seems to involve the same phenomenon. The first reported case of someone walking on water is none other than Jesus and his disciple, Peter. It was on the Sea of Galilee. As it says in the *Gospels* of the Bible, "Jesus constrained his disciples to get into a ship…the ship was now in the midst of the sea….Jesus went onto them, walking on the sea. And when the disciples saw him walking on the sea, they were troubled…And Peter said, Lord, if it be thou, bid me come unto thee on the water. And he said, Come. And when Peter was come down out of the ship, he walked on the water, to go to Jesus."

At this point, Jesus then calmed the storm and pulled Peter, who was sinking, back into the boat.

While Jesus was the first to walk on water, he certainly wasn't the last. In the fourth century, St. Bessarion reportedly walked across many rivers, including the Nile, the Takazze River, and the River Chrysoroas. In the early 1500s, St. Peter of Alcantara was observed to walk across the Guadiana River in Spain. In the 1800s, Dengnabine, an Azande Medicine man from Africa, walked on water after being bound by stones. The late 1800s case of Mademoiselle Hauffe of France, as investigated by Dr. Kerner, also involved unexplained floating. St Basil (18??) and St. Zachary of Russia (d1936) were both reportedly seen by witnesses to "walk on water"—an ability exhibited by many other saints.

Jesus Christ is the first recorded case of walking on water. (Kesara)

Leroy lists more than a dozen such cases of water-walkers. Though he provides no details, Leroy's list includes Bernardin of Sienne, Bertin, Birin, Bogomile, Francois de Paule, Jean Capistran, Jean the Hermit, Jutta, Marie D'Oignies, Mathieu de Bascio, Nazaire, Pierre Regalati, Raymond de Pennafort, Sebald, and others.

The ability to walk on water is obviously connected to levitation. And while such accounts might seem to be limited to antiquity, the truth is that like other cases of levitation, they start in ancient history and continue to the present day.

After Jesus, there is the case of St. Ammon (d350), a well-known Egyptian hermit. He lived the first half of his life quietly with his wife, spending the day in manual labor and the night in prayer. He later left his wife and retired into the desert, eating only bread and water, and spending all his time in prayer. As written in the *Acta Sanctorum,* St. Ammon became known for producing miracles, one of which involved walking on water.

St. Ammon was with his disciple, Theodore, when they had to cross an overflowing river. They withdrew from each other to undress. St. Ammon, however, was too shy to undress and suddenly found himself transported over the river. When Theodore saw that his friend had gotten across without getting wet, he begged St. Ammon to reveal what happened. Ammon reluctantly said that it had been "a miracle" and not to tell anyone until after his death.[354]

The following case from the sixth century could also be classified as a crisis levitation, but it fits just as well in this section. St. Benedict lived in Subiaco, Italy, where he cared for several of the children of various noble families. One day, St. Benedict had a vision that one of the children, named Placid, had fallen into the lake and was drowning. He shouted to his friend, Maurus, to rescue the boy. Maurus without thinking, "ran to the lake and walked on the water, a bow-shot from the bank, to the place where Placid had been struggling, and, taking hold of him by the hair, returned with the same speed. When he got to the shore and looked behind him he saw that he had walked upon the water, which he had not noticed till then." As a result, Placid himself became very religious and was later canonized as a saint.[355]

Blessed Alvarez of Cordova, Italy (d1430) founded several chapels in his area. He practiced severe penances and spent much of his time in prayer. One night, he was returning to his monastery when a violent storm struck. Alvarez's path was blocked by a brook that had been transformed into a swollen torrent. Alvarez knelt down and spent a few moments in prayer, then removed his cloak, spread it on the surface of the water and used it to walk safely across the river. He then put his cloak back on, which was miraculously dry, and returned to his monastery in time to take his place in the choir.[356]

Another early account is that of St. Seraphino (1540-1604). As a child, he worked as a shepherd. He was then orphaned and cared for by his elder brother, who treated him very badly. Seraphino ran away at age sixteen and joined the Capuchins, working as a bricklayer. He eventually became a very popular preacher. His gifts of healing and reading the future attracted wide crowds, including civil and ecclesiastical dignitaries.

Two miracles are ascribed to him, one involving walking on water. He was on a pilgrimage to Loreto, but the river Potenza was impassable due to floods. Seraphino, however, was able to traverse the river by walking on the surface of the water, and reached the other side completely dry.[357]

St. Gerard Majella (1726-1755) experienced numerous levitations and other supernatural experiences in his life, including at least one incident involving walking on water. Gerard was at the bay of Naples when a storm threatened to sink a small ship. A huge crowd had gathered on the beach, and they pleaded to him for help. Gerard made the sign of the cross then and stepped out onto the water, saying out loud, "In the name of the Most Holy Trinity, pause!" Then he either commanded the ship to "come here" or actually laid hold of it and drew it after him safely towards the shore. The crowd became maniacally enthusiastic and mobbed Gerard, who quickly fled to Naples and hid himself in a friend's home until the furor died down. Afterwards, Father Margotta asked him how he was able to perform such an amazing miracle. Gerard replied, "O Father, when God wills, everything is possible." Later, Father Cajone asked him the same question. Gerard elaborated, "I caught it [the ship] with two fingers, and drew it to shore. In the state in which I then was in, I could have flown in the air."[358]

A more modern case occurred on July 18, 1837, to Nikolai Yurlov (age eight) of Russia. On that evening, Yurlov was woken up by a ghostly apparition of a "tall bald-headed elderly man" next to his bed. Gripped with uncontrollable terror, Yurlov jumped up and ran out of the house, across the garden and *across* the nearby Sviyaga River.

Servants were chasing the boy and found him "absolutely dry" on the far side of the large river. Says Yurlov, "Several of our servants were running after me. They swore that they had seen me flying across the river with my feet touching the water sometimes."[359]

While walking on water is one of the rarer forms of levitation, plenty of other examples exist. One of the most dramatic is the incident witnessed by Baird T. Spaulding. In December of 1894, Spaulding joined an expedition of eleven men to undertake "metaphysical research" in India. After two years of studying, Baird Spaulding met a group of yogis who appeared to exhibit numerous supernatural powers.

Spaulding and his group were amazed at the way the yogis were able to communicate with wild animals, or seemingly appear out of nowhere. They displayed an incredible range of knowledge, and also appeared to be unaffected by the elements.

However, nothing could have prepared Spaulding for what happened next. Spaulding and his group were invited by the men to travel with them into the Himalayas. They accepted the offer and began the expedition. As they reached the foothills of the Himalayas, they came upon a large river "about two thousand feet wide, running bank-full, and the current was at least ten miles per hour."

Spaulding and his group assumed that they and the yogis would go upstream and cross over the river on a bridge. Instead, one of the yogis, Jast, told Spaulding that they planned to cross the river without a bridge. Spaulding and his group assumed that Jast meant that he and the other yogis were going to swim across the river—a feat that Spaulding considered dangerous and foolhardy.

However, to the surprise of the group, Jast and the twelve other men used another method. Writes Spaulding, "When Jast rejoined the group, the twelve, fully dressed, walked to the bank of the stream, and with the utmost composure, stepped on the water, not into it. I shall never forget my feelings as I saw each of those twelve men step from solid ground upon the running water. I held my breath, expecting, of course, to see them plunge beneath and disappear. I found out afterwards that that was the thought of all our party. At the time, I think each of us held his breath until they were all past midstream, so astonished were we to see those twelve men walking calmly across the surface of the stream and not sinking below the soles of their sandals. When they stepped from the water to the farther bank I felt that tons of weight had been lifted off my shoulders and I believe this was the feeling of everyone of our party, judging from the sighs of relief as the last man stepped ashore. It was certainly an experience that words fail to describe….There was little discussion regarding what we had witnessed, so engrossed were we with our own thoughts."

Spaulding and his group were forced to go upstream to find a place to cross. When Spaulding later asked Jast about the incident, Jast replied, "Do you think that the men you saw walk across the stream yesterday to save themselves the inconvenience of this trip are in any way special creations any more than you are? No. They are not created in any way different from you. They do not have one atom more power that you were created with. They have, by the right use of their thought forces, developed their God-given power. The thing you have seen accomplished while you have been with us, you, yourselves, can accomplish just as fully and freely. The things you have seen are accomplished in accord with definite law and every human being can use the law if he will."[360]

While saints and Enlightened Masters are undoubtedly the most famous water-walkers, another group of people who supposedly could walk on water were witches. A popular belief in medieval times was that witches could not be drowned. The term "witch hunt" was born during these times for one simple reason: numerous people were executed for displaying paranormal abilities. While some people were put on trial, others were lynched by public mobs. A popular method of this kind was known as "swimming." The accused was thrown into a body of water and if they floated, they would be found guilty.

On June 5, 1696, several people were accused of sorcery and put on trial in Montigny, France. The witnesses were bound by hand and foot and thrown in the Sein River, where they "didn't sink in the water, no more than gourds."[361]

In July, 1737, an anonymous young woman was accused by the townspeople of Bedfordshire, England of witchcraft. She was surrounded and "swum." She reportedly floated like a cork three times, but finally drowned after being tied down. This ritual of "swimming" witches was still practiced by fearful citizens as late as 1931.[362]

For those who are still skeptical of the accounts of walking on water, or witches who cannot be drowned, the following case provides a modern example. Throughout the 1920s, Angelo Faticoni of Jacksonville, Florida publicly displayed his talent as the *"Human Cork."* Without the use of any devices, Faticoni (also known as "The Man They Could not Drown") was able to stay afloat in water indefinitely. He could assume virtually any position, lying on his side, his back, or curled up in a ball. He was even able to sleep on the water. He was able to swim great distances with metal weights tied to his body. During one experiment, he was observed to float in the water for a period of fifteen hours with a twenty-pound lead weight tied to his ankles. On another occasion, a twenty-pound cannonball was lashed to his legs; he was then sewn into a sack and thrown into the water. Faticoni remained motionless, floating on the surface of the water, for a period of eight hours.

Faticoni's fame grew quickly, and he attracted more people who wanted to study his case. His abilities intrigued doctors at Harvard University, who agreed to examine him. They theorized that a peculiarity in his physiology would account for his unnatural buoyancy. However, a thorough medical examination by doctors and students failed to reveal any physical abnormality. A photograph of one of the experiments shows Faticoni floating in the water while tied to a weighted chair. His arms lay on his chest and his head rests just above the water with a calm expression on his face.

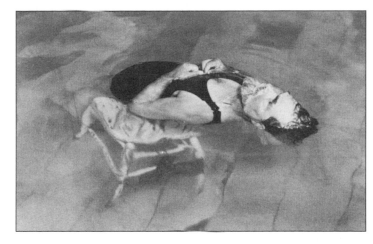

According to Faticoni, he acquired his ability as the result of a traumatic childhood incident. He often promised to reveal

Bernard Faticoni, aka the "human cork," exhibited the supernatural ability to float on the surface of water, despite being tied down with heavy weights. (New York Harold Tribune/UPI)

exactly how he became the "human cork," but unfortunately this was not to be. On August 13, 1931, the New York Harold Tribune announced the death of Angelo Faticoni, with the headline: "'Human Cork' is Dead; His Secret Unrevealed."[363]

The ability to walk on water may seem like magic, but the above cases show that it is available to anybody. The ability to remain dry after being exposed to water has a parallel to other abilities reported by saints and yogis, including incombustibility and immunity to cold. Could it be that the levitators are producing some sort of electromagnetic field around their bodies which can repel fire, water and earth?

24. Modern Eastern Levitations

Eastern countries like India and Tibet have produced a disproportional large number of levitation accounts. Unlike most cultures, the eastern cultures seem to have a very advanced understanding of levitation. Many of the cases involve levitators who have a large measure of control over their flights. The twentieth century produced nearly a dozen high-quality cases of this kind.

An early 1900 account comes from highly advanced Indian Yogi, Ram Gopal, who witnessed and recorded the levitation of two other yogis. The incident took place in an isolated cave in the Himalayan mountains of Tibet.

The event began when Gopal was called to visit Babaji, known to many as the "the Yogi-Christ of Modern India." Babaji is credited with numerous super-human abilities, among them levitation.

Gopal arrived at the prescribed location and waited. It was around midnight when he saw a figure arrive. As he says, "The draped form of a young and surpassingly lovely woman emerged from the cave and levitated high in the air. Surrounded by a soft halo, she slowly descended in front of me and stood motionless, steeped in ecstasy. She finally stirred, and spoke gently."

The lady revealed that her name was Mataji, the sister of Babaji.

Gopal then witnessed the levitation/teleportation of two other yogis. "A nebulous light was rapidly floating over the Ganges; the strange luminescence was reflected in the opaque waters. It approached nearer and nearer until, with a blinding flash, it appeared by the side of Mataji and condensed itself instantly into the form of Lahiri Mahasaya. He bowed humbly at the feet of the woman saint."

Gopal then looked up and saw "a circling mass of mystical light traveling in the sky. Descending swiftly, the flaming whirlpool neared our group and materialized itself into the body of a beautiful youth. I understood at once that he was Babaji."

Gopal had been called to witness a solemn ceremony between the yogis. Afterwards, he watched Babaji and Lahiri Mahasaya as they "slowly levitated and moved backward over the Ganges. An aureole of dazzling light surrounded their bodies as they vanished into the night sky. Mataji's form floated to the cave and descended."[364]

Another 1900s case comes from Herbert Benson, who traveled to India specifically to see some Lamas who could reportedly levitate. Unfortunately, they were unable to produce a conclusive display and appeared simply to be hopping from a lotus position. Benson was understandably disappointed and inquired if this was the limit of their abilities. As he wrote, "I later asked them whether it was possible to stay up in the air. The younger monk said his great-grandfather had been able to do so, but he knew of no one doing it today. I then asked the older man if he knew of anyone who could carry out such a feat. He said it was an ability that was present many hundreds of years ago, but not today. I asked the older monk if he would like to levitate, and with a twinkle in his eye, he responded, "There is no need. We now have airplanes."[365]

While Benson was unable to view a levitation, other explorers have had much better luck. In July of 1916, P. Muller, a German veterinarian, was ordered to Turkey during World War I. While there, he had the opportunity to visit a group of Rufai dervishes in Scutari.

Muller sat in the audience and watched in fascination as the dervishes formed a circle and began moving and dancing in "curious jerking motions." As the hour progressed, the music and dancing intensified. Suddenly one of the dancers jumped into the center of the circle, raised his arms up and began to float upwards.

Having never witnessed anything like this, Muller was understandably shocked. As he wrote later in a letter to a friend, "And now the incomprehensible happened....slowly the whole tense body of this man elevated itself about eighteen inches off the floor and remained there, floating in the air with the toes pointing down....How long? That I cannot exactly say, for in such surprising situations the sense of time is, I suppose, always suspended. I estimate that it must have been at least a half minute to a minute before the ecstatic man, despite all the shouting of the dancers and of the faithful audience, slowly descended, touching the floor first with the tips of his toes, and then collapsed and was caught up by his companions who rushed up to him." This is highly reminiscent of the account of Zangi Bashgirdi, a dervish from the fifteenth century who would often be seized with ecstasy and would then levitate and perch on the shoulders of other whirling dervishes.[366]

Sometime in the early 1900s (exact date not given) well-known yogi, Paramahansa Yogananda of India, visited his friend Nagendra Nath Bhaduri, who was widely known as "the Levitating Saint." When Yogananda's friend, Upendra Mohn Chowdhury, said, "I saw a yogi remain in the air, several feet above the ground, last night at a group meeting," Yogananda could only smile.

As Yogananda writes in his autobiography, "The yogi lives so close to my home that I often visit him. I have seen his remarkable feats. He has expertly mastered the various pranayamas mentioned in the ancient eightfold yoga outlined by Patanjali....I am vastly entertained by the wit of his wisdom. Occasionally my prolonged laughter mars the solemnity of his gatherings. The saint is not displeased, but his disciples look daggers!"[367]

By this time, India and Tibet were attracting more and more visitors to view levitation events. Probably one of the most famous levitation demonstrations of the early 1900s occurred in 1936. At that time, British news reporter P. T. Plunkett, a tea-planter and one-time reporter for the *Illustrated London News*, observed and photographed a display of stick levitation on his tea plantation in India. The levitation was performed by the fakir, Slubbayah Pullavar, who had been training in this particular yogic practice for more than twenty years.

In preparation, the yogi had a tent set up, around which he sprinkled water. He went inside, drew a circle on the ground and forbade anybody from entering it. He then entered the circle and grabbed his walking stick lightly with one hand outstretched from his body. Then he slowly lifted up his legs and hung suspended in the air.

At this point, the tent was removed, and Pullavar allowed the spectators to roam around him. Plunkett took several now-famous photographs of the yogi that were published in the *Illustrated London News* on June 6, 1936.

The photographs—each from a different angle—show the yogi's body lying horizontal in the air, as if resting on an invisible couch, with his right arm outstretched in front of him, gripping the top of a stick. He appears to be relaxed, and seems to use the stick more for balance or keeping contact with the earth than to support his weight.

Afterwards, the tent was replaced to hide the yogi from view. Plunkett, however, spied through a hole in the tent, and watched as the yogi slowly lowered to the ground. Says Plunkett, "After about a minute he appeared to sway and then very slowly began to descend, still in a horizontal position. He took about five minutes to move from the top of the stick to the ground, a distance of three feet."

Afterwards, the tent was removed and spectators were again invited to inspect the yogi. Says Plunkett, "When Slubbayah was back on the ground

Indian Fakir Slubbaya Pullavar put on this impressive display of stick levitation in 1928 on the location of a tea plantation in India. (London Illustrated News Picture Library.)

his assistants carried him over....and asked if we would try to bend his limbs. Even with assistance, we were unable to do so."

Plunkett was convinced. As he wrote, "I have witnessed the performance with several of my planters, I am quite convinced of the total absence of trickery."[368]

In the 1940s, author Ernest Wood traveled to India to view firsthand the feats of levitation. He was not disappointed. As he writes, "Levitation, or the rising of the body from the ground and its suspension a few feet up in the air above the seat or couch, is a universally accepted fact in India. I remember one occasion when an old yogi was levitated in a recumbent position about six feet above the ground in an open field, for about a half an hour, while the visitors were permitted to pass sticks to and fro in the space between."[369]

In 1950, American journalist and paranormal investigator John Keel, traveled through Tibet looking for interesting paranormal accounts. While he was staying in a monastery bungalow, he was visited by a monk named Nyang-Pas. Keel was delighted as he had heard from the locals that this man was a great Siddha with awesome powers. Nyang-Pas, however, denied this, saying he was only "a simple Lama."

Keel pleaded with him to show or teach him something. Nyang-Pas replied, "It would take you a lifetime of solitude....Perhaps I can introduce you to the principals."

It was then that Keel was privileged to a very unusual display of stick levitation by the lama. Writes Keel, "He struggled to his feet, pressed one hand on the top of his stick, a heavy branch about four feet long, frowned with a little effort, and then slowly lifted his legs up off the floor until he was sitting cross-legged in the air! There was nothing behind him or underneath him. His sole support was his stick, which he seemed to use to keep his balance. I was astounded."

Keel asked how this amazing feat was accomplished and the lama replied that it took years of study and meditation, and conducted the rest of the conversation while "sitting there in empty space."

Keel asked the lama to accompany him to Gangok for further displays, but Nyang-Pas declined saying, "It's too big a place for me. I am a solitary man."[370]

Sometime in the 1950s, explorer and adventurer Fosco Mariani traveled through Tibet and Sikkim. Because of his high social standing, he was invited to go on a ski trip with Prince Thondup and his sister, Princess Pema Choki. In the evening, they held deep conversations on a number of subjects, including the supernatural feats of Buddhist holy men.

Princess Pema Choki then revealed her experiences with her incredible uncle Says Choki, "He was the most extraordinary man I have ever met. I remember that when I was a little girl he lived in a completely empty room and flew."

Fosco Mariani was amazed at this claim and asked Choki, "Weren't you afraid? Did you actually see him?"

Choki replied, "Yes. He did what you would call exercises in levitation. I used to take him a little rice. He would be motionless in mid-air. Everyday he rose a little higher. In the end he rose so high that I found it difficult to hand the rice up to him. I was a little girl, and had to stand on tip-toe....There are certain things you don't forget!"[371]

A similar account (no date given) comes from Patricia Palden, who writes that her father, Lama Lobsang Palden, told her that he had seen his grandfather (her great grandfather) in a state of levitation. As she writes of her great grandfather, who was also a Buddhist monk in Tibet, "He left to spend the last years of his life in a cave. Lobsang would often bring food to his grandfather, and once he found him in meditation, levitating above the ground."

Explorer and author Douchan Gersi has witnessed levitations in numerous primitive cultures. His first such experience occurred in a Buddhist monastery near Cashmere, India. He was twenty years old and was given permission to stay and do research at the monastery for five days. While there, he talked to the monks, learning about spirituality and philosophy. On his last night, he saw something that would leave a vivid impression on his mind for years to come. Writes Gersi, "That night, I saw the lama, who was sitting in the lotus position, praying, rise slowly upward in the air until he was about two feet above the floor, where he stayed for at least three or four minutes."

Gersi crept away and vowed to ask the lama about the incident, but it was not to be. Writes Gersi, "The next morning I knew I couldn't leave the monastery without asking him a few questions about what he had done. Looking for him, I stumbled upon a monk who was carrying the little bag containing my personal belongings. 'Our spiritual leader has said that you must go now,' he whispered in broken English, leading me to the monastery's exit."[372]

In 1968, the world-famous musical group, the Beatles, visited India to have an audience with the also world-famous, Maharishi Mahesh Yogi. While there, the subject of levitation came up. As Paul McCartney revealed in the Beatles' Anthology, "I don't buy any of those stories about flying and levitation, although it interests me now because you can actually take courses where you learn these 'siddhes,' as they call them, and you fly—you bounce off the ground a bit. I well remember a little chat we had with Maharishi when we asked him if levitation was possible. He said, 'Well, *I* can't do it, but I know a fellow in the next village who can.' And we said, 'Can we get him here? We'd love to see it.' That would have been something to write home about, but we never did get to meet him."[373]

A truly incredible modern case of levitation occurred in 1971 near the Mae Pang mountain of Thailand. The levitator in this case was Luang Pu Waen, born in 1888. Waen began his religious studies at age twelve and soon became an ordained Monk, specializing in Saiyawet or "magical knowledge and practices" originally formulated by Indian Brahmans. Waen soon gained a reputation in the area for being able to chase away wild animals that were terrorizing local villagers.

In 1971, a Thai Air Force pilot received the shock of his life. During a practice flight, he clearly saw the form of a monk sitting in serene meditation on a cloud. The pilot was forced to swerve to avoid a collision. Later, he identified the monk as Luang Pu Waen. According to Waen's biographer, Stanley Jeyarajah Tambiah, several other pilots had the same experience, and also traveled to Waen's monastery to identify him as the one they saw levitating several thousand feet in the air, the single highest recorded levitation in history.[374]

In 1984, researcher Paul Dong released his book, *The Four Major Mysteries of China,* in which he describes the case of two anonymous doctors of Chinese medicine who have both mastered the ability of levitation. According to Dong, the two men learned to levitate as a result of long practice of a specialized aspect of the traditional Chinese breathing technique called *qi gong*. The variation is called *ching gong*, or "lightweight" gong.[375]

As can be seen, the eastern countries' reputation for producing levitation demonstrations is well deserved. And with their track record, it won't be long before further dramatic cases will be revealed.

25. The Indian Rope Trick

While this book is about human levitation without the aid of any physical devices, one cannot discuss it without including the incredibly famous *Indian Rope Trick*. It is difficult to trace exactly when this trick was first performed, and nobody seems to know exactly who invented it. And yet, the trick itself is very well known.

In most cases, the performance is done at night and involves a yogi, a child, and a rope. The yogi throws the rope up into the air where it magically stays floating in space. The child then climbs up the rope. At this point, the story varies. In some cases, the child disappears, the rope falls down, and to the amazement of the onlookers the child reappears in a different location. In another more gruesome variation, the yogi climbs up the rope after the child and with a scimitar, cuts his

Not much is known about this rare photo. It was taken by an anonymous sailor in the 1930s in India and shows either a staged "stick" levitation or perhaps a genuine version of the Indian Rope Trick. (Mary Evans Picture Library)

body into pieces, which fall to the ground. The yogi then climbs down the rope, puts the pieces of the body in a basket and covers them with a cloth. At that point, the child jumps out of the basket, healthy and whole.

Researcher Pran Nevile has traced the origins of the trick back to the fourteenth century. Writes Nevile, "It finds a mention in the Jatakas and also in the commentary on the Mandukya Upanishad. Shankaracharya speaks of 'the magician, the mayavin who throws a cord up into the air, and armed, climbs up it, beyond the range of sight, to enter into battle and be dismembered; after his bodily parts have fallen to the ground, he is seen to rise up again and there is no concern over thinking about the reality of the magic trick that has been performed.'"

According to Sir Henry Yule, Marco Polo saw or heard about the feat during his explorations of the Far East. Ibn Batuta reportedly witnessed a demonstration

The Indian Rope trick has yet to be explained by modern science. What kind of force can make the rope become stiff? (Mary Evans Picture Library)

in Delhi in the fourteenth century. He wrote that he observed Chinese jugglers take a rope "fifty cubits in length, and in my presence threw one end of it towards the sky, where it remained, as if fastened to something in the air." At that point, animals instead of humans ran up the rope and disappeared.[376]

The trick is mentioned again in the memoirs of Jahangir who witnessed it in his court. It is mentioned by Chinese author, P'u Sung-Ling (1640-1715), in his story *Theft of a Peach*. According to Nevile, "By the end of the nineteenth century, newspapers in India and abroad carried reports by travelers who clamed to have witnessed the rope trick."

Some of these witnesses are prominent people in society, whose word on any other subject would be taken very seriously.

One newspaper, *The London Morning Post*, carried the testimony of Sir Ralph Pearson, the Lt. Governor of the North West Frontier Province, who claimed to have seen the trick performed in the west Khandesh district of Bombay.

Another good witness is Colonel Bernard, Commissioner of Police in Calcutta. Colonel Bernard was invited to attend a private exhibition of the rope trick. He sneaked in a camera and during the performance, snapped several pictures. The trick was performed as normal: the boy climbed up the levitating rope, disappeared, and then reappeared standing next to the yogi. However, when the photographs were developed, they told a different story. The photos reportedly showed that the rope and the boy were lying on the ground when they were supposed to be levitating. The colonel's conclusion was that the trick was an illusion caused by mass hypnosis.

Another case that supports the hypnosis theory was published on March 15, 1902, in the *Calgary Herald*. Captain James Palmer wrote that he observed the trick and believed it to be true until he observed it on a second occasion from an outside perspective. Palmer wrote that a fakir performed the trick for his friends while he hid in the background. Writes Palmer, "The man placed a drawn knife between his teeth, took the usual ball of twine in his right hand, made a motion as if throwing it into the air, and then stood perfectly quiet. My friends on the veranda were looking into the upper air with astonishment on their faces, which in a minute turned to a look of horror as their eyes came back to the ground. In another minute, their countenances lighted up with pleasure, and they applauded roundly. They could not say enough about the wonderful performance they had seen and they were astonished beyond measure when I told them I had been as near the fakir as they, and had seen nothing of what had so wonderfully impressed them. If that was not hypnotism, what was it?"[377]

Some cases, however, might not be explained so easily. One such case comes from Lady Waghorn who observed the trick in 1892 in Madras. She gave a detailed description, saying that she was only fifteen feet away from the yogi when he threw the rope about twelve feet into the air. When the rope became stiff, a young boy climbed up to the top and disappeared. Seconds later, he reappeared in the branches of a tree one hundred yards away.

Another account comes from Mr. Bodalin, a Dutchman living in Calcutta in the late 1890s. He observed the boy climb the rope and disappear. The yogi followed him up the rope and swung wildly with a sword above him. The yogi came back down with the sword covered in blood. Seconds later, the boy reappeared in the crowd of stunned onlookers.

Is the Indian Rope Trick real or an optical illusion? Writes researcher, A. C. Brown, "The rope trick is more talked about than seen. But nevertheless, there is a certain amount of truth in the story of this Eastern Magic."[378]

Researcher Peter Lamont, however, is not convinced. In his book, *Rise of the Indian Rope Trick: How a Spectacular Hoax Became History,* he contends that the Indian Rope Trick was actually a hoax originating from the *Chicago Tribune* who ran a fictionalized article on August 8, 1890, describing the trick as witnessed by "Fred Sellmore." The article concluded by saying that the trick was probably caused by mass hypnosis. Although the Chicago Tribune later admitted that the article was not true, by then many other witnesses were coming forth with their own accounts.

The trick has been filmed at least twice. One is an obvious hoax, with the rope only appearing to float because the film is being played in reverse. This film was made in 1937 on an army base. The other, however, appears to be genuine. In the 1930s, the magician's group "the British Magic Circle," offered a reward of 500 guineas to anybody who could perform the trick. A magician named Karachi took up the offer and performed the trick in front of famed investigator, Harry Price. The film shows the rope being thrown up and remaining erect in the air, although for only a few feet. At that point, Karachi's young son climbs up the mysteriously rigid rope. Unfortunately, the boy did not disappear, and Karachi did not earn the reward.

In 1955, an Indian guru named Sadju Vadramakrishna said that he had performed the rope trick and would reveal the secret. According to the guru, there is no actual levitation involved. Everything is done through sleight of hand and trickery. The stunt is performed in evening. By placing torches around the perimeter of the crowd, visibility upwards is limited to fifteen feet in the sky. Before the trick is performed, a wire is tied between two distant trees. The rope is thrown up and hooked to the wire, and the child (a skilled acrobat and tightrope walker), climbs up the rope and only seems to disappear. In fact, he travels the tightrope and comes down via the distant tree. Meanwhile, the body parts are actually those of a "dead monkey" which are concealed in the boy's cloak and thrown out prior to his departure.

Another guru named Sorkhar offered the same theory, saying that the wire could also be run between two hills. John Keel offered this theory in his 1957 book about eastern mysteries, *Jadoo*.

Researcher, Richard Wiseman researched many of these early stories and claims to have found no less than fifty independent accounts from English citizens who had seen the trick. However, none of these cases involved the gruesome aspects of the trick—only a levitating rope, which a young boy would ascend and descend or disappear and reappear.

And here the story ends. While the origins and veracity of the Indian Rope trick remain unknown, the controversy has had the effect of popularizing the subject of levitation and introducing millions of people to the idea that human beings can somehow defy the laws of gravity.

26. Modern Ecstatic Levitations

A common misperception about levitation is that it is a "lost art." Perhaps people could levitate in the distant past, but not today. However, if levitation were a true phenomenon, then one would expect a continuity of cases stretching from early history to the present day. And, of course, this is exactly the case. While levitating saints may seem to be a throwback to the Dark Ages, the truth is that many modern cases exist. Here we examine sixteen modern cases from the nineteenth and twentieth centuries.

Louise Lateau (1850-1883) was a well-known stigmatic from Belgium whom Dr. Imbert-Gourbeyre personally studied. According to him, he personally observed her not to actually levitate, but to balance in positions that defied gravity. She also displayed the phenomenon of inedia, or survival without food.[379]

In 1851, Monsieur Brown-Sequard of France recounted that he witnessed a case of levitation involving a young girl who experienced ecstatic trances. Every Sunday, she fell into a trance and climbed up onto the round, polished headboard of her bed. Standing up on her tiptoes, she perched in a half-levitating position of prayer which she would maintain until eight o'clock in the evening.[380]

Marie Julie Jahenny (1853-1879) was another ecstatic who was personally studied by Dr. Imbert-Gourbeyre. According to him, he and several other competent people verified her "ecstatic lightness."[381]

In 1855, Maria Domenica Barbagli of San Savino, Italy experienced several levitations. As one witness reported, "I saw the ecstatic of San Savino in Toscane…she was kneeling, her arms crossed, and raised up in the air with her feet above her bed. The ecstasy lasted one hour. I put my hand under her knees. I was able to raise her more. She weighed like a feather. I blew on her and her body balanced lightly in the air, like a leaf blown gently by the wind. I was well aware of all these phenomena; I experienced it. The next day she had three ecstasies, one of which was aerial."[382]

On September 8, 1861, the German newspaper, *Frankfurter Zeitung,* published the report of a Catholic priest who unintentionally provoked the levitation of an audience member in his congregation in the Church of St. Mary in Vienna Italy. According to the article, "Soon after the commencement of the sermon, a girl of about twenty years of age, showed all signs of ecstasy, and soon, her arms crossed upon her bosom, and with her eyes fixed on the preacher, she was seen by the whole congregation to be raised gradually from the floor into the air, and there to rest at an elevation of more than a foot until the end of the sermon. We are assured that the same phenomenon had happened several days previously at the moment of her receiving communion."[383]

Marie of the Passion (1866-1912) of Italy began experiencing levitation shortly before her death. In 1912, she fell ill and had to be helped to and from services. Sister Marie Prassede, who was put in charge of this duty, reported, "Hardly had we left the choir when I saw the servant of God, even though she was very sick, to climb the stairs in an instant, as if she flew on wings. And I who was in good health wasn't able to follow her. She appeared not to touch the ground and to actually fly up the staircase to her cell." Marie of the Passion died within the year.[384]

St. Gemma Galgani (1878-1903) was born in Tuscany, Italy. She was poor and suffered from tuberculosis. From an early age, she experienced numerous visions and apparent demonic attacks. Her relatives and neighbors initially scorned her as a dreamer; however, she eventually became famous for her supernatural manifestations of stigmata and ecstatic trances, during which she would give long religious discourses, many of which were recorded. She was also "plagued" by repeated levitations. She was sometimes apparently able to use them to her advantage to reach a certain favorite crucifix that was normally high up on a wall beyond her reach.

Galgani later went to live with the Giannini family of Lucca, Italy. On the dining room wall of the Giannini home hung a large painting representing the crucifixion of Christ. It was this painting that sometimes sent Galgani into levitation. The first time it occurred, she observed the painting and became overwhelmed with love for Jesus. Seeing his wounds, she desired to kiss them. As she told her spiritual director, she suddenly felt herself lifted up several feet to the height of the painting, where she gently kissed his wounds.

Elena Giannini was one member of the family who observed Galgani in levitation. She was a young child at the time, and seeing the woman in levitation, ran from the room screaming, "Aunty, come see Gemma. She's flying!"

Here Gemma describes in her own words what she felt during her ecstasies. "Try to think of a light that fills the whole universe, that penetrates it and kindles it. At the same time, a light that gives life and animation to all things, so that all things that exist are imbued with it, or encircled in it, and in it and through it have life. Thus I see God and in him all creatures. He is a burning fire. It burns but does not consume. On the contrary, it gives light and warmth and joy. The more it burns, the more happy and perfect it makes those encircled by its rays."

Several miraculous healings are attributed to Gemma Galgani. Despite considerable opposition, she was beatified in 1933 and canonized in 1940.[385]

Sister Marie Baourdie (d1878) was a Syrian Carmelite nun in Bethlehem whose levitations were recorded in her biography. Over a period of two years, 1873-1874, no less than eight public levitations were recorded. In most cases, Baourdie was seen to rise to the top of a particular lime tree on her convent grounds whose company she enjoyed. Its height was estimated at nearly fifty feet.

The first incident occurred on June 22, 1873, when it was realized that Sister Marie was missing. A search entailed, and Baourdie was finally discovered "at the absolute summit" of the lime tree. The prioress arrived and ordered Baourdie to come down.

The Mother Superior asked her how the levitations occur. Baourdie replied, "The Lamb [Jesus] carries me in his hands....If I obey quickly, the tree becomes like this," she placed her hand low to the ground.

Baourdie's levitations caused a sensation in her convent. Several of the sisters tried to spy on her to verify the levitations. One of the sisters was successful. As she says, "She had seized the extremity of a branch so little that a bird would have bent it, and from there, in an instant, she had been raised on high."

Looking up, the sister watched Baourdie float to the top of the tree, touching the branches lightly on the way up as if to sustain the levitation.

On July 19, 1873, Baourdie experienced another levitation and rose to the top of the lime tree. The Prioress ordered her down. At that moment, Baourdie's ecstasy ended, and she found herself trapped at the top of the tree, and had to climb down slowly and carefully.

On another occasion, Baourdie felt a levitation coming over her. She ordered the nun next to her to turn around. The nun did so, and then looking back, saw Baourdie already at the top of the tree, singing of the love of God.

One witness who saw Baourdie in levitation wrote that she moved "like a bird from branch to branch with great lightness and modesty."

Baourdie also experienced one crisis levitation. Following a long illness in which Baourdie claimed she was being attacked by evil spirits, she spontaneously recovered. Immediately following her recovery, she was seen floating "several hand spans" above her bed, in an ecstatic trance.[386]

Another famous nineteenth century levitator was Victoire Claire (d1883), a young girl from Ardeche, Coux, France. One witness, Mademoiselle D., witnessed many of the episodes. As she said in an interview with Colonel Rochas, "I saw her with great amazement remain with her eyes fixed but lively, and gradually raised above the chair whereon she was sitting. She stretched forth her arms, leaned her body forward, and remained thus suspended, her right leg bent up, the other touching the earth but by a toe. I saw Victoire in this position, impossible for anyone to keep up normally, every time she was in an ecstatic trance. I had the good fortune to visit twice a week. During these visits, she had two or three ecstasies which lasted for ten to fifteen minutes. I have seen her in this state more than a thousand times, mainly during the first years of our relationship."

Another firsthand witness to Victoire's levitation was Mademoiselle Regnier, who testified, "Victoire-Claire was kneeling behind us against the confessional; in turning my head, I saw her elevated in the air about one meter from the ground. The Sister, in seeing my amazement, made us leave quickly."[387]

Paranormal researcher Colonel Rochas reports the case of a lady who lived in the late 1800s in a convent near Grenoble. She was witnessed by a priest, a professor, and his student to fall into a trance and *nearly* levitate. According to one of the witnesses, "Her body would sometimes become stiff and so light that it was possible to lift her up like a feather by holding on to her elbow."[388]

According to Colonel Rochas, the lady was an "ecstatic" who was retired. She suffered from occasional fits during which she would lie down and become totally rigid. While in this state, her body was so light that it could be lifted easily, as if it had no weight whatsoever.[389]

An undated account probably from the 1800s comes from Abbot Petit of France, who reported to Colonel Rochas that he has experienced levitation at least twice and found it "terrifying."

He actually left a descriptive firsthand narrative. "In this that concerns levitation, I have experienced two different kinds in a church. One time, it was a simple raising up of the body which I attributed to an expansion of the astral body. Another time, there was a transport. In the first case I experienced an intense tingling in the hands and feet with a feeling of an escaping force. In the second case, the sensation was totally different. It seemed to me that a strange force was pulling me towards the altar."

Petit denied that his levitations were miraculous or contrary to the laws of nature. Instead, he believed that levitation is a natural event whose causes remain unknown.[390]

Yet another late 1800 case reported to Rochas involved a young French girl who would fall into trances and exhibit "supernatural agility" during which she was seen by her family to "climb without effort along the walls."

The child's mother consulted several doctors who were unable to help. Then one day, the child fell into a trance and dictated a cure involving a certain concoction which she must drink. This was done and proved to be an effective cure.[391]

An astonishing modern case is that of Father Padre Pio (1887-1968) of Benevento, Italy. Pio joined the Franciscans at age seventeen. At age twenty-one, he began to experience pains in his hands and feet which doctors were unable to diagnose. Three years later, Padre Pio collapsed from the pain. His fellow priests found him unconscious, bleeding from the hands and feet. Pio had become a stigmatic. Following this, Pio performed a number of well-verified miraculous healings. A few accounts of his life mention briefly that Pio was occasionally seen levitating while in prayer. One witness was Padre Ascanio, who writes, "We were waiting for Padre Pio was who coming to hear confessions of the penitents. The church was crowded and everybody watched the door through which Padre Pio would enter. The door stayed closed, but suddenly I saw father Pio walking above the heads of the people, he reached the confessional, and then disappeared. After some minutes, he started to receive the penitents."

Padre Ascanio later approached Pio and asked him how he was able to walk in the air. Pio responded, "I can assure you, my child, it's just like walking on the floor."

Padre Pio also reportedly levitated above his home town during World War II, warding off enemy planes and pushing bombs off target. He was canonized in 2002.[392]

Father Padre Pio experienced numerous paranormal manifestations as a result of his religious fervor, including stigmata, miraculous healings, bi-location, and levitation. (Self Realization Fellowship)

Teresa Neumann (1898-1962) of Konnersreuth, Germany is one of the best-verified cases of modern mysticism. On Christmas day in 1922, Neumann experienced a mystical vision. Following this day, Neumann displayed the phenomenon known as inedia, or survival without food. This soon developed into survival without food or water. Neumann then began to display the wounds of stigmata, and had precognitive visions. Neuman's inedia was verified numerous times under strictly controlled conditions. It was also discovered that like many other saints, she needed little sleep, averaging less than two hours a night.

Towards the end of her life, Neumann experienced ecstatic levitations, as witnessed by an abbess, several priests and numerous visitors. One near levitation occurred when observers heard her cry out, "Take me along!" She was in the middle of a rapturous ecstasy. The observers then observed that Neumann was "standing on the very tips of her toes so that you had to look to see whether she was still on the floor or not."

Abbess Maria Benedicta von Spiegel reports that she witnessed Neumann to fall into ecstasy and levitate about one foot above the floor.

One of the best verified of her levitations occurred on August 15, 1938, when a group of priests and visitors all observed Neumann "actually raised a little bit from the floor and hovering in the air for a while." Today, live films exist showing Neumann in ecstasy, displaying wounds of the stigmata.[393]

In the early 1950s, Father Aloysius Ellacuria (1906-1981) of southern California, began to experience raptures that usually occurred during the most devotional portions of his mass. During one mass, three sisters reported that when Father Aloysius fell into ecstasy, they watched his body rise "several inches" above the floor. Expert on modern mysticism, Patricia Treece tracked down the story and was able to confirm many details.

Apparently, the levitations were well known among those who knew the father, but the subject was rarely spoken of to outsiders. Treece located two sisters who each heard firsthand accounts of the father's levitations.

Treece spoke with firsthand witness, Katherine Morrow, who joined Father Aloysius on a pilgrimage in 1968. While saying mass, she observed the Father to suddenly rise up in the air. According to Morrow, the father appeared to be struggling to return to the ground. Morrow observed another levitation shortly thereafter, and a third episode in Los Angeles. On each occasion, Aloysius attempted unsuccessfully to end the levitation.

Treece also interviewed Paul Chacon, a banker from Los Angeles, who witnessed an apparent partial levitation of Father Aloysius around the same year. "One day Father Aloysius was giving us a day of recollection. As he was talking about the Lord, I noticed he was standing on the tips of his toes. He maintained this odd position for perhaps five minutes, and during this time he was extending his arms without any trembling of the body of legs that would seem normal in that circumstances. I said to myself, 'This guy's going to take off.' But he didn't."

In 1975, Mother Marguerite Carter went on a pilgrimage with Father Aloysius. She was praying with the Father in a chapel when she suddenly heard him cry out, "Oh, my God!" Says Carter, "Naturally everyone looks up and there is

Father Aloysius lost in ecstasy and a good four inches off the floor. You could see the space under his shoes." Father Aloysius died a few months later at age seventy-five.[394]

In 1970, Father John Nicola and a Passionist monk named Candido Amantini (then the official exorcist of Rome), conducted a days-long exorcism of a young nun who was suspected of being possessed. During an interview with the nun, Amantini, Nicola, and three others observed the nun to rise from her bed six feet into the air where she remained suspended for a period of thirty seconds.

Father Nicola was so stunned by this turn of events that he had trouble believing his own eyes. As he says, "Everyone in the room saw her levitate. At least this was our experience. We saw it."

Today Nicola has difficulty absorbing the event, and wonders if there might be another explanation other than physical levitation. As he says, "We may have been involved in a situation of mutual hypnosis. Or, from my researches in parapsychology, I'd propose it might have been psychokinesis. The point is, you can't jump to conclusions."[395]

While levitations are still occurring today, observers are apparently as mystified about the phenomenon as they have been for centuries. In many cases, levitation accounts are still being covered up and treated as a miraculous event that should not be questioned or even talked about. One can only wonder how many devoutly religious people are currently flying around in their rooms, performing incredible miracles and telling nobody.

27. Modern Mediumistic Levitations

By the time the 1900s came around, documentation of levitation events had reached a dramatic new level. Now numerous scientists were looking into cases and not only recording them, but were conducting live fieldwork. For the first time, investigators began to take convincing photographs of people in an actual levitating state. Gone are any arguments about hypnosis, hallucinations, or exaggerations. For the first time, actual proof of levitation was within grasp.

Just this event happened in 1908, when Amedee Zuccarini, (Zucarini) a state employee Bologna, Italy, attracted the attention of scientists with his ability to levitate. His case was closely studied by Dr. L. Patrizi, Professor of Physiology at the Universe of Modena and Professor Oreste Murani of the Milan Polytechnic in Italy, who were able to take photographs of him during

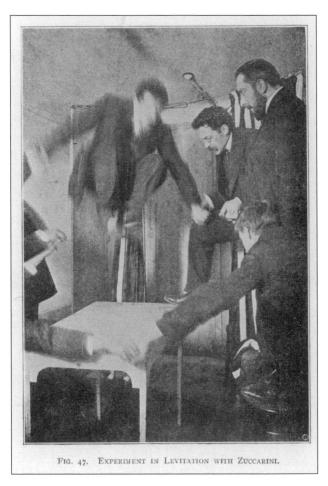

FIG. 47. EXPERIMENT IN LEVITATION WITH ZUCCARINI.

Italian medium Amedee Zuccarini obtained one of the first convincing photographs of mediumistic levitation in action. Only able to levitate in darkness, Zuccarini used flash-photography to obtain this impressive photograph. (Mary Evans Picture Library)

his levitation episodes. Zuccarini was only able to levitate in complete or near-complete darkness. To overcome this obstacle, the scientists used magnesium flash photography. They would conduct a séance, and at the moment of levitation, they took the photographs. Using this method, the scientists took numerous photos of Zuccarini levitating. The most famous photo shows the circle of five people in the séance, with Zuccarini floating about three feet above the floor in a perpendicular position, still holding the hands in the circle. His levitations were invariably brief, lasting twelve to fourteen seconds. Yet the stringent laboratory conditions and the photographs make the case particularly reputable.[396]

In the 1920s, English medium Jack Webber rose to fame because of strong abilities of physical mediumship. While seated in a darkened room, Webber would enter into a trance and ectoplasm would escape from his body and lift various objects throughout the room. The ectoplasm was photographed numerous times using flash photography and remains one of the best verified cases of physical mediumship on record.

On occasion, Webber also physically levitated himself. Probably the most famous event occurred during a séance involving more than twenty sitters, all situated along the walls of a narrow rectangular room, in the center of which was a long table. Once the room was plunged into near-total darkness, Webber and his chair rose up to the ceiling and hovered there momentarily, then came back down on the other side of the table, a maneuver normally impossible in the crowded room. Once the lights were turned on, Webber was found in his new position. Looking up, witnesses saw an oily smudge from Webber's hair products where his head had struck the ceiling.[397]

One of the most successful modern European physical mediums was Polish bank clerk, Teofil Modrzejewski, aka Franek Kluski (1873-1943). Modrzejewski's abilities as a medium didn't manifest until he was forty-five years old, in 1918. At that time, he was invited to his first séance, during which, paranormal activity seemed to center around him. Further sittings revealed that he was in fact a powerful medium, capable of producing a wide range of paranormal phenomena.

As with other mediums, during the séances, Modrzejewski's weight would sometimes fluctuate. As his fame grew, he was examined closely by prominent investigators who declared the medium genuine. Colonel Okolowicz wrote a book about the case and attended many of the séances, which took place from 1918 to 1925. On one occasion, he observed the medium to fall into a cataleptic trance, his body becoming completely rigid. Okolowicz decided to try and move the medium. To his shock, Modrzejewski's body was "extremely light." By pressing down on his legs that extended beyond the couch, Okolowicz was able to bring the medium to a standing position. After repeating this maneuver several times, he then physically lifted the medium. He did so easily, and estimated that Modrzewski's body had lost approximately two-thirds of its normal weight.[398]

An undated case, probably from around the 1920s, concerns a young medium named Maria Vollhardt whose case was studied by the eminent English physician, Dr. Schwab. After several sittings, Dr. Shwab succeeded in photographing Maria Vollhardt in a levitating state.[399]

In 1928, Father Theophilus Riesinger, a priest from Marathon, Wisconsin, conducted an exorcism on an anonymous woman from Earling, Iowa. The woman had been very religious from an early age, and all her life, had experienced symptoms of demonic possession. Despite her piety, she would become enraged at being blessed or when in the presence of religious objects. She understood languages unknown to her and experienced many other unusual events.

She lived with her bizarre symptoms until age forty, when she finally decided to undergo an exorcism. On the first day of the rite, the woman was laying on her bed contorting her body as Father Theophilus began the ritual. As Reverend Carl Vogel writes, "….a hair-raising scene occurred. With lightning speed the possessed dislodged herself from her bed and from the hands of her guards; and her body, carried through the air, landed high above the door of the room and clung to the wall with a tenacious grip….Real force had to be applied to her feet to bring her down from her high position on the wall. The mystery was that she could cling to the wall at all!"

Said Father Riesinger, "Think, the body of the possessed person floats in the air."[400]

While Home, Mirabelli and Eglinton made a name for themselves as levitating mediums; a young British man by the name of Colin Evans was not to be left out. Throughout the early 1930s, he held numerous séances and levitated in front of large crowds. Like Home and others, he credited his levitations to the intervention of spirits. However, unlike most levitating mediums, Evans was able to repeatedly photograph himself in a state of levitation. In 1938, Evans conducted a séance in Conway Hall, London. Evans, like other levitators, was only able to levitate in total or near-total darkness. To prove the genuineness of his levitations, he brought a flash camera with a remote control switch. The camera was aimed at him and he held the switch in his left hand. The séance began and Evans felt his body being lifted up. He quickly snapped the picture, which clearly shows him hovering in the air.

Evans was able to perform this feat on numerous occasions. Some of the photos were taken in series, seeming to indicate that Evans remained in the air for at least several moments.[401]

British Medium Colin Evans was able to levitate repeatedly in front of large crowds. Here he takes remote control flash-photographs of himself in a state of levitation. (Mary Evans Picture Library)

Nandor Fodor was one of the early pioneers of levitation research. Throughout the 1930s, Fodor traveled across Europe visiting mediums who claimed to be able levitate. Most were unable to do so. However, his patience was rewarded when he met house-painter, Harry B. Brown. Interestingly, Brown himself said that he had no direct knowledge that he could levitate. All he knew was that during the séances he attended, he fell into an unconscious trance-like state. It was his friends who claimed that Brown would levitate. Like many mediums, Brown did so only in darkness. The sitters would sit around a table and hold hands in the darkness. Brown would fall into a trance and be pulled upwards towards the ceiling.

Fodor felt that Brown was "honest and straightforward." A séance was quickly arranged. To Fodor's amazement, Brown levitated as his friends said he would. Writes Fodor in his 1959 book, *The Haunted Mind,* "I cannot say that I 'saw' him floating in the air, for the sitting at the Institute was held in total darkness " The sitters all took their places and the light was extinguished. After a few moments, Brown fell into a trance and the levitation began immediately. Writes Fodor, "I felt an upward pull on my hand. Both Mrs. Bell and myself had to climb onto the seat of our chairs to follow a rising hand. We had to reach higher and higher. Soon I was standing on my toes. We could not see Harry Brown's body. It was too dark for that, but we could feel it behaving oddly. It swayed as if rocked by a gentle breeze. It changed its angle, it twisted and twirled about, just as a body would, over which gravity no longer had a hold. His head must have almost touched the ceiling. Now he was slowly coming down, then he went up again."

Fodor was hoping to obtain a photograph of the levitation using flash photography, as had other levitators, including Zuccarrini and Evans. Writes Fodor, "It was our agreement that we should take his photograph at the most auspicious moment. He should give the word by saying: *go!* Suddenly a strangled cry broke his lips, the prearranged signal; there was a dull red flash, and the next moment Harry Brown fell with a thud that shook the floor. He landed on his feet, fell back to his chair—and in a short while he was out of trance and the lights were turned on. We were, of course, devoured with curiosity as to what the photograph would show."

To Fodor's delight, the photograph showed Brown in a state of genuine levitation. Writes Fodor, "It [the photo] showed a good deal: Harry Brown standing in the air, his coatline dead straight, and the buttons showing no sign of blur. Control experiments proved that if, contrary to our own feelings about his movements in the dark, the coat would have flapped. These two features of the photograph—the coat and the unblurred buttons—were in favor of genuine levitation."

Some remarkable levitation research was conducted over a period of several years in the mid-1940s in Copenhagen, Denmark. Psychical researcher and professional photographer, Sven Turck, headed the project, which had specific and lofty goals in mind. As he wrote, "I subjected most of our mediums here in Copenhagen to critical investigation, and, afterward, organized a little group of ten members of the highest capacities....we got together twice weekly at my laboratory at Vesterbro....Our intent was to make a completely technical attempt to bring about telekinesis and levitation—two groups of phenomena which are well-suited to photographing."[402]

The first sessions produced few results, however, as the meetings progressed, the phenomenon grew in strength. After several months of regular meetings, the group had successfully levitated several heavy pieces of furniture. They were able to record these events on a trio of cameras that had been placed at strategic locations to capture any activity which might occur.

After one year of the experiments, the group finally succeeded in levitating a human being. During one of the sessions, one of the members of the group, Mr. Borge Michelson, suddenly found himself rising up to the ceiling. Writes Turck, "He circled around up there above the table and then fell to the knees of Madame Melloni, softly, without the least bump. Madame Melloni scarcely felt the force of his fall. The three cameras had flashed and presented us with proof that we had not been victims of hallucination. I succeeded in photographing five such air rides."

Psychic and medium, Olof Jonsson, was a member of Turck's group. Writes Jonsson, "Big heavy tables lifted themselves to the ceiling, in spite of several persons 'on board' as passengers. One medium who sat in our group was named Michelson. He was able to bring about veritable flights to the ceiling."

Turck's experiments and especially his photographs, sent shockwaves through Denmark's scientific community. Writes Brad Steiger, who interviewed and wrote the autobiography of Olof Jonsson, "The series of photographs taken during Turck's experiments in Copenhagen were carefully examined by five of Denmark's foremost photographic technicians, among them the director of the Danish photographic professional school, Theodore Andresen, who had full access to the photographic negatives. Each of the photographers agreed that no manipulations what-

Medium Borge Michealson in levitation. One of a series of photographs taken by Dutch investigator Sven Turck. This group of mediums was able to produce several successful levitation events under controlled conditions. (Sven Turck)

soever had been worked upon with the negatives."[403]

In 1949, a poltergeist haunting in Mount Rainier, Maryland culminated in the apparent possession of a thirteen-year-old boy. During the haunting, the thirteen-year-old, Roland X., was seen by his family to levitate. They would be awakened by his screams, run into his bedroom, and find he and his bed levitating and pounding on the floor.

When Roland began exhibiting a 'secondary personality,' he was placed in a Catholic hospital where more levitations took place. Finally, an exorcism was ordered, during which Roland exhibited superhuman strength, the ability to read minds, understood Latin, and levitated. One of the priests observed a levitation. As he later wrote, "One night the boy brushed off his handlers and soared through the air at Father Bowdern standing at some distance from his bed." After a long, grueling exorcism, the boy was finally cured. This case eventually inspired the blockbuster movie, *Exorcist*.[404]

In the early 1960s, world famous English medium, Brian Hurst, attended a séance in London with the unusually powerful physical medium, William Olsen. Because of his ability to consistently produce physical paranormal phenomena, Olsen was widely sought by people wishing to sit with him. Typically, Olsen would be physically tied to a chair while other sitters sat around the table. Musical instruments would be placed on the table. During the séance, the instruments would be lifted and played by the spirits. Other spirits would lift the trumpet and speak through it. Olsen could produce these feats in a room lit with red light, removing any suspicion of hoax.

During one séance, Brian Hurst and others observed Olsen to physically levitate. The spirits suddenly announced that they would attempt a levitation. Then, as Hurst writes, "We all watched, frozen with astonishment, as the wooden armchair [with Olsen] began to rise towards the ceiling. The light became dimmer and I could barely see the chair floating above us. After a moment, we heard the voice of the guide speaking from above and from a different location in the room. 'Keep in your feet! We bring the medium down!'

"There was a quick shuffling sound as people tucking their feet under their chairs. We heard a loud thump on the floorboards and the guide's voice, now speaking from our level, said, 'That is all for tonight. God bless you! In a moment, you may turn on your white light.' When Mrs. Olsen switched on the light, we were surprised to see the medium still roped to his chair, but sitting in a completely different part of the room. He groaned, came out of his trance and looking around in a rather dazed manner said, 'Oh, I see you've had results!'"[405]

An astounding case of modern mediumistic levitation occurred in 1977 to a young English schoolgirl named Janet Harper. The Harper family of Enfield, England had their first clue that they were destined for the unusual when their home—suddenly and without warning—became severely haunted. Violent poltergeist activity seemed to center around one of the three young children, Janet Harper, who was just entering puberty.

The haunting started out innocuously, with small objects moving, doors opening and closing. However, it soon escalated to furniture being tumbled and objects thrown at people's faces. The activity was photographed and witnessed by numerous credible observers, including scientists and police officers. Then in 1978, Janet Harper began falling into trances. She was rushed to the hospital but the doctors were unable to diagnose the trance-states. Then came the levitations.

The levitations started with Janet and her sister Rose being thrown out of bed by an unseen force. It soon escalated to sleeping levitations. While asleep, Janet was repeatedly floated out of her bed, across the room and deposited on a dresser, where she would wake up with no knowledge of how she got there.

By this time, investigators were on the scene nearly constantly and were documenting the activity. Janet continued to be pulled out of bed. On the next occasion, she was floated asleep into the corner of the room, a distance of fourteen feet.

On another occasion, Janet was awake during a levitation. She walked next door and knocked on the neighbor's door, when it opened by itself. Said Janet, "Peggy's front door opened on its own. I looked behind, and there was no one there, and it just shut....I looked in the front room, and no one's in there. When I came in, someone lifted me upstairs....as I came in, I got lifted halfway up the stairs....and I came rolling down. I nearly fell down dead when that happened.... it frightened the life out of me."

A few days later, Janet was woken up out of a sound sleep and levitated/dragged down the staircase. Says Janet, "I was in bed, asleep. All of a sudden, I felt something pull me by the arms out of bed—and I tripped over—and I went there—and then it lifted me up and the door opened and I went flying downstairs."

Janet's mother observed part of the incident. As she says, "I saw the door open....it seemed as if she was being pulled along the floor."

Two of the investigators, Grosse and Burcombe, caught the end of the incident and observed Janet "lying head downwards on the staircase, slowly sliding down it, still half-asleep."

As the activity escalated, the investigators engaged the poltergeist in communication, first through automatic writing and then by using direct channeling through Janet. Many of these conversations were recorded on audiotape.

During one such occasion, one of the investigators asked the poltergeist, "Will you do some tricks for us?"

"Leave the room," the spirits said through Janet.

As soon as the investigators left the room, Janet called out, "I'm being levitated!" There was a loud crash, and the investigators found that the mattress had been flung across the room, blocking the doorway. Although the investigators didn't witness the levitation, they could see that Janet herself was convinced. She had a look of total astonishment and kept repeating, "I've been floating in the air....I've just been floating."

The investigators were intrigued and determined to get proof. A few days later, Janet reported that she had been levitated and pulled *through* a solid wall into the adjoining bedroom. As she says, "I was sitting on the bed....and I sort of sprang into the air and started whizzing around the room. Then I went through the wall."

It wasn't long before other people began to witness Janet's levitations. One such witness was Hazel Short, who looked inside Janet's bedroom window from the sidewalk outside the house and saw her floating. As she said, "I was standing there looking at the house, when all of a sudden, a couple of books came flying across and hit the window. It was so sudden. I heard the noise because it was so quiet....then after a while, I saw Janet....she was going up and down as though someone was just tossing her up and down bodily, in a horizontal position, as if someone had got hold of her legs and back and was throwing her up and down. I definitely saw her come up to window height, but I thought if she was bouncing, she'd bounce from her feet, she wouldn't be able to get enough power to bounce off her back, to come up that high. My friend could see her as well, we both could see her. It was as though her arms and legs were going everywhere. I mean, if you were doing it to yourself, you'd keep your arms and legs to your body, if you know what I mean. But she was definitely lying horizontal, coming up and down."

Another witness was a gentleman who insisted upon anonymity. As he says, "I saw this child, whom I now know to be Janet, well inside the room, and in the first instance I saw her head bobbing up and down, just as if she were bouncing up and down on her bed. Then articles came swiftly across the room towards the window. They were definitely not thrown at the window, as the articles were going round in a circle, hitting the window and then

When a young English girl named Janet Harper began levitating in the middle of a poltergeist haunting, investigators set up remote cameras and captured this amazing series of photos. There were also other eyewitnesses who testified to the reality of Janet's "episodes." (Bruce Schmidt @ www.Zurich-Mansion.org)

bouncing off, to continue at the same height, in a clockwise direction....the articles appeared to be books, dolls and linen articles. There were five or six articles and by their movement they acted as though there were attached to a piece of elastic. They appeared to be traveling with considerable force, and all were going around at the same time. The child then appeared on two occasions, floating horizontally across the room, and twice her arm banged forcibly against the window. I was frightened at the time that she would come right through the window. At the same time as the articles were going around the room, the curtains were blowing upwards, into the room....I was very upset and disturbed by what I saw."

The investigators decided to set up a remote control camera in an attempt to catch Janet's levitations on film. To their amazement, they succeeded in getting several clear photos of Janet levitating in the center of her room. One particularly impressive photo shows Janet hovering in a kneeling position in mid-air in the center of the room, leaning forward with her arms outstretched in front of her. In the background, her sister looks on in stunned amazement.[406]

While levitating mediums were very common during the mid-nineteenth century, several modern twentieth century cases have surfaced. Roberto Setti (1945-1984) of Florence, Italy first produced mediumistic phenomena at age fifteen, following the death of his brother. The Setti family began holding regular séances, during which many physical phenomena were produced. Setti soon became a very powerful medium, holding séances every Saturday for decades. Setti insisted upon total anonymity and only allowed outside visitors on rare occasions.

Dr. Paolo Giovetti, author of a dozen books, was one of the few scientists allowed in the circle. Giovetti claims to have observed Setti to levitate on several occasions. Writes Giovetti, "Almost at every séance a very mystical personality was manifested who called herself 'Teresa' and who talked about love for people and the importance of praying. On these occasions the medium levitated and produced a strong smell of roses that lingered for a long time. During the levitation his voice came from above. Then, as I could personally verify on several occasions, the medium would ask for hands and fall on his chair."[407]

A 1970s case involves an Italian nun, "Sister Rosa," who was suffering from attacks of possession. During one such attack, the sisters who were presiding over her were shocked to see Sister Rosa "rise up in the air, float slowly up to the ceiling, and pass right through it." The sisters ran up the stairs to the room above and found Sister Rosa standing there. As we have seen, this is only one of several cases of a levitator moving through a solid wall.[408]

A disturbing case of mediumistic levitation comes from demonologists, Ed and Lorraine Warren. In the mid-1980s, they received a call from a southern California woman who had heard their lecture about ghosts at a local college. She told them, "Last Sunday my brother levitated. I was sitting ten feet away. I saw it for myself."

Upon further questioning, the Warrens learned that the lady's brother, Milton, had been exhibiting this bizarre trait for a few months.

The Warrens visited the home. Milton was upset that they had been called, but his mother was concerned. As she told him, "You can't imagine what it was like. You were lying right down on that couch over there. Asleep—and then your whole body began rising in the air." As the Warrens continued their investigation, Milton was seen again by his sister to levitate.

After several interviews, the Warrens got an unbelievable confession from Milton that, during his job at a Funeral home, he had participated in gruesome and unspeakable acts. According to the Warrens, this led to demonic possession, which was evidenced by Milton's levitation. As Ed Warren writes, "He turned to perhaps the worst sin of all—necrophilia—and in so doing, handed his life over to the Devil." Apparently this act caused a "demonic" haunting, leading to the levitation events.[409]

While some people seek out levitation, others experience it as a result of moving into a haunted house. In 1973, John and Janet Smurl and their four daughters moved into a home in West Pittston, Pennsylvania. Shortly after they moved in, they began to experience poltergeist-like phenomena, including lights turning on and off, unusual stains, objects moving. Over the next ten years, the activity gradually intensified into a full-blown attack with the full range of paranormal phenomena, including, on one occasion, levitation.

By 1986, Janet Smurl had become somewhat used to unexplained events. They contacted demonologists, Ed and Lorraine Warren, who believed that Smurls were dealing with a demon.

Janet Smurl had good reason to believe that she was being pushed around by something, when on one occasion she was lifted out of her bed and thrown across the room. As she says, "Obviously it's not something I'll ever forget. It twisted me around several times and then hurled me into the far wall. Just before I crashed, I crossed my hands over my skull to protect it from the collision. Then the demon turned me over very quickly and at such an angle that my hands and arms were outstretched. I only had a few seconds to put myself into the fetal position because I could see the demon was going to catapult me into the wall, this time trying to break my hands and arms....What happened finally I can't really describe. All I could think of was being in a trance. I saw everything in our shadowy bedroom very clearly but at the same time I had a sense of being in two worlds, this one and the life after, almost as if I was hanging between life and death itself—and then suddenly I was lying next to Jack and I was sobbing, really out of control, and he woke me up and tried to calm me down, asking me what had happened, and I showed him the bruises from where the demon had slammed me into the wall...."[410]

As we have seen, in many cases levitation occurs as a result of spirit influence. The conclusion is undeniable: in some cases, dead people are able to levitate living people. An unusual case occurred in the 1980s and involved a levitating bed. In 1980, hotel renovator Frances Kerman purchased a large plantation and hotel in Louisiana. She was delighted by its architecture and was determined to make it like new. Called the Myrtles Plantation, it was already a widely known haunted place. Visitors showed up regularly from across the United States specifically to see the ghosts. At first Kerman was skeptical, but it wasn't long before she, too, experienced all kinds of ghostly encounters including cold spots, footsteps, strange noises, full-color apparitions and more.

Numerous other guests and visitors also reported all kinds of bizarre experiences. One particular room, the Bridal Suite, she soon discovered, had a "levitating bed." The first indication of this came from a photographer who was doing a story on the ghostly activity. The photographer spent the night in the bridal suite. In the morning, she quietly pulled Kerman aside and said, "You won't believe this! The bed lifted up in the middle of the night! I had just gone to bed when it started vibrating. The next thing I knew it lifted up in the air and was floating about a foot from the floor. I pulled the sheet over my head."

Kerman looked at the photographer with disbelief. Although she knew from personal experience that the Myrtles plantation was haunted, she just couldn't bring herself to believe in levitation. Then came more reports, and more after that. She could no longer deny the truth. Writes Kerman, "We became astounded as one guest after another told us that the bed in the bridal suite had floated in the air with the guests in the bed along for a ride....I attributed these wild stories to the spirits in the bottle, not the spirits in the house, until a sweet retired couple stayed with us for several days. They never knew about the ghosts. On the third morning of their stay, I joined the wife on the verandah for a cup of coffee and a biscuit. 'You know, I don't know if I should bring this up or not. I feel pretty silly telling you this, as you probably won't believe me,' she confided. 'But in the middle of the night last night the bed started shaking, and it lifted right up off the floor with both of us in it.' I suddenly knew better than to discredit anyone's story ever again, no matter how outrageous."[411]

In 1989, a small family in Indiana complained to their local pastor that they were victims of a strong poltergeist attack. Bob Mueller was pastor of the Zion Lutheran Church, but this was his first exposure to the paranormal. He was shocked at what he heard. Says Mueller, "They said they'd experienced a frightening poltergeist phenomenon in their house that morning. Their nine-year-old daughter had somehow been picked up and levitated. These people seemed sane and sensible; I couldn't write them off as lunatics."

The pastor blessed the house and to the great relief of the family, the manifestations promptly ended.[412]

In the 1990s, prominent social anthropologist and author Michael Cuneo conducted a years-long field study of exorcism across the United States. He witnessed more than fifty exorcisms firsthand. Not once did he see anybody levitate, however, he did hear of several firsthand accounts. Writes Cuneo, "I never personally witnessed levitation or any other spectacular effects—demonic or otherwise. I did, however, hear reports of such effects taking place at exorcisms I was unable to attend—a middle-aged man rising four feet in the air during the preliminary stages of an exorcism conducted on the East Coast; a hugely obese woman in the Midwest levitating in her chair, despite the efforts of three people to hold her down. I have no way of vouching for the historical truthfulness of reports such as these, which were relayed to me by people of considerable intelligence and integrity, if not exactly sterling impartiality."[413]

Even people who experience levitation themselves can remain skeptical of the event. Lisa Cain was seven years old when she and her mother moved into a haunted house. Immediately they both began to encounter the ghost. Cain reports that she would feel an invisible hand on her shoulder, feel odd cold spots, and see actual apparitions out of the corner of her eye. Meanwhile, her mother was pushed down the stairs more than once by an invisible force. Then came the levitations.

Writes Cain, "Another experience that I had was that I actually levitated off the bed several times and kept thinking that I would hit the ceiling at any moment."

Cain didn't tell her mother about the levitation incidents because she could hardly believe them herself. And by that time, they both knew the house was haunted and they'd moved out. It wasn't until years later that the subject came up again. Writes Cain, "As I got older, I brushed it [the levitations] off as a dream until my mother and I talked about that house and I told her about my dream. My mother turned white as she told me that she had walked in to check on me and I was levitating off the bed and then immediately fell. She said that she had never mentioned it to me because I was a child and she didn't want to frighten me."[414]

Another modern account of levitation (exact date not given) comes from an anonymous family who suffered a severe poltergeist attack in their home in the Midwest. The attack came suddenly and seemed to be focused primarily around the ten-year-old daughter, Hanna. The mother, Kristi, was in her bedroom one evening when she woke up to hear her daughter screaming for help. Kristi ran down the hallway and attempted to open her daughter's bedroom door. The door was being held shut by some mysterious force. Assuming it was her daughter, Kristi shouted at her to move away from the door. Hanna screamed that she wasn't by the door and continued to cry for help.

Using all her strength, Kristi finally slammed the door open with her body. Says Kristi, "The door flew open. I flicked on the light switch and what I saw was the scariest thing I had ever seen in my life! Hanna, who had a wrought iron canopy bed, was hanging on to the post and levitating in mid-air! She was holding on for dear life. Black shadows flying around the room quickly gathered and flew out the window. Normally this window needed something to prop it open, but it was staying open by itself. When the shadows flew out the window, the window crashed shut and Hanna slammed down to her bed." After this incident and others, the family moved out of their home and across several states to Florida.[415]

Prior to the 1900s, levitation events, while well documented, were still largely anecdotal. But with the advent of photography, we no longer depend solely on eyewitness testimony. The levitation photographic evidence, combined with the testimony of witnesses and the levitators themselves makes these cases hard to dismiss. Exactly how much evidence is needed to prove that levitation is true?

28. The Strange Case of Ted Owens

In 1924, in Bedford, Indiana, well-known and controversial psychic Ted Owens (1920-1987) experienced the first of several spontaneous levitations. Says Owens, "I was only four years old and was playing out in the yard. I was standing outside of the house when suddenly I began to float up the side of the house, way up to the top of the house. Then I floated back down again; of course, back then I had no idea of time. So I don't know how long it took. I definitely floated up in the air. When I got back down again, I knocked on the door and told Queenie [his grandmother] about it, and she laughed and thought I was making it up."

Owens grew up in a family where psychic events were accepted. As a child, he developed a strong interest in hypnotism and the paranormal, and as a teen-ager, would hypnotize his friends or give psychic readings. It was in this environment that Owens experienced his second episode of spontaneous levitation. Unlike his first

The late and controversial psychic, Ted Owens, had a long track record of accurate predictions and weather-control experiments. He also experienced three dramatic episodes of levitation. (Robert Mishlove)

episode, this one involved an outside witness. Says Owens, "I was about thirteen years old. I was at the country club that was just outside of Bedford where there was a swimming pool. It was in broad daylight. I climbed up on the ten-foot board and did a swan dive up in the air, spreading my arms out. Then I didn't come down. I was so astounded and amazed, I couldn't believe it, but I kept my arms outstretched and it was the most wonderful, exhilarating feeling I'd ever had in my life. I stayed up there what seemed like a long time. Then finally I went down into the water."

Like many people who experience an episode of spontaneous levitation, Owens found himself doubting the experience—that is, until he was confronted by an outside witness. Says Owens, "I might have thought it was my imagination because I couldn't figure it out. I knew that what goes up comes down. But when I climbed out of the pool, Bob Armstrong came up, a redheaded kid with freckles, and he said to me....'I knew you could do tricks, but how did you stay up in the air all that time?'"

Ted grew up and got his first job as a store clerk, and then worked in the office of famous psychic investigator J. B. Rhine, where he himself displayed psychic abilities. After several months, he decided to leave the job and join the military.

In 1943, at age twenty-three, he experienced his third and final episode of levitation. At the time, he was in the U. S. Navy aboard a ship in the Pacific. On this occasion, there were scores of witnesses. Says Owens, "One day I was outside on the ship's deck. I climbed up on a hatch. There must have been fifty to sixty men up there, lying around looking at the ocean. I gave a little jump to go down two or three feet off the hatch—and instead of coming down, I went into the air and just sort of floated. All of the sailors were pointing and saying, 'Look at that!' I was just floating and finally came down near the rail some distance away. It was really weird. I'll never forget it. It was definitely levitation. But I don't know what caused it. The sailors' eyes were all bulging out. I lost all sense of time, just as I had done when it happened in Bedford."

After a few years, Owens realized the military life wasn't for him. He left the service and decided to make a career as a psychic. He soon had a group of followers who helped support him. He went on to experience numerous other kinds of paranormal events, claiming to be able to control weather events, cause power outages, manipulate sporting events, call down UFOs, conduct spiritual healings, predict earthquakes, and more. While these claims may seem extreme, Owens has a surprisingly strong track-record. As the number of his "hits" mounted, investigators were forced to take notice. Writes researcher Colin Wilson, "I think there seems to be no reasonable doubt that he had astonishing capacity for causing changes in the weather."

Many other researchers confirmed that Owens displayed considerable psychic abilities. Author and researcher Robert Mishlove Ph.D. documented many of these events and hundreds of other paranormal incidents in the life of Ted Owens in his outstanding book, *The PK Man*. Regarding Owens' levitations, he writes, "Admittedly, these accounts of spontaneous levitation stretch Owens' credibility. This is probably because such a phenomenon is extremely rare; but it is not unknown in the annals of psychic science…if the great saints could levitate, there is no logical reason to doubt that some of us living secular lives could similarly be endowed with this same ability."

Owens died on December 28, 1987, leaving behind an enduring legacy of mystery.[416]

29. The Floating Stage (When Children Fly)

The vast majority of levitations occur to people who are spiritually inclined—a saint, priest, nun, friar, shaman, psychic, magician, sorcerer, medium…the list goes on. However, one small subcategory of levitations involves a unique group of people—young children. In case after case, children ranging in age from about six to thirteen spontaneously levitate. In fact, the cases are so consistent, that it's almost as if there is a developmental stage in which levitation is facilitated. Perhaps it's because pre-pubescent children have a super-abundance of psychic and emotional energy, which may be related to poltergeist-type activity. Or perhaps it's because children have not yet placed limits on their abilities or been spoiled by society's prejudices that people cannot fly. In any case, the floating stage appears to be a very real phenomenon.

The following case was personally investigated by the author, and involves a lady by the name of Mary Frank. Today, Mary works as a producer for a northern California radio station. I can personally vouch for her integrity and have known her for more than thirty years. She rarely revealed her experience with levitation, as it occurred only once, and she had learned that many people were skeptical. However, because of my interest in the paranormal, and because I asked, she agreed to share her account.

Back in 1951, at age eight, she had an experience she will never forget. It is a perfect example of a spontaneous levitation. She says, "My parents were taking me to the doctor. And the doctor's office was in a fairly large office building, an older building in Chicago. We got off the floor at the doctor's office. It was a square-shaped building, and to get to the office that I had to go to, I had to walk three-fourths of a square all the way around to the other side.

"I ran ahead of my parents, and I had a sensation of light changing in the corridor. It wasn't a bright light, but it was more like a glowing feeling. I felt like the faster I ran, this glowing feeling around me—not in myself but in the exterior around me—intensified. And I felt my legs no longer touching the ground, but I felt that I could fly. And I looked down and I *was* flying. And I would say it was—I didn't go very high because I was inside, but I was at least three feet off the ground. And it lasted for however long it took me to go around the corner, probably about thirty seconds….[I flew] around the corner inside the building…. Nobody was there. See, I was ahead of my family. I was going fairly fast, but not like a car. It was more like a floaty—it wasn't probably too much faster than a real fast run, except I wasn't running anymore….I remember the sensation of flying, and I felt elevated obviously. I was steady as a bird. I remember thinking, 'Oh, my God! I'm flying!' In other words, recognition came right away….I remember being very, very astounded by it, totally astounded by it….It was amazing but not scary because I felt very safe. I was amazed! It was neat. I wasn't thinking anything but how neat it was. You know, I was a kid, and at that age, anything seems possible, sort of, 'Wow, I learned to fly.'

"When I came to my feet, I had the sensation of being placed down as opposed to falling or all of the sudden not flying. I felt almost placed back down on the ground. That's what I remember. I remember running back to my mom and dad and telling them, saying, 'You won't believe what just happened to me. I just flew around the corner!' When I tried to, of course, tell them about it, they said, 'Yeah, sure, sure, sure.'

"But no one could ever talk me out of the fact that I had flown, because I felt I had."

Mary has no idea why she flew or the cause. In fact, even as the event was in progress she tried to figure out what was happening. Her first thought was that somebody must have come up behind her. But when she turned around, nobody was there. Still, today she speculates that something or someone invisible was there. As she says, "I felt definitely in somebody's company, because I had the feeling of looking around to see who was with me, and not being able to see anything, but feeling, as I said, a kind of glowing atmosphere."

Shortly following the incident, and many times afterwards, Mary tried to duplicate the event and levitate again. Unfortunately, she was unsuccessful. As she says simply, "It never worked!"[417]

Another modern account of levitation for which I can personally vouch comes from another friend, Kelly Marley (pseudonym) from southern California. She is employed as an author and has completed several children's books. When she heard of my interest in levitation, she revealed that she had experienced levitation not once or twice, but *numerous* times. All of the incidents occurred in the early 1950s and were confined to her childhood for a period of two years, between ages six to eight.

Says Kelly, "We lived in a house on the second floor. We rented the second floor of a duplex and in order to get upstairs to our house, there was a long flight of stairs, and then a turn with a short flight of stairs. And I can remember as a child just going up and down those stairs from time to time *without* running up and down. I would just levitate. I got up the stairs.

"The first time I didn't know how I did it. But I knew I started out at the top. The first time I did it I went from the top and I went down to the bottom. I went around the corner and down. It must have been about a dozen steps and it just went really fast...my experience was that I was very close to the ceiling. It was the same way I was standing, but maybe tilted a little bit....I started off at the top and the next thing I knew I was through the air and at the bottom. I was so utterly confused that I just sat at bottom for a long time. I couldn't understand what had been going on."

Kelly reports that her landing was "soft, very gentle and on my feet."

At first, she assumed that this was a once-in-a-lifetime event. However, only a few weeks later it happened again; but this time she was going the other direction. "And I remember once going up that way. I called it flying. I don't remember flapping my arms or anything like that. But I do remember that I didn't use any kind of energy at all. I was transported back and forth. It was very confusing to me."

Kelly was unable to control her flights, and they only occurred on the one staircase, usually when she was descending. After the levitations had occurred repeatedly, at least a half-dozen times, she decided that she had better tell somebody. She first revealed her secret to her teenage cousin, telling him matter-of-factly, "I can fly up and down the stairs."

He replied, "Show me!"

Kelly replied, "Can't you do it too?"

That's the first time Kelly actually realized just how unusual it was. As she says, "I thought everybody could do it."

Kelly became even more confused when she tried to duplicate the experience for her cousin. To her disappointment, she was unable to do so. As she says, "I couldn't do it for him, and it was very frustrating. I couldn't show him. It wouldn't happen."

To her relief, however, her cousin believed her. He could see that she was genuinely confused and sincere. Kelly then decided to tell her mother. It became her first lesson in skepticism. Says Kelly, "I can't talk to many people about it, because people think I'm weird. That's what happened. When I flew, I remember telling my mom who told me I was crazy and I better be careful whom I told that to. And soon after that I stopped flying....I was too frightened and I stopped doing it. I was so afraid that I was doing something bad...nobody wanted to talk too much about it. They just thought that I was fantasizing and imagining, and there she is telling stories. They didn't understand that they were true....It was very distressing."

Kelly's story, however, does not end there. As a child, she had what she called a secret way of running which allowed her to run faster than anybody around, including boys who were much older than she. As she says, "I remember when I was a young girl, I could run really *very* fast. And that was the closest I ever got to the experience I had on the stairs. I could outrun all the boys three blocks around, fast. I could run *really* fast. And sometimes I would be afraid that I'd trip on the sidewalk, but there was a way that I could run that I wasn't that close to the ground. But everybody else who saw me—it looked like I was running on the ground. But I knew I wasn't. You know how sidewalks bump up and down, that sort of thing."

Kelly's description sounds amazingly similar to the Native American's method of "supernatural running" or the Tibetan *lung-gom*. Interestingly, Kelly reports a variety of other psychic experiences, including premonitions and memories of a past-life as a Native American.[418]

Another similar account occurred in the mid-1900s (exact date not given) to a young girl from Churchill, Oxford in England. Felicity X. was six years old when her parents divorced. As a result of the disharmony in the family, Felicity soon experienced "tension" which gave her the ability to levitate. Interestingly, these are the same conditions that in some cases foster poltergeist activity. In this case it manifested as levitations.

Felicity explains, "When I was very young, I used to stand at the top of the winding stairs and fly down. I used to count every step—there were thirty. It happened in the evenings when I had been sent to bed. I was afraid of something upstairs and felt I had to get to the bottom. But I also had a tremendous feeling of power. I used to jump off the top step and land on my feet. The staircase was old and winding with a thick rope instead of a banister. I somehow got round the corner and touched the rope at one point in the middle. I never told anyone I was terrified at the top of the stairs. I knew it was going to happen as it happened most evenings....All this went on for years and finally ended when I was six when my parents divorced and I moved with my mother to a modern house."[419]

There are many accounts of children who have flown. A remarkably similar account comes from a man known only as "Spencer," today a television anchorman turned entertainer. Spencer reports that there was a short period during his early childhood when he also was able to fly. He called it "the floating stage."

As in the other cases, Spencer reports that his many flights took place exclusively on one particular staircase, usually when he was running. Says Spencer, "I'd hit the landing and I swear to you that I'd float up over that landing. Sometimes I thought I'd hit the ceiling. But then somehow I'd end up down at the bottom of the stairs without ever having walked down them. At a certain point in my life, it happened a lot. I didn't make anything of it. I just thought I was at, you know, *the floating stage.* I didn't know. I was a kid. I thought *everybody* floated."

A final twist to this particular case is that Spencer is a UFO abductee. UFO researcher, Budd Hopkins, who uncovered this case theorizes that Spencer's flights may have been the result of UFO experiences, and that instead of flying, he was levitated up a beam of light from a UFO. However, Spencer did not recall any light beams during these experiences, and the fact that Spencer's flights were so numerous and closely match other accounts of non-abductees, opens the possibility that Spencer really did fly, and that there actually is a "floating stage" during which young children have access to this normally latent ability of levitation.

Hopkins recounts another case involving the brother of an abductee. Peter X. who reports that he often flew as a young child, not only at his home, but at his friend's home. Says Peter, "I was doing it in my bedroom, and I was doing it at Eric Avallar's house. I'm flying around his room. That's right. I remember that, in the bedroom. I can even tell you what it feels like...I honestly do remember floating around in our bedroom and also over at Eric Avallar's house, floating around their house. It was a kick. I know what it feels like to be flying around. I'd be way up there too. I'd be almost at the ceiling. But I don't think I was steering or in control."

Again, Hopkins theorizes that these are likely half-remembered UFO abduction experiences. And in fact, there are at least two other similar cases. One involves a French doctor who experienced two spontaneous levitations following his own abduction experience. The other involves famed abductee and author, Whitley Strieber, who experienced a spontaneous levitation episode in his cabin in upstate New York. [420]

While explanations for the spontaneous levitation of children remain a mystery, the cases speak for themselves. Clearly something unusual is happening here.

30. The Levitations of Rajalakshmi

A truly compelling mid-twentieth century case (exact date not-given) account was investigated by Doug Boyd, author, Native American civil rights leader, and founder of the Cross-Cultural Studies program in Tucson, Arizona. In the 1980s, he was funded by the Menninger Foundation to travel to across the world to interview a variety of yogi adepts and study their ability to control states of consciousness and psychophysiological states, or in other words, mind-body connections.

One of their subjects was an extraordinary woman by the name of Mahayogini Rajalakshmi of Tirupati, India. At the time, Rajalakshmi was the professor of biochemistry at the University of Sri Padmavathi. Boyd couldn't help but notice that Rajalkshmi was different from the many other yogis he had met. She was young, female, drove a fancy sports car, dressed with expensive jewelry, and was strikingly beautiful.

However, Boyd was assured by those around her that she was a genuine yogi. As a child, she had created a local sensation because of her ability to levitate. Writes Boyd, "Rajalakshmi had been somewhat of a legend in her own hometown during her childhood, we were told. As a child, she had begun to meditate and had experienced many occurrences of transcending gravity. At times she would levitate, and at times she would turn upside down and levitate on her head.... She was so often and so long in levitation that people came from near and far to see her. These things occurred spontaneously...and were not entirely in her control. It created a problem for the wealthy family and they had to hire guards because of the crowds."

During his meeting with Rajalakshmi, Boyd was shown photographic evidence of her levitations. "Among the snapshots of Rajalakshmi were several photographs taken by a newspaper journalist, showing her sitting in a lotus-posture and levitating about a foot off the floor. On one of these in particular, it looked as though some external force—almost like a great wind, or perhaps vacuum—were acting upon her and lifting her into the air. Her hair and clothing seemed to be blowing in several directions, while her expression and her posture appeared still and calm."

Boyd was amazed by the photos and learned that Rajalakshmi had given demonstrations of her levitating abilities on prior occasions, including once for a group of students and faculty at the university where she taught.

Boyd finally asked her about her ability to levitate. Rajalakshmi replied, "It does not happen nowadays...well, not spontaneously as before. And it was never an objective of mine—not something I was seeking. It was like an automatic sort of thing, and it gave me problems at times. In college I had to stay alone because I had several times alarmed my roommates. This is a surprising thing, you see, when it is so unusual for them and unexpected....As a young girl when this happened, I was amazed, I can say, but I was not frightened. Yet it startled my parents. To them it appeared an emergency, something dangerous happening to their daughter, so they were quite upset enough to seek help, not the first time—the third or fourth time, perhaps. You see, I went straight up from my bed, which was against the wall. We have these high windows with inside shutters... and I hit the shutter. Normally I could not reach the shutter, and it made such a loud sound in the night, my parents came rushing in. Seeing me suspended in the air in that manner, they were startled, and my father shouted at me. Perhaps that in itself brought me down, and I became fully conscious."

Rajalakshmi also knows exactly what first caused her ability to levitate. "I was in meditation, and even though I was not fully conscious of my body, I knew what had happened and why...you see, my teacher chose for me this wonderful book, *The Gospel of Ramakrishna*....So I would read this book, and it was so, so inspirational for me, it opened me to something. I used to meditate on this, though I had not been doing meditation. I would read some pages and become so moved, and I would meditate on this emotion. I read it in the evening instead of my homework. I had not much worry for homework, as I was excelling in my class work, and I read this book instead when my parents thought I was doing homework. So this thing did it—it put me into levitation. This book was the cause of it in the beginning."

The book is more than 1,000 pages and details the life of spiritual master, Ramakrishna, himself a levitator. To stop the levitations, Rajalakshmi's parents forbid her from reading the book and sought help from the leading sage of their village, who advised them that their daughter was a yogi and to seek a guru. The guru instructed the parents to have no fears, that levitation was natural and to allow her to read the book.

The parents agreed, but were not mollified. Says Rajalakshmi, "So then it went on for a time. I went on reading my book and remained long hours in meditation and long hours in levitation....so the villagers learned of this and they came. Others began to arrive from here and there. My father would not let them see me, and at last there were crowds of people—men, women, children—sleeping and washing and preparing meals on our property."

The police were called, who said that they were unable to order the people away and the best solution would be a compromise. Allow them to view the levitating girl for short periods. The parents reluctantly agreed. Says Rajalakshmi, "So the days of the week and the hours were set, and the people could come in, a few at a time, in one door and out the other. There were ropes put between so they could not touch me."

After a few months, Rajalakshmi was advised by her guru to stop the levitations as she was "lost in bliss" and becoming "useless in your lifetime." At that point, Rajalakshmi stopped the levitating trances. Today she has focused her energy on more practical pursuits including running a yoga institute, teaching at a university and working at a health clinic. One of her students credits her with helping to cure his diabetes.[421]

31. Levitations Today

While we have already examined several current cases of levitation, this chapter will focus on some additional cases which have occurred in the twentieth and twenty-first centuries. Far from being a phenomenon relegated to the Dark Ages, levitation continues to occur at a steady rate.

The phenomenon of out-of-body travel is, in some cases, closely linked with levitation. This is typified in the following case that occurred sometime in the 1920s to French author Yram (pseudonym.) Yram achieved fame for his book on personal experiences of astral projection. On several occasions, he would return from his out-of-body experiences with such an increased sensation of energy that he felt he should be able to physically fly. On at least one occasion, he nearly did. Writes Yram, "The following instance is rather unusual. I slept for six hours and awakened in an apparently normal state. As soon as I had risen, I felt extraordinarily light. I felt as if I were walking on air and my legs were moving far too quickly. At first this amused me. I had the impression of being in an inter-mediary condition between earth and a less material substance, and this form of disequilibrium was new to me. At last, I remembered my social obligations and, walking down on the street, boarded a tram. This semi-exteriorization had not come to an end, though, and it somewhat diminished my nervous sensitivity. It therefore happened that on stepping off the tram, I was nearly run over. No longer having a full control over my body, I still had the feeling of walking on air. On stepping off the tram it seemed as if a chasm were opening at my feet, and I reacted violently in order to keep my balance. All this took scarcely a second. Anyone looking on would only have seen me take a few steps faster than was necessary. I did not fall, but the vividness of the impressions which I experienced in so minute a fraction of time is beyond imagination. At all events, I do not consider that such states of spontaneous levitation are to be encouraged."[422]

A compelling and well-verified account of a partial levitation comes from Captain J. Alleyne Bartlett of England. On May 3, 1931, during a lecture before the London Spiritualist Alliance, Captain Bartlett revealed that he had the unusual ability to reduce his weight using mere will power. He reported often having the feeling of being able to lighten his weight, and agreed to test his strange talent before the lecture audience. A scale was procured, and Bartlett stepped onto it. His weight was measured and then Captain Bartlett willed that his weight become lighter. To everyone's amazement, Bartlett was, in fact, able to reduce his weight by "several pounds." Incidentally, Bartlett also worked extensively with automatic writing and probably had some mediumistic abilities himself.[423]

As we explore the modern accounts of levitation, several facts become clear. First, the accounts haven't changed much. Over the centuries, the same story has been heard again and again. What differentiates modern accounts from earlier ones is the quality of evidence. Gone are all myths and legends. Most modern accounts have firsthand written testimonies by living witnesses and/or percipients.

An interesting 1960s account comes from Mikhail Drogzenovich, a fifty-three-year-old Bulgarian farmer from the village of Stara Zagora who was well known locally for his ability to levitate. A newspaper article profiling the farmer provoked crowds of people to visit his farm for a demonstration. Among these were several scientists. Drogzenovich was happy to oblige. He sat down in a field on his farm and intensely concentrated as the crowd surrounded him. Slowly, Drogzenovich rose about four feet into the air, where he remained suspended for ten minutes while the visitors and scientists tried to determine if there was any evidence of hoaxing or trickery. None was detected, and Drogzenovich sank down to the earth. When asked what his secret was, Drogszenovich replied, "Once I'm in the air, I'm unable to change my position. I get there by will power."[424]

Another 1960 account of partial levitation also involves a seemingly normal person. Reported by John Weed, the incident occurred during a visit to a small traveling fairground in the United States. One of the booths contained a lady who, like Captain Bartlett, claimed to have the ability to reduce her body weight by mind power alone, allowing visitors to lift her with one hand.

As Weed writes, "Levitation: this gravity-defying performance was apparently a lot more common in ancient times than it is today. Yet occasionally even now one runs into evidence of the ability to lift the body into the air without artificial aid. Not long ago I saw a stage performer who could change her weight. It was no trick. Curious, I went to the stage when people were called from the audience and found to my surprise that I could lift her easily with one hand as she sat in a basket-like contrivance with a handle at the top. Yet on a scale her size indicated the 140 pounds it recorded was correct. She could levitate to a small degree."

Weed inquired on how she was able to do this, she replied simply, "It's a knack. My mother could do it and I can. You can just make yourself feel light in here." She put her hand over her chest.

Weed then asked her if she had ever been able to truly levitate. The lady replied, "No. I tried several times and although I felt very light once or twice I was never successful in actually getting off the ground. However, when I was younger, about eight or nine, I had no fear of heights and would jump off walls and down flights of stairs. I never came down hard, never hurt myself, but always floated down gently like a thistledown." Age eight or nine? Sounds like the floating stage.[425]

Another 1960s (exact date not given) incident occurred to an anonymous gentleman in the United States. After developing an interest in levitation, he decided to attempt it. To his surprise, he succeeded and found himself rising spontaneously into the air with little control on his own part. He soon learned to regret his decision to attempt levitation.

Often while he walked his dog, he found himself rising uncontrollably into the air.

Thankfully, he lived in the country on a large parcel of land with many trees that he used to arrest his levitations. As he says, "My dog would just stand and wait until I was able to balance myself. Such a nuisance....how I wish it would stop....I've never told anyone but you about my levitating. I know I would be a deranged character."[426]

In 1967, Boris Ermolaev (Yermolayev), a young man from Leningrad, Russia was invited to a party near his home. Little did he know that his life was about to change forever. There were various games planned to entertain the guests, one of which involved levitation. Apparently, some of the members of the party came from a family whose members had the peculiar ability to levitate either themselves or small objects. First one of the members levitated a flower between his hands. Ermolaev was impressed and told the young man so. He said, "That's nothing, you should see my sister self-levitate."

Ermolaev asked for a demonstration, and was taken to meet the sister, a slightly overweight teenager. As he says, "He introduced me to her. 'Will you show me?' I asked her. 'I will,' she said, 'but no other audience.' With that she led me into the bedroom next door, stood up on a couch—it sank in under her weight—and she squinted her tiny eyes. Suddenly the couch straightened out under her feet, and then she rose, like a balloon, into the air. She stopped about two feet up....then she came back down onto the couch. I left the room without saying a word. I was stupefied. I asked my host, 'Is your whole family this way?' He shrugged, 'Maybe.'"

Ermolaev was so impressed that he returned several times for further demonstrations to learn as much as he could. He became determined to learn the process himself. To his surprise, he was extraordinarily successful, eventually becoming one of the Soviet Union's top psychics. Throughout the 1970s he performed many feats of levitation, usually of small objects, but sometimes of actual people. Interestingly, the length of his levitations usually corresponded to the length of his breath retention. His case is among the best-verified accounts of the twentieth century. Says Luisa Georgyevna of the *Literary Gazette*, "[He's] a very remarkable man. Lifts people and keeps them in mid-air with sheer will power."

Victor Ladyshev, a science editor for the *Literary Gazette* says of Ermolaev, "I was attending the screening of a movie in the main projection room when a young fellow rushed in all excited, calling out, 'Ermolaev has just suspended Shipkhina in mid-air and she is up there right now, floating.' I'll never forgive myself for not dashing out there to see the famous woman film director [and actress] float in mid-air. But others did, and they said they actually caught her slowly descending to the divan in the reception room where it all took place."

Says Victor Adamenko, "Many people have told me of the levitation of the actress. The people who witnessed it are solid and upstanding citizens."

One of the witnesses was Boris Groshikov, a dancer of the Bolshoi theater ballet. "I was there and saw Ermolaev perform the levitations. I could not believe my eyes, but it happened. The woman was motionless, but floating two feet above the sofa. She left no indentation on the surface of the sofa. We were all around

Ermolaev and the woman, as close as we wanted to be. The people at the party included some of the top people of stage and screen in this country. There was no trick. We were not hypnotized, there were no ropes or mirrors. We were not fooled. It was a spontaneous demonstration."

Says Ermolaev of the event, "I was demonstrating my power to make things hang in mid-air when she asked me if I could lift her....I had never done anything like this before. But she kept on asking and I finally agreed to do it. She was so light that I could have lifted her physically. That is important in levitation. You must know that you can physically lift the object. I can't make houses float in mid-air; it has to be something fairly light. I told the actress to lie down, because somehow I knew that she would have to be in a horizontal position to levitate. I was right. I've had several experiments with others since, but I usually fail when I try to float people standing up. Apparently this is very difficult. And on this occasion, improvising as I went, I tried to imagine that in fact she was not lying down, but was over my head, as though the ceiling was the floor, and that I was holding her up—that I was keeping her from falling. I concentrated on this. My hands were about two feet above her at all times. When she moved upwards, my hands maintained the two-foot distance. Although I was later told that I appeared to be pressing down with my hands, all that was in my mind was that I was supporting her. It is reverse thinking....Slowly she moved up from the sofa. I held her there for as long as I could. But in my mind, I became too tired of holding up her weight. I had to drop her. She sank slowly back onto the sofa. At no time did I touch her. I was standing close to the sofa. Afterwards, she did not feel anything unusual."

Russian scientist and engineer Genady Sergeyev studied Ermolaev's case in depth and came away convinced. "He has the unusual ability of concentrating his energy into a focal point in mid-air and causing objects [and people] to be suspended in the air for many seconds."[427]

In 1977, Maharishi Mahesh Yogi received a lot of publicity when he announced that he was teaching courses in transcendental meditation and levitation. At least one student, Albertine Haupt, was allegedly successful. As she told a newspaper reporter, "I suddenly found myself six feet above the floor and thought, 'Heavens, I've done it!'" While the course may be effective, no students have yet claimed or publicly exhibited levitating abilities equal to the majority of cases. However, even today, there are courses available to learn this type of "yogic flying."[428]

Sometime in the mid-1970s, an anonymous family in the United States befriended a man and his son, Joaquin, who had come from India where they had studied in various ashrams to "attain different disciplines and practices." One day, two members of the family observed their two new friends perform an amazing feat. Writes the anonymous witness, "This man let us know that what they were doing required a lot of concentration, so they needed some quiet, regardless of what happens. So we agreed and just sat around to watch whatever was going to happen. Then he turned to us and said that he was going to float. So I was like, okay, go ahead. The man faced the wall, folded his hands in front of him and stood in concentration. Then he began to teeter slightly back and forth. Then his feet lifted off the ground as he carefully wiggled his toes underneath to tell whether he was off the carpet or not, or maybe to tell how far up. Granted it was no more than an inch or so, but he eventually rose higher to approximately six inches and was in fact floating. When he got to this height, he held his hand out to the wall to stabilize himself and then drifted down. I remember being quite amazed and then it was Joaquin's turn. His father stood behind him as if to help if he was to fall or something, and sure enough the boy rose off the ground about six to eight inches."

The witness asked how they were able to do this. The man explained that he focuses on a spot on the planet Mars, and by connecting to it and concentrating on it, he is able to levitate. The witness says he attempted the strange technique on a few occasions. He felt a "sense of light in my body…a sensation of smoothly lifting upwards, but I can't get off the ground. I always sense like I am falling forwards, which makes me nervous and totally breaks my focus."

The witness, however, is convinced. As he writes, "This is a true story, but there are secrets to it that I have yet to figure out. But please let me attest to this as an actual witness of this. Human levitation is a real phenomenon."[429]

An absolutely astonishing case of a mid-1980s levitation comes from author and teacher Helen Hadsell of Dallas, Texas. She became interested in levitation after taking a course in the Silva Mind Control program. After following the exercises, she was delighted to discover a strong increase in her psychic abilities. She soon began lecturing on the power of positive thinking, and thought to herself that levitation would definitely be an interesting experiment. As she says, "That's when the idea to levitate first surfaced. Why not? It could probably draw more people into my lectures than a Billy Graham service. I'd be able to show skeptics and non-believers that everything is possible. Whatever the mind can conceive, it can achieve, I reasoned….whatever your reason, mine was to show off and attract attention."

Out of the blue, Hadsell was approached by a gentleman who had seen her on a TV talk show and somehow knew of her interest in levitation, although she had never voiced it publicly. He warned her, "You don't really want to levitate, but I don't think you will believe me until it happens to you." He said that it had happened to him, and he found it a nuisance as he was unable to control the spontaneous events. But seeing that Hadsell was not convinced, he gave her recommendations. "I'll tell you what you need to do. Pretend you are swimming but hold your arms out like this."

Hadsell filed the man's advice in the back of her mind and continued her efforts. She looked into yoga, but found the positions excruciating. She considered losing weight, until she read that some of the levitating saints were known to be overweight. She started meditating daily. She bought a trampoline and as she jumped on it, she visualized herself levitating. Nothing, however, seemed to work.

After a few months of this, however, she woke up one morning feeling "charged, balanced and grateful for all my blessings." Not even thinking about levitating, she drove to the chapel for morning services at the University of Dallas near her home. As she left her car, she spontaneously levitated. All her practice and meditation finally paid off and to her utter astonishment she found herself suddenly flying through the air.

Says Hadsell, "After I left my car and walked fifty yards toward the chapel, something happened. Looking down at the ground, I realized it was below me—my body was floating, six inches in the air. The path to the chapel was downhill and there were no trees or bushes nearby. I panicked. That's when I remembered what the man had told me in Detroit, and I began stroking in mid-air as though swimming. I balanced myself and began moving forward toward the chapel. I locked my mind onto one of the pillars which bordered the entrance way. I planned to wrap my arms around it and get myself back on the ground. I kept my eyes firmly on my goal and soon was able to accomplish this maneuver although I was operating in a totally unfamiliar environment. As I hastily returned to solid ground, I felt tremendous relief. I kept clinging to the pillar until, with a sudden jerk, the voices of students arriving for services brought me back to reality."

Hadsell, like many levitators, was thankful that nobody had seen her antics. She attended services and in fear of a repeat performance, waited until everyone else had left before she returned to her car. Says Hadsell, "It hasn't happened since."[430]

A mid-1980s account comes Father Richard McAlear, a healing and deliverance preacher from New York. During his service, he has conducted numerous deliverances or mini-exorcisms. In the vast majority of these cases, no paranormal events occurred. However, Father McAlear admits that on a few occasions, he saw things that bordered on the miraculous. Says McAlear, "You're going to find some of this hard to believe, and if I were in your shoes, I'd also find it hard to believe. But I was there, and I can only report what I saw. And I was sober and sane. I have only mentioned this particular case to a few people, but feel free to write it up. It really happened....There was a woman in her early forties who went to a charismatic prayers group for a healing...But during the prayers she threw herself on the floor, and then she levitated. The group tried to perform deliverance on her over a period of weeks, and they eventually put in a call to Betty and me. We went out, and she levitated right before our eyes. She was the first case of full-fledged possession we'd ever seen."[431]

It is difficult to account for cases of spontaneous levitation. The case of Jeffrey Greenberg is a good example. Writes Greenberg, "On some twenty occasions over the years of 1981-83, I levitated. Sometimes this was a mere floating, at others, actual flying and swooping about."

Greenberg has no idea what first triggered the experience, but after several episodes, he noticed patterns. "I didn't prepare to levitate; that is, I didn't wear any special clothing, diet in any way, change my breathing, nor attempt to hop in the air from the lotus position. Instead, I would be sitting in a chair, or pacing in my studio, thinking, gathering my thoughts—*in some way gathering together a pool of anger*—and, then, as if an explosion had taken place, I would be in flight. I would tend to assume a kind of 'zooming' position, leading with my chin, legs and arms following sometimes stiff, sometimes loose. Landing sometimes was a slow motion stroboscopic process, sometimes a simultaneous vanishing from flight and reappearance at rest."

Greenberg soon learned that flying around had its drawbacks. "How did I levitate? The happy secret is not so much that I caused it, but that I permitted it to happen. You might think this was trivially easy: simply granting oneself permission to do something, but in these matters, where great pressure is exerted to stay in line, it is not so easy. Usually I was exhausted and for several hours quite useless. This tiredness never diminished, not even over the repeated acts and it lessened the usefulness of the flying....Levitation is amusing only for so long. In and of itself, it leads nowhere. Still, it was fantastic."

Greenberg has no plans to attempt a repeat performance. "These levitations are difficult to take. I have trouble reconciling them with what is certain and solid. Then I thought these acts powerful. After all, who can boast that they have violated physical laws; are these not the acts of a super creature? Then I saw my acts as proof that reality could be radically interpreted....Now I see the desperation in that flight. Six years later, I have no longing for those events to repeat themselves....I have been silent about these acts till now, but they must be presented." (www.inventivity.com)

A 1990 account comes from Edmund X., a resident of Los Angeles, California. During an informal interview with the author, Edmund revealed that he successfully levitated following years of meditation. For several years, Edmund had been studying the philosophy of a well-known Mexican spiritual leader, Samael Eon Weor, founder of the Gnostic Movement. Edmund had been doing various exercises to provoke astral-travel experiences.

According to Weor, humans also have the ability to levitate, and he provides exercises to achieve levitation. Weor says that humans can levitate if they achieve what he calls the "djin state" which involves meditation and raising the body's vibratory rate. Once you achieve a certain level of vibration which you can physically feel, you are supposed to jump up and levitate.

One evening, while lying down and meditating, Edmund felt the vibrations that are indicative of the djin state. He quickly got out of bed and jumped up. As he said, "I jumped up and my body flew up in the air and went forward across the room and hit the wall."

As he explained what happened in broken English, Edmund was clearly sincere and excited. He said that the experience shocked him and even though he was working towards it, it was totally unexpected.[432]

An outstanding modern case comes from Yogi Masaharu Naruse of Japan. At age twelve, Naruse began to practice yoga with the hopes of freeing himself from all bondage and reaching Nirvana. Throughout the 1970s, he visited many yoga masters throughout India. In 1976, he began teaching yoga himself. Years later, in 1982, he began to levitate. In April 1983, a series of eight photographs were taken of Naruse while levitating. Five years later, he levitated more than one meter high and was again photographed. In 1990, he allowed himself to be photographed in a levitation for one final time, but never again. In 1992, he wrote the Japanese book, *Levitation by Method of Yoga*. In 2001, he was conferred the title of Yogi Raj. Today he is considered one of the highest practitioners of kundalini yoga. He currently heads the Naruse Yoga Group in Tokyo. Yoga classes are open Monday through Saturday, from 10:30 in the morning to 8:00 in the evening. (www.naruse-yoga.com.)

In 1992, an anonymous woman from Crestone, Colorado was in her home meditating. She had been a regular meditator for many years. As she told me during an informal interview, "I was meditating in a cross-legged position. After a while, I opened my eyes and I was hovering a few inches off the ground! As soon as I noticed I was hovering, I fell back down gently."

The lady was astonished as she had never experienced levitation before and had no idea that she was hovering until she opened her eyes.[433]

An incredible modern case of levitation occurred in 1997, in the Polish town of Goshkovice, as reported in the local *Zycie Warszawy* newspaper.

Yogi Masaharu Naruse is one of today's leading teachers and practitioners of kundalini yoga. Says Naruse, "This photo is taken in the most relaxed manner. The timing of this photo was just when I sat on a very thin air film (layer) and my waist just started sinking into it. You may feel how comfortable I am on this air film…I am sure this is going to be the last photo of my levitation." (April 26, 1990) (Pravda.ru/www. naruse-yoga.com.)

Local fortune-teller Marisa Lozinskaya was having a good day. She had a line of customers in front of her booth and was in the process of giving readings as she did everyday. One of the customers in line, Anneli Vozgolskaya, describes what happened next. "All of a sudden she said she had a headache. She stopped reading cards, turned ashen-faced and even screamed with pain. Right at that moment I saw her rising above the ground slowly. Her body remained motionless there. Everybody on the square was flabbergasted at the sight of the woman hanging in the air three meters above the ground. She was hovering for two minutes and then started going down. As soon as her feet touched the ground, she fell face-down."

Dozens of people observed the incident. Authorities were immediately called. The first physician to examine Lozinskya was Doctor Dobzinsky. Says Dobzinsky, "Her eyes were shut. She had a weak pulse. When she recovered, the first question she asked was, 'Why am I lying here?' As it turned out, she did not remember what happened to her."[434]

In 1999, Joan Hartmann of Florida spontaneously experienced a typical OBE (out-of-body experience) during which she floated about her room. She found the experience very pleasant and decided to try it again. A few days later, Joan attempted to initiate an OBE. While she was successful, her attempts also resulted in a full-blown levitation episode. Writes Joan, "I had an out-of-body experience. I spontaneously popped out of my body and hung out up in a corner of the bedroom but didn't know what to do, so I just looked down at my body and that of my sleeping husband. After about fifteen seconds, I snapped back into my body. I thought this was really cool and tried to repeat it. A few days later, it happened again, only this time, I watched my body actually levitate off the bed before I snapped right back."[435]

Marilynn Hughes is a leading expert and practitioner of astral projection. She has written a fascinating series of books about her own personal experiences while out of the body, which began shortly following the birth of her first child. She has also experienced numerous highly mystical experiences involving precognition, miraculous healing and other phenomenal events, including at least two dramatic episodes of levitation.

For years, she had wondered about the phenomenon. Then one evening in the late 1990s, she received her answer. She lay in bed having just returned from a major out-of-body journey. Suddenly, she felt strong energetic vibrations pulsing through her body. Writes Hughes, "A massive energy surge overtook my body, thousands of times stronger than I'd ever felt before. Scared, I'd never felt anything like this, but suddenly, my whole *body* and *spirit* lifted up out of bed, beginning to fly around the room. 'It is possible!' I screamed out, trying to get Andy's attention, but he was deeply asleep.... For the next hour or so, the energy beam came and went, taking me on bodily flights around the room."

Marilynn Hughes is one of today's leading pioneers in astral projection and spiritual enlightenment. She has experienced two spontaneous episodes of levitation in her bedroom. (Marilynn Hughes)

A few years later, Hughes experienced a repeat performance. Again, she was lying in her bedroom meditating when she sensed (but could not see) the presence of two spirits. She felt that the spirits were performing some type of "energetic adjustment" on her body. Evidently, the adjustment was effective, because Hughes found herself promptly levitated. Writes Hughes, "Suddenly, two spirits were lifting my body and soul up off the bed, as I began levitating. What wonder! What malaise! It was so spectacular; I cannot even fathom the words to tell! As my body and soul floated about the room in the hands of my unseen quests, I awaited the end of this levitation to bid them with a question. Lasting for about five minutes, they slowly began lowering my body onto the bed." Hughes then asked for the invisible spirits to reveal themselves. She saw two glowing human-looking figures quickly appear and disappear, one male and one female.

Hughes's case is highly reminiscent of those of the saints. Today she continues to teach and write about out-of-body experiences and spiritual enlightenment.[436]

Levitations, as can be seen, are currently taking place all over the world. However, society still has trouble dealing with the phenomenon. Australian researcher Simon Harvey-Wilson illustrates this dilemma with an interesting current case. Writes Harvey-Wilson, "The Catholic church's apparent ambivalence about miraculous phenomena makes human levitation harder to investigate because it reduces the number of witnesses and subsequent documentation of such events. For example, the Croatian stigmatist, Father Zlatko Sudac, who visited America early in 2002, claims to have the 'gifts of levitation, bilocation, illumination, and the knowledge of upcoming events.' However, when asked about them during a recent interview, he declined to elaborate until the Catholic hierarchy had made a pronouncement about the matter."[437]

In the early 1990s, a young man named Jeffrey Grant Oswald picked up Steve Richards' book, *Levitation*, and became immediately obsessed with the subject. He began doing levitation exercises and seeking out people who could levitate. Writes Oswald, "I knew it was possible, and in 1995 I was magically introduced to three people in three different countries who had actually levitated. Two of them could float three feet above the ground for several minutes and the other still flies to this day." While Oswald himself denies being able to levitate, he later had many incredible spiritual experiences that so transformed him, he changed his name to Jafree. (see: www.enlightenedbeings.com.)

Another current case is that of Maha Yogi Alfred S. Narayana. In his on-line book, *Super Psychic*, Narayana tells how, as a child he was trained in the secret yoga arts and attained the use of up to twenty of the siddhis, as outlined by Patanjali, including levitation. Writes Narayana, "I levitated four feet off the ground in front of a camera....I shall of course, refrain from ever levitating in public, as a matter of fundamental principle, for that would be a sacrilege. Furthermore, like several of my siddhis, levitation is an involuntary occurrence that happens in rare moments of religious ecstasy, perhaps as few as one or two times a year."

A 2005 levitation account recently took place in Japan. The television cable program, *Sushi TV*, features people with unusual talents. Some of their guests are contortionists, acrobats, martial artists and others, including at least one levitator. Mr. Osami, a handsome middle-aged man of Japanese ancestry, appeared on the program as a "magician." First he demonstrated his ability to move a compass-needle with the energy emitted from his hands. By just passing his hand a few inches above it, he was able to make the compass needle spin erratically.

Next he demonstrated his ability to levitate outside in broad daylight. He walked out into the middle of a field and sat down in the lotus position, spine erect, palms upraised. He closed his eyes and remained still. As the film clearly shows, suddenly, he slowly and softly lifted up about three feet above the ground. The host of the program approached in astonishment. He waved his hands around Mr. Osami searching for any wires or ropes. The cameraman then approached and walked around him proving that there were no hidden devices.

Mr. Osami remained hovering in a cross-legged position, about three feet in the air, for a few more moments. Then he slowly and gently lowered back down to the ground. Although the footage is only a minute long, the film could be the best photographic evidence to date.

And so closes the modern accounts of levitation. The same trend that has endured for centuries continues. The main difference is, the modern accounts are more numerous, better verified with more witnesses and more detailed firsthand testimonies. Cases such as Boris Ermolaev and Captain Bartlett, join the ranks of well-verified cases of levitation. But again, the sheer volume of cases speaks more for their veracity than does the quality of the cases.

In fact, the testimonies are so numerous that it becomes impossible to classify all of them as hoaxes, misperceptions or delusions. The consistency of their content coming from a wide variety of independent sources points towards the conclusion that these accounts are actually taking place as described. It would be extremely unscientific to ignore the evidence, and if one examines it carefully, it becomes very difficult to reach any conclusion other than that levitation is a valid phenomenon, one that occurs regularly throughout history to all kinds of people, including men, women, and children, in all different cultures, and in a wide variety of situations. The next logical step is to analyze the cases, to determine the scope of the phenomenon, and draw whatever conclusions we can, based on the evidence.

32. The Secret Behind Levitation

Levitation remains mysterious, however, by now several facts should be clear. First, levitation is true. With more than 330 reported cases, we can safely conclude that levitation is a valid phenomenon that has occurred regularly throughout history. With so many cases, from such a wide variety of credible sources, each following similar patterns—it would be exceedingly unscientific to reject the testimony as being "too incredible."

Nor can the accounts be relegated to blanket explanations of hoaxes, hallucinations, or misperceptions. Again, there are too many accounts involving too many witnesses of unimpeachable integrity. And there is, of course, the photographic and laboratory evidence. The experiments of Baron Schrenk-Notzing, William Crookes, Charles Richet, Hereward Carrington, and others have proven conclusively that levitation is real.

First let us analyze the reported cases and break them down into the seven categories.

Ecstatic Levitation

These cases involve levitations, usually of nuns, monks, priests, etc...caused by religious prayer. It can last for seconds, minutes, or even hours. It usually occurs spontaneously, but can be induced. It is the second most common type of levitation.

Meditational Levitation

These cases involve yogis, mystics, sorcerers, etc...who, through meditative and physiological techniques, are able to initiate and control levitation events. It is the third most common type of levitation.

Crisis Levitation

These cases involve all kinds of people. The vast majority involves falls with a few cases of illness. In most cases, the episodes last only a few seconds though they *can* last minutes or even hours.

Mediumistic Levitation

By far these are the most common, most demonstrated, and most studied. They can be induced or sometimes involve uncontrolled poltergeist-like manifestations, including in extreme cases, possession. In about one third of the cases, the victims were reported to be possessed. These cases can usually only be performed under séance conditions and are only partially controllable.

Spontaneous Levitation

The vast majority of these involve children, though there are a few adult cases. Several of the cases involve children who fly down staircases. Many children express the belief that they can fly. In fact, according to biographer Tolpin, the Russian author Tolstoy may have experienced a levitation episode during his childhood. At age nine, Tolstoy believed he had the ability to fly, and he actually leapt out of a two-story window and suffered a concussion. However, even into adulthood, he firmly believed he had the ability to levitate. Winston Churchill also expressed similar beliefs, and at age eighteen, leapt off a bridge into the treetops below, believing he could fly.[438]

Many people, especially children, believe they can fly. And in some cases, they seem to be right.

Traveling Levitation

The second rarest category, the accounts of running levitation, are remarkably consistent. Whether it involves a fifteenth century nun, a Tibetan *lung-gom-pa*, Native American "swift runners," Holy lamas, or an American schoolgirl, the effect is the same. As Ikawai's tracks showed, as Alexandra David-Neel witnessed, and as Kelly Marley so vividly described, saying, "I had a way of running where I was barely touching the ground"—it is clear that the same phenomenon is involved. In most cases, it appears to take specific training; however, in others it appears to manifest naturally. Cases of walking on water fit well in this category.

Sleeping Levitation

This rarest type of levitation occurs only when the percipient is sleeping, therefore, there are few actual firsthand reports coming from the levitators themselves. In a few cases, people did wake up to find themselves levitating (Johnson, Smurl), however, both were living in haunted houses, so this phenomenon could be related to mediumistic levitation. In one case, the ability was carried from mother to daughter.

While levitation remains mysterious, there are obvious patterns. Many cases of levitation share several common elements. According to researcher David Orme-Johnson, these include: an awareness that the body is pervaded by space, a sense of lightness, an upward current of energy, trembling and fast breathing, hopping, and finally hovering. This pattern is exhibited only in certain cases of meditational levitation.

There are other patterns. In most cases there is a degree of dissociation involved. With meditative, mediumistic, and ecstatic levitation, the levitator is often in a trance state. With crisis levitation, there is dissociation caused by trauma. Running levitation is also very meditative. Sleeping is a profound form of dissociation and perfectly fits this pattern.

Dissociation is an experience of mind-body separation. Examples include meditation, prayer, sleep, hypnosis, out-of-body experiences, use of the Ouija Board, physical trauma, etc.

Frequently, there are peculiar physiological effects as a result of levitation. In some cases, the limbs will become temporarily rigid, and the levitator may feel an electrical-type force lifting the body. In most cases, there is no sensation of hands lifting the body. Rather, the body seems to rise not by being pushed or pulled, but drawn upwards. However, some mediumistic levitators do report feeling hands lift them into the air. Some levitators report a shortness of breath. In a few cases, the levitators were exhausted by their ordeal. Others are energized. Some report healings. In a small percentage of the cases, levitators emit white light from their bodies.

Levitation may be hard to believe, but it comes down to one simple fact: levitation is real and is happening across the world. The next step is to analyze the various aspects of the phenomenon.

Strength of Levitations

Levitation is an extraordinarily complex phenomenon. One curious aspect of the experience is the sheer force involved. Out of the hundreds of cases, there are several in which witnesses have attempted to end the levitation or pull the levitator down. In most cases, they are unsuccessful. In several cases, even the strength of several full-grown men was insufficient to pull the levitator down. Clearly, a great amount of force is in operation. According to Von Gorres, it is impossible to physically push levitators to the ground. While some accounts support this assertion, others involve accounts in which witnesses were easily able to move the levitators by lifting them lightly or even blowing on them.

Interestingly, some levitators also report increased strength. One example is St. Joseph of Cupertino who was able to lift a heavy wooden cross which ten men couldn't lift. Daniel Home also reported an event in which he was able to lift a heavy log. St. Bosco could reportedly hammer nails with his bare fist.

Multiple Levitations

The force which causes levitation can be contagious. In several accounts (Cupertino, Kellar, Vollhardt), those who physically grabbed or even touched the levitator were also levitated. There are a few cases of three people being simultaneously levitated, though none of four or more. One possible theory then is that the (as of yet) unidentified section of the electromagnetic spectrum which causes levitation creates a field around the levitator which is, in some occasions, large enough or strong enough to levitate others who are adjacent to or physically touching the levitator.

This theory is also supported by the many accounts in which people have been levitated along with their chair, stool, bed, or other furniture.

What Triggers Levitation?

Most of the saints found themselves levitating as a result of intense, prolonged, and fervent prayer. The events occur spontaneously, though for some it may be provoked by mere exposure to religious paraphernalia or even something beautiful, like pomegranate seeds or music. On the other hand, meditational levitators simply have to concentrate and are able to levitate at will. Spontaneous levitation occurs for no apparent reason, but most often to young children. As we have seen, illness and sleep can provoke levitation.

Another repetitive cause includes falls. In several mediumistic cases, levitation was caused when onlookers either began an exorcism ritual or specifically asked the alleged spirits for a levitation display. Rajalakshmi reported that her levitation occurred as a direct result of reading the book, *The Gospel of Sri Ramakrishna*. The book is a thousand pages in length and outlines inspirational conversations about God between the spiritually enlightened master, Sri Ramakrishna (himself a levitator) and his devotees.

Is Levitation Hereditary?

Leroy doubted that levitation had any genetic component. At that time, the only evidence supporting this was the case of the royal family of Hungary, which involved the levitation of several family members. However, today, several other cases have surfaced. The case cited by Joseph Weed involved a lady who could reduce her weight, an ability that her mother also had. Another case, cited by Hadsell, involved a mother and daughter who both experienced episodes of sleeping levitation. There are a few cases of mediumistic levitating families, such as the family that Ermolaev was introduced to in Russia. Other examples are Rudy and Willy Schneider, the Harper sisters, and the Davenport brothers, all of whom experienced mediumistic levitation. There is also one case of an anonymous man and his son, Joaquin. The above cases, however, appear to be the exceptions. The great majority of cases involve unrelated people. While there may be some genetic factors involved, clearly anybody can levitate.

Can Levitations Be Stopped?

In the vast majority of cases, the levitators are not disturbed. In some cases, however, onlookers attempt to end the levitations. In most cases they are unsuccessful, though in a few cases, witnesses were able to stop the levitations by physically restraining the person. In a few cases, the levitators could be brought down by calling their name or playing music. St. Joseph of Cupertino stopped levitating for two years following severe reprimands from his superior. He was also called down on at least two occasions by name, though usually he was insensible during his trances. Sometimes the levitators themselves tried to stop their episodes from occurring. In some cases they were successful, (Rajalakshmi), in other cases they were not (Teresa of Avila.) Mediumistic levitations have the same paradox. In some cases, the levitations are easily stopped (Home), while in others, all efforts to end it fail (Fontaine, Riesinger.) Meditational levitators can apparently start and stop the episodes at will. The ability to stop a levitation event appears to depend mostly upon the levitator's experience with or understanding of levitation.

Control of Levitation

The levitators report widely varying degrees of control of their flights. The saints generally reported little or no control. Most could neither start nor stop the episodes, nor control their flights. Furthermore, their bodies often became rigid, and their awareness of their surroundings sometimes diminished. Cupertino did report some control, in that he was able to lift a cross and maneuver around objects to reach the altar. Other times, however, he remained insensible. St. Francis of Assissi also apparently could levitate at will as he used his ability to convert followers.

Meditational levitators, however, report much better control, with several yogis reporting the ability of traveling levitation (the most highly controlled form of levitation) or the ability to move long distances while avoiding obstacles such as walls, trees, and doorways, or reach considerable heights.

Mediumistic levitators seem to levitate only at the whim of their spirit friends, and usually only during séance conditions. However, the best mediums were able to produce levitation phenomenon fairly regularly.

Crisis levitation is, by nature, not controllable as it only occurs during accident or illness, and then only rarely. Sleeping levitators obviously have no control whatsoever.

Spontaneous levitators do report a small measure of control, being able to turn corners and fly up and down staircases.

The control of levitation seems to correspond to the levitator's experience with the phenomenon. Meditational levitators, therefore, have the greatest degree of control.

Length of Levitations

How long is the average levitation? Writes Fodor, "Mediumistic levitation seldom exceeds a few minutes....ten minutes is far behind the achievements of the saints."

The average length of levitations is hard to ascertain. Crisis and spontaneous levitations are typically brief, lasting seconds, with one outlying case lasting an hour. Mediumistic levitations typically last from fifteen seconds to three minutes with a few longer cases, particularly those involving demonic possession, the longest lasting thirty minutes. There is very little information on the length of running levitations, through some Native American runners were reportedly able continuously to run for three days or more. The length of sleeping levitation is also hard to determine for the obvious reason that the levitator is not aware of levitating. However, it appears that these episodes last anywhere from a few seconds to a few hours. This brings us to ecstatic and meditational levitation, both of which typically last a few minutes to a few hours, or in a few outlying cases, up to twenty-four hours.

Height of Levitation

The height of the average levitation varies from one or two inches to several thousand feet. The vast majority of cases, however, involve levitation between a few inches and three feet off the ground. According to some sources, the height of levitation corresponds to the spiritual level of the levitator. A few of the cases support this theory, (ie: Princess Shoki, Naruse). Some saints reportedly levitated up to the height of the tallest trees. There are several cases of meditational levitators reaching one hundred feet or more. The highest reported case is the monk, Luang Pu Waen, seen at several thousand feet by several airline pilots.

Credibility of Evidence

The main argument against the validity of levitation is the perceived lack of hard evidence. Mainstream science will never accept these accounts until levitation can be demonstrated as a repeatable controlled experiment using scientific methodology. This has actually occurred with several levitators, including the cases of Palladino, Faticoni, Mirabelli, Zuccarini , Home, Indridason, Ruggieri, Schneider, and others.

Lack of evidence, however, doesn't mean that levitation isn't a valid phenomenon. How many people have photographed somebody getting struck by lightning? Almost none. And yet it happens hundreds of times a year. As Murphy writes, "Levitation may only occur during rare and spontaneous ecstasies that cannot be programmed to meet the requirements of a scientific experiment. Superordinary lifting from the ground, if it in fact occurs, would require an improbable set of circumstances, which a scientist would be lucky to witness. Levitation, like other holy powers, would have to be 'caught in the wild.'"[439]

And remember, levitation has actually been photographed many times, including Mirabelli, Faticoni, Zuccarini, Melloni, Harper, Evans, Owaka, Vollhardt, Pullavar, Rajalakshmi, Osami, Naruse, and others.

The foundation of science is observation, and anecdotal evidence is crucial to the process. While the hard evidence supporting levitation is limited to a few dozen studies at most, the circumstantial evidence is mountainous and of the highest quality. With so many accounts, levitation as a phenomenon is firmly established.

The credibility of the levitators and witnesses is, in many cases, beyond reproach—particularly in the case of the saints who lived exceedingly austere and moral lifestyles, and as a rule, tried to hide and end their levitation episodes, rather than flaunt and encourage them. Leroy writes, "The chances of willful deception diminish to the proportion that the witnesses are more honorable and more numerous."[440]

Of the saints, Leroy wrote, "It is necessary to insist here that the moral quality of these witnesses is exceptional and vetoes any fabrication of their depositions."[441]

In the second half of Leroy's book, he conducted an analysis of the evidence. He was surprisingly skeptical of many of the cases, claiming that hagiographers may have exaggerated accounts of levitation out of a devotional zeal. He believed that subjective impressions of levitation could be rejected out-right as being un-verifiable. As he says, "For this reason, the sensation of levitations described by Saint Teresa of Avila, Saint Catherine of Sienna, or Saint Phillip of Neri will be regarded a priori as imaginary." While he later affirmed these cases—because they had outside witnesses—he approached the subject from a very skeptical viewpoint.[442]

With a strong religious prejudice, Leroy rejected virtually all cases not involving saints. However, even then, he concluded that levitation is a reality, one that demands objective analysis. As he wrote, "If levitation is a true fact, historically proven, it takes a new interest for us, more immediate, more material. As far as we believe it is a subjective impression, it barely matters to us. But now that we know we are dealing with a physical objective phenomenon of the mystical life, we are deposed to examine it more closely, and to particularly note the details and surroundings....The historic proofs for the reality of levitation are both numerous and solid…if the reality of this phenomenon must be rejected, it is not able to be by virtue of prior views on its possibility, but on the study of the testimonies which affirm it."[443]

An objective look at the study of levitation reveals a surprising number of cases with considerable evidence, certainly enough evidence to hold up in a court of law.

Again several of the levitations were performed under controlled laboratory conditions in front of eminent scientists (Home, Palladino, Schneider, Mirabelli, Zuccarini). Hereward Carrington was actually able to prove levitation as a demonstrable scientific fact using an ingenious experiment (see next chapter).

Skeptics will have to explain the photographs of levitations, not to mention the number of witnesses to these events. The levitations of Cupertino, Home, Liguori and Avila are supported by literally *hundreds* of witnesses.

The evidence collected in this book, I think, conclusively proves that levitation is a fact.

Of course, some cases are better than others. Although the sheer volume of accounts is more than enough to convince any reasonable person, many cases lack good documentation. The ideal case involves multiple living witnesses of high credibility, repeated levitations, photographs, and statements from the levitator, also of high credibility. No single case fits all these criteria.

Using these criteria, however, the ten best cases of levitation (in my opinion) in ascending order are:

10. Janet Harper: This case is particularly solid because the phenomenon surrounding her was observed by so many people and occurred in modern times. Her case of levitation was observed by multiple living witnesses who provided testimonials and were also affirmed by her. Finally, the levitations were also photographed.

9. Rajalakshmi: This case is well-verified in many respects. The main witness is still living (as of the printing of this text) and is of high credibility, holding

a position as a professor and leader of a yoga institute. Her levitations were witnessed by numerous people and were also photographed.

8. Alphonse Liguori: Although this case occurred a long time ago, an extremely large number of credible witnesses left written testimonies under oath testifying to the veracity of his levitations.

7. Zuccarini: This case is reputable because it involves several scientists who were able to photograph the levitations of the medium on multiple occasions under controlled conditions.

6. Mirabelli: The fact that this man was able to levitate before a group of scientists for a period of ten minutes, during which time they closely observed and photographed him makes this case hard to dispute. He was also seen to levitate on several other occasions in front of numerous witnesses.

5. Stainton Moses: As a minister and college professor, Moses' integrity is impeccable. Combined with his own testimony of his levitations and the fact that they were witnessed by multiple people on at least ten separate occasions makes his case one of the best verified in history.

4. Joseph Cupertino: Although this case occurred hundreds of years ago, the enormous number of witnesses (92) and their credibility (Popes, Dukes, priests, nuns...) makes the case particularly hard to dismiss. Also, the fact that the witnesses were under oath makes their testimonies even more credible.

3. Eusapia Palladino: The levitations of this medium were witnessed by numerous very influential scientists (Crookes, Richet...) across Europe. Her levitations were consistently produced in controlled laboratory conditions. She was able to produce levitations across Europe for more than a decade.

2. Teresa of Avila: This case is supported not only by voluminous statements from St. Teresa herself, but by numerous highly reputable eyewitnesses who left testimonials under oath.

1. Daniel Home. This is the single best case of all time simply because so many credible people observed Home to levitate on so many different occasions under so many different conditions. He levitated before numerous heads of state, kings, queens, dukes, before leaders in the fields of science, art, and literature. He was never once caught in fraud and produced numerous other miracles, including healings, elongation, incombustibility, superhuman strength, prophecy, and more. But it was his levitations that were verified on at least one hundred occasions.

Other highly credible levitators also deserve special mention including the cases of Schneider, Indriddason, Ermolaev, Ruggieri, Bartlett, Naruse, and Melloni, to mention only a few. Anyone skeptical of levitation must explain these cases.

Is Levitation Generated Internally or Externally?

The force that causes levitation is invisible, powerful, and, in some cases, controllable. But is it generated by an outside force such as spirits, or an inside force, such as the human body? The evidence is strong for both theories. Mediumistic levitation seems to be caused by spirits of deceased people: these levitations often occur simultaneously with haunting activity attributed by ghost researchers to spirits. Some of the mediumistic levitators also report feeling the sensations of hands gripping and lifting them. In a few cases, hands are seen or the identity of the affecting spirit is actually named and identified.

On the other hand, the evidence is fairly conclusive that meditational levitation is internally generated by the human organism. According to Yogic tradition, levitation is an ability that is potentially available to anyone. Many levitation accounts originate from people who have learned to levitate, as a skill, using specific procedures.

Most types of levitation such as sleeping, running, and spontaneous levitation, also appear to be internally generated—whereas with crisis levitation, it is difficult to say.

It appears that levitation is, in some cases, caused by an outside force (mediumistic) and in other cases is internally generated (meditational). Interestingly, while many mediumistic cases only take place in low light levels, many meditational levitations involve light being emitted by the body. However, some mediumistic levitators also emit light. In either case, however, it seems clear that the same actual force is involved.

Locations of Levitations

An analysis of the locations of these events shows that they take place virtually everywhere, in all cultures. They take place inside and outside, in darkness and light. In churches, homes, courts, buildings, hallways, fields, forests, gardens, over rivers...even on boats. The majority of levitating saints come from Europe, with many from Italy. Eastern countries such as Tibet and India are the leading producers of meditational levitators. Otherwise, levitations are distributed rather equally throughout the world.

As we have seen, however, the era and location of a levitation event can have a profound effect on how the event is interpreted, with two extremes being canonization as a saint, or execution as a witch. Researcher Douchan Gersi personally witnessed several shamans perform ceremonies in which they levitated, disappeared, or dematerialized.

After witnessing several such events, he became aware of a peculiar detail. Writes Gersi, "I noticed that my eyes picked up a distinct image. This image was always the same: the person who had just disappeared, seen from the back, appeared to be followed by something that looked like a bunch of feathers. In pondering this, my first thought was that it looked like someone riding a broom, an image similar to representations of witches traveling to their Sabbaths."

Could this be the origin of witches flying on brooms? Gersi thinks it may be. He later had the opportunity to visit a sorcerer in Papua, New Guinea. The sorcerers are called Cassowary Men, after a native ostrich-like bird with large tail feathers. The reason for this name is because witnesses to the dematerialization or teleportation of the

The only real difference between witches on brooms and magicians on flying carpets may be a matter of cultural interpretation. (illustration by Kesara)

sorcerers receive the visual impression that the sorcerer is flying away riding on a cassowary. Gersi was given a demonstration and reports that he saw exactly the same optical effect that he had observed in Haitian Voodoo ceremonies.

Gersi received further confirmation of this worldwide phenomenon when he visited the Middle East. Writes Gersi, "In Arabia, when people saw a magician dematerializing—I have met some Arabs who claim that such magicians still exist nowadays—they also picked up the image I have described. Since their cultural references include neither cassowaries nor brooms, Arab witnesses perceived the image as being the tasseled end of a carpet. This gave rise to tales of people traveling on flying carpets. In each of these cultures, people ascribed the image their eyes picked up…to whatever it was that they already knew—a broom, a cassowary, a carpet….This phenomenon at least gives evidence that something powerful goes on at that specific moment; otherwise, why would people of different cultures, living in different times, experience the same image?"[444]

Witnesses to Levitations

While there are many firsthand accounts of levitation in this book, most accounts are recorded only if there are outside witnesses. Anyone can claim to levitate, but those who were able to demonstrate it in front of witnesses comprise the majority of the accounts. Interestingly, because the ability to levitate attracts so much attention, the witnesses are often people of extremely high social standing. The roster of witnesses attesting to these events is impressive and includes not only the ordinary person, but influential leaders in science, medicine, religion, politics, business, arts, and literature. Kings, queens, heads of state, emperors, popes, cardinals, dukes, famous authors, leading scientists, prominent physicians, professors, archbishops, politicians, business leaders…all are among the witnesses to various levitations. In fact, it is their testimonies that form the bulk of the evidence supporting the veracity of levitation.

What Kinds of People Levitate?

An analysis of the kinds of people who levitate reveals that an equal number of men and women levitate. People of all ages in virtually all cultures report levitation. There is strong evidence that people who are spiritually inclined are more likely to levitate. Each culture has their holy person—a priest, a shaman, a medicine man, a sorcerer, a psychic, a medium, a saint, a yogi, a fakir, a mystic, a clever man, a magician…etc. These are the types of people who levitate.

Therefore, it appears that the differences between the various types of levitation may be a matter of cultural interpretation. In other words, despite the dissimilarities in the accounts, again it appears that the same basic phenomenon is in operation. Some cultures may have been able to evolve further with their understanding and use of levitation, however, it may be that there is little fundamental difference between any types of levitation.

Writes Fodor, "Such clear contemporary testimony makes Home's levitations vie in importance with any hagiographic account. Olivier Leroy, with ecclesiastic bias, attributes mediumistic levitations to diabolic agency but it is difficult to see more than a quantitative difference of levitating power between saints, demoniacs and mediums."[445]

D. Scott Rogo has also noticed that each culture interprets levitation uniquely. "Every culture is automatically prejudiced in believing that it, and only it, is scientific and sophisticated, and that earlier reports and studies are either invalid or suspect….as for levitation phenomena, certain physical mediums have been known to be levitated during well-controlled experiments. Because of this, levitations reported by the saints probably represent a peculiar form of telekinesis."[446]

Researcher Colin Wilson states the case wryly, "Under Christianity, magic became Black Magic, and its power derived from demons or angelic intervention, instead of from man's own hidden faculties…a monk who happened to possess mediumistic powers might find himself burnt alive or canonized."[447]

Andrew Lang succinctly summarizes the controversy: "Saint or sorcerer has always been a delicate question."[448]

Lang was one of the first paranormal investigators to realize that accounts of levitation were truly worldwide. As he writes, "When we find savage 'biraarks' in Australia, fakirs in India, saints in medieval Europe, a gentleman's butler in Ireland, boys in Somerset and Midlothian, a young warrior in Zululand, Miss Nancy Wesly at Epworth in 1716, and Mr. Daniel Home in London in 1856-70, all triumphing over the law of gravitation, all floating in the air, how are we to explain the uniformity of stories palpably ridiculous?"[449]

Good question. How can this happen? Doesn't levitation defy everything we know about gravity?

The problem is, we don't know much about gravity, as these types of accounts so painfully point out. This is the crux of the problem in solving the mystery of levitation. It all comes down to explaining the phenomenon of gravity. Unfortunately, mainstream science has never been able to fully explain the force of gravity. How can we understand levitation if we don't even understand gravity?

Writes Steve Richards, "The fact that science cannot explain gravitation means that science cannot condemn levitation."[450]

Charles and Jordan write, "Unaided human flight, no matter how astounding and mystifying, is not contrary to natural law. It is simply an event in nature that science has not yet explained."[451]

Authority on modern mysticism, Patricia Treece astutely points out that the fantastic nature of levitation has caused it to be largely ignored by mainstream science. As she writes, "Science has no help to offer as to how the phenomenon works. Insisting that gravity is not breachable, scientists have never taken levitation seriously enough to even postulate how it might work."[452]

Writes Australian researcher Simon Harvey-Wilson, "Religion and science have always had an uneasy relationship…research into levitation is hampered by centuries of prejudice about witches, possession, and spiritual abilities…explanations for human levitation seem to depend on the spiritual beliefs of those concerned…with minor variations, [the] explanation for human levitation is that spiritual forces are responsible…on the other hand, some people claim that they alone are responsible for their levitation….It may eventually be discovered that human levitation is a load of nonsense, but I doubt that this will turn out to be the case. There have been too many surprisingly similar reports throughout history from all over the world. I suspect that where there's smoke there is probably fire. Any scientist who asserts that levitation is impossible because science cannot currently explain it is, frankly, just an idiot and should hand his lab coat over to someone who understands that research is about exploring the unknown, not ignoring it."[453]

Of course, some scientists have looked into the situation. After witnessing Home's levitations under controlled conditions, scientist William Crookes concluded, "These experiments appear conclusively to establish the existence of a new force, in some unknown manner connected with the human organization, which for convenience may be called the Psychic Force."[454]

Physicist Bruce Smith points out that superconductors are known to be surrounded by a field of energy known as a Meissner Field, which actually has the effect of neutralizing gravity. While scientists are able to produce mechanical superconductors with which they have levitated live frogs, Smith speculates that the human body itself might be a superconductor under the correct conditions. As he writes, "Our bodies might be able to create superconductivity within them via the pathway of trance-inducing practices. This internal superconductivity may be like a switch that we turn on to enter a levitating state."[455]

Nandor Fodor writes, "How is levitation done? We know nothing and suspect but little of the power which accomplishes it.…The loss of weight in the levitated body may be an appearance due to the effect of a force which lifts or, if internally applied, makes the body buoyant."[456]

According to the Catholic Church, there are three explanations for levitation: the Grace of God, the Influence of the Devil, and Outside Forces.

Unfortunately, this does little to explain levitation. As Patricia Treece writes, "In theory, then, I could propose St. Teresa levitated because her body was acted on by God, Daniel Home levitated because he had rare psychic gifts, and Mahasaya levitated, aided by the Devil, to torment his poor wife! I am kidding, of course. Distinctions are not so easy."

While admitting that levitation may have different causes, Treece notes the obvious relationship between levitation and holiness. "Because it is so difficult to distinguish the purely supernatural from the psychophysical even in saints, levitation is never accepted as 'miraculous proof' of sanctity in Catholic investigations. Assuming the presence of the crucial virtues of heroic charity, heroic humility, heroic trust in God, etc., well verified levitation can be accepted as 'corroborative evidence' of sanctity, however. This is important for us because it means testimonies of levitation are not just ignored, but looked at carefully to rule out fraud, delusion, and hearsay…Genuine levitation among Catholics is regularly associated with holiness. Testimonies from Beatification Processes and other trustworthy sources simply contain too many eyewitnesses, broad-daylight accounts for the relationship to be coincidental…If—as perplexing as the thought may be—it appears that humans do levitate, and that those who do so are holy, the obvious question is, can we finger the psycho spiritual-physical connection between sanctity and levitation? To a degree, I think we can. Speaking in nontheological terms, levitation of the primary type appears an extreme manifestation of the 'walking on air' sensation of blissful love.…If your first love made you feel like you were walking on air, isn't it possible the sanctified body, ravished by the love of God, at times breaks through gravity and actually rises in bliss?"[457]

Writes Fodor, "In Catholic mysticism, levitation is ascribed to the grace of God. Ecclesiastically this is a final explanation; scientifically it is entirely meaningless. How does religious ecstasy counteract or at least partially, gravitation? The question leads us back to the ancient conflict between matter and spirit.

Are there spiritual laws as well as material laws? Is the material law subservient to the spiritual law?"

Pioneering levitation researcher Olivier Leroy attempted to refine the Church's theories, writing that mediumistic levitations were caused by diabolical agency whereas ecstatic levitations were caused by a divine agency. While he remained skeptical of many accounts, calling them "divine hallucinations," his final conclusion was unambiguously positive. As he writes, "Following very ancient traditions from diverse origins, the human body is able to escape under certain conditions the law of gravity."

As to how levitation occurred, Leroy's thoughts were more vague. He wrote that levitation seemed to rely upon the level of spiritual advancement of the would-be levitator. "The moral dispositions and the way of life of the subjects to levitation are a necessary condition to take into consideration as to the causes of the phenomenon...a moral ambience seems required for the production of the phenomenon in question....Indeed, levitation has a constant precedent of moral circumstances, a manner of thinking, of perceiving, of living."[458]

While this may be true for saints and mystics, there are many cases of spontaneous and mediumistic levitation involving people of normal or even dubious moral circumstance.

Despite his belief in levitation, Leroy was unable to reconcile its seemingly paranormal attributes with the known laws of science. As he wrote, "The problem of levitation is posed in terms which are repugnant to the methods of physics. The pseudo-scientific solutions proposed in order to explain the origins of this phenomenon are without value and there is no indication that one will be found in the future."[459]

Most early levitation researchers postulated theories involving spirits. Writes medieval scholar, Augustin Calmet, "It is not absolutely impossible that a person may be raised into the air and transported to some very high and distant place, by order or by permission of God, by good or evil spirits; but we must own that the thing is of rare occurrence....Was it by ministration of angels, or by the artifice of the seducing spirit, who wished to inspire her [a levitating nun] with sentiments of vanity and pride? Or was it the natural effect of Divine love, or fervour of devotion in these persons?...The writers who give us these particulars do not say what was the cause, whether these ecstatic elevations from the ground were produced by the fervour of the Holy Spirit, or by the ministry of good angels, or by a miraculous favour of God, who desired thus to do honour to his servants in the eyes of men."[460]

Writes Father Herbert Thurston, "Assuming, then, that we have reasonable ground for crediting the fact of levitation, there remains the question of its possible explanation. Theologians for the most part offer the rough and ready solution that in the case of holy people it is a manifestation of divine power, effected perhaps through the ministry of angels; but that in such cases as those of Simon Magus, sorcerers, and spiritualistic mediums, it is the work of the Devil. Without venturing to reject this explanation outright, I find certain difficulties, too complex to summarize here, which suggest that it would be wise to suspend our judgment. I may confess that as regards the levitation of material objects without contact, the spiritualistic evidence seems to me quite convincing, and if a table can be suspended in the air, it is hard to see why a man cannot. Sir Oliver Lodge adumbrated a spiritistic theory to explain these phenomena, Professor Charles Richet, a materialistic one. They attribute strange activities to the ether, to teleplasm, to cryptaestheisa, etc....but it seems to me that in the present state of our knowledge we cannot even decide whether the effects observed do or do not transcend the possible range of what may be called the psycho-physical forces of nature."[461]

Even today, the belief that levitation is caused by demons persists. In 1973, modern witchcraft historian, Montague Summers wrote, "Angels, be they blessed spirits or demons, have the power to move matter. The levitation of sorcerers is effected by the agency of evil forces, devils who bestow this favour upon an auxiliary and a companion....It stands to reason that Satan, the ape of God, must imitate and caricature the divine phenomenon of mystical levitation."[462]

J. J. Von Goerres was among the first modern European writers on the subject to state that levitation is an innate human ability, but one which is activated only in "a soul well-prepared by the ascetic life."

He wrote that levitation occurs as the result of a "kind of interior tempest aroused by the equilibrium of the mechanical forces of the organism being suddenly upset."[463]

Early researcher Abbott Ribet wrote that most cases of levitation can be explained by the "preponderance of the spirit to seize the body."[464]

This popular idea is echoed by Abbot Hanapier who wrote, "The body and the soul, the spirit and the material are united so that the two substances nearly make one…in a way that one is able to say that the body is spiritualized or that the soul is materialized. It is of the same nature of the soul to command the material. In the ordinary state, we know very little to be able to understand this ability of the soul on the body…We must assume that, disengaged from the bonds of the body, it takes superiority over it…and the body becomes its slave."[465]

In his comprehensive study of shamanism across the world, Mircea Eliade found that many cultures used similar ceremonial techniques, often involving levitation, to initiate the would-be shaman into occult mysteries. This means that many shamanic cultures regard levitation as an innate human ability that can be manifested through specific rituals. Writes Eliade, "The initiatory ascent gives the future magician the power to fly....It is difficult to determine if all magicians who believe that they can travel through the air have had an ecstatic experience, or been exposed to a ritual ascent, during their period of apprenticeship—that is, if they obtained their magical power of flight as the result of an initiation or of an ecstatic experience that announced their shamanic vocation. It may be supposed that at least some of them did obtain this magical power after and through an initiation. Many of the documents attesting the ability of shamans and sorcerers to fly fail to state how these powers were obtained; but it is quite possible that this silence is due to the incompleteness of our sources. However this may be, in many cases shamanic vocation or initiation is directly connected with an ascent to the sky."[466]

Eliade's research revealed that levitation can be achieved using different methods. "The power of flight can, as we have seen, be obtained in many ways (shamanic trance, mystical ecstasy, magical techniques), but also be a severe psychological discipline, such as the Yoga of Pantajali, by vigorous asceticism, as in Buddhism, or by alchemical practices. This variety in techniques doubtless corresponds to a variety of experiences and also, though in lesser degree, to different ideologies (for example, abduction by spirits, 'magical' and 'mystical' ascent, etc.). But all these techniques and mythologies have a common characteristic—the importance accorded to the ability to fly through the air."[467]

Field researcher Douchan Gersi, who witnessed multiple levitation events in various primitive cultures writes, "It is interesting to note that I witnessed these levitation phenomena when the believers were in a state other than the normal one—that is, when they were meditating, in a trance, or in a possession state. Perhaps the intoxication brought on by meditation, by the trance state, or by possession helps to shut down the negative beliefs—those that keep us from levitating, for instance—and liberates the unconscious, which gives us the power to perform such feats."[468]

Dr. Fugairon, a French doctor of science and medicine, theorized that levitation was caused by a bio-electric force emitted from the body. "Is it not possible that a subject gifted with electricity, standing on their tiptoes on the floor, and producing a very intense discharge of electric fluid through their toes, to elevate himself above the ground? Is it not possible for this effect to take place if the subject, in ecstasy, allows his fluid to escape at that time, through his toes or bent knees?"[469]

Writes Natts, who witnessed a levitation, "Levitation in the air, to the contempt of the law of gravitation proved by modern science, is able to be explained by the theory of universal attraction and repulsion. If the mediums are raised up, it's because they are, for a time, rendered completely positive. There is in each human organism, as in the rest of nature—two magnetisms, positive and negative. What we call life is the result of the constant action and reaction of these positive and negative forces; the cessation or the equilibrium of these forces, this is death. But this observation doesn't apply to the Yogis; the occultists are able to produce at will this equilibrium in their physical nature without dying. If we are totally negative, we are rooted to the ground like the trees; if we are completely positive, we are not able to stay on the ground for a single moment, but are always repulsed from the surface because the positive forces repulse…because our will power isn't developed, and as a consequence also not as strong such as an occultist's, we are not able to levitate ourselves."[470]

Author William Q. Judge writes, "Levitation of the body in apparent defiance of gravity is a thing to be done with ease when the process is completely mastered. It contravenes no law. Gravitation is only half of a law. The Oriental sage admits gravity, if one wishes to adopt the term; but the real term is attraction, the other half of the law being expressed by the word repulsion, and both being governed by the great laws of electrical force. Weight and stability depend on polarity, and when the polarity of an object is altered in respect to the earth immediately underneath it, then the body may rise....The human body will rise in the air unsupported, like a bird, when its polarity is thus changed."[471]

Ramtha (as channeled by J. Z. Knight) explains that with practice, a person can levitate by controlling their fields or "bands" of energy in their body. Says Ramtha, "When an entity levitates, it is because they have changed the resonant field of their bands. They are actually encased in a bubble of frequency that is greater than the time/space dimension that they are presently existing in...the field is antigravity because it is not resonating at B-flat [gravity] any longer. It is resonating at a higher harmonic, thereby consuming gravity, thereby allowing the entity to lift off...it is actually eating the B-flat fields around you and taking them into a vortex of energy which allows antigravity to exist, which brings upon the state of levitation."[472]

Colonel Albert Rochas completed the first truly comprehensive study of levitation. He believed that it had different causes, but seemed to involve an electrical force. "It is strongly probable that the phenomenon is very complex, and that it isn't always from the same cause....Some of the experiments from the end of the last century seem to prove that electricity diminishes the weight of bodies."

He believed that mediumistic levitation, however, was attributable to "the action of intelligent and invisible entities (elementals, angels, or demons)."

He wrote that ecstatic levitation was caused by prolonged meditation on God, which allowed the soul to become increasingly powerful. This eventually translated into supernatural abilities. Writes Rochas, "They are produced mainly in ecstasy and at diverse degrees. There are few ecstatics who haven't been observed, at one time or another in their raptures, to be lifted above the ground suspended in the air without support, floating sometimes and balancing themselves on the slightest breath."[473]

Colin Wilson echoes most modern researchers, believing that levitation is an innate talent potentially available to anyone. After examining the accounts of Cupertino, Home, Schneider, and others, he wrote, "Friar Joseph flew. There can be no possible doubt about that. It would be pointless to ask, 'How do we explain it?' because we cannot even make a start on understanding the mechanisms involved. Home attributed his flights to spirits, rather than to his own powers. Friar Joseph's flights undoubtedly proceeded from his own powers. The most sensible attitude is to assume that all human beings are potentially capable of flying....Whether the forces that made St. Joseph float like a balloon were 'telekinetic,' or whether St. Joseph and Willie Schneider somehow provided the energy for extrahuman agencies, is a matter upon which no opinion can be ventured at this stage. But that these forces are, potentially, in the control of every human being, surely there can be no doubt. "[474]

According to Eastern Yogic tradition, levitation is, in fact, an ability available to all human beings. During his expeditions through India and Tibet, Baird T. Spaulding not only witnessed levitating yogis, he was given an explanation by Master Puraji, who also displayed the ability of levitation. Says Master Puraji, "There are a number among you who have never witnessed body levitation and they wonder. Let me say this about it, it is a power which belongs to man. We look upon it as knowledge of ancient Yoga. Many people have used it in the past and it was not looked upon as miraculous. Guatama Buddha visited many distant places through the levitation of his physical body. Thousands of people have I seen that have made the accomplishment and there are much greater evidences of power than these that you will see, evidences of a great irresistible force that can be used to move mountains when brought under complete control."[475]

Unfortunately, none of these insights reveal the true mechanics behind the phenomenon.

According to eastern philosophy, the universe is made up of planes or dimensions starting with the physical dimension, with each dimension becoming progressively finer. One of the ruling forces in the Universe is consciousness or thought. In other words, our physical laws are in fact ruled by consciousness. The finer the dimension, the more easily it is manipulated by the power of thought.

Under this model, the secret to levitation is found with knowledge to manipulate consciousness to the degree where one can affect matter on the physical plane.

All of this becomes much clearer when we examine who the levitators are and why their levitations occurred.

Clearly, levitation is connected to spirituality. In the vast majority of cases, levitators are described as being deeply spiritual. The great majority claim to have experienced a many different kinds of psychic events, not just levitation.

However, the real question remains, what causes levitation? Can it be duplicated by others? What are the actual mechanics behind the phenomenon?

This book focuses only on the phenomenon of levitation. However, throughout my research, it has been impossible to ignore a wide variety of other paranormal phenomena that seem to be intrinsically connected to levitation. These include out-of-body experiences, ghosts, poltergeists, mediumship, possession, channeling, telekinesis, healings, supernatural strength, teleportation, inedia, bilocation, incombustibility....the list goes on. The vast majority of those who levitate have experienced many other paranormal events of these kinds.

While I would prefer not to explore tangential subjects in a book about levitation, it seems unavoidable. To explain levitation, we need to understand the other phenomena that come with it, in particular, the astral body.

The Astral Body and Levitation

A disproportional large number of levitators also report out-of-body experiences. Robert Monroe is one example. Prior to his two levitations, he had hundreds of out-of-body experiences. The same is true for St. Teresa of Avila. In her autobiography, she recorded numerous out-of-body experiences. In fact, she describes them as being very similar to levitations, the only difference being that with levitations, her body rises up following her astral body. St. John Bosco reported out-of-body experiences. Christina the Astonishing's levitations began as the result of a near-death, out-of-body experience. Many projectors report feeling like they should be able to fly. Patricia Garfield and Sylvan Muldoon, both accomplished astral projectors, also report that following their OBEs, they felt like they should be able to physically levitate. Yram and Marilynn Hughes actually did.

The theory behind out-of-body experiences is that each person has an astral body. We all have out-of-body experiences every night as we sleep, however, most do not remember them. By transferring and maintaining waking consciousness in the dream-state, one is able to recall out-of-body experiences.

Does astral travel provoke levitation, and if so how?

For most people, the dominant body is the physical body. This is where they spend most of their time and waking consciousness. However, repeated out-of-body travel apparently strengthens the astral body. The more out-of-body experiences one has, the stronger the astral body becomes. Just as one can exercise the physical body and make it stronger, the same holds true for the astral body.

Could it be that the astral body, once it becomes sufficiently strengthened by repeated use, becomes the dominant body? Once this threshold is reached then it should be easy for the astral body to take control over the physical body.

Under this theory then, levitation would simply be an out-of-body experience during which the astral body remains in coincidence with the physical body, lifting it up.

The law of gravity is never really defied. Instead, the human organism itself becomes transformed into, or encompassed by, an energetic field originating from the astral plane, with the atoms vibrating at a much higher frequency. This is actually the basic theory of most modern researchers.

As Madame Blavatsky writes, "...the Adepts of Hermitic Science explain the levitation of their own bodies by saying that the thought is so intently fixed on a point above them, that when the body is thoroughly imbued with the astral influence, it follows the mental aspiration and rises into the air."

Researcher Lynn Picknett has reached a similar conclusion. As she writes, "Perhaps those rare beings who find themselves levitating physically are subconsciously releasing the trigger and allowing an enormous surge of the energy used in OBEs to take hold of their bodies and up they go, briefly."[476]

Write Charles and Jordan, "....whether levitation is intentional or spontaneous, the mechanics are the same: when the spirit takes flight, the body may sometimes follow."[477]

After investigating a wide cross-section of accounts, world-renowned psychic Sylvia Browne concludes, "What lies at the heart of levitation, in my opinion, are astral projection and/or astral travel, physically manifested through either a deliberate or spontaneous disbursement of the body's cellular energy."[478]

Parapsychologist D. Scott Rogo speculates that the body may become weightless as the result of an unknown "biogravitational force" which is somehow created from the human organism. Writes Rogo, "The notion that levitation occurs when a psychic field is created around the body, or affects the physical area surrounding the levitator is an intriguing possibility....the mind of the levitator somehow physically alters the area about him so that the laws of gravity are temporarily suspended and weightlessness ensues....a theory of levitation is that some invisible force actually leaves the body when the miracle takes place and produces a psychic support system."[479]

A similar theory is postulated by anonymous researcher, Commander X, who writes, "At first glance, cases such as these seem to suggest that weight, as if it were a substantial corporeal entity, had been withdrawn from the body. However, this is not the proper way to look at the situation. Weight is not such an energy; weight is the quality of a reaction. That is, weight is the reaction of a mass to the gravitational attraction of another mass....It would seem then, that somewhere between the center of gravity of a levitator and the center of gravity of the Earth, a line of force is set up that has the effect of neutralizing the pull of gravity on all other points in the elevated body....It is entirely within the realm of possibility that a link may exist between the gravity waves and certain waves generated in the nervous system of the human body....According to this idea, electric waves generated with the levitator would oppose the force of gravity along a thin line extending between their center of gravity and that of the Earth."[480]

Madame Blavatsky writes, "Until gravitation is understood to be simple magnetic attraction and repulsion...it is neither fair nor wise to deny the levitation of either fakir or table. Bodies oppositely electrified attract each other, similarly electrified, repulse each other. Admit, therefore, that any body having weight, whether man or inanimate object, can by any cause whatever, external or internal, be given the same polarity as the spot on which it stands, and what is to prevent its rising?"[481]

Some of the answers behind the mechanisms of levitation may have been revealed through the study of a remarkable Russian psychic, Nina Kulagina (1925-1990). A housewife from Leningrad, Kulagina rose to celebrity status with her ability to move small objects with her mind. From 1968 to 1978, her telekinetic abilities were studied extensively by numerous leading scientists. Kulagina proved herself able to levitate objects up to thirty grams even when placed behind shields of wood, paper, glass, plastic, steel, copper, aluminum, and other materials. Her feats were filmed and photographed and repeatedly declared genuine. Physicists from leading technological institutions were brought in to study her with sensitive instruments. They found that Kulagina's hands emitted acoustic impulses ranging from 25 to 10,000 Hertz with a magnitude of 70 to 90 decibels. Even more remarkable was that her hands also emitted magnetic fields that measured up to .027 Tesla, exceeding the Earth's magnetic field by about 100 times! The ordinary person has a magnetic field between 100,000 to 10,000,000 times less. Not surprisingly, when Kulagina is performing her telekinetic feats, researchers repeatedly recorded a "considerable loss of weight" from her physical body. Clearly, our understanding of the potential powers of the human body remain incomplete.[482]

Writes Rampa, "Gravity, which gives a thing apparent weight, is merely a magnetic attraction between the object and the core of the Earth. Under certain conditions the magnetic attraction can be lessened or entirely removed, so that the material object becomes less heavy or actually without weight. This process is adopted when an article is teleported. It is also a system in use during levitation."[483]

Theosophist Arthur E. Powell conducted a comprehensive study of the astral body. He writes, "There is known to occult science a method of neutralizing or even reversing the force of gravity, which is in fact of a magnetic nature, by means of which levitation may be easily produced."[484]

After studying accounts of "phantom limbs," British researcher and President of the International Spiritualist Federation, Dr. Karl E. Muller, concluded that the phenomenon was caused by the astral body. As he writes, "Cases have been reported of people, who shortly after the amputation of a leg, forgot to use their crutches and walked several steps on their phantom legs. It sounds unbelievable but might be explained by the unconscious action of the etheric counterpart, similar to other physical effects reported, or a kind of telekinesis."[485]

Swami Panchadasi writes that levitation is caused by manipulating the astral body. "Under certain conditions there may appear in the case of a person strongly psychic, and also strongly charged with prana, the ability to extend a portion of the astral body to a considerable distance, and to there produce an effect upon some physical object. Those with strong clairvoyant vision may actually perceive this astral extension, under favorable circumstances. They perceive the astral arm of the person stretching out, diminishing in size as it extends...and finally coming in contact with the physical object it wishes to move or strike. Then is seen a strong flow of prana along its length, which by a peculiar form of concentration is able to produce the physical effect....This astral body extension produces spirit raps on tables; table-tilting and movement; levitation, or the lifting of solid objects in the air....In the case of the levitation of the person himself, the astral arms, and sometimes the legs as well, extend to the floor and push up the physical body into the air, and then propel it along."[486]

A similar theory is raised by Rene Sudre, who writes that levitation is caused by an invisible ectoplasm which exudes from the medium's body. Writes Sudre, "From a theoretical point of view the levitation of a person is as easy to understand as that of an object. The teleplastic [ectoplasmic] levers have naturally their fulcrum on the floor. Their shape is not definite; it may be that of a simple stay, of a cloudy cushion, or even a complete human materialization. The force of gravity is not eluded, but simply opposed by a contrary upward power."[487]

Clearly, there is some force involved, but what is it? As it is invisible, it seems logical to assume that it is electromagnetic in nature. In support of this theory is the fact that several cases of levitation do involve radiation emissions of visible light and even heat.

Leroy writes, "In a considerable number of cases, it is reported that the body of the levitators radiates a light, more or less bright. In the case of Bernardino Realino, the deposition is so precise and affirmative that it gives credit to the more vague references that have been made to this phenomenon in the other biographies."[488]

The fact that many levitation cases involve luminescent bodies (Johnson, Home, St. Francis of Assisi, Realino, Stainton Moses, Suarez, Mahasaya, Ramakrishna, Palladino…) indicates that the human body is, in fact, capable of emitting visible electromagnetic radiation. Certainly humans emit infrared radiation in the form of heat. It appears then that levitation could be caused by a form of radiation emitted from the human body, physical, or astral. Perhaps the light being emitted by levitators is the same light as reported by near-death experiencers.

The fact that some of the levitators can only levitate in low light levels, red light, or in complete darkness also supports the theory that a "field" of energy is responsible for levitation. Apparently, this field is so sensitive that it can be disrupted by visible light. In Home's case and others, a touch or even a prolonged stare from a witness could disrupt the energy field. Writes Fodor, "In modern experience the power which effects levitation is often short-circuited as soon as the chain of hands is broken, the gaze of the sitters is too intense, the light is switched on, or the levitated body is touched."

This bizarre side effect has occurred several times. Could this be because each person generates their own bio-electric field around their body? Can this explain how it is sometimes possible to feel a person's stare?

That there is a field of energy around levitators seems to have been conclusively proven by the photographic experiments of researcher Douchan Gersi. As we have seen, while levitation has been photographed, it has not been without difficulty. In many cases, levitation occurs only in complete darkness, making photography nearly impossible, though even this obstacle has been overcome through the use of flash photography.

During his field research, Gersi tried many times to get a photograph of a levitation in progress. However, he soon found that this was easier said than done. Writes Gersi, "It is interesting to note that I have never successfully photographed or filmed these phenomena. Each time, something has interfered with my ability to record the incident on film. Frequently the batteries supplying power to my movie camera died just as the levitation began. As a matter of fact, my camera batteries would not be the only ones to go; the batteries supplying the portable lighting system and those of the tape recorder, as well as my watch's battery, would all give up just at the time someone began levitation."

Gersi is certain that this was not a coincidence, as it happened too many times. "One set of batteries that dies suddenly can be explained as a technical failure; two separate sets dying at the same time may be considered a coincidence. But the fact that all these separate sets of batteries died at once, and repeatedly—more than twenty times, each time a levitation phenomena occurred—poses serious questions that I don't believe have a purely technical explanation."

Gersi says that on two occasions, his camera didn't fail, but when the film was developed, it showed either complete blackness or was so dark and out of focus as to be useless. This was true for moving films and still photographs. Gersi successfully filmed people immediately prior and following levitations, but was never able to catch one in the act.

He did notice other odd effects. "I must admit that each time a levitation occurred, I felt the hair rise all over my body—I have a hairy body—in the same way it does when I get very close to a TV screen." Gersi asked the other attendees, who also reported feeling a "kind of shivering along the body" when they stood next to a levitator. Gersi has also felt intense heat coming from the levitators.

All of these details clearly indicate the presence of some kind of electromagnetic field. Writes Gersi, "Might it be that in order to overcome the forces of gravity and perhaps other principles of physics, someone levitating needs such an enormous amount of energy that it discharges all nearby batteries? Or should we perhaps consider that the state of levitation—that is, the manipulation of gravitational forces and perhaps forces related to other principles of physics—itself develops such a quantity of energy that it short-circuits all batteries, killing them instantly?"[489]

Lucid Dreaming and Levitation

Lucid dreaming is when you are awake in your dream, *while* you are dreaming. It differs from the out-of-body experience only in that the images seen are generated from your own mind.

However, this can be very confusing because the astral plane is governed by your thoughts. As you think, so shall you experience.

The Tibetan Buddhists use lucid dreaming as a pathway to enlightenment. First they learn to wake up in the dream state. They then learn to control the dream state. They then realize that all things in the physical world are illusory, like dreams. The final step, enlightenment, comes when the dreamer realizes that the physical world is just like the dream world, and can be manipulated in the same way.

Once this realization is reached, all things are possible, including teleportation, levitation, materialization, invisibility, immortality and more. This is the explanation that Milarepa used to account for his ability to levitate. All his supernormal abilities first appeared in the dream state and then manifested in physical reality. Interestingly, all of us already have the ability to fly in our dreams.

Demonic Possession and Levitation

Demonic possession can be defined as a severe dissociative personality disorder. The cause is unknown, but it seems to occur spontaneously, often through careless use of the Ouija Board or other dissociative device. Most victims are children.

To be officially diagnosed by the Catholic Church as demonically possessed, there are several qualifications, including supernatural knowledge, superhuman strength, or levitation. Typically, the disorder involves a suppression of the primary personality to be replaced by a personality that is generally focused on negative emotions such as fear, hatred, lust, despair…etc.

How is it that demonically possessed people levitate? It seems clear that the same mechanics are involved in ecstatic levitation and mediumistic levitation. Both involve rigidity in the body. Both involve dissociation. Both involve numerous other paranormal phenomena. And yet there are obvious differences.

While demonic possession can cause levitation—it can also cause the opposite of levitation, or *increased* weight. There are several cases on record where people, instead of levitating, actually gain weight!

I first discovered this was while investigating a ghost case. A young girl named Happy had begun experimenting with a Ouija Board. Her father was recently deceased, and Happy believed she had contacted his spirit. At first the messages were comforting, but Happy soon became obsessed with the board, using it daily. One day she was with her friends and was using the board when she fell into an unconscious trance. Her concerned friends planned to rush her to the hospital, but to their shock, were unable to lift her up. Said one witness, "It felt like she weighed hundreds of pounds."[490]

Another case occurred in 1928, during an exorcism. The possessed woman's body would contort and change shape and weight. As the report reads, "At times her abdominal regions and extremities became as hard as iron and stone. In such instances the weight of her body pressed into the iron bedsteads so that the iron beams of the bed bent to the floor."[491]

This is true for some mediums also, such as Home. Another example occurred in 1864, during a séance in Nashville, Tennessee. The séance produced a number of spiritualistic phenomena. Then, at one point, one of the men at the table became stuck to the floor. As one witness, Dr. J. B. Ferguson, later wrote, "We noticed the gentleman referred to and found him firmly seated, his feet and chair riveted to the floor. Several persons of great physical strength attempted to remove his chair and failed....The company seemed confounded."[492]

This phenomenon of increased weight seems to be related to a phenomenon sometimes referred to as the *Odic* force. On a television talk show, I saw a young girl who claimed to possess the "Odic force." By concentrating, she was able to increase her weight so that a full-grown man was unable to lift her. It is also one of the siddhes as outlined by Patanjali.

Writes Fodor, "In religious chronicles one event meets with the antithesis of the phenomenon: excessive gravitation...hysterics often claim such an increase of energy that they are unable to stir. That the feeling may not be purely imaginative is indicated by the case of Alberto Fontana, the medium, who, after a levitation, remained as if nailed to the floor and nobody was able to remove him."[493]

In any case, it appears again that the physical body becomes stronger when the astral body is activated. This would explain the cases of supernatural strength reported by several mediums and saints, and the occasional normal person under extreme stress. Certainly a large number of the levitation cases seem to be the result of possession.

Explorer Douchon Gersi writes, "It is interesting to note that all the innumerable levitation phenomena I observed in Haiti involved people who were experiencing a state of possession during a ceremony. They didn't always travel long distances, following a complicated or zigzag path, but they did all levitate by jumping into the air, staying above the ground for much longer than a normal jump would keep them there, and hitting the ground, not always falling straight down."[494]

Illness, Trauma and Levitation

A small portion of the levitation episodes were caused by illness, trauma, or even approaching death. The theory behind this would be that the physical body, having become temporarily weakened, is dominated by the astral body.

Some illnesses can actually cause increased weight. Writes Professor Petty, "In several diseases, as for instance nervous fever, the weight of the body appears to be increased..."[495]

In 1920, a group of prisoners at Clinton Prison in New York State contracted botulinus poisoning. During their illness, the patients' bodies became mysteriously charged with electricity, causing metal objects to fly around their vicinity. Significantly, the poltergeist effects varied in intensity corresponding with the severity of their conditions.[496]

In February, 1976, twelve-year-old Vyvyan Jones of Bristol, England broke his arm, causing his body to become electrically charged. For a period of two days, his hair stood on end, he emitted electric shocks whenever touched and caused interference in electrical machinery. He was able to make light bulbs glow by merely holding onto them. The effect faded as his arm healed.

In 1877, seventeen-year-old Caroline Clare of London, England suffered a severe and unexplained illness involving seizures and weight-loss. After her recovery one year later, Clare manifested the bizarre symptom of becoming magnetic. Metal cutlery would stick to her skin and had to be pulled off by another person.[497]

There are many other such cases of so-called "electric" or "magnetic" people. Clearly, the human body is both electric and magnetic, and illness can have a profound effect on this bio-electromagnetic field.

Writes Rampa, "Under certain conditions a lama who is desperately ill can use a modified form of levitation to get himself off the ground in order that he may cope with an emergency. Of course he has to pay for it after, but the energy can then be paid back in small installments over a week or so." [498]

Why do some people levitate during a fall? Under this model, it would be because the astral body is jolted into a connection with the physical body, becoming for a split-second the dominant body. Because the "victim" is awake and moving, the astral body remains locked to the physical body, physically lifting it into the air.

Poltergeists and Levitation

The poltergeist phenomenon stretches back thousands of years and remains remarkably consistent. Modern researchers have uncovered the mechanics behind some of the activity. In a large proportion of the cases, there is the presence of an emotionally disturbed teenager. The theory is that repressed emotions and feelings become exteriorized into an independent personality fragment that wreaks havoc on the home. Others feel that poltergeist phenomenon is really just uncontrolled mediumship.

Whether all forms of levitation are attributable to people who have medium-istic talent is a valid question. A medium is someone who reportedly has a strong avenue of communication with the astral world. The difference in various cultures may be due to a matter of interpretation and ability to control this force.

Interestingly, many of the saints suffered from poltergeist attacks.

Writes Commander X, "We find levitation associated with a few poltergeist cases....The nature of levitation suggests that the ability may draw upon the same source of energy as does poltergeist activity....It seems reasonable to sup-pose that the force emanating from the target subject, in a manner science does not fully understand, and capable of moving relatively heavy objects such as furniture, could, if directed toward the ground, effectively lift the subject's body into the air."[499]

It may be important to note that at least one mediumistic levitator (Schneider) lost his ability to levitate after going through puberty. Perhaps also important to note is that the vast majority of the levitating saints and yogis remained chaste, and this may have been a contributing factor to their levitations.

Channeling and Levitation

Channeling and demonic possession are flip sides of the same coin. Many of the saints displayed both types of behavior. Both involve a subjugation of the primary personality. Both cause the victims to be able to levitate, read minds, and have supernatural strength and psychic knowledge. One is generally emotionally positive, the other negative.

How can this be? Where do all these psychic powers come from? The one commonality again is dissociation. By dissociating, the personality has opened a psychic doorway to the astral dimensions. It again appears that the secret lies on the astral plane.

Multiple Personality and Levitation

Virtually every case of MPD (multiple personality disorder, now called dis-sociative identity disorder) involves extreme abuse which causes the victim to dissociate. As with channeling or demonic possession, the primary personality is subjugated and a new one takes its place. What many people don't know is that MPD victims are, almost without exception, extraordinarily psychic. A typical example is the case of Chris Sizemore, who experienced a lifetime of paranormal events, including levitation. Her levitation seems to have been the result of extreme abuse, which caused her to dissociate. Again, it seems clear that dissociation is the answer.

Interestingly, several MPD sufferers have personalities that define themselves with polarizing names such as God or the Devil. Many also experience typical poltergeist phenomenon. Some modern researchers have postulated that, in the past, MPD was often misdiagnosed as demonic possession. While MPD and demonic possession are clearly separate phenomena, their similarities are undeniable.

Telekinesis and Levitation

Telekinesis has been demonstrated numerous times under strict laboratory conditions. The case of Nina Kulagina is a perfect example. Parapsychologists believe that it is a latent ability in all humans, but that some are more proficient than others. The force is unknown, but seems to be connected to mind power, through the use of will, imagination, and intent. Many researchers have postulated that levitation and telekinesis may involve the same force.

Sleep and Levitation

Again, some cases of levitation occur when the person is asleep (Harper, Smurl, Hadsell, Slade, Hartmann). Sleep is the most obvious and profound form of dissociation. Presumably, in cases where levitation occurs during sleep, the astral body has again become dominant and instead of going out of the physical body, lifts it upwards, as the astral body's normal mode of travel is flying.

Lightning and Levitation

Rochas was the first to note a relationship between electricity and levitation. Recounting several accounts of lightning strikes levitating both people and objects, he concluded that the force involved is likely electrical in nature. Today, several modern accounts have surfaced involving lightning and levitation.

Back in the mid 1800s, Professor Steiglehner experimented with electrifying objects and discovered that he was, in fact, able to reduce weight through this process. This was verified in 1847 by Abbot Nolet who wrote to the Royal Academy of Sciences that he also obtained similar results.

Today, research is more promising. Using superconductors which generate intense electrical fields, scientists have successfully levitated small living frogs. The electrical fields seem to have no effect on the frogs other than completely canceling the weight of their bodies, making them exactly as light as air.

Scientists have also been able to levitate extremely small objects using powerful lasers. Today, magnetic levitation is widely used in society in everything from kitchen appliances to subway trains.

Conclusions

Again, the main undeniable conclusion is the obvious connection between dissociation and levitation. Writes Commander X, "The one thing that stands out in all levitation cases is that the levitator was in an altered state of consciousness. It seems clear that the ecstatic reaches levitation through meditation of an intense sort. The medium achieves something similar by going into trance....Levitation then seems to depend upon a trance or altered mental state of consciousness."[500]

Dissociation has long been known to be an important factor in producing a wide variety of paranormal manifestations. As Rene Sudre wrote, "The production of metaphysical phenomenon always accompany with the subject a particular organic state which is called 'trance.'"[501]

Writes Harvey-Wilson, "One way to find useful clues as to how human levitation might work is to analyze what the various groups that occasionally produce such reports have in common. Several connections are obvious. A belief in spirits and/or a spiritual realm is integral to shamanism, mysticism, spiritualism, spirit possession and poltergeist activity....The people who belong to these groups often enter trances or altered states of consciousness, either voluntarily or involuntarily, and many of them develop paranormal abilities other than levitation. This introduces the closely related subjects of parapsychology and consciousness research."[502]

Writes Fodor, "Many mediums go into trance and do not rise up in the air. The state of trance, mysterious as it is, is not an explanation. The rate of breathing undergoes an alteration in trance....Some secret may exist between the rate of breathing and loss of weight....We do not know what is the force that accomplishes such feats. It should be sufficient to know that such a force exists. Religious ecstasy may also liberate a force."

In 1875, Sir William Crookes published a list of forty levitating saints in the *Quarterly Journal of Science*, of which he was editor. Originally a skeptic, Crookes' list caused an uproar among the conservative English society. Crookes, however, was able to draw solid conclusions about the nature of levitation. Regarding these forty levitators, Crookes writes, "As the lives of all these are pretty fully recorded, we have means of drawing several generalizations. It is plain that all displayed the qualities most distinctive of today's 'spirit-mediums,' and many were accompanied from childhood by some of the same phenomenon....A feature common to the whole forty is great asceticism. Only four married, and all were in the habit of extreme fasting, 'mascerating' their bodies either with hair shirt or various irons under their clothes, and many submitting to bloody flagellations. Again, all, without exception, were ghost-seers, or second-sighted; and all subject to trances, either with loss of consciousness only, or of motion and flexibility too....Many were levitated only in these unconscious states, others as Joseph of Cupertino, both in trance and the ordinary state, and (like Mr. Home) most frequently in the latter, while a very few, as Theresa, seem to have been always conscious when in the air."

Crookes also noted that many of the levitators on his list were "fire-handlers," some had the "gift of tongues," and that most were "great preachers." He finds it significant that his list contains the founders of six major religious orders, showing that the levitators were often profoundly influential. Finally, he noted one of the most obvious and pervasive patterns exhibited among the levitating saints. Writes Crookes, "In all cases the subjects were either praying at the time, or speaking or listening to a particular religious topic that, in each case, is recorded to have generally affected that person either with trance or levitation."

The conclusion is inescapable: whether one is put into an ecstatic trance, or is so abused that they shut their awareness off, or meditates to achieve dissociation, or falls down, or the person is sleeping, or very ill, the principal is exactly the same. The person is dissociating, or transferring awareness to other aspects of the mind. They have dissolved the borders of mind that most people have.

Many people feel that they exist alone in a limited physical body with their own thoughts. Meditation or dissociation makes one realize that we are connected to all things and beings, that we are, in fact, all things and beings. It is this realization, as one moves into awareness of these aspects of self, that the so-called siddhis, or psychic powers, become activated.

Levitation then, seems to be a natural ability that will eventually occur in everybody at some point during their spiritual evolution towards enlightenment. It appears to be caused by a dominant astral body, which is actually the superior body in terms of ability, both physical and mental. Obviously, the human body is more than just flesh and blood. It is also an electrically supercharged dynamo of energy with enormous potentials at which we have only begun to guess.

33. So You Want to Fly?

Is it possible for anybody to levitate?

As we have seen, the answer is yes. People of all types levitate. You don't have to be a saint, yogi, medium, psychic, or astral-traveler, though this certainly seems to help.

Nor do you have to believe that levitation is even possible. Several of the levitators had no prior beliefs concerning the subject when they started levitating. If you've read this far into the book, you obviously have an interest in spirituality, and are, therefore, an ideal candidate.

As we have seen, the secret behind levitation is dissociation. Whether it's through prayer, meditation, mediumship, sleep, trance, austerities, illness, or trauma, the one constant is dissociation.

The next question would be then, how does one dissociate to induce levitation?

Not surprisingly, there are several different ways. While illness or trauma are obviously not feasible (nor are drugs recommended), there are many other methods you can use to achieve levitation.

Writes Joseph Weed, "To levitate skillfully and successfully the physical organism must be purified. A diet is prescribed and one must be rid of all excess weight. Along with the physical training, mental exercises are recommended and, of course, an increase in psychic energy is essential. Those who have succeeded explain that it is not too difficult to repeat once achieved, not too unlike learning to swim."

Weed believes that the ability to levitate is "inherent" in everybody, otherwise "it would not be possible for so many individuals of so many different races and places and with such different backgrounds of experience and culture to perform them."[503]

While Weed writes that excess weight must be removed, the cases show that several overweight persons have, in fact, levitated. Though conversely, there are virtually no cases of levitating alcoholics, drug addicts…etc. Spiritual and physical purification, therefore, seems to be an obvious factor.

Ramtha, as channeled by J. Z. Knight, explains that levitation can be accomplished through a process of focusing one's consciousness. Says Ramtha, "So now if we are going to accept a philosophy as outrageous as levitation, we have to change some conventional views. We have to change them because if we don't, we will never get to levitate…So now I teach you—which one day you will do—how to levitate, once we have worked on your focus. What you would start to do is that you would alter the resonant field that you are currently in. Now let's interject something here…about field phenomenon. Field phenomenon is sort of like radiation, microwave fields, electromagnetic fields. Listen to me very carefully. All fields are a product of a stream of consciousness. They are a phenomenon of consciousness. Now with that in mind, then all fields—all fields—known and unknown are subject then to streams of consciousness. And what is the greatest accelerator that you now possess that can tune into different streams of consciousness? The brain….To learn to levitate is to change the resonant frequency field that you currently inhabit….So when I say then that when you change your resonant field, you alter the field in which you are in, that the field becomes pliable according to focused consciousness. That field, overlapped in this field, will be an antigravity field because it will eat gravity to sustain its higher resonance."[504]

There are apparently many different ways to levitate. What follows are six of the major methods that are used by various cultures to achieve the mystical state of levitation.

Pranayama

Levitation can be achieved through the practice of pranayama, an ancient eastern practice involving control of the breath. It should only be done by a true Yoga initiate with a qualified teacher.

This can be a rather complicated process, so pay attention. The student is instructed to sit in a full lotus posture and inhale. After inhaling, you hold your breath until it becomes uncomfortable, counting the number of seconds. Then exhale.

Now you are instructed to time your inhalation to be one-fourth the length of the time you comfortably held your breath. Inhale for this length of time, and hold your breath as before.

Next, time your exhalation to be one-half the length of time you held your breath.

In other words, you breathe with a timed ratio of one [inhalation]—four [retention]—two [exhalation]. If this sounds complicated, it is.

This is one method of pranayama. According to one source, if you can perform the pranayama for one hundred repetitions by inhaling for sixteen seconds, holding your breath for sixty-four seconds, and exhaling for thirty-two seconds, then you have reached the threshold necessary for levitation. Of course, it will take time to work up to this point.

This breathing practice will reportedly bring about a number of physiological changes. First there is a feeling of lightness. The body will then perspire. This is followed by a trembling of the body, which then starts to hop about like a frog and then finally rises into the air. This is the true practice of yogic flying.

This practice may take years to achieve, and students are again very strongly advised to see a yoga instructor if they want to use this method. Another very important note: Pranayama is normally practiced only by students who have already mastered the various yoga asanas (postures) and samyamas (meditation and concentration). Included in these are several other steps, (good thought, good action, abstinence, meditation, concentration…) **Again, this method should**

only be used by serious students who are already under the guidance of a qualified teacher.

Masaharu Naruse is one of the few modern living levitators. In regards to how to levitate, he writes, "It is to use instantaneously prana, or vital energy permeating the universe. Place one's consciousness on the destination point for floating. According as the amount of consciousness increases, existential reversal takes place and the physical self becomes evacuated. Then, the physical body gets attracted towards the consciousness which has been already shifted to the destination. One can thus levitate." (www.naruse-yoga.com)

Some Indian fakirs seem to use a similar method. As Kellar writes of a first-hand case, "....the magician laid himself flat upon the earth, face downwards, for a minute or a minute and a half, then arose, and, pressing his arms tightly against his sides, stepped forwards and upwards as if upon an aerial stairway, walking up into the air to an altitude of several hundred feet....my informant said he thought this might be done through an occult knowledge of electrical currents, as if these fakirs changed at will the nature of the electrical current with which their body was charged from negative to positive, or vice versa, inhaling an electrical influence from the earth which had the effect of destroying the force of gravity."[505]

This idea is echoed by Blavatsky who writes, "The altitude of levitation would be measured by his ability to charge his body with positive electricity. This control once obtained, alteration of his levity or gravity would be as easy as breathing."[506]

Says yoga teacher, I. K. Taimini, "Levitation is a very common phenomenon in pranayama practice and is due to the pranic currents flowing in a particular way."[507]

Writes Rampa, "Levitation is accomplished by a very special form of breathing which actually raises the frequency of the body's molecular oscillations, so that it is able to induce a form of contra-gravity. If one is expert enough, one can control the height at which one floats. If one is not so expert, well, it is to be hoped that they said goodbye to their friends and relations before practicing. In the East, in the great lamaseries where such things are taught, all practices are first conducted indoors, so that the worst that can befall a novice is that he gets thumped on the head by the ceiling, and that often serves to teach him to study more assiduously. Levitation cannot be done while there are scoffers gaping at one because it demands concentration and a special form of breathing."[508]

Some of the best evidence for the veracity of levitation comes from an ingenious yet simple experiment designed by pioneering paranormal researcher Hereward Carrington. It involves the use of breathing and the common schoolyard game known as "finger levitation." Carrington's repeated experiments prove conclusively that rhythmic breathing can, in fact, reduce the weight of a human body.

The experiment involved five people, a wood chair, and a large-sized, self-registering weight scale. The chair was placed in the center of the scale and one person sat on it. The other four people also stood on the scale on each side of the sitter. At this point, their combined weight, including the chair, measured 712 pounds.

Then all five were instructed to inhale and exhale deeply, several times, in unison. On the fifth count, everyone was instructed to retain their breath, and the four lifters would then quickly insert their fingers beneath the arms and legs of the sitter and lift him up with their fingers.

To Carrington's shock and delight, he was able to scientifically prove that levitation was occurring. As he writes, "On the first lift the recorder stated that the dial had fallen to 660 pounds, a loss of 52 pounds. On the second lift there was an apparent loss of 52 pounds. On the third lift of 60 pounds; on the fourth lift of 60 pounds, and on the fifth lift of 60 pounds. No gain of weight was at any time recorded, invariably a loss, which, however, slowly returned to normal as the subject was held for some considerable time in the air. I have no theory to offer as to these observations which I cannot fully explain."[509]

Writes Fodor, "Carrington's experiments with the lifting game [finger levitation] have actually proved that, for some mysterious reason, rhythmical breathing may considerably reduce the weight of the human body."[510]

Another experiment was performed by Abbot Nollet in the latter part of the 1800s. This involved the magnetizing of small animals placed on scales to record their weight. Using these methods, Nollet was able to significantly reduce the weight of a cat and a pigeon.[511]

Patanjali's Methods

Yogic methods to achieve levitation are thousands of years old and have been traced to their point of origin. They were first recorded by Patanjali, an Indian yogi who lived twenty-five hundred years ago. Levitation is one of eight major siddhis, or psychic powers. Patanjali's *Yoga Sutras* describe how one can achieve numerous siddhis.

Patanjali presents two methods to achieve levitation.

According to Sutra 111.40, "By mastery of udana vayu, the yogi can walk over water, swamps, and thorns without touching them. He can also levitate."

Sounds simple enough. But the Yoga Sutras are famous for their seeming simplicity. What exactly is the *udana vayu,* and how does one gain mastery over it?

The udana vayu is one of the five vital pranas, or energies. It is associated with the throat chakra. Mastering control of this particular energy is then a matter of samyama, or meditation. Richards recommends visualizing "a very thin white line, the thickness of a human hair, extending from the region of your throat to the forepart of your nose, then to the space between your eyebrows, and finally to the top of your head."

If you can visualize this clearly enough, Richards says, "The first few times, you may feel a tingling sensation in the area of the Udana, later, you may feel some pressure as the energy becomes stronger. And later still, you will feel a very definite, pulsating, upward current of energy that manifests most strongly in the upper part of your head."

After this, Richards recommends visualizing the energy of the Udana growing stronger and more powerful until it literally lifts you off the ground. In his book, Richards hints that he has found this method to be successful. As he writes, "You will find this an exhilarating meditation to perform, even before you begin to get objective results."[512]

While this Sutra seems to be effective, it is Sutra 111.43 which is usually cited to achieve true levitation. According to this Sutra, "By knowing the relationship between the body and ether, the yogi transforms his body and mind so that they become as light as cotton fibre. He can then levitate in space."

Another translation, "By Samyama [meditation] on the relationship between the body and the Akasa [space] and on the lightness of such things as cotton down, the yogi acquires passage through the sky."

This particular siddhe is considered one of the eight major siddhis, called *laghima*, meaning to become light as cotton.

To perform this meditation, simply visualize your body being filled with space. Recognize that your body is made of vibrating molecules which contain more space between them than matter. Remember that physical reality is an hallucination which can actually be manipulated.

Writes Richards, "As you imagine your body becoming pervaded with space you will feel a gradual feeling of lightness coming over you. This is the lightness of which the Sutra speaks. If you feel it, that is your assurance that you are performing the siddhi correctly....If your effort is great, then your result will be great also."[513]

Meditation and Prayer

Pretty much all methods to achieve levitation require some form of meditation. Many of the saints levitated apparently as a result of long meditation upon God. This is a simple, but surprisingly effective method to achieve levitation, and should not be underestimated. Most people who levitate not only have a strong belief in the existence of God; they have made a career of it. A life devoted to the meditation of the Divine can provoke levitation. The conclusion is inescapable.

It doesn't matter who or what you think God is, as this works in any culture, under any belief system. The obvious factor is the level of devotion and practice. The more effort, attention and discipline that is applied to meditating and praying on the perfection, love and glory of God, the better will be the results.

To levitate using prayer, simply find a quiet, comfortable area where you won't be disturbed. Then depending upon your religion or spiritual inclinations, you may surround yourself with sacred, holy, or religious paraphernalia. Anything that inspires spiritual feelings within you should suffice. Then simply relax and concentrate all your attention on God, the Spirit-Which-Moves-Through-All-Things, All That Is, Nature, the Universe, or whatever you conceive of as God. Recognize that you yourself are made in God's image, that you are a part of God, that God exists within you. Appeal to your spirit guides, to other Enlightened Masters, to your Higher Self, to God, whatever you feel comfortable with. The point is to build a bridge from the physical world to the spiritual realms.

However, belief in God is not necessarily required to levitate. There are many different meditational methods to achieve levitation.

According to Swami Bhakta Vishita, anyone can achieve levitation through a very simple meditation. He instructs the would-be levitator to sit down with the spine, neck and head in a straight line. Then allow your body to relax. Next, quiet your mind by allowing all thoughts to pass. Vishita then says, "Now we come to an important stage. Shut out all external and internal thoughts, and think of that only which leaves the body at the time of death. Focus all your mental energy inwardly on your soul, and, as you begin to realize this more and more, a veritable blaze of illumination will rise within you. This is a wonderful experience—this bathing in the great ocean of soul-force; it will develop startling powers in anyone. It is capable of charging your being with powerful energy; it will brighten your intellect, lighten your physical weight, and may even give you the power of rising in the air, levitation."[514]

According to Buddhist tradition, levitation will result after long meditation on either the third-eye chakra and/or the heart chakra. To use this method, simply find a quiet, comfortable location, clear your mind of all thoughts, and focus your attention on either of these two areas. Imagine your chakras becoming active. If you do this correctly, you may feel a spinning, buzzing or warmth in the area of your attention. This is a good sign and means you are making progress. Meditating on these chakras will also activate and awaken other psychic abilities including astral travel, precognition, clairvoyance, and more. According to the well-known ancient Chinese book on esoteric knowledge, *The Secret of the Golden Flower,* "When one sits in meditation, the fleshly body becomes quite shining like silk or jade. It seems difficult to remain sitting; one feels as if drawn upward. This is called: 'The spirit returns and touches heaven.' In time, one can experience it in such a way that one really floats upward." People who have reached this stage are said to have obtained "the Rainbow body."

In the *Tripitaka,* or the teachings of Buddha, he describes that one can float or walk in air through a process of determination and resolution. All that is needed is total faith and complete resolve.

Many of the saints achieved mystical states of consciousness through a process of severe austerities—including chastity, abstinence from food or eating polluted food, restricting the hours of sleep, sleeping on hard boards with a rock for a pillow, mortifying the flesh in a multitude of ways, wearing heavy chains or hair shirts, wearing only light clothes in cold weather, and much more. While not all of them tortured their physical bodies, most led very chaste and ascetic lifestyles. Austerities are clearly a powerful factor in leading many of the saints to the state of consciousness where levitation is possible. On the other hand, many levitators limited the austerities of their students. **Because of health dangers, this method is not preferable. Extreme austerities are, therefore, not recommended.** However, fasting and other minor austerities may be very helpful. In any case, always practice your austerities with extreme caution.

As can be seen, there are many different ways to induce meditational levitation. Choose the method that feels most comfortable to you. If you meditate regularly, on a daily basis, you will likely have the best results. Again, your progress will mostly depend upon the degree of effort you put forth.

Mediumship

While the popular belief is that mediumship is a congenital talent, there is evidence that it can be developed. In most cases, mediumship involves the use of dissociative devices such as a Ouija Board, table tipping, automatic writing, pendulum, a trance state, or in some cases, direct voice channeling.

Developing mediumship again involves dissociation. The medium attempts to allow the ego to step aside and permit the consciousness of another to communicate telepathically. Mediums are apparently able to raise their vibration so that they are in coincidence with the astral energies.

This evidently creates a bond between the medium and the spirit world, whereby energy can be taken from the medium and manipulated by the spirits to produce mediumistic phenomenon, including levitation. This would be a form of physical mediumship, which is much rarer than mental mediumship. Also, it is a rare physical medium who can also levitate.

That said, you will want to start out slowly. Mediumship is not always an easily controlled ability. The beginner is first encouraged to seek out a professional medium to expose themselves to the process, and to study the mediumship literature. One then forms a small group of persons, usually from four to ten people, equally divided between men and women, who meet for séances regularly, at the same time each week. If there is a medium in the group, after several sittings you should start to get results.

To practice with the Ouija Board, pendulum, automatic writing, or table tipping, it is also best if you can learn this with an experienced medium. However, failing that, you can try it on your own. Begin with a cleansing meditation. Surround yourself mentally with white light. Then ask, mentally or out loud, specifically for guidance from entities who are at or above your level of spiritual development. Maintain a positive attitude and radiate only love. This should protect you from a poltergeist haunting, which is sometimes the fate of those who mess around with dissociative methods to contact spirits, without knowing what they are doing. Afterwards, always close with another cleansing white light meditation.

Remember, mediumistic levitation is apparently caused by ghosts, so it's important to remain aware of what you may be getting into. The chances are, if you going to levitate through mediumistic methods, you already possess strong abilities in this direction. It is quite easy to prove to yourself that levitation is possible using these methods.

Simply get a Ouija Board or small table. Gather a small group of people you trust *implicitly*. Then place your fingers as lightly as possible on the pointer; ask the spirits to come. If you are using a Ouija Board, you ask questions and the pointer should move seemingly by itself. The process is the same with table-tipping. With your same group, gather round a small table and as lightly as possible, place your fingers on the top of the table. Do not attempt to tip it by pressing down your fingers. Simply ask for contact. If you succeed in making contact, you then start asking for physical manifestations, such as rappings or levitation.

Again, this works best with experienced mediums, but if you gather enough people, it is easy to produce inferior levitation effects, such as the table tilting on edge or standing on one leg.

Before and after each session, be sure to meditate again on positive energies, white light, and closing any spiritual doors you may have opened. Again, this may safeguard you against any unwanted malicious poltergeist activity.

Mediumship is a very powerful method of levitation, and some researchers feel that there is little qualitative difference between levitating saints and mediums.

Astral Travel

As we have seen, there is a strong connection between astral travel and levitation. Apparently, by achieving the ability of astral travel, one is able to have access to astral energies on the physical plane. There are many methods to achieve astral travel, and the reader is encouraged to review the voluminous literature on the subject (see my book: *Out of Body Exploring: a Beginner's Approach*). In a nutshell, OBEs can be initiated in several ways including lucid dream control, affirmations, relaxation, and visualization exercises. Again, repeated astral travel leads to the development of numerous siddhis, including telepathy, precognition, and levitation.

To try this process, find a place you can relax without distraction. Sit or lay down. Spend about twenty minutes without moving. Relax every muscle in your body until you begin to feel a heaviness, lightness, numbness, tingling, or vibration. These are "exit sensations" that are often felt immediately prior to exiting the physical body.

Once you are physically relaxed to the point where you cannot feel your physical body, you must become mentally relaxed. Focus your attention away from your body and onto your thoughts. Allow your thoughts to pass, while at the same time, observing how they begin to become images in your mind's eye. Once you reach the point where you are nearly asleep, you are ready to exit.

At this point, visualize, intend, imagine, desire, affirm, remember, and will yourself to get out of body. Imagine yourself running out of your body. Imagine yourself climbing a rope or ladder. Imagine yourself rolling over and out of bed. Imagine yourself floating upwards, or spinning. Imagine yourself already out of your body.

That's all there is to it. If you persist, you will find yourself able to travel out-of-body. This can activate numerous psychic abilities including precognition, clairvoyance, healing, and, of course, levitation.

Will Power

Some people have been able to levitate without years of meditation or prayer. They simply use mind power, or a combination of imagination, desire, will, and intent. As the levitating Bulgarian farmer, Drogzenovich, said simply, "I get there by will power."

Ermolaev said, "I imagine I'm holding her up—reverse thinking." The anonymous lady at the fair said, "You can just feel light in here," and tapped her chest. Captain Bartlett reported a feeling that he could lighten his weight "at will," a talent he was able to demonstrate. Helen Hadsell practiced this method for months before she found herself suddenly flying.

Each of these people are essentially doing the same thing. They are able to intensely focus their mind power to achieve levitation.

To try this method, focus your desire, your will power, your imagination, and your intention on one goal: levitation. Simply imagine yourself becoming light as air. Imagine your body is filled with space, and your arms and legs are attached to helium balloons. Vividly picture your body being drawn upwards. Use all your will power to will yourself to levitate. Strongly focus your intent and attention on rising up. Will yourself with intense concentration to rise into the air. Desire it. Put emotional energy into your act. Know you can do it. You just may be surprised at the results.

＊   ＊   ＊

With the above six methods, and with enough practice and persistence, levitation is within your grasp. In reality, there are infinite pathways to achieving levitation. Each person who has ever levitated, reached this mystical state in their own unique way.

Choose the method that works best for you.

If you are able to produce levitation, there is another thing to consider. There is a controversy among levitators. On one side, there are those who feel that levitation should never be demonstrated, nor should it be a goal. While *enlightenment* always remains the ultimate goal, levitation and other siddhis are known to be powerful obstacles on the pathway to enlightenment by tempting the ego with pride and power, as well as leaving the levitator vulnerable to accusations of fraud or constant requests for further and better demonstrations. In a section of the *Vinya*, Buddhist monks are specifically banned from levitating in public. This occurred after a monk showed off his levitating abilities to Buddha, and the Buddha scolded him for being like a "prostitute."

On the opposite extreme are those who display their abilities of levitation openly, not for self-aggrandizement or thrills, but as a display of their devotion to God and to inspire others to follow the pathway to enlightenment. This was much more common in ancient times, whereas today, modern levitation demonstrations are very rare. Then, of course, there is every range in-between.

If levitation is true, it is inevitable that there will be more accounts. Sooner or later, another prolific levitator like Daniel Home or Joseph Desa will show up and turn modern science upside down.

Conceivably, if enough people openly display the talent to levitate, it won't be so strange. It will be accepted as an odd human talent, but one that is potentially achievable for the masses.

Judging from the consistency of the levitation reports, it is, I think, safe to conclude that there are many people living today who have the ability to levitate. And yet, very few are displaying this ability in a way that is generating significant publicity.

Still, I can't help but wonder that if levitation is a sign of progress on the pathway to spiritual enlightenment, why would one want to hide this fact? Levitation is, in and of itself, so incredibly spectacular and dramatic—literally flying in the face of the known laws of gravity—that it seems meant to be a spectacle. Can you imagine, in the future, the *International Yogic Olympics*? Many people who have fantastic talents provide demonstrations. Why not levitation?

Signs of spiritual advancement could just as easily have been, and often are, invisible to outside observers. However, levitation is so fantastic, it is impossible to miss. And yet, those who levitate seem to learn very quickly that it is in their best interests to keep it a secret to all but a choice few.

*   *   *

So there you go. Now you know the secrets that used to be taught only in hidden ancient occult schools to a select few persons, but are now public knowledge, available for anyone. Give it a try. You have nothing to lose and much to gain. Just think, *you could actually fly*. Or even better, maybe become *enlightened*! Doesn't that sound like an experience worth having? I think you can do it!

Epilogue

When I first began my research into levitation I was very skeptical. Years later, I am forced to reverse my opinions. I am now totally convinced that levitation is a reality. I honestly cannot imagine any other explanation for the huge number of accounts told by so many credible witnesses from so many different cultures throughout recorded history.

I can only conclude that human potential is much greater than most people realize. Levitation is only one of the many superhuman abilities, or siddhis, that can be activated in anyone willing to follow the spiritual path. Achieving these abilities is simply a matter of applied knowledge. Those who actually try the methods to levitate may be surprised by their success.

Again, my interest in levitation was sparked when a family friend revealed to me that she had levitated as a child. A few weeks later, I found another person who made the same claim. I later met several other levitators. After talking to so many people who claim to have levitated, I realized that it is an ability that *anyone* can learn. I also quickly discovered that the main obstacle to the advancement of knowledge about levitation is skepticism. The only thing stopping most people from levitating is that they don't think they can do it.

And yet the amazing fact is, they can. Anybody can.

Many "coincidences" brought this book into being, the most amazing was the fact that I actually knew people who had levitated. Then there were the many times that difficult-to-find books, or obscure levitation accounts seemed to be guided to me. But there was one incredible incident that still makes me wonder. During my research into levitation, I went to visit a spiritual medium who had witnessed a levitation firsthand. In the audience was an older lady named Yvonne. We began talking. She told me about how she had experimented with a Ouija Board. She stopped using it immediately because, she explained, the pointer kept levitating by itself. She denied ever levitating herself, or even trying. That would be much too scary. Then she blurted out, "Did you know that my relative was a saint?"

"Really? Which saint?" I asked, immediately intrigued.

"Anne Catherine Emmerich," she replied. "Have you heard of her?"

Appendix

Below is a chronological list of all known and recorded levitators. More than two-dozen cases of anonymous or un-named levitators/levitation events are not listed.

1. Siddhartha Guatama Buddha (563-483? BC)
2. Kuang T. Zhu (179-157 BC)
3. Brother Schnoudie (100s BC)
4. Jesus Christ (0-33? AD)
5. St. Ammon (d350)
6. St. Bessarion (300s)
7. Marie the Egyptian (430)
8. St. Aedh. (d589)
9. St. Milburga (700)
10. Shankara (788-820)
11. Padma Sambhava (700s?)
12. Tongjung Thuchen (700s)
13. Maurus (700s?)
14. Andrew of Salus (880-946)
15. Luke of Soterium (890-946)
16. St. Dunstan (910-988)
17. St. Stephen I, King of Hungary (978-1038)
18. Al Hosayn-Ibn-Mansour (d993)
19. Simon Magus (900s?)
20. Maxime (900s?)
21. St. Richard (1036)
22. Ladislas I, King of Hungary (1041-1096)
23. Milarepa (1052-1135)
24. St. Bernard of Clairvaux (1091-1153)
25. Ibn al-Qal'lyyah (1100s?)
26. Ibn al-Hakim (1100s?)
27. Christina the Astonishing (1150-1220)
28. St. Dominic (1170-1221)
29. St. Hedwig (1174-1243)
30. St. Edmund of Abingdon (1180-1240)
31. St. Francis of Assissi (1181-1226)
32. St. Lutgard (1182-1246)
33. Gilles the Blessed (1190-1267)
34. Agnes of Bohemia (1205-1281)
35. Jalalu d'Din Rumi (1207-1230)
36. Princess Elizabeth of Hungary (1207-1231)
37. Franco Lippi of Grotti the Blessed (1211-1291)

38. St. Philip Benizi (1233-1285)
39. St. Douceline (1214-1274)
40. Jutta of Prussia (1215-1264)
41. Humiliano of Florence (1219-1246)
42. Ambrose Sausedonius (1220-1287)
43. St. Bonaventura (1221-1274)
44. St. Thomas of Aquinas (1227-1274)
45. Bentivoglio the Blessed (d1232)
46. Peter Armengol the Blessed (1238-1304)
47. St. Albert Trapani (1240-1306)
48. Princess Margaret of Hungary (1242-1270)
49. Gerardesca the Blessed (d1243)
50. St. Marguerite of Cortone (1247-1297)
51. Agnes of Montepulciano (1268-1317)
52. Gerard Cagnoli (1270-1345)
53. St. Robert of Solentum (1273-1341)
54. Phillipin the Blessed (1200s?)
55. Pierre of Monticello (1200s?)
56. Sheikh Djilani of Baghdad (1200s?)
57. St. Qutb uddin Haydar (1200s?)
58. Bartholous of Vado (d1300)
59. Blessed Peter of Treia (d1304)
60. Marguerite of Castello the Blessed (d1320)
61. St. Flora of Beaulieu. (d1347)
62. Catherine of Sienna (1347-1380)
63. St. Vincent Ferrer (1359-1419)
64. Coleta of Ghent (1381-1447)
65. Pierre-Jeremie of Panormo (1381-1452)
66. Catherine Columbina (d1387)

67. St. Antonine Pierozzi (1389-1459)
68. Nicolas of Ravenne (d1398)
69. St. Pierre Regalati (1300s?)
70. Guilemette de la Rochelle (1300s?)
71. St. Francois de Paule (1416-1507)
72. Alvarez of Cordova the Blessed (d1430)
73. Eustochium of Padua (1443-1463)
74. Blessed Giles of Lorenzana (1443-1518)
75. Ladislaw of Gielniow the Blessed (1440-1505)
76. Osanna Andreasi of Mantus (1450 1505)
77. Jean-Ange Porro the Blessed (1450-1506)
78. J. Savaranola (1452-1498)
79. Archangela Girlani (1460-1494)
80. St. Diego (d1463)
81. Columba of Rieta (1468-1501)
82. St. Angela Merici (1470-1540)
83. Blessed Antonia of Florence (d1472)
84. Blessed Louisa Albertoni (1473-1533)
85. Christine D'Aguila (1480-1543)
86. Blessed James of Illyria (d1485)
87. St. Cajetun (1480 1547)
88. Bernard Scammacca (d1486)
89. Thomas of Villanova (1488-1555)
90. St. Ignatius of Loyola (1491-1556)
91. St. Peter of Alcantara (1499-1562)
92. Brother Antoine de Saint-Reine (1400s?)
93. Zangi Bashgirdi (1400s)
94. St. Francis Xavier (1506-1552)
95. Bartholomew of Anghiers (d1510)
96. St. Teresa of Avila (1515-1582)

97. St. Philip Neri (1515-1595)
98. Dr. Torrabla (1525)
99. Salvator de Horta (1520-1567)
100. Nicholas Factor the Blessed (1520-1583)
101. St. Catherine of Ricci (1522-1589)
102. St. Luis Bertrand (1526-1581)
103. Conradin de Brecia the Blessed (d1529)
104. St. Caspar de Bono (1530-1604)
105. St. Bernardino Realino (1530-1616)
106. John de Ribera the Blessed (1532-1611)
107. St. Alphonsus Rodriguez (1533-1617)
108. Marguerite Agullona (1536-1600)
109. St. Pascal Baylon (1540-1592)
110. St. Seraphino (1540-1604)
111. John of the Cross (1542-1591)
112. Rabbi Hayyim Vital (1542-1620)
113. Ursule Benincasa the Blessed (1547-1618)
114. Francis Suarez (1548-1617)
115. St. Camille de Lellis (1550-1614)
116. Marie Raggi (1552-1600)
117. St. Joseph of Leonissa (1556-1612)
118. Francois Dorothee of Villa (1558-1605)
119. St. Laurence of Brindisi (1559-1619)
120. Dominque Ruzzola de Jesus-Marie (1559-1630)
121. Jacquette de Bachelier (1559-1635)
122. St. Mary Magdalen Dei Pazzi (1566-1607)
123. Marie Acarie of the Incarnation the Blessed (1566-1618)
124. Damien de Vicaro (1569-1613)
125. Leonard de Lettra (1569-1621)

126.St. Martin de Porres (1579-1639)
127.Humile di Bisignano the Blessed (1582-1637)
128.Jeanne Rodriguez of Jesus-Marie (1584-1650)
129.Maria Villanie (1584-1670)
130.St. Giacinta Mariscotti (1585-1640)
131.Jean Massias the Blessed (1585-1645)
132.J. S. Piscator (d1586)
133.St. Michael of the Saints (1589-1625)
134.St. Pierre Clavet the Blessed (1589-1654)
135.Francoise Fontaine (1591)
136.Elisabeth De Ranfaing (1592-162?)
137.Lha-Tsu Ch'em-Bo (1595-1661)
138.St. Marie Madeline of Cordoue (1500s?)
139.Luc de Medina del Campo (1500s?)
140.Alphonse Rubius (d1601)
141.Andrew Hiberon the Blessed (d1602)
142.Maria Coronel de Agreda (1602-1665)
143.St. Joseph of Cupertino (1603-1663)
144.Thomas of Cori (1603-1709)
145.Jeanne-Marie of the Cross (1603-1673)
146.St. Seraphino (d1604)
147.St. Bernard Latini of Corleone (1605-1667)
148.St. Francois de Saint-Nicholas (1608-1678)
149.Passitea Crogi (d1615)
150.Collette Dumont (1617)
151.St. Marianne of Jesus of Paredes (1618-1645)
152.Marguerite Parigot of the Saint-Sacrament (1618-1648)
153.Veronica Laparelli (d1620)
154.Sister Beatrice Mary of Jesus (1632-1712)
155.Marie Paret (1636-1674)
156.Onofrio de Fiamenga (d1639)
157.Francois de Posadas the Blessed (1644-1714)
158.St. Joseph Oriol (1650-1702)
159.Bonaventura of Potenza (1651-1711)
160.St. Pacifico Divini (1653-1721)
161.St. John Joseph Calosirto of the Cross (1654-1734)

162.Mr. Jones (1657)
163.Mary London (1661)
164.Julian Cox (1663)
165.Ange d'acri the Blessed (1669-1739)
166.Margaret Rule (1660s?)
167.Maria Minima Strozzi (d1672)
168.St. Veronica Giuliani (1676-1727)
169.Marcelline Pauper (1668-1708)
170.Therese of the Cross (d1673)
171.Francis Fey (1682)
172.Blaise de Caltanisetta (d1684)
173.St. Paul Francois Danei of the Cross (1694-1775)
174.St. Alphonse Liguori (1696-1787)
175.Dominic de Jesus-Marie Carme Dechaux (1600s)
176.Juana de la Encarnacion (d1705)
177.Jean-Baptiste de Mastena (d1713)
178.Saint Marie-Francoise des Cinq Plaies (1715-1791)
179.Nancy Wesly (1716)
180.Patrick Sandilands (1720)
181.Angiolo Paoli (d1720)
182.Anthony Margil (d1726)
183.St. Gerard Majella (1726-1755)
184.Didacus (1743-1801)
185.Clara Isabel de Funariis (d1744)
186.St. Benedict Joseph Labre (1748-1783)
187.Gertrude Salandri (d1748)
188.St. Andrew Fournet (1752-1843)
189.Mary Magdalen Postel (1756-1846)
190.Abbe Claude Dhiere (1757-1820)
191.St. Seraphim of Serov (1759-1833)
192.Mr. Giles (1761)
193.Anne Catherine Emmerich (1774-1824)
194.St Maddalena di Canossa (1774-1835)
195.Marie of Jesus Crucified (1782-1826)
196.Joachima de Mas Y de Vedruna (1783-1854)
197.St. Gaspar del Bufalo (1786-1837)
198.St. Joseph Benoit of Cottolengo (1786-1842)
199.St. Jean-Marie Baptiste of Vianney (1786-1859)

200.Marie de Jesus, the Mother of Bourg (1787-1862)
201.Michael Garicoits the Blessed (1797-1863)
202.Shaikh Muhammad Quaili (1700s?)
203.Seraphina (1700s?)
204.St. Bernard Ptolomei (1700s?)
205.Mademoiselle Thevenet (1700s?)
206.Margaret Hallahan (1802-1868)
207.St. Anthony Claret (1807-1870)
208.Marie de Morel (1812-1863)
209.St. John Bosco (1815-1888)
210.Xavier Seelos (1819-1867)
211.Francis Luycks (1824-1896)
212.Lahiri Mahasaya (1828-1895)
213.Dengbagine (1830s?)
214.Helene Blavatsky (1831-1891)
215.Daniel Dunglas Home (1833-1886)
216.Ramakrishna (1836-1886)
217.Nikolai Yurlov (1837)
218.Mademoiselle Pourrat (1840)
219.Eugene Vintras (1840)
220.Andre Bessette (1845-1937)
221.Mary of Jesus Crucified (1846-1878)
222.Harry Phelps (1850)
223.Louise Lateau (1850-1883)
224.St. Frances Cabrini (1850-1917)
225.Monsieur Brown-Sequard (1851)
226.Ms. Atwood (1851)
227.Ira Davenport (1851)
228.Henry Gordon (1853, 1864)
229.Mademoiselle French (1853)
230.Marie Julie Jahenny (1853-1879)
231.Jean Eouard Lamy (1853-1931)
232.Eusapia Palladino (1854-1918)
233.Maria Domenica Barbagli (1855)
234.Roland Squire (1855)
235.Narayenanand (1856)
236.Victoire Vullet (1858)
237.Henry Cathcart (1859)
238.Mademoiselle A. (1859)
239.Joseph X. (1860)
240.Charles Reed (1863)

241.Covindasamy (1866)
242.Marie of the Passion (1866-1912)
243.Helene-Josephine Poirier (1867)
244.Amarchand Maitreyer (1860s)
245.William Stainton Moses (1870)
246.Florence Cook (1870)
247.Teofil Modrzejewski (1873-1943)
248.St. Gemma Galgani (1878-1903)
249.Marie Baourdie (1878)
250.Victoire Claire (d1883)
251.Indridi Indridason (1883-1912)
252.Ramagiri Swami (1885)
253.Padre Pio (1887-1968)
254.Carmine Mirabelli (1889-1951)
255.William Eglinton (1880s)
256.Mr. Williams (1880s)
257.Mr. Herne (1880s)
258.Mr. F. (1888)
259.Mr. C. (1888)
260.Alberto Fontana (1893)
261.Arturo Ruggiero (1893)
262.Nicholas Santangelo (1893)
263.Jast (1894)
264.Teresa Neumann (1898-1962)
265.Part-Sky Woman (1800s?)
266.Abbot Petit (1800s?)
267.Mrs. Volckman-Guppy (1800s?)
268.Mr. Foster (1800s?)
269.Mademoiselle Hauffe (1800s?)
270.Mundauin (1800s?)
271.David Du Plessis (1905-1987)
272.Father Aloysius Ellcuria (1906-1981)
273.Ngudeng (d1906)
274.Claire-Germaine Cele (1907)
275.Zuccarini (1908)
276.Mr. Slade (1909)
277.Mataji (1900s)
278.Babaji (1900s)
279.Nagendra Nath Bhaduri (1900s?)
280.Maria del Passione (d1912)
281.Ted Owens (1924)
282.Willie Schneider (1927)
283.Kaawia (1920s)
284.Jack Webber (1920s)
285.Yram (1920s)
286.Maria Vollhardt (1920s)

287.Captain J. Alleyne Bartlett (1931)
288.Angelo Faticoni (d1931)
289.Slubbaya Pullavar (1936)
290.St. Zachary (d1936)
291.Blanche Swisher (1937)
292.Colin Evans (1938)
293.Harry Brown (1930s)
294.Robert Setti (1945-1984)
295.Roland X. (1949)
296.Rabbi Israel Spira (1940s)
297.Borge Michaelson (1940s)
298.Nyang-Pas (1950)
299.Mary Frank (1951)
300.Kelly Marley (1950s)
301.Felicity X. (1950s)
302.Spencer X. (1950s)
303.Peter X. (1950s)
304.Martha Sherman (1950s)
305.Mikhail Drogzenovich (1960s)
306.William Olsen (1960s)
307.Luang Pu Waen (1971)
308.Dolores Cazares (1975)
309.Albertine Haupt (1977)
310.Janet Harper (1978)
311.Robert Monroe (1970s)
312.Ms. Shipkhina (1970s)
313.Sister Rosa (1970s)
314.Lisa Cain (1970s?)
315.Hanna X. (1970s?)
316.Joaquin X. (1970s)
317.Jeffrey Greenberg (1983)
318.Nana Owaka (1984)
319.Christ Costner Sizemore (1984)
320.Janet Smurl (1986)
321.Heather Bonser (1986)
322.Milton X. (1980s)
323.Rajalakshmi (1980s)
324.Helen Hadsell (1980s)
325.Dana X. (1980s)
326.Masahara Naruse (1990)
327.Edmund X. (1990)
328.Doretta Johnson (1992)
329.Joan Hartmann (1999)
330.Marilynn Hughes (1990s)
331.Marisa Lozinskaya (1997)
332.Alfred Narayana(2005)
333.Mr. Osami (2005)

Endnotes

1. Richards, 31
2. Leroy, 130
3. Calmet, 80
4. Rochas, 5
5. Leroy, 5
6. Thurston, 1952, 4, 26
7. Eliade, 61, 126, 140, 409, 477, 481
8. Treece, 251, 254
9. Picknett, 13
10. Charles & Jordan, 11
11 Inglis, 161
12. Summers, 1973, 134-136
13. Rampa, 70
14. Childress, 169-171
15. Fodor, 194
16. Rogo, 1983, 13
17. Murphy, 109, 517, 520
18. Rickard and Michell, 81
19. Commander X, 6, 93-94, 101
20. Browne, 167
21. Eason, 194
22. Charles & Jordan, 70-71
23. Leroy, 54-55
24. Leroy, 54; Delaney, 392; Ghezzi, 508-509
25. Thurston & Attwater, ed., vol. 4, 308-309 (also vol. 1, 405-406)
26. Charles & Jordan, 20-21
27. Charles & Jordan, 54-55 (www.theosophy.org)
28. Rinpoche, 72-74
29. Rochas, 45; Leroy, 57; Richards, 143
30. Rochas, 45; Leroy, 56; Thurston & Attwater, ed., vol. 1, 271; Delaney, 367-368; Richards, 143
31. Calmet, 79; Leroy, 59-60; Thurston, 1952, 26; Thurston & Attwater, ed., vol. 2, 349-351; Delaney, 187-188; Ghezzi, 180-181; Rogo, 1982, 13
32. Calmet, 79
33. Rochas, 7; Leroy, 17; Richards, 36. (www.theosophy.org.)
34. Leroy, 17-18 (www.theosophy.org.)
35. Rochas, 21; Leroy, 27; Richards, 65-66
36. Rochas, 21; Leroy, 28-29
37. Rochas, 21; Leroy, 18-19
38. Leroy, 23; Treece, 255
39. Milarepa, 122-123; Charles & Jordan, 59-60
40. Leroy, 61; Thurston & Attwater, ed., vol. 3, 360-366; Delaney, 101-102; Ghezzi, 86-87
41. Charles & Jordan, 120
42. Charles & Jordan, 121
43. Calmet, 78-79; Rochas, 38-39; Leroy, 62-63; Thurston & Attwater, ed., vol. 2, 176-178; Delaney, 145; Richards, 143
44. Calmet, 78; Rochas, 45; Leroy, 61-62; Thurston, 1952, 7-8; Delaney, 181-182; Richards, 143; McBride, 58-63; Rogo, 1982, 13
45. Leroy, 67; Thurston, 1952, 26; Thurston & Attwater, ed. vol. 4, 357-358; Fodor, 194; Delaney, 190-191; Rogo, 1983, 14
46. Leroy, 63-65; Thurston, 1952, 5-7; Thurston & Attwater, ed. vol. 4, 29; Delaney, 234-235; Ghezzi, 236-237; McBride, 64-69; Charles & Jordan, 162-163
47. Leroy, 23
48. Leroy, 65
49. Rochas, 45; Leroy, 67; Thurston & Attwater, ed., vol. 2, 557-558; Delaney, 368; Richards, 143
50. Leroy, 68; Thurston & Attwater, ed., vol. 2, 308; Fodor, 198; Delaney, 258
51. Leroy, 22
52. Eliade, 126, 402
53. Leroy, 22-23; Charles & Jordan, 128-129; (www.khamush.com.)
54. Calmet, 78-79; Thurston & Attwater, ed., vol. 3, 385-388; Ghezzi, 606-607
55. Leroy, 69-71
56. Rochas, 45; Leroy, 64-65; Delaney, 336; Richards, 143
57. Rochas, 45; Richards, 143
58. Rochas, 45; Leroy, 72-73; Thurston & Attwater, ed., vol. 1, 644-646; Delaney, 508; Richards, 143
59. Rochas, 45; Leroy, 71; Delaney, 110; Richards, 143
60. Rochas, 45; Leroy, 71; Thurston & Attwater, ed., vol. 1, 509-513; Delaney, 552-553; Richards, 143; Rogo, 1983, 14
61. Leroy, 66; Thurston & Attwater, ed., 458-459; Delaney, 100
62. Rochas, 45; Leroy, 76; Thurston & Attwater, ed., vol. 2, 174-175; Delaney, 458-459; Richards, 143
63. Calmet, 78; Rochas,

45; Thurston & Attwater, ed., vol. 3, 276-277; Delaney, 38; Richards, 143

64. Leroy, 66-67
65. Leroy, 73-74; Thurston & Attwater, ed., vol. 1, 396-399; Delaney, 381-382; Ghezzi, 472-473
66. Rochas, 45; Thurston & Attwater, ed., vol. 2, 135-137; Delaney, 32
67. Thurston & Attwater, ed., vol. 4, 460
68. Calmet, 78; Rochas, 45; Leroy, 77; Richards, 143
69. Leroy, 73; Thurston, ed., vol. 4, 542; Delaney, 237
70. Rochas, 46; Leroy, 75; Thurston & Attwater, ed., vol. 4, 560; Richards, 144
71. Charles & Jordan, 15-16; _____ www.isidore-of-seville.com.
72. Thurston & Attwater, ed., vol. 1, 360-361
73. Leroy, 76-77; Thurston & Attwater, ed., vol. 2, 87; Delaney, 381
74. Thurston & Attwater, ed., vol. 4, 38
75. Leroy, 78-79, 337-338.; Thurston, 1952, 26; Thurston & Attwater, ed., vol. 2, 192-197; McBride, 70-76; Charles & Jordan, 169
76. Richards, 144; Rochas, 46; Leroy, 79; Thurston & Attwater, ed., vol. 2, 31-34
77. Rochas, 46; Leroy, 79; Thurston & Attwater, ed., vol. 1, 506-508; Delaney, 153; Richards, 144
78. Rochas, 45; Leroy, 80; Richards, 144
79. Calmet, 78; Rochas, 46; Leroy, 77; Richards, 144
80. Rochas, 46; Leroy, 80; Delaney, 469; Richards, 144
81. Leroy, 80; Thurston & Attwater, ed., vol. 2, 303
82. Leroy, 79

83. Rochas, 23; Leroy, 82
84. Leroy, 86; Thurston & Attwater, ed., vol. 2, 10-13; Delaney, 235; Richards, 144
85. Thurston & Attwater, ed., vol. 1, 89-90
86. Leroy, 84-85; Thurston & Attwater, ed., vol. 2, 592-596; Delaney, 54; Richards, 144
87. Leroy, 86
88. Fodor, 194
89. Leroy, 81; Thurston & Attwater, ed., vol. 4, 327-328
90. Leroy, 87; Thurston & Attwater, ed., vol. 2, 359-361; Delaney, 155; Richards, 144
91. Leroy, 87-88; Thurston & Attwater, ed., vol. 1, 117
92. Fodor, 194
93. Leroy, 82
94. Rochas, 45; Leroy, 60-61; Thurston & Attwater, ed., vol. 3, 466-469; Delaney, 332; Richards, 143; Ghezzi, 670-671; Charles & Jordan, 166-167.
95. Rochas, 45; Leroy, 61; Thurston & Attwater, ed., vol. 2, 654-655; Delaney, 344; Richards, 143
96. Rochas, 46; Leroy, 66; Thurston & Attwater, ed., vol. 4 pp 386-391; Delaney, 194-195; Richards, 144; Ghezzi, 190-191
97. Leroy, 67; Delaney, 277; Thurston, ed., vol. 4, 124; Ghezzi, 292-293
98. Leroy, 72; Thurston & Attwater, ed., vol. 1, 462-464; Delaney, 32; Richards, 143
99. Rochas, 45; Leroy, 69; Thurston & Attwater, ed., vol. 1, 176-178; Delaney, 382; Richards, 143
100. Thurston & Attwater, ed., vol. 2, 432-434
101. Calmet, 78; Thurston & Attwater, vol. 3, 272-274; Delaney, 127-128; Rogo, 1983, 13
102. Calmet, 78; Rochas, 46; Leroy, 89-90; Thurston,

1952, 8-9; Thurston & Attwater, ed., vol. 3, 221-227; Delaney, 298; Richards, 145; McBride, 103-109; Rogo, 1982, 13; Rickard and Michell, 83
103. Leroy, 90-91; Thurston & Attwater, ed., vol. 4, 144-148; Fodor, 194; Charles & Jordan, 174
104. Thurston, 1952, 8-9; Thurston & Attwater, ed., vol. 4, 474-481
105. Leroy, 93; Thurston & Attwater, ed., vol. 1, 328-331
106. Rochas, 46; Leroy, 92-93; Delaney, 105; Richards, 145
107. Leroy, 105-107; Thurston, 1952, 22-24; Thurston & Attwater, ed., vol. 3, 13-14; Delaney, 488; Rogo, 1982, 21-22; Rickard and Michell, 81-82
108. Leroy, 94; Thurston & Attwater, ed., vol. 2, 333-337
109. Leroy, 94; Thurston, 1952, 24; Delaney, 320; Richards, 145
110. Calmet, 72; Leroy, 94-96; Thurston, 1952, 15; Thurston & Attwater, ed., vol. 2, 395-399; Delaney, 420-421; McBride, 110-116; Rogo, 1982, 13; Ghezzi, 608-609; Inglis, 162; Charles & Jordan, 156
111. Leroy, 104; Thurston & Attwater, ed., vol. 3, 134-136
112. Leroy, 104; Thurston & Attwater, ed., vol. 1, 253-254; Delaney, 331
113. Leroy, 103-104; Thurston, 1952, 14; Thurston & Attwater, ed., vol. 2, 416-419; Delaney, 453-454; Rogo, 1983, 36
114. Leroy, 112; Thurston, 1952, 31; Thurston & Attwater, vol. 2, 66, (and vol. 1, 206-27)
115. Rochas, 47; Leroy, 117-118; Thurston, 1952, 31; Thurston & Attwater, ed., vol. 3, 519-524;

Delaney, 150-151; McBride, 124-130; Ghezzi, 592-593
116. Leroy, 27-28
117. Rochas, 30
118. Ibid, 31
119. Leroy, 33-34; Ebon, 90-99
120. Summers, 138
121. Ibid, 139
122. Rochas, 23
123. Gordon, 163
124. Leroy, 29-32; Fodor, 194-198; Commander X, 99-101
125. Rochas, 30
126. Home, 272; Fodor, 195; Brookesmith, 75; Commander X, 124
127. Fodor, 195; Inglis, 113
128. Fodor, 198; Inglis, 160
129. Summers, 141
130. Home, 282; Rochas, 31; Fodor, 198
131. Lang, 111-117
132. Home, 273; Fodor, 195
133. Richards, 51; Commander X, 126
134. Rochas, 24; Leroy, 33-35; Rogo, 1983, 45-46
135. Rickard & Michell, 6
136. Avila, 1565, 189-204; Avila, 1577, 133; Leroy, 97-101, 237; Thurston, 1952, 9-13; Thurston, 1954, 9-12; Thurston & Attwater, vol. 4, 111-121; McBride, 96-102; Rogo, 1983, 14; Reader's Digest, 284-285; Picknett, 15; Time-Life, 116-117; Treece, 252-253; Murphy, 110, 518-519; Charles & Jordan, 159-161; Commander X, 97-98
137. Leroy, 85-86; Thurston & Attwater, ed., vol. 2, 276
138. Thurston & Attwater, ed., vol. 1, 325-326
139. Ibid, 327-328
140. Ibid, 446-447
141. Ibid, 447-448
142. Ibid, 354-355
143. Rochas, 47; Leroy, 89; Thurston & Attwater, ed., vol. 3, 613-617; Charles & Jordan, 155
144. Rochas, 46; Leroy,

86-87; Richards, 144

145. Rochas, 46; Leroy, 91-92; Thurston & Attwater, ed., vol. 1, 630; Delaney, 507; Richards, 145

146. Thurston, 1952, 31; Thurston & Attwater, ed., vol. 4, 562-563

147. Leroy, 87

148. Thurston, 1952, 31; Thurston & Attwater, ed., vol. 3, 104-105

149. Thurston, 1952, 31; Thurston & Attwater, ed., vol. 1, 43-44

150. Thurston, 1952, 31; Thurston & Attwater, ed., vol. 4, 225-227

151. Leroy, 102-103

152. Ibid, 110

153. Leroy, 107-110; Thurston, 1952, 26-28; Read ers Digest, 285-286; Rogo, 1983, 21-22; Childress, 169; Rickard & Michell, 67-68, 83

154. Leroy, 103

155. Leroy, 111-112

156. Thurston, 1952, 31; Thurston & Attwater, ed., vol. 3, 172-173

157. Leroy, 113-114

158. Ibid, 114-115

159. Leroy, 110-111; Thurston & Attwater, ed., vol. 2, 24-126; Delaney, 23; Ghezzi, 484-485

160. Leroy, 104

161. Ibid, 111

162. Thurston, 1952, 24; Thurston & Attwater, ed., vol. 4, 269-270

163. Leroy, 117

164. Leroy, 120; Thurston, 1952, 13-14; Rogo, 1983, 15-16; Murphy, 519; Charles & Jordan, 12

165. Leroy, 115; Thurston, 1952, 26; Thurston & Attwater, ed., vol. 3, 593-594; Delaney, 393-394

166. Rochas, 26; Richards, 144

167. Leroy, 96

168. Leroy, 103

169. Rochas, 35; Leroy, 118-119, 240; Thurston, 1952, 28-29; Reader's Digest, 286; Rogo, 1983, 48; Childress, 168

170. Thurston, 1952, 31; Thurston & Attwater, ed., vol. 2, 124

171. Leroy, 123-139, 232-234; Dingwall, 9-29; Thurston, 1952, 15-18; Thurston, 1954, 16; Thurston & Attwater, ed., vol. 3, 587-591; Fodor, 194, 199; Delaney, 330-331; Ghezzi, 408-409; Childress, 169; Readers Digest, 286-288; Rogo, 1983, 23-28; Inglis, 159-160; Time-Life, 116; Treece, 258; Auerbach, 58; Murphy, 110, 519-520; Charles & Jordan, 171-173

172. Leroy, 144-145; Thurston, 1952, 25-26; Thurston & Attwater, ed., vol. 1, 127-128; Delaney, 554; Charles & Jane, 155

173. Leroy, 121

174. Leroy, 119-120; Thurston, 1952, 31; Thurston & Attwater, ed., vol. 1, 124-125; Delaney, 348 175. Leroy, 121

176. Leroy, 105; Thurston, 1952, 28-29; Rickard & Michell, 83; Treece, 251-252, 294

177. Leroy, 115; Delaney, 465

178. Leroy, 115-117

179. Rogo, 1983, 48

180. Leroy, 121

181. Leroy, 142-143; Thurston, 1952, 31; Thurston & Attwater, ed., vol. 3, 608-609

182. Leroy, 140-141; Thurston & Attwater, ed., vol. 1, 666-667; Delaney, 438; Charles & Jordan, 155

183. Leroy, 115

184. Rochas, 46; Leroy, 141-142; Thurston, 1952, 31; Thurston & Attwater, ed., vol 4, 207-208; Delaney, 111; Richards, 144

185. Leroy, 143-144, Thurston, 1952, 31; Thurston & Attwater, ed., vol. 3, 631-632; Delaney, 181

186. Leroy, 145; Thurston, 1952, 24-25; Thurston & Attwater, ed., vol. 1, 490-493; Delaney, 129

187. Leroy, 145-146; Thurston, 1952, 31; Thurston & Attwater, ed., vol. 4, 228-229

188. Leroy, 144; Thurston, 1952, 6; Thurston & Attwater, ed., vol. 3, 57-59; Delaney, 258

189. Leroy, 141

190. Ibid, 120-121

191. Ibid, 121-122

192. Leroy, 148-149; Ghezzi, 574-575

193. Calmet, 80; Rochas, 35; Thurston, 1952, 25; Fodor, 198

194. Leroy, 151-159, 238; Thurston & Attwater, ed., vol. 3, 242-249; Fodor, 194; Delaney, 360-361; Ghezzi, 20-21; Rickard and Michell, 83

195. Charles & Jordan, 142

196. Ibid, 62-63

197. Ibid, 122

198. Yogananda, 323-324

199. Charles & Jordan, 37; Nikhilananda, 10.

200. Rochas, 11-12; Richards, 88-89

201. Rochas, 14

202. Rochas, 8-11; Rogo, 1983, 32-34; Time-Life, 117; Charles & Jordan, 24-25

203. Rochas, 17-18

204. Richards, 88

205. Summers, 138

206. Fodor, 200

207. Charles & Jordan, 108

208. Inglis, 159-162

209. Hodgson, 354; Leroy, 45-47

210. Leroy, 25-26

211. Ibid, 26-27

212. Charles and Jordan, 106

213. Rodewyk, 120-127; Ebon, 154-164; Readers Digest, 103-104; Rogo, 1982, 45

214. Gersi, 153

215. Childress, 171

216. *Journey Into the Beyond*, Director: Rolf Olsen

217. Leroy, 25; Charles & Jordan, 96-97

218. Elkin, 64-65; Eliade, 127

219. Leroy, 24-25; Summers, 1973, 134-135

220. Eliade, 243

221. Long, 230

222. Gersi, 144-145, 153

223. Ibid, 153-156

224. Ibid, 174-184

225. Leroy, 143

226. Leroy, 150; Thurston, 1952, 31

227. Thurston, 1952, 19-22

228. Thurston, ed., vol. 1, 672-673; Delaney, 178

229. Saint-Osmer C.SS.R., 45, 67-69, 90, 122-124; Leroy, 146-148; Thurston, 1952, 24; Thurston & Attwater, ed., vol. 4, 131-134; Ghezzi, 266-267; McGreevy C.SS.R., 10-11; Charles & Jordan, 179-180

230. Leroy, 149-150; Thurston & Attwater, ed., vol. 2, 106-108; Delaney, 343; Charles & Jordan, 155

231. Rochas, 46; Leroy, 162-167; Thurston, 1952, 31; Thurston & Attwater, ed., vol. 2, 303-305; Delaney, 233; Treece, 267-270; Charles & Jordan, 157-158

232. Leroy, 169-173; Thurston & Attwater, ed., vol. 3, 120-122; Delaney, 477-478; Charles & Jordan, 168

233. Rochas, 46; Leroy, 161-162; Fodor, 194

234. Leroy, 57-58; Ghezzi, 652-653; Charles & Jordan, 178

235. Leroy, 161-162. Fodor, 194. Time-Life, 116-117. Charles & Jordan, 164-165.

236. Thurston & Attwater, ed., vol. 2, 309-310; Treece, 272-273

237. Leroy, 162

238. Thurston & Attwater, ed., vol. 2, 374-375; Treece, 274

239. Thurston & Attwater, ed., Vol. 1, 25-26; Treece, 147, 270-272

240. Leroy, 167-169, 240; Thurston, 1952, 31; Thurston & Attwater, ed., vol. 2, 191-192; Delaney, 162; Treece, 273

241. Leroy, 173; Thurston & Attwater, ed., vol. 2, 285-292; Delaney, 570-571; Ghezzi,

398-399; Treece, 262-263

242. Rochas, 92; Leroy, 174-177; Thurston, 1954, 155; Treece, 273

243. Leroy, 177-178; Thurston & Attwater, ed., vol. 2, 312-313; Delaney, 245; Ghezzi, 532-533

244. Calmet, 78-79

245. Strieber, 160

246. Rochas, 26; Leroy, 32-33; Fodor, 198

247. Rochas, 21

248. Rochas, 25; Leroy, 29

249. Fodor, 195

250. Leroy, 177-178

251. Thurston & Attwater, ed., vol. 1, 208-212; Treece, 110, 280-281

252. Treece, 275

253. Ibid, 69-71, 282, 294

254. Treece, 285

255. Leroy, 178-179; Thurston, 1952, 29; Charles & Jordan, 155

256. Home, 38-39

257. Ibid, 121

258. Ibid, 137-138

259. Ibid, 146-147

260. Ibid, 151-152

261. Ibid, 159-160

262. Ibid, 163-164

263. Ibid, 172

264. Ibid, 178-179

265. Ibid, 184

266. Ibid, 190

267. Ibid, 194

268. Ibid, 195

269. Ibid, 196-197

270. Ibid, 200-201

271. Burton, 183; Rogo, 1983, 37-38

272. Picknett, 33-34

273. Mulholland, 85

274. Ibid, 85

275. Fodor, 197

276. Fodor, 196; Richards, 35; Rogo, 1982, 38

277. Home, 168

278. Ibid, 10-11

279. Ibid, 39, 138

280. Home, 39; Leroy, 38-41

281. Leroy, 195-196

282. Leroy, 322; Readers Digest, 293-294

283. Rochas, 93; Leroy, 44-45

284. Rochas, 94; Leroy, 44-45

285. Rochas, 51

286. Rochas, 51; Leroy, 35-36

287. Rochas, 55-56

288. Ibid, 28

289. Rochas, 93-95; Leroy, 45-46

290. Thurston, 1954, 21; Fodor, 195

291. Summers, 1987, 245-246

292. Hardinge, 78

293. Hardinge, 155; Mulholland, 49-51; www.survivalafter-death.org.

294. Hardinge, 99

295. Hardinge, 101; Fodor, 195

296. Hardinge, 279; Fodor, 195

297. Rochas, 57-58

298. Hardinge, 267-268

299. Ibid, 451

300. Hardinge, 338; Fodor, 199

301. Hardinge, 290

302. Rochas, 66-68; Leroy, 42-43; Fodor, 197; Commander X, 125

303. Inglis, 304; Picknett, 49

304. Leroy, 44; Fodor, 200; Picknett, 42, 76-79, 83; Imich, 1-26

305. Inglis, 159-162

306. Pearsall, 109

307. Fodor, 198

308. Rochas, 70-72

309. Rochas, 68-70; Fodor, 198

310. Fodor, 198-199

311. Ibid, 198

312. Ibid, 199

313. Rochas, 85-90; Fodor, 199

314. Fodor, 199

315. Rochas, 72-84; Leroy, 41-43; Fodor, 199, 271; Rogo, 1975, 190; Rogo, 1983, 38-39; Auerbach, 63; Imich, 27-29

316. Thurston, 1954, 17; Imich, 47-98

317. Leroy, 43-44, 272-273; Muldoon, 276; Fodor, 200, 337

318. Calmet, 80

319. Rampa, 71

320. Treece, 191

321. Murphy, 470-471

322. Charles & Jane, 98

323. Rochas, 24

324. Treece, 295-296

325. Hardinge, xii

326. Charles & Jane, 100

327. Treece, 299-301

328. Thurston, 1952, 30; Rogo, 1983, 36-37

329. Charles & Jordan, 98-99

330. David-Neel, 194-195; Fodor, 201; Charles & Jordan, 57-58

331. Rogo, 1983, 36

332. Rochas, 28-29

333. Treece, 297

334. Thurston & Attwater, ed., 179-180; Treece, 299

335. Fodor, 31

336. Thurston & Attwater, ed., 593-597; Treece, 298

337. Leroy, 182-183

338. Richards, 122-123

339. Swisher, 99-100

340. Treece, 301-302

341. Sherman, 62

342. Nebel, 123-127

343. Monroe, 9-10

344. Miracles & Mysteries, 1986

345. Treece, 289-290

346. Sizemore, 246-247

347. Guggenheim & Guggenheim, 264

348. Bonser, 55-56

349. Rochas, 26; Leroy, 32-33; Fodor, 198

350. Fodor, 199

351. Hadsell, 90-91

352. Johnson, 217

353. Dennett, personal files

354. Thurston & Attwater, ed., vol. 4, 32-33

355. Thurston & Attwater, ed., vol. 4, 34; Sudakov, 3

356. Thurston & Attwater, ed., vol. 1, 378-379

357. Thurston & Attwater, ed. vol. 4, 141

358. Saint-Osmer C.SS. R., 153; McGreevy C.SS.R., 10-11

359. Sudakov, 2

360. Spaulding, 1924, 52-55

361. Leroy, 313

362. Summers, 236-238

363. Reader's Digest, 273-274

364. Yogananda, 351-353

365. Benson, 157-158; Murphy, 109-110

366. Charles & Jordan, 132

367. Yogananda, 70-76

368. Hitching, 104-106; Reader's Digest, 304; Rogo, 1983 p33; Childress, 171

369. Richards, 36

370. Charles & Jordan, 64-65

371. Maraini, 55; Charles & Jordan, 66

372. Gersi, 152

373. The Beatles, 283

374. Charles & Jordan, 53.

375. Dong, 167

376. Nevile, 1-3; Carroll, 2

377. Benedict, 42

378. Nevile, 1-4

379. Leroy, 181; Treece, 175-177

380. Rochas, 27

381. Summers, 136

382. Leroy, 174, 240

383. Fodor, 195

384. Leroy, 182-183; Thurston, 1952, 30; Treece, 296-297

385. Leroy, 182; Thurston, 1952, 29-30; Thurston & Attwater, ed., vol. 2, 75-76; Delaney, 243; Ghezzi, 258-259; Rogo, 1983, 23; Treece, 283-285

386. Rogo, 1983, 23, 34-35; Treece, 276-280

387. Rochas, 26-27; Leroy, 179-181; Fodor, 197

388. Fodor, 201

389. Rochas, 91.

390. Leroy, 321; Fodor, 195

391. Rochas, 91-92

392. Reader's Digest, 272-273; Mishlove, 47-48; http/www. padrepio.catholic-webservices.com

393. Treece, 262, 285-286

394. Ibid, 248-249, 261

395. Cuneo, 264

396. Fodor, 198, 416; Rogo, 1983, 39

397. Edwards, 71

398. Imich, 123-157

399. Fodor, 200

400. Ebon, 218-219, 249; Reader's Digest, 104-105; Rogo, 1983, 44

401. Time-Life, 10

402. Steiger, 130

403. Ibid, 130-132, 144

404. Rogo, 1983, 41-43; Allen, 5-50

405. Hurst, 122-125

406. Playfair, 96-156.

407. Imich, 34-40

408. Gordon, 162

409. Warren, 113-131

410. Curran, 184

411. Kerman, 215-220

412. Cuneo, 232-233

413. Ibid, 264

414. Cain, 30

415. Wagner, 1-2

416. Mishlove, 45-49

417. Dennett, personal files

418. Ibid
419. Eason, 141-142
420. Hopkins, 298, 324
421. Boyd, 80-103
422. Yram, 110-111
423. Fodor, 201
424. Ostrander & Schroeder, 291
425. Weed., 161-162
426. Hadsell, 88
427. Gris & Dick, 29-43; Imich, 175-177
428. Time-life, 118
429. Anonymous, 1-2
430. Hadsell, 87-89
431. Cuneo, 133-138
432. Dennett, personal files
433. Ibid.
434. Sudakov, 1-2
435. Hartmann, 159
436. Hughes, vol. 3, 31-32; vol. 5, 67
437. Harvey-Wilson, 6
438. Monroe, 271-272
439. Murphy, 536
440. Leroy, 206
441. Ibid, 241
442. Ibid, 221

443. Ibid, 243, 307
444. Gersi, 185-186
445. Fodor, 198
446. Rogo, 1983, 33-34
447. Wilson, 218
448. Burton, 127
449. Richards, 51
450. Ibid, 31
451. Charles & Jordan, 11
452. Treece, 253
453. Harvey-Wilson, 7-10
454. Picknett, 46
455. Smith, 5
456. Fodor, 200-201
457. Treece, 257-260
458. Leroy, 258
459. Ibid, 350
460. Calmet, 78, 82
461. Thurston, 1952, 30-31
462. Summers, 135
463. Leroy, 33; Fodor, 200
464. Rochas, 97
465. Leroy, 331
466. Eliade, 140-141
467. Ibid, 410-411
468. Gersi, 158
469. Rochas, 98

470. Ibid, 18-19
471. Judge, 336
472. Knight/Ramtha, 41-46
473. Rochas, 34, 102
474. Wilson, 219, 221
475. Spaulding, 1935, 115
476. Picknett, 43
477. Charles & Jordan, 12.
478. Browne, 167
479. Rogo, 1983, 49-50
480. Commander X, 127-128
481. Blavatsky, 244
482. Imich, 170-174
483. Rampa, 122-123
484. Leadbetter, 159
485. Sculthorp, 144
486. Panchadasi, 237-238
487. Fodor, 201
488. Leroy, 251
489. Gersi, 156-157
490. Dennett, personal files
491. Ebon, 226
492. Hardinge, 410
493. Fodor, 195
494. Gersi, 153-154

495. Richards, 9
496. Rickard and Michell, 72
497. Ibid, 70-71
498. Rampa, 71
499. Commander X, 125-126
500. Ibid, 128
501. Leroy, 271
502. Simon-Harvey, 5
503. Weed., 162
504. Knight/Ramtha, 43-46
505. Richards, 67
506. Blavatsky, 497-498; Richards, 68
507. Richards, 85
508. Rampa, 70
509. Fodor, 37
510. Ibid, 201
511. Rochas, 100
512. Richards, 116-117
513. Iyengar, 211; Richards, 122, 128-129
514. Vishita, 126-127

Sources

Anonymous. "Witness to Levitation." *Paranormal Phenomena: Your True Tales.* http://paranormal.about. com/library/blstory_march04_12.htm. March 2004.

Auerbach, Loyd. *Mind Over Matter.* New York: Kensington Books, 1991.

Avila, St. Teresa. *The Interior Castle.* New York: Paulist Press, (1577) 1979. p133.

———. *The Life of Teresa of Jesus: The Autobiography of Teresa of Avila.* (translated and edited by E. Allison Peers from the Critical Edition of P. Silverio De Santa Teresa, CD) New York: Doubleday, (1565) 1960, 1991.

Beatles, The. (editor: Derek Taylor) *The Beatles Anthology.* San Francisco: Chronicle Books, 2000.

Benedict, W. Ritchie. "The Magic of Old India: Myth or Mystery?" *Fate.* Lakeville, MN: Fate Magazine, Inc., November 2005.

Benson, Herbert. *Beyond the Relaxation Response.* New York: Times Books, 1984, pp 157-158.

Blavatsky, Helena. *Collected Writings.* Wheaton, IL: Theosophical Publishing House, 1950, 1991.

Bonser, Heather. "We Are Never Alone." *FATE.* Lakeville, MN: Fate Magazine, Inc. March, 2003, pp 55-56.

Boyd, Doug. *Mystics, Magicians and Medicine People: Tales of a Wanderer.* New York: Marlow & Company, 1991.

Brookesmith, Peter. *When the Impossible Happens: Unnatural Events That Defy Science.* MacDonald & Company Publishers, 1984, 1988.

Browne, Sylvia. (with Lindsay Harrison). *Phenomenon.* New York: Dutton Books, 2005.

Burton, Jean. *Heyday of a Wizard: Daniel Home, the Medium.* New York: Warner Books, 1944.

Cain, Lisa. "Levitated." *Paranormal Phenomena: Your True Tales.* http://paranormal.about.com/library/ blstory_may05_30.htm. (May 2005)

Calmet, Augustin. *The Phantom World.* Woburn Square, London: Wordsworth Editions. 1746, 2001.

Carroll, Robert Todd. "The Indian Rope Trick."   http://skepdic.com/indianrope.html.

Charles, Rodney and Ann Jordan. *Lighter Than Air: Miracles of Human Flight from Christian Saints to Native American Spirits.* Fairfield, IA: Sunstar Publishing, 1995.

Childress, David Hatcher (editor.) *The Anti-Gravity Handbook.* Kempton, IL: Adventures Unlimited Press, 1985, 1998.

Commander X. (Introduction by Timothy Green Beckley.) *Invisibility and Levitation: How-To Keys to Personal Performance.* New Brunswick, NY: Abelard Productions Publications, 1998.

Cuneo, Michael W. *American Exorcism: Expelling Demons in the Land of Plenty.* New York: Broadway Books, 2001.

Curran, Robert with Jack and Janet Smurl & Ed and Lorraine Warren. *The Haunted: One Family's Nightmare.* New York: St. Martin's Press, 1988.

David-Neel, Alexandra. *Magic and Mystery in Tibet.* New Hyde Park, NY: University Books, 1965.

Delaney. John J. *Dictionary of Saints.* New York: Doubleday, 1980.

Dennett, Preston. *California Ghosts.* Atglen, PA: Schiffer Books, 2004.

———. *Out-of-Body Exploring: A Beginner's Approach.* Charlottesville, VA: Hampton Roads Publishing, 2004.

Dingwall, Eric John. *Some Human Oddities*. London, England: Home and Van Thal, 1947.

Dong, Paul. *The Four Major Mysteries of Mainland China*. Englewood Cliffs, NJ: Prentice-Hall, 1984.

Eason, Cassandra. *The Psychic Power of Children: Extraordinary Experiences of Ordinary Families*. London, England: Rider, 1990.

Ebon, Martin. *Demon Children*. New York: The New American Library, 1978.

Ebon, Martin (ed.) *Exorcism: Fact Not Fiction*. New York: Signet Books, 1974.

Edwards, Harry. *The Mediumship of Jack Webber*. London: Harry Edwards Foundation, 1928. P71.

Elkin, Adolphus Peter. *Aboriginal Men of High Degree*. Sydney, Australia: Elkin, 1946.

Eliade, Mircea. *Shamanism: Archaic Techniques of Ecstasy*. Princeton, MA: Princeton University Press, 1964.

Fodor, Nandor. *Encyclopedia of Psychic Science*. London and New York: University Books, Inc. 1966.

———. *The Haunted Mind: A Psychoanalyst Looks at the Supernatural*. New York: Garrett Publications, 1959.

Gersi, Douchan. *Faces in the Smoke: An Eyewitness Experience of Voodoo, Shamanism, Psychic Healing and Other Amazing Human Powers*. Los Angeles, CA: Jeremy P. Tarcher, Inc., c1991.

Ghezzi, Bert. *Voices of the Saints: A Year of Readings*. New York: Doubleday, 1985.

Gordon, Stuart. *The Book of Miracles*. London: Headline Books, 1996.

Gris, Henry and William Dick. *The New Soviet Psychic Discoveries*. New York: Warner Books, 1979.

Guggenheim, Bill and Judy Guggenheim. *Hello From Heaven!: A New Field of Research — After-Death Communication — Confirms That Life and Love Are Eternal*. New York: Bantam Books, 1995.

Hadsell, Helen. "Levitating — A Nuisance!" *Fate*. St. Paul, MN: Llewellyn. Nov 1993. pp 87-91.

Hardinge, Emma. *Modern American Spiritualism: A Twenty Years' Record of the Communion Between Earth and the World of Spirits*. New Hyde Park, NY: University Books, Inc., 1970.

Hartmann, Kelly S. *Enlightened Through Darkness: A True Story of the Exorcism of a 6-Year-Old Boy*. Shining light Press: www.shininglightpress.com., 2001.

Harvey-Wilson, Simon. "Human Levitation." *The Australian Ufologist Magazine*. Australia. Vol. 6 No 6, 2003. (www.homepage.power.com.au/~tkbnetw/simon_harvey-wilson_13.htm)

Hasted, John B. *The Metal Benders*. London: Routledge & Kegan Paul, 1981.

Hitching, Francis. *The Mysterious World: An Atlas of the Unexplained*. New York. Holt, Rhinehart and Winston, 1978.

Hodgson, M. "Indian Magic and The Testimony of Conjurers." *SPR Journal*. London: Society for Psychical Research. vol. 1893-94.

Home, Daniel D. *Incidents In My Life*. Secaucus, NJ: University Books, Inc., 1864, 1971.

Hopkins, Budd. *Sight Unseen: Science, UFO Invisibility and Transgenic Beings*. New York: Atria Books, 2003.

Hughes, Marilynn. *Medicine Woman Within a Dream: Book 3 of the Mysteries of the Redemption Series*. www.outofbodytravel.org.

———. *The Mystical Jesus: Book 5 of the Mysteries of the Redemption Series*. www.outofbodytravel.org.

Hurst, Brian Edward. *Heaven Can Help: The Autobiography of a Medium*. 1st Books Library: http://www.ktb.net/~hurani/, 2001.

Imich, Alexander. (editor) *Incredible Tales of the Paranormal: Documented Accounts of Poltergeist, Levitations, Phantoms and Other Phenomena*. New York: Bramble Books, 1995.

Inglis, Brian. *The Paranormal: An Encyclopedia of Psychic Phenomenon*. London: Paladin, 1985.

Iyengar, B. K. S. *Light on the Yoga Sutras of Patanjali*. San Francisco, CA: Harpercollins, 1966, 1993.

Johnson, Doretta with Jim Henderson. *The People In the Attic: The Haunting of Doretta Johnson*. New York: St. Martin's Press, 1995.

Judge, William Q. *Echoes of the Orient*. San Diego, CA: Point Loma Publications, 1975.

Kerman, Frances. *The Myrtles Plantation: The True Story of America's Most Haunted House*. New York: Warner Books, 2005.

Knight, J. Z. (aka Ramtha) *Buddha's Neuronet for Levitation: Opening the Lotus of a Thousand Petals*. Yelm: WA: JZK Publishing, 2002.

Lang, Andrew. *The Book of Dreams and Ghosts*. New York: Causeway Books, 1897, 1974.

Leroy, Olivier. *Levitation: An Examination of the Evidence and Explanations*. Paris: Librairie Valois. 1928. (In the French Language, translation by Preston Dennett.)

Long, Max Freedom. *Recovering the Ancient Magic*. Cape Girardeau, MO: Huna Press, 1934, 1978.

Maraini, Fosco. *Secret Tibet*. New York: Viking Press, 1952.

McBride, Rev. Alfred. *Saints Are People: Church History Through the Saints*. Dubuque, IO: William C. Brown Co. Publishers, 1981.

McGreevy, C.SS.R., Michael. *Gerard Majella: The Mother's Saint*. Liguori, MO: Ligouri Publications, 1994.

Milarepa. (original translation by W. Y. Evans-Wentz) (Edited by J. L. Cranmer-Byng.) (as told to Lobzang Jivaka) *The Life of Milarepa: Tibet's Great Yogi*. New York: Paragon Books, 1928, 1962.

Mishlove Ph.D., Jeffrey. *The PK Man: A True Story of Mind Over Matter*. Charlottesville, VA: Hampton Roads Publishing Company, Inc., 2000.

Monroe, Robert. *Far Journeys*. New York: Doubleday & Company, Inc., 1987.

Muldoon, Sylvan and Hereward Carrington. *The Projection of the Astral Body*. York Beach, Maine: Samuel Weiser, Inc., 1929, 1973.

Murphy, Michael. *The Future of the Body: Explorations Into the Further Evolution of Human Nature*. Los Angeles, CA: Jeremy Tarcher, Inc., 1992.

Nebel, Long John and Sanford M. Teller. *The Psychic World Around Us*. New York: Hawthorn Books, Inc, 1969.

Neville, Pran. "Forgotten Feats of Indian Jugglers." *The Sunday Tribune, India*. December 30, 2001. www.tribuneindia.com.

Nikhilananda, Swami. *The Gospel of Sri Ramakrishna*. New York: Ramakrishna-Vivekananda Center, 1942.

Ostrander, Sheila and Lynn Schroeder. *Psychic Discoveries Behind the Iron Curtain*. Englewood Cliffs, NJ: Prentice-Hall, Inc., 1970.

Palden, Patricia. "Midnight Fire Puja in the Snow." *Lama Lobsang.com*. http://www.lamalobsang.com/FirePuja.htm.

Panchadasi, Swami. *Clairvoyance and Occult Powers*. Chicago, IL: Yogi Publication Society, 1919.

Pearsall, Ronald. *The Table Rappers*. New York: St. Martin's Press, 1972.

Picknett, Lynn. *Flights of Fancy? 100 Years of Paranormal Experiences*. New York: Ballantine Books, 1987.

Playfair, Guy Lyon. *This House is Haunted: The True Story of a Poltergeist*. Briar Cliff, NY: Stein and Day Publishers, 1980.

Powell, A. E. *The Astral Body and Other Astral Phenomenon*. Wheaton, IL: Theosophical Publishing House, 1927, 1996.

Rampa, Tuesday Lobsang. *Wisdom of the Ancients*. Corgi Books: London, England, 1965.

Reader's Digest (editors). *Mysteries of the Unexplained*. New York: the Reader's Digest Association, Inc., 1982

Richards, Steve. *Levitation: What It Is - How It Works - How To Do It*. Hammersmith, London: The Aquarian Press, 1980.

Rickard, Bob and John Michell. *Unexplained Phenomena: A Rough Guide Special*. Shorts Garden, London: Rough Guides, 2000.

Rinpoche, Tenzin Wangyal. (editor: Mark Dahlby.) *The Tibetan Yogas of Dream and Sleep*. Ithaca, NY: Snow Lion Publications, 1998.

Rochas, Colonel Albert D. (Editeur: P. G. Leymarie) *La Levitation*. Paris: Librairie des Sciences Psychiques, 1897. (In the French Language, translation by Preston Dennett)

Rodewyk, Adolf. *Possessed by Satan*. Aschaffenburg, Germany: Paul Patloch Verlag, 1963.

Rogo, D. Scott. *Miracles: A Parascientific Inquiry into Wondrous Phenomena*. Chicago, IL: Contemporary Books, 1983.

——. *Parapsychology: A Century of Inquiry*. New York: Dell Publishing, 1975.

Saint-Osmor C.SS R., Father Edward. *St. Gerard Majella: The Wonderworker and Patron of Expectant Mothers*. Rockford, IL: Tan Books and Publishers, Inc., 1907, 1999.

Sculthorp, Frederick C. *Excursions to the Spirit World: A Report of Personal Experiences During Conscious Astral Projection*. Holland Park, London: Almorris Press, Ltd., 1961.

Sherman, Martha. "True Mystic Experiences." *FATE*. St. Paul, MN: Llewellyn. December, 1993.

Shirokogoroff, Sergei M. *General Theory of Shamanism Among the Tungus*. JRAS, North-China Branch (Shanghai), LIV, 1923, pp 246-49.

Sizemore, Chris Costner. *A Mind of My Own*. New York: William Morrow and Company, Inc., 1989.

Smith, Bruce. "Levitation 101: Human Levitation." *AmericanAntigravity*. www.americanantigravity.com/levitation101.shtml, 2003.

Spaulding, Baird T. *Life and Teaching of the Masters of the Far East: Volume 1*. Marina Del Rey, CA: DeVorss Publications, 1924, 1937.

——. *Life and Teaching of the Masters of the Far East: Volume 3*. Marina Del Rey: De Vorss Publications, 1935, 1962.

Steiger, Brad. *The Psychic Feats of Olof Jonsson*. Englewood Cliffs, NJ: Prentice-Hall, Inc., 1971.

Strieber, Whitley. *Breakthrough: The Next Step*. New York: HarperCollins Publishers, Inc., 1995.

Sudakov, Dmitry. (translator, from Russian). "Phenomenon of Levitation Comes Into Everyday Life." *Pravda. RU*: http://english.pravda.ru/science/19/94/378/14253_levitation.html.

Summers, Montague. *The History of Witchcraft*. New York: Dorset Press, 1923, 1987.

——. *A Popular History of Witchcraft*. New York: Causeway Books, 1973.

Swisher, Blanche F. "What Held Me Up? True Mystic Experiences." *Fate*. St. Paul, MN: Llewellyn, October, 1992.

Thurston, Herbert. *Ghosts and Poltergeists*. Chicago: Henry Regnery, 1954

——. *The Physical Phenomena of Mysticism*. London: Burns Oates, 1952.

Thurston, Herbert and Donald Attwater. (editors) *Butler's Lives of the Saints*. Allen, TX: Christian Classics, 1756-1759, 1956. Volumes I, II, III, IV.

Time-Life, (editors.) *Mysteries of the Unknown: Mind Over Matter*. Alexandria, VA: Time-Life Books, 1988.

Treece, Patricia. *The Sanctified Body: A Gripping Investigation of Bilocation, Levitation, Supernatural Energy and Other Mystical Phenomena*. Liguori, MO: Triumph Books, 1989.

Vishita, Swami Bhakta. *Seership — the Science of Knowing the Future: Hindoo and Oriental Methods*. Chicago, IL: Yogi Publication Society, 1918.

Wagner, Stephen. "The Poltergeist Levitation." *Paranormal Phenomena: Your True Tales*. www.paranormal. about.com. Oct 2005.

Warren, Ed and Lorraine. *Ghost Hunters: True Stories from the World's Most Famous Demonologists*. New York: St. Martin's Press, 1989.

Weed, Joseph J. *The Wisdom of the Mystic Masters*. West Nyack, NY: Parker Publishing Company, 1968.

Wilson, Colin. *The Occult: A History*. New York: Random House, 1971.

www.catholic-forum.com. (website detailing the lives of catholic saints)

www.levitation.org. (website detailing various stage levitation or street levitation techniques.)

Yogananda, Paramahansa. *Autobiography of a Yogi*. Los Angeles, CA: Self-realization Fellowship, 1977.

Yram. *Practical Astral Projection*. New York: Samuel Weiser Inc, 1972.

Contact:

To contact the author, email: prestone@pacbell.net or write c/o the publisher.